The Pursuit of Division
Race, Gender, and Preferential Hiring in Canada

The topic of equity policies and identity politics in Canada is at the forefront of public and media discussion, and Martin Loney adds fuel to the fire. In *The Pursuit of Division* he provides a provocative critique of recent government policies with respect to race, gender, and preferential hiring, exposing the suspect methods of so-called progressive thinkers in their pursuit of the politics of difference.

Loney takes issue with popular attitudes towards race and gender, whereby to be born a woman or a member of a visible minority is to enter life at a disadvantage and therefore be entitled to compensatory provisions. Arguing that social class not group membership determines life chances, he refutes the claims of those who detect systemic prejudice and discrimination and reap considerable public subsidy in return.

Loney sets the growth of federal involvement in preferential hiring in the context of a growing industry whose success depends on the constant affirmation of group grievance based on gender or race. He argues that preferential hiring policies and a muddled multiculturalism lead to the continual assertion of the primacy of race even as the government officially opposes racial thinking.

Among his many up-to-date and high profile examples Loney includes Bob Rae's preoccupation with skin and gender politics, Brian Mulroney's attempts to strengthen the Conservative Party's ethnic constituency by funding ethnic groups and maintaining high levels of immigration, and former defence minister David Colenette's extensive use of public funds to court ethnic voters in his Toronto constituency.

The Pursuit of Division is essential reading for anyone concerned about where government-mandated policies on equity and multiculturalism may be taking us and about the implications of emphasizing the politics of difference over that of shared community.

MARTIN LONEY has taught at universities in Canada and the U.K. and is currently a social policy consultant living in Manotick, Ontario.

THE PURSUIT OF DIVISION
Race, Gender, and
Preferential Hiring in Canada

Martin Loney

McGill-Queen's University Press
Montreal & Kingston · London · Buffalo

© McGill-Queen's University Press 1998
ISBN 0-7735-1744-8 (cloth)
ISBN 0-7735-1769-3 (paper)

Legal deposit second quarter 1998
Bibliothèque nationale du Québec

Printed in Canada on acid-free paper

McGill-Queen's University Press acknowledges the support of the
Canada Council for the Arts for its publishing program.

Canadian Cataloguing in Publication Data

Loney, Martin, 1944–
The pursuit of division : race, gender, and preferential hiring
in Canada
Includes bibliographical references and index.
ISBN 0-7735-1744-8 (bound)
ISBN 0-7735-1769-3 (pbk.)
1. Affirmative action programs – Canada. 2. Women –
Employment – Government policy – Canada. 3. Discrimination in
employment – Canada. 4. Minorities – Employment – Government
policy – Canada. 1. Title.
HD8108.5.A2L65 1998   331.13'3'0971   C98-900396-5

Typeset in Sabon 10/12 with Frutiger Condensed display by
Caractéra inc., Quebec City.

Contents

Acknowledgments

This book was made possible by a grant from the Donner Canadian Foundation, whose support is gratefully acknowledged. The grant was made through the Society for Academic Freedom and Scholarship.[1]

Nathan Greenfield offered continual support and encouragement, lent books, and exchanged ideas. Linda and Paul Chappin and Malcolm and Judy Cairns swapped anecdotes and outrage. Chris Miller and Anne Rutledge commented on various chapters. Ian McKelvie suggested publishers and helped with production of the final manuscript. Greg Hutton and the Manotick Library provided exemplary assistance in locating books through the inter-library loan service. Rainer Knopf made a number of helpful suggestions, and Maureen Garvie's editing tightened the prose and sharpened the argument.

My family, Chris, Suzi, and Amy, lived through the demanding research and writing process. This book is dedicated to them and to the reassertion of the prior claims of our common humanity over the sirens of identity politics.

Introduction

My interest in preferential hiring policies was, not surprisingly, sparked by personal experience. In 1988 I gave up an academic appointment in Britain and returned to Canada. I was aware that opportunities for academic employment were limited but assumed that over time some would materialize. In this I had failed to take note of the increasing importance of group membership rather than merit in the appointment process. It quickly became clear that in many university departments race and gender loom far larger than such traditional questions as teaching record, scholarly publication, or even formal qualification. Increasingly candidates must also offer endorsement to the precepts of radical feminists and other ideologues of contemporary orthodoxy.

The election of the Rae government in Ontario gave a significant boost to preferential hiring advocates and provided a fertile climate for the thriving culture of complaint. There is much that could be written about Bob Rae's tenure in office, an event from which Canadian social democracy may never recover. The government enthusiastically endorsed the politics of grievance. The inclusive egalitarian demands that had underpinned the appeal of the left were usurped by the demands of those who claimed injustice arose not from generic factors such as social class, poverty, inequality of opportunity, or social marginalization but from group membership. In this new mantra white men were inherently powerful; others not blessed with this biological categorization were disadvantaged and thus entitled to preferential treatment.

The Rac government is no longer, but the politics it espoused and so liberally funded are still with us. The Harris government repealed the employment equity legislation, but within the Ontario Public Service the claims of group membership over merit have sunk deep roots. The repeal of Bill 79 has had little effect on the burgeoning equity bureaucracy in municipalities, hospitals, school boards, and large private-sector companies. The diversity training industry, meanwhile, provides ideological backing to those who would reduce humanity to discrete groups bounded by race, gender, and sexual preference. Universities in Ontario and elsewhere continue to privilege those with the right racial and gender attributes even as academic ideologues declaim against the continuing domination of a Eurocentric curriculum and a white male pedagogy.

Initially my response to the antics of the preferential hiring advocates and Rae's employment equity bureaucrats was confined to the occasional newspaper article. Grant support from the Donner Canadian Foundation provided the opportunity for more extensive research embracing the critical role of the federal government as midwife to Canada's grievance industry. The lack of any convincing evidence that racial minorities or women experienced the contemporary systemic discrimination so frequently claimed on their behalf raises other questions. How did an industry based on a proverbial stack of cards become so well entrenched? How did Canada, a country which on any international scale appears to enjoy considerable racial harmony, come to be portrayed as profoundly racist, a country in which colour is said to be the defining issue in the life experience of every visible minority?

The search for answers leads time and again to the actions of politicians and bureaucrats in endorsing the agenda of a politics based on group identity. Considerable tax funding and political recognition have been provided to those who claimed to speak for vast constituencies of those whose putative oppression results from their biological characteristics. Federal government departments, the Canada Council, and, particularly in Ontario, a range of provincial and municipal organizations have not only enthusiastically embraced the demands of preferential hiring advocates but have also actively sponsored the development of a politics in which the claims of group membership predominate.

The result of the proliferation of policies purporting to address racial discrimination is the entrenchment of racial thinking. The obsession with race, once the prerogative of white supremacists, is now mainstream, and skin politics the mark of progressive thinking. This is evident in the acceptance that there is a collectivity of people in Canada who can be usefully encompassed by the label "people of colour." The origins of this terminology, which carries the implicit assumption that there are people without colour, lie in the politics of the radical feminist movement. The phrase has now permeated our national discourse, gracing not only the CBC, always an ardent purveyor of group grievance, but even the sober pages of Canada's national newspaper, the *Globe and Mail*. It is worth pausing to reflect on the route by which this loaded term has received such wide currency. It is underpinned by the assumption that what unites a wide range of people – some of them immigrants, others descendants of those who arrived in Canada a hundred or more years ago, from diverse ethnic backgrounds, with an enormous variance in skills, income, and wealth – is colour.

This is racial thinking, a sociological characterization of apartheid South Africa or the Deep South in the Jim Crow era. What does it have to do with a country where, in spite of the best efforts of racial zealots, race has remarkably little salience for our national politics or sense of nation? Identity politics serve not to diminish the accident of race and ethnicity but to endlessly proclaim its importance in asserting the putative oppression experienced by those who are thus identified.

That the preferred terminology should emphasize the centrality of supposed racial difference is not surprising. The time when the agenda was driven by those who preferred to judge people on the content of their character rather than the colour of their skin has passed. We have in a bizarre way come full circle: now we must recognize the inherent victim status that derives from skin colour and welcome the array of special entitlements that must in consequence follow. Where once those who claimed the progressive mantle urged that we ignore race or gender in making decisions, casting votes, and allocating resources, now we must prioritize such matters. Support is commanded not because individuals offer intellectual ability, integrity, or an attractive political platform but because their race and gender entitle them to demand such support. Those who comply apparently confirm that they are repositories of some historic guilt which can only be expiated by acts of self-effacement. No thoughtful observer of the politics of identity could be in any doubt that the goal is not integration, or the rejection of racial thinking, but rather the legitimation of a new hierarchy in which those who can lay a dubious claim to historic disadvantage assert a contemporary right to preference.[2]

The same transformation is evident in the rapidly spreading diversity training cult. Where once liberal values gave support to the idea of treating people equally and recognizing that ethnicity, skin colour, sexual preference, and gender were not defining characteristics, now we must learn that such characteristics are indeed defining and that people must be treated differently, depending on which they exhibit. Sensitivity is to be encouraged through official endorsement. The only group not entitled to such protection are heterosexual white males, whose caricatured world views and ostensible privileges provide much of the diversity training script.

Federally, Canada's ill-conceived multicultural policies have evolved from the reasonable acknowledgment that the country was built by a variety of ethnic groups who must be seen as more than a footnote to the British and the French, to the development of policies in which the concept of "Canadian" takes second place to the prior claims of ethnicity. Government policy is to foster the creation of a polyethnic state, a mission acknowledged to be unique in the world. The goal is not assimilation or integration but government assistance to groups wishing to retain a discrete ethnic identity in perpetuity. In the words of a contemporary government report, "Canada has charted a unique course among nations in pursuit of a sometimes elusive, and controversial vision of a society in which people retain their heritage languages and their cultural identification while enjoying the full benefits of a citizenship founded on shared rights, freedoms and obligations" (Canadian Heritage 1996: 5).

The emphasis on group distinctiveness is consistent with the larger embrace of the supremacy of group over individual rights. Preferential hiring provides a quintessential example of the policies that flow from this approach; justice for the individual, which might be assured by an insistence on merit, is secondary to group justice, secured by an insistence on the proportionate representation of each group, in every economic sector, at every level.

Ironically, the origins of multiculturalism go back to the Trudeau era – an astonishing legacy for a politician who, in his attacks on Quebec separatists, dismissed the over-arching claims of ethnicity and history in favour of the assertion that all citizens must be equal before the state. In retrospect, policies that sought to build national unity by incorporating a diverse range of groups spawned a growing constituency dependent for support on their ability to articulate group grievance.

Identity politics offers great scope for manipulating the political agenda and seeking support through networks of patronage. For the political and bureaucratic classes the vision of a collection of disparate ethnic groups locked in a historic eternity of separation, sharing a vast continent while a benevolent government manages their common citizenship, has obvious attractions. It's much easier to manage an ethnically divided, patronage-dependent population than to deal with a united citizenry with no doubt of their common identity.

The exposure of then Defence Minister David Colenette's extensive use of public funds to court ethnic voters in his Toronto riding no doubt affords an extreme example of the political uses which may be made of such policies. The report that $5,000 had been provided to Mahmood Khan to "informally assess and subsequently advise the minister" on Muslim views on the Canadian armed forces must have left Muslim constituents wondering why they had not merited the $116,000 handed over to Stefanos Karabekos to provide advice on the Greek community's views (*Globe and Mail*, 25 October 1996).

The Liberals have historically been assiduous in courting ethnic constituencies. Under Brian Mulroney the federal Conservatives sought to emulate such policies to strengthen their ethnic constituency. The maintenance of high levels of immigration, even as the economy went into deep recession, was explicitly linked to fostering ties with ethnic constituencies – a reflection of the old political adage that when it came to casting a vote, immigrants and their children would remember the government that granted them entry. Funding for ethnic groups was also linked to the party's electoral strategy. Funding to the Canadian Ethnocultural Council, for example, rose from some $164,500 in 1987 to $321,000 in the election year of 1989 (Bryden 1994: 24).

The most striking aspect of the progressive agenda's dominance by the champions of identity politics is the convergence of interest between those who believe they are at the forefront of progressive thinking and bureaucrats and politicians who represent the existing order. The emergence of grievance politics in Canada has been centrally dependent on the feminist movement and more particularly on the National Action Committee on the Status of Women, an organization that owes its existence to sponsorship by the federal government. The growing acceptance that racial minorities in Canada experienced pervasive discrimination has received considerable impetus from NAC, whose leadership has never found it necessary to limit its interventions to claims that might be supported by empirical evidence.

The 1980s and early 1990s witnessed an explosion of books, articles, magazines, and journals that gave voice to those who claimed that women and "people of colour" were perennially victimized and marginalized. Again the striking conclusion is that much of this would never have been published without generous subsidy from various public purses, whether at the Canada Council, Canadian Heritage, or the Ontario Arts Council. Fertile soil was also found within the universities, where preferential hiring policies and federal sponsorship to a number of chairs in women's and ethnic studies were backed by generous "research" support to those who sought to declaim against their victim status. The legacy of the various initiatives that have been undertaken, and of the plethora of groups whose existence is dependent on the continuing demonstration of the victim status that defines their entitlement, is a society more divided by race and gender. Issues that fail to mesh with the new agenda are largely marginalized.

The contemporary debate is dominated by apparent evidence of the grossly discriminatory nature of the Canadian labour market. Much of this supposed evidence of racial discrimination rests not on careful analysis but on a comparison with the wider population of the labour market experience of groups disproportionately comprised of recent immigrants, often fluent in neither of Canada's official languages, lacking in Canadian qualifications and experience. Such comparisons are used to support preferential hiring policies giving those who exhibit the right group characteristics significant advantages at the expense of able-bodied white males – of whom it is always possible to employ too many but never to employ too few. Canadians might be excused for assuming that discrimination against many native-born Canadians is justified by conclusive evidence of gross discrimination against others. They would be wrong. Canada's preferential hiring legislation can be traced to many influences, including the American experience and a well-funded feminist lobby. It has not been driven by hard evidence of discrimination.

In the last twenty years women have made quite extraordinary gains in the labour market, frequently at the expense of male competitors. The public sector has been a particular target of preferential hiring advocates; it has afforded rewarding careers to those who have entered the expanding equity industry and rich prizes for the beneficiaries. Public sector employment in Canada is significantly more generously rewarded than private sector employment. In 1995 39 per cent of public sector employees had incomes of $40,000 or above, compared to a little less than 21 per cent of private sector employees. Average earnings for women in the public sector are almost double those of women in the private sector. Ninety per cent of full-time, public sector workers have an occupational pension plan, 51 per cent of full-time private sector employees. Eighty-eight per cent of full-time public sector employees have a medical plan, 64 per cent of their private sector counterparts (Clark 1997: 9–25). Public sector workers comprise some 25 per cent of the work force but account for 50 per cent of pension plan members and a staggering 70 per cent of pension plan assets and contributions (Corcoran 1997).

Women's gains in public sector employment in the last 20 years are as notable as men's losses. Between 1976 and 1996 the number of women employed in the public service increased by 47 per cent, while the number of men employed fell by 14 per cent. Women now constitute a majority of public sector workers, but while the number of men employed fell by 95,000 during the down-sizing between 1992 and 1996, the number of women employed fell by only 25,000 (ibid.).

The historic decline in Canadian male incomes, a phenomenon from which only upper income males have been immune, has been driven by a number of factors, including immigration levels which are now, on a per capita basis, the highest in the world. A recent study for the Canadian Institute for Advanced Research reported that male graduates in 1964 could expect incomes nearly 50 per cent higher by the time

they reached their mid-thirties than those 1990 graduates might anticipate (*Globe and Mail*, 18 September 1997). Even assuming that the
smaller proportion of those graduating in the earlier period resulted in
a higher earnings premium, this is a major shift. This generational
inequity has been compounded by the distributional effects of soaring
debt, which allowed older Canadians to enjoy government services at
the expense of future generations, and by the structure of the Canada
Pension Plan. The CPP was set up on the altruistic proposition that
those who had not yet entered the labour market, and were without a
vote, would happily pay premiums far in excess of the returns they
could expect, in order that older Canadians, who did vote, might enjoy
pensions far higher than their contributions merited.

Preferential hiring advocates regale Canadians with specious comparisons between men's and women's earnings with, as we will see,
scant regard for whether apples are being compared with apples. The
leaders of the movement, women in their mid-thirties and beyond,
might be thought representative of a group that has experienced some
marked hardship. In contrast, they represent the only group in the
Canadian labour force that can boast quite striking gains. For many
Canadians the last two decades have seen little progress in earnings,
with any gains quickly absorbed by tax increases; some have experienced a sharp fall in earnings. A study reported in the Statistics
Canada's *Canadian Economic Observer* (October 1997) highlighted
the marked decline in income, and the share of total employment,
experienced by entry level workers, male and female. In contrast, the
group categorized as "Prime Women" (aged 35 to 54) recorded large
increases in employment and striking increases in earnings. Between
1983 and 1992, women in this group had earnings growth of a little
over 18 per cent, compared to "Prime Men," who saw earnings
increases of only 2.5 per cent. The group experiencing the greatest
losses was clearly young males (20–24), with entry level males experiencing a "dramatic" decline in earnings of nearly 24 per cent. There
are no tax-funded lobbies who claim to speak on their behalf, no
government departments mandated to address their "marginalization."

Historically, those who spoke for a politics premised on the demand
for greater social equality sought to give voice to the concerns of those
who were victims of diminished employment opportunities and falling
incomes. In the contemporary Canadian context a generous platform
is afforded to those who have experienced significant gains; meanwhile, white young males find themselves the subject of a discourse
in which their real world experience is redefined with an emphasis on
the continuing advantages purportedly flowing from white skin colour
and male gender. Not surprisingly, many interpret failure in personal
terms and respond by withdrawing from the competition. Women now

predominate among those entering university and colleges. Those white males who do persevere will, in contrast to feminist rhetoric, frequently find that their group membership is less an advantage than a singular barrier to appointment, not least to the academic positions from which many contemporary advocates of grievance politics make their pitch. That a politics which fails to root itself in the lived experience of ordinary people should lack popular appeal, finding its support in public funding and sponsorship by bureaucratic and political elites, is unsurprising.

The backlash to the Rae government's embrace of preferential hiring and its enthusiastic endorsement of grievance politics helped the Conservatives to victory; but in general there has been remarkably little populist reaction, beyond growing cynicism about a politics dominated by what are seen as special interest groups. Ironically, the United States, whose racially divided history inspired the birth of affirmative action programs, has increasingly turned against such measures. Critics have argued that what has been created is an invasive bureaucracy that has contributed to racial tension without securing the promised upward mobility for poorer American blacks. Instead, advocates of preferential policies have secured the implementation of a plethora of policies and programs and financing for a burgeoning constituency of organizations and individuals whose continued funding and employment depends on articulating evidence of group grievance. In the last thirty years the entirely laudable objective of securing equality of opportunity has given way to the goal of equality of outcome. This, in turn, has led to a frontal assault on standards and the merit principle, in order to ensure that groups gain a strictly proportionate share of college places, government contracts, and employment.

The relative absence of debate in Canada may owe much to the ability of government-funded preferential hiring advocates and an array of unrepresentative grievance groups to dominate the agenda. In this they are immeasurably assisted by the nation's public broadcaster, whose commitment to represent a wide range of opinion seems at variance with the views that actually predominate, most notably on CBC Radio. Changes in the nature and availability of work, nonetheless, combine with preferential policies to create a potentially explosive mix.

Those who have a vision of social justice that amounts to more than a reordering of group representation must articulate a new politics of inclusion. The purpose of this book is more modest; it is to expose the fraudulent claims, nepotism, shoddy research, and self-serving rhetoric that have propelled the politics of grievance. In order to move forward, it is necessary to unmask this dubious inheritance.

The Pursuit of Division

1

The New Orthodoxy

Race, Gender, and the Politics of Grievance

> Practitioners of orthodoxy claim to be profoundly concerned
> about the plight of victims ... The key to social and intellectual
> legitimacy is to be a victim, or, if one has little or no concrete
> personal experience of being a victim, to be a member of a
> recognised victim group. The list of such groups is extensive.
> There is, indeed, a place for everyone who is not an able-
> bodied, heterosexual, white male ... orthodoxy ... obviates
> any need for the concrete analysis of real social conditions.
>
> Robert Martin, *Orthodoxy and Research*

THE MANUFACTURE OF GRIEVANCE: ENGINEERING EQUITY

It has become commonplace to describe Canada as a country characterized by profound racial and gender divisions. A multi-million dollar
industry has been created committed to achieving equality for women
and racial minorities. Specific concern is focused on those said to
experience double or even triple discrimination, notably so-called
women of colour.

The furore over group disadvantage has occurred at a time when
the number of women in the labour force has risen sharply and
Canada's demographics have undergone a marked shift. Changes in
Canadian immigration policy in the late 1960s resulted in the transformation of the ethnic and racial make-up of Canada's major cities.
This has been accompanied by a cacophony of demands that a range
of public policies, most notably employment legislation, be changed to
accommodate the needs of recent arrivals. Generous public funding of
advocacy groups who purport to speak for large constituencies of

grievance has ensured in public debate the portrayal of Canada as a society riven by conflicts over race and gender.

The actions of successive federal and provincial governments have created formidable numbers of those whose politics, cultural expression, and, frequently, jobs are crucially dependent on group identity. Thousands of people now make a living in the preferential hiring industry or the linked field of "diversity training," which urges managers in dealing with their employees to focus on their group membership. Individuals are to be seen first and foremost as members of identity groups: gay or heterosexual, male or female, Chinese, South Asian, black or white; it is these identities that mediate their relationship with society. In the mantra of the industry, justice no longer requires treating individuals equally, but rather groups must be treated differently to accommodate the needs presumed to flow from intrinsic group characteristics. It is an approach that seems driven by its own stereotypes, even while declaiming against the negative stereotypes held by others (Bernstein 1994).[1]

Managing diversity has become a major theme in contemporary human resources policy. When TV Ontario produced a four-part series under the title, the programs featured predictable claims about the existence of widespread systemic discrimination together with the stereotypical middle-aged white manager who failed to appreciate the merits of diversity or recognize his own counterproductive bigotry. Able-bodied white males may, in these politically correct times, be the only group who can be caricatured with impunity.

The popularity of diversity training in corporate North America may rest on more than a fad. The message of diversity training is that the corporate employer cares for your discrete, group-determined identity; the problem is not with the corporation but with the potential bigotry or insensitivity of colleagues whose essential "difference" is the diversity training text. The answer lies not in solidarity but dependence on the employer's benevolent paternalism. The ideological appeal scarcely needs spelling out.

Diversity training is now well established within government and the wider public sector. In the face of growing pressure on health care budgets, St Joseph's Health Centre in Toronto advertised the senior position "Valuing Diversity Coordinator," to administer the "comprehensive Valuing Diversity Program" which the centre had in place (*Globe and Mail*, 18 September 1996). Training extends into the most improbable areas: in 1997 the Department of Fisheries and Oceans announced its interest in recruiting a consultant who might develop "an effective marine diversity training session and implement a pilot program in Newfoundland and Labrador" (Consulting Services Solicitation No. HWT0670).

The National Film Board, even as it struggled with budget cuts, announced the recruitment of a "documentary producer, cultural diversity." The lucky incumbent was not actually expected to make films but, under the direction of an executive producer, "stimulate and encourage the conception and development of film *ideas* by film makers from cultural communities in Western Canada that are currently underrepresented in the film industry" (advertisement, *Globe and Mail*, 27 September 1996, emphasis added). Apparently at the NFB, films are made not by creative individuals, and certainly not by the burgeoning bureaucracy, but by representatives of "cultural communities." Obviously encouraged by this experience the NFB advertised (widely and at considerable expense) for another "documentary producer, cultural diversity" based in Toronto (*Globe and Mail*, 5 February 1997). Among the modest specifications, the successful candidate was expected to have a "thorough knowledge of the realities of cultural communities." It is in the nature of such initiatives that they acquire ever wider dimensions. The successful candidates would be joining a "Special Mandate Team for Cultural Diversity." In its enthusiasm for fostering the realities of cultural communities, the NFB's already minor contribution to a Canadian culture will, no doubt, be further marginalized and fractured.

The advocates of identity politics are assured of generous funding, as the growing equity industry has access to an increasing client base in the public and private sector. Their critics enjoy no such advantages. Not surprisingly, many of those who might benefit from policies that afford preferential treatment to the group of which they are a member eagerly embrace any evidence purporting to document their disadvantage. Consequently, many of the assumptions that drive identity group politics go unchallenged, not least the claim that "systemic discrimination" in employment results in pervasive disadvantages for women, visible minorities, aboriginals, and the disabled. This is the new orthodoxy; the traditional concern with the divisions of social class and income have been usurped by claims that victim status is inherent not in a particular social position but in group membership.

Orthodoxy does not require that the individuals claiming victimization furnish evidence; the justice of the claim is inherent in the membership of the group. Individual visible minority women may hold positions of considerable prestige, garnering incomes far higher than many other Canadians, while portraying themselves in all seriousness as members of a persecuted and marginalized minority entitled, in consequence, to special rights. Self-styled feminists with six figure incomes, living in exclusive residential areas, seriously proclaim their victim status and entitlement to special consideration.

The inclusion of aboriginal Canadians in the embrace of employment equity legislation may appear to address some of the historic injustices Aboriginal Canadians have suffered. But employment equity has had little impact on the problems facing Canada's First Nations, not least the failure of successive provincial and federal governments to acknowledge the obligations flowing from conquest and settlement. These largely arise not from discrimination at the point of entry into training or employment but from inadequate labour market preparation, geographic location, aboriginal ambivalence towards success in the mainstream economy, and government failure to protect traditional aboriginal economic activities from the deleterious effects of resource mega-projects (Loney 1987, 1995a). This legacy and the ill-considered welfare measures that have fostered a culture of dependency will not be effectively resolved by preferential hiring policies. Legislated employment equity may serve to create the illusion of political action without the substantial expenditures and controversial measures required to address the real issues.

The employment problems of Canadians with disabilities may, uniquely, merit legislative redress, but the statistical abuse and empire-building evident in the broader preferential hiring industry create a distorted picture. Advocates funded by government and charities claim to speak for the 15 per cent of Canadians with disabilities. This figure includes many, particularly older Canadians, whose disabilities, while real, have little impact on their job performance and are unlikely to appear on any employer "equity survey." The real needs of severely disabled Canadians for specific measures to provide employment accommodation are lost beneath inflated allegations of gross discrimination against hundreds of thousands of Canadians who neither sought nor mandated action on their behalf.

Politicians anxious to show that they are at the forefront of progressive thinking are quick to endorse claims of grievance. Activists compete in offering ever more dramatic descriptions of "systemic" injustice. What is striking, looking back over the last twenty years, is how quickly orthodoxy has dominated the progressive agenda and how little the claims of gross discrimination have been underpinned by scholarship. Equally notable is the alliance between mainstream politicians and bureaucrats and the self-styled radicals. The former have provided funding that has ensured the growth of grievance politics; the latter, in embracing the divisive demands of identity politics, have ensured that traditional populist and inclusive demands of the left for a more egalitarian social order have been drowned by the cacophony of voices claiming to speak for competing constituencies of grievance.

Few progressive voices have been raised to oppose the insistent claims of identity politics, but not all those who are concerned to fight racism and address issues of social inequality have been captivated by the insistence on the biological basis of guilt and virtue. A. (Siva) Sivanadan, head of Britain's Institute of Race Relations, and editor of its journal, *Race and Class*, has long declaimed against the lure of "skin politics," which attributes all the problems of racial minorities to the legacy of imperialism and the endless culpability of whites, advocating, with commendable tenacity, an inclusive politics of radical social change.[2] In a coruscating attack on racism awareness training (in many ways the precursor of the contemporary plague of diversity training), Sivanandan describes it as "the blight of the black struggle," riddled with "psycho-spiritual mumbo-jumbo" that reduces social problems to questions of individual attitude (Sivanandan 1985).

The Royal Commission on Equality in Employment under Judge Rosalie Abella evidenced the influence of orthodoxy in Canada. The targets of the judge's measured sympathy were portrayed as victims, with scant regard to the requirements of social analysis. The disadvantage of visible minorities in the labour market was never documented, though a casual reader could have been excused for assuming the learned judge had seen overwhelming evidence (Abella 1984). In fact, analysis of 1971 and 1981 census data showed no generalized trend for visible minorities to be concentrated at the bottom of the labour market. In 1971, for example, Asian Canadians were in the second highest earning group, and in 1981 Japanese Canadians were the third highest earners in all ethnic groups (Winn 1985: 686). Such findings are profoundly disturbing for preferential hiring advocates, for if some non-white groups out-perform some white ethnic groups, the claim that non-whites experience pervasive discrimination at the hands of whites becomes questionable. If some racial minorities succeed where others fail, explanations more complex than discrimination begin to intrude.
┃ In contrast to claims of "systemic discrimination," based on "visibility," an analysis of income data indicates that some "non-visible" ethnic groups experience less favourable labour market outcomes than other "visible" ethnic groups. An examination of 1986 census data, the year the first federal employment equity legislation was introduced, is instructive.┃

Chileans are excluded from the groups defined as visible minorities, but 1986 census data indicate that their average male employment income was lower than that for Brazilians, Peruvians, and Mexicans, who were included. Jamaicans, also included, had an average male income that placed them between Greeks and Portuguese, two other groups with large numbers of recent immigrants but not beneficiaries of employment equity legislation.

Incomes of Haitian males were 72 per cent of the national average income, and that of Jamaicans 85 per cent; both groups are black. Lebanese, Syrian, Indonesian, Turk, Japanese, Thai, and Egyptian males, however, were among the groups in which males had higher than average earnings. All are beneficiaries of employment equity legislation (Harvey and Wortley 1993: table 6.2). Chileans were among the five out of forty-six ethnic groups surveyed who were disadvantaged on five out of six measures. The Japanese, Indonesians, and Egyptians, beneficiaries of preferential hiring programs, were among the five groups who did not score highly on any of the measures of disadvantage (ibid.: 18–19). Such evidence would seem to cast substantial doubt on the proposition that labour market outcomes are driven by "visibility."

Analysis of 1991 census data indicates that among those aged 15–64, 13 per cent of those reporting Greek and Portuguese ethnic origin reported incomes above $40,000, compared to 14 per cent of those reporting Chinese and 16 per cent of South Asian ethnic origin (Canadian Heritage 1994: 7). Further analysis indicates the importance of such factors as language capacity, immigrant class on entry to Canada, and length of time in the Canadian labour market.

Japanese Canadians, who unlike Greek, Portuguese, Chinese, and South Asian Canadians include relatively few first generation immigrants, belong to the ethnic group that experienced the most overt discriminatory treatment in the twentieth century, including property seizure, internment, and deportation (Adachi 1976). Today, on any measure, they are among the most successful ethnic groups in Canada – scarcely evidence that historic mistreatment and contemporary discrimination against visible minorities is a powerful factor in affecting success.[3]

Abella subsequently summarized her thinking on equality rights and the case for preferential hiring programs in a collection of essays examining Canada's future. She borrowed heavily from the rationale developed in support of American affirmative action programs, designed to address that country's very different historical legacy. Voicing a view that had become commonplace but which was gaining ever wider meaning, Abella argued that while civil rights required everybody to be treated in the same way, human rights required people to be treated differently:

The reason in human rights that we do not treat all individuals the same way is that not all individuals have suffered historic generic exclusion because of group membership. Where assumptive barriers have impeded the fairness of competition for some individuals, they should be removed even if this means treating some people differently. Otherwise, we can never correct disadvantage, chained as we would be to the civil libertarian pedestal of equal treatment of every individual.

There is nothing to apologize for in giving the arbitrarily disadvantaged a prior claim in remedial responses (Abella 1991: 273).

There are two linked flaws in this approach. Firstly, any evidence for historic group exclusion depends on selection of particular moments or geographic areas. This has little contemporary salience and none for the recent immigrants who are the primary beneficiaries of the muddled attempt to address "historic generic exclusion," a concept borrowed from the United States. The group that experienced the most exclusionary policies in Canada in this century, the Japanese, is as we have noted among the most successful. The second flaw lies in the assertion that if such exclusion had existed, the removal of barriers would in itself be insufficient. If a case can be made for the need for action beyond equal treatment, it can gain credence only in the context of a legacy of gross exclusionary policies. Who are the "arbitrarily disadvantaged"? Women whose mothers did not work? Women who choose to stay home and raise children? The 83 per cent of visible minority adults who are first generation immigrants?

Abella leaves unanswered the question as to why contemporary targets of preferential hiring should be compensated for the discrimination experienced by previous generations. She similarly fails to explain why contemporary able-bodied white males should pay a penalty for the "advantages" of previous generations.

Abella's embrace of the argument that some individuals, because of group membership, are entitled to different treatment leads to other consequences. The imposition of universal requirements for employment and training is eroded in the face of demands for compensatory provision. Standards must be varied; qualification requirements for one group need not be as high as those for other groups; indeed, whole curricula might be transformed and adapted to the supposedly unique requirements of a particular group. What starts as an apparent demand for equal treatment and an end to arbitrary exclusion is transformed into a case for special treatment and the consequent marginalization of those not possessing desirable group membership. The pattern is evident in the United States, as Christopher Lasch notes: "The civil rights movement originated as an attack on the injustice of double standards; now the idea of a single standard was itself attacked as the crowning example of 'institutional racism'" (Lasch 1995: 136).

Abella's claim for differential group entitlements is consistent with biopolitics, what Trent University professor John Fekete calls "a regression *from* politics to a new primitivism which promotes self-identification through groups defined by categories like race or sex ... The concern is to promote the group and to advance the group's cause *against* its enemies" (Fekete 1994: 22, emphasis in original).

We return to Abella's legacy and the federal government's enthusiastic if ill-informed pursuit of preferential hiring in chapters 7 and 8.

THE POLITICS OF RACE AND GENDER

Canadian feminists, backed by substantial government funding, have played a critical role in the development of the politics of grievance and legislated preferential hiring. Paul Malvern's account of the Canadian lobbying industry highlights the role played by feminists in promoting racial hiring policies that might have otherwise encountered substantial resistance. In allying "with one group that does count for a great deal in government eyes – the feminist lobby," Malvern suggests, ethnic leaders advocating preferential policies showed "a touch of genius" (Malvern 1985:176).

The striking change in women's labour force participation and the rapid growth in the number of women in professional and managerial positions in the last twenty-five years might have suggested that legislation, at least so far as gender equity is concerned, was unnecessary. Women's position in the labour market has changed rapidly, driven by changing social mores and the increasing economic pressure on households, which has created growing dependence on a second income. The proportion of women with a university degree more than tripled between 1971 and 1991 from 3 per cent to 10 per cent. The number of women in post-secondary education increased at every level. Women's share of those pursuing first degrees rose from 42.6 per cent in 1972–73 to 53.4 per cent in 1992–93. At the master's level the share rose from 26.7 per cent to 46.2 per cent, while at the doctoral level the rise was from 19.4 per cent to 35.2 per cent (Statistics Canada 1995a: 58–60). By 1993–94 women obtained 58 per cent of all bachelor's degrees (HRD 1995b: 33).

The increase in women's representation in higher education has been matched by the growth in the number of women in the better paid positions in the labour force. In 1994 women made up 43 per cent of

those employed in management and administration as compared to
29 per cent in 1982. Women made up 32 per cent of all doctors and
dentists in 1994, compared to 18 per cent in 1982 (Statistics Canada
1995a: 67).

The earnings gap between men and women has been closing steadily:
for full-time workers the ratio declined from 58.4 per cent in 1967 to
73.1 per cent in 1995. In recent years the growth in female earnings
has been paralleled by a real decline in male earnings. Expressed in
1995 dollars, male earnings for full-time, full-year workers fell from
$41,236 in 1975 to $40,610 in 1995. In the same period full-time, full
year female earnings rose from $24,876 to $29,700 (Statistics Canada
1997: 11). Earnings of males in full-time employment fell 2 per cent
from 1989–93, while female earnings rose 8 per cent (Statistics Canada
1995a: 86). If attention is focused on never married earners, the female
to male earnings ratio was 94.1 per cent in 1995: "there was almost
no difference in average earnings for university-educated single males
and females (95.7 per cent)" (Statistics Canada 1997: 14). Marital
status and the division of responsibilities within the family, not labour
market discrimination, drive such figures. The thriving employment
equity industry, in contrast, prefers to cherry-pick statistics that purport to reveal gross discrimination, particularly in representation in
higher paid positions. Such statistical comparisons often eschew age
standardization, qualifications, distinction between part-time and full-
time workers, and continuity of labour force participation.

There are strong parallels between the efforts of feminists to find
gender disadvantage and discrimination in the most unlikely places, and
those who attribute all of life's misfortunes to race. Carleton University
professor Jill Vickers, co-author of a history of the government-
sponsored National Action Committee on the Status of Women (Vickers *et al.* 1993) and former president of the Canadian Association of
University Teachers, claims the attenuated careers of Audrey McLaughlin and Kim Campbell resulted from the operation of a ruthless male
political machine: "They were sacrificial lambs in both instances. The
women were chosen as the sacrificial standard bearers when it was
quite clear the parties were going to be defeated" (Dawson 1996). In
contrast to Vickers' view, which suggests a degree of feminist paranoia,
conjuring up male conspiracies to humiliate women, Campbell was
perceived as a potential winner who emerged after a tough convention
fight and quickly, if briefly, overcame Mulroney's unpopularity to
establish a strong lead in the polls. McLaughlin's victory in the NDP
leadership campaign owed much to her gender, but the vigorous
opposition she encountered from other candidates, including veteran

B.C. politician and former premier Dave Barrett, is scarcely consistent with the idea that the party was on the ropes. Before Ed Broadbent's disastrous performance in the 1988 election the federal NDP had gone through an unprecedented period of popular support.

If gender is to account for the callous sacrifice of McLaughlin and Campbell, then race explains the fate of Rosemary Brown and Howard McCurdy, both at different times candidates for the leadership of the federal NDP. Barbadian-born writer Cecil Foster argues that Brown, a backbench MLA from British Columbia, lost the 1975 leadership convention to Ed Broadbent "partly because he was a man and white" (Foster 1996: 148). Foster, who has a finely honed sense of racial grievance, reports: "This story is told many times over in the Canadian black community as an example of how integration does not work, of how the best often doesn't win when race becomes the ultimate factor" (ibid.: 148). Foster offers no evidence that race was the ultimate factor. Brown offered herself as a radical feminist candidate and lost to a federal MP. Whether Brown was the best is a matter of judgment; she had relatively little experience, having served only a few years in the B.C. legislature. She subsequently served as chief commissioner of Ontario's fractious Human Rights Commission.

McCurdy's defeat in 1989 is also, apparently, attributable to his race. He was, of course, beaten by McLaughlin. McCurdy, Foster reports, knew that the only reason he failed to get the votes and dropped off after the first ballot was "because he was black" (ibid.: 154). Foster supports McCurdy's superiority as a candidate by noting McLaughlin's "inexperience" – precisely the same criticism that might have been levelled at Brown.

Faced with the strident claims of identity politics, many Canadians have retreated in confusion from traditional liberal values. Where once an emphasis on race as a basis for qualification or exclusion would have been an anathema, it is now a legitimate concern. The former book reviews' editor at the *Ottawa Citizen*, Charles Gordon, in a hand-wringing soliloquy on the challenge of selecting an appropriate reviewer asks, rhetorically: "Should books by black writers be reviewed by black reviewers? A white reviewer might not have a full enough understanding of the experience" (*Ottawa Citizen*, 16 February 1997).[4] If such a question might reasonably be asked, then it follows that we must ask whether a black reviewer can review a book by a white writer, or a man review a book by a woman. Apparently the idea that universal standards might apply to both fiction and non-fiction has been swept out on the tide of cultural relativism. Those who thought the debacle that followed the Canada Council's culturally illiterate musings on "voice appropriation" had ended such nonsense were wrong.

LEGISLATED DISCRIMINATION

Advocates of preferential hiring policies frequently cloak their demands with the rhetoric of social justice and appeals to combat racial or gender prejudice. The effect of preferential hiring policies is, in fact, the exacerbation of group conflict, sometimes with disastrous consequences. Thomas Sowell, in his international review *Preferential Policies*, notes the case of Sri Lanka where the Sinhalese majority adopted increasingly onerous measures to remedy the perceived over-representation of Tamils in positions demanding higher education. These included specific steps to reduce Tamil access to higher educational opportunities. Sowell notes the good ethnic relations that existed at the time of independence and the confident predictions for the future and roots the increasingly bloody ethnic conflict on the island in the pursuit of such preferential policies: "The worsening of relations between the Sinhalese majority (about 70 per cent of the population) and the Tamil minority (about 20 per cent) began with preferential policies" (Sowell 1990: 77).

The divisive nature of preferential policies is not difficult to understand. Candidates for employment or promotion who find their application blocked by reason of group membership are unlikely to share the view that this is a reasonable price to pay to address some perceived historic wrong. The continual emphasis on group membership as the basis for entitlement or disqualification leads not to a reduction in the significance attached to gender or race but to an increase. Polarization, not harmony, is the inevitable outcome. White male workers who are denied equal treatment and then condemned as racist for protesting preferential policies may come to embrace the charge, and students subjected to a relentless barrage of "multicultural" education may not always react in the intended fashion.[5] Observes Lasch, "Since opposition to an 'affirmative' double standard is routinely dismissed as racist, one reaction to this insult, from working- and lower-middle-class people harassed by affirmative action ... and now from college students harassed by attempts to enforce politically correct language and thought is to accept 'racism' as a badge of honour, to flaunt it, with studied provocation in the face of those who want to make racism and minority rights the only subject of public discussion" (Lasch 1995: 91).

The introduction of preferential hiring may give a significant advantage to recent immigrants who are designated group members over Canadian-born, white male applicants. Canada has continued to admit large numbers of immigrants even as' unemployment has increased. Only a small proportion of immigrants, the so-called independent class, have been admitted because of presumed labour market skills. Most have been family class immigrants, many fluent in neither English or French. Legislation, nonetheless, may require employers to give preferential consideration to such immigrants in competition with able-bodied white males. The economic and social rationale for this combination of policies is unclear. In effect Canada has frustrated the ambitions and hopes of many young white males in pursuit of preferential hiring policies and immigration policies which have become disconnected from labour demand generated by economic growth.

The creation of numerical targets intended to ensure that the workforce mirrors the rapidly changing population inevitably places at a disadvantage those whose group characteristics are already well represented. The disproportionate number of white males in senior positions results from the predominance of white males in the labour force in an earlier period. In any workforce in which white males historically predominated, the implication of legislated employment equity has been that able-bodied white male applicants are placed at a disadvantage for new hiring and able-bodied white male employees are placed at a disadvantage for promotion.

Preferential policies provide legitimation to those who prefer to portray individual or group failure as driven by discrimination rather than broader problems such as global restructuring, falling wage levels, high levels of unemployment, or many other factors that affect individuals irrespective of group membership. One result of the eager embrace of the claim of "systemic racism" by academics, politicians, and bureaucrats is that members of racial minorities are encouraged to conclude that many of the misfortunes they encounter can indeed be reduced to such abstractions.

Able-bodied white males may also experience discriminatory treatment in the context of downsizing. Many workers are protected by seniority provisions, but in the context of reductions in the Ontario Public Service, Rosemary Brown, then chief commissioner of the Ontario Human Rights Commission, warned the Ontario government that since women and racial minorities tended to have less time in the work force they would be disproportionately affected. Brown claimed that apparently neutral layoff procedures could contravene the Human Rights Code (*Globe and Mail*, 21 June 1996). Brown's intervention brought the issue into the open, but equity activists had already been seeking to use downsizing to advance equity targets.

In the industry newsletter *Managing Diversity*, Paul Scott, who subsequently served as executive director of the Ontario Office of the Employment Equity Commissioner, reported on the ways in which the Municipality of Metro Toronto had used the opportunities provided by restructuring and downsizing to target designated groups for retraining, available promotions, and any new positions that became available (Scott 1993). Metro Toronto's approach was not unusual; the City of Toronto quantified its success in protecting designated group members impacted by "streamlining": 49.2 per cent of affected designated group members remaining with the city were found permanent positions, in comparison with only 28.6 per cent of able-bodied white males. Designated group members were overwhelmingly favoured in retraining expenditures, receiving 94.4 per cent of all expenditures in the first six months of 1995 (City of Toronto 1995: 2).

The logic of legislated employment equity is the requirement that group membership take precedence over merit. This is invariably denied by equity advocates but easily demonstrated. Labour turnover varies between industries; in some areas where pay is low and skills easily transferable, there may be considerable fluidity. In other occupations, for such groups as firefighters, police, teachers, and many other public sector positions, employees may envisage continual service until retirement.

Most Canadian university professors will remain employed at the same institution for the whole of their working life. This means that very few positions fall vacant in any one year; when this is combined with cut-backs, new recruitment will be minimal. This has implications for meeting employment equity targets. A university with one thousand academic staff might, over a ten-year period, see 250 resignations or retirements (this is a generous estimate). If it is assumed that racial minorities are proportionately represented in 1986, that two hundred new academic staff are hired, and that racial minorities are represented in appointment according to their growing number in the population, at the end of the period racial minorities will be under-represented. They will receive a growing share only of the new appointments, not of the positions already occupied. The only way a university can ensure that its work force reflects the wider population is to give a dramatically disproportionate share of new appointments to racial minority candidates, to match the increase in racial minorities in the wider population. Universities also face incentives to preferential hiring in attempting to meet equity goals for female academic staff. The rapid increase in the number of females with a PHD degree will not be immediately reflected in the overall composition of the university's academic staff without preferential hiring.[6]

Employment equity policies set targets not only for proportionate employment but also for representation in senior positions. Since visible minorities and women have lower average seniority and labour force experience, proportionate representation in senior positions will not be achieved by merit but will require preferential promotion policies.

Preferential policies may affect access to relevant study and training opportunities. Even though women constitute a large majority of Canadian undergraduates, the Canada Scholarships Program run by Industry Canada, providing support to students in science and technology, gave explicit preference to female applicants, who were guaranteed at least 50 per cent of the places. In 1989 scholarships were awarded to 43 per cent of female applicants and only 34 per cent of males (Industry Canada 1990: 22). The following year the disparity was less marked; 36.9 per cent of women were successful compared to 31.9 per cent of men – a difference it was noted "lower than in the previous years" (Industry Canada 1991: 19). The requirement that women secure at least 50 per cent of the scholarships resulted in some disciplines in higher scoring males being rejected in favour of lower scoring females. A similar program provided scholarships to technology students at community colleges, where again women who make up only a small proportion of such students were guaranteed 50 per cent of the grants. No similar program affords support to male students in disciplines dominated by women. Following cut-backs, no new scholarships are offered under the Industry Canada program, but Human Resources and Development offer grants of $3,000 a year to women doctoral candidates in any field in which the female participation rate is below 35 per cent. No similar financial support is offered to male doctoral students in areas dominated by women.

Men now constitute only 42 per cent of those graduating with first degrees from Canadian universities, but there is a striking absence of concern over this trend, or proposals for special programs, from those who elsewhere demand measures to ensure proportionate representation in every area of the economy for other groups. A majority of those admitted to medical schools are now women, and research by the Canadian Medical Association suggests that male applicants face significant discrimination. Eva Ryten, director of research, told Canadian Press that no less than 70 per cent of high performing candidates who were rejected were men. Overall, in 1993–94, the acceptance rate for women was 12 per cent higher than for men (*Globe and Mail*, 18 October 1994).

A number of scholarship programs offered by universities are also specifically targeted on the basis of gender and race. The University of Windsor provides racially exclusive scholarship support to visible minorities pursuing doctoral studies. The scholarship carries the promise of a tenure track appointment on completion. The rationale for such racial provision is not readily apparent. Some 20 per cent of

Canadians graduating with PHDs are members of a visible minority – twice the proportion in the Canadian population (Wannell and Caron 1994a: 4). Were such racially exclusive provision afforded to white candidates, the Ontario Human Rights Commission would impose a substantial penalty.

At the Faculty of Education at York University, which has a wide range of preferential admissions, applicants can take advantage of York's "Access Initiative" by submitting an autobiographical statement. Included in its "Initiative" are those who might want to claim special consideration because of "first language, race, ethnic background, place of birth, parental education, family size and economic circumstances, and physical, sensory or learning disabilities" (Nikiforuk 1994). One such student had made fifteen unsuccessful applications over five years to various education faculties, but with marks averaging in the seventies she failed to meet the standard. York offered her a place, in preference to applicants with higher grades, as "differently abled" (Kreuger 1996).

The School of Social Work at Carleton University even identifies sexual preference as a criteria in selection. Under the heading "How Do I Qualify," the school's prospectus identifies a cast of underdogs who will find particular welcome:

Admissions to Social Work are governed by the following policy:

The Carleton School of Social Work is committed to educational equity. The society in which we live and of which social work is a constituent part is composed of groups with differential access to power – economic, political and social. The School affirms that all these groups should have the opportunity to learn in a supportive environment. Specific groups include, but are not limited to, persons of Aboriginal and racial, cultural, and/or ethnic minority origin, persons with disabilities, lesbian, gay, and bisexual persons, and persons disadvantaged by their gender or economic position (Carleton 1993).

Transparently, here as elsewhere, merit is of little concern.

That many of the more extreme preferential hiring and training excesses occur in the public sector is not surprising. Discrimination has an economic cost, a point long familiar to economists who have argued that market forces work to diminish discrimination by imposing a penalty (Friedman 1962: 21). Employers who discriminate against potential employees because of skin colour will, it is argued, be less successful than those who recruit solely on merit. In the public sector, the costs will be indirect, borne by the taxpayer. In racially divided societies this may result in discrimination being more prevalent in the public sector than in the private (Sowell 1990: 20 and *passim*). Sowell's observation was made after examining discriminatory policies against blacks, often reinforced by legislation, as in South Africa or in the American South during the Jim Crow era. The same argument can, however, be made in regards to reverse discrimination or preferential hiring. Employers who hire to meet equity targets or offer preference to candidates on the basis of desirable group characteristics rather than merit will experience an economic cost. The evidence suggests that the public sector will be much more willing to bear such costs. In the Ontario public service, equity activists were successful in some departments in raising the proportion of visible minorities above 30 per cent, an outcome difficult to reconcile with the merit principle.

FUNDING THE CULTURE OF GRIEVANCE

Assertions of gender and racial disadvantage have been put forward by those who claim to speak for large constituencies. When those who are alleged to suffer some disadvantage are added together, they embrace a substantial majority of the population. Closer examination suggests that those giving voice to these claims, and the ever more sweeping demands for mitigatory action, speak not for social movements but government funded bureaucracies. Legitimacy rests not on any grass-roots mandate but on a generous public subsidy to those who have found a sympathetic ear among politicians and bureaucrats. The National Action Committee on the Status of Women and the plethora of women's groups that have emerged in the last twenty-five years reflect less some popular ground swell than the generous funding of government social engineers.

Funding of groups that purport to identify racial disadvantage and speak for the victims of discrimination ensures the constant production of evidence that appears to confirm the existence of gross prejudice. No similar platform is provided for those who might offer a more balanced view of Canada's record. There are many whose job descriptions include broadcasting evidence of failure: If racial minorities are "under-represented" in senior management, it is evidence of racism. If blacks are disproportionately dropping out of the school system, it is evidence of racism. But if racial minorities constitute 20 per cent of those currently pursuing PHDs in Canada, if students of Chinese ethnic origin dominate the honour rolls in many schools, what is that evidence of? We do not know. The grievance industry is thriving, the celebration of success unfunded.

The consequence is the production of the poisoned race relations the race industry claims to be addressing. In a competitive market economy there are inevitably winners and losers. Global economic changes and the fiscal mismanagement of successive governments has resulted in a job market that offers diminishing prospects to young Canadians. Many will be frustrated in realizing their ambitions. The conclusion urged on those who are members of racial minorities is that they are victims not of political incompetence, opportunist immigration policies, social injustice, or economic adversity but racism. Others, witnessing the proliferation of programs seeming to offer special assistance to anyone except able-bodied white males, might reasonably conclude that discrimination of a different kind is becoming institutionalized. It is a curious vision of racial harmony that requires a constant emphasis on race to establish entitlement or disqualification.

The increasingly strident voice of Canadian feminism has been orchestrated by the tax-subsidized National Action Committee on the Status of Women. The failure of NAC to secure financing from its members is indicative of the disproportionate role of federal bureaucrats and politicians in shaping the Canadian women's movement. In 1980, for example, NAC lobbied government for a four-fold funding increase to the women's program of $4.1 million. In the same year, in a major campaign explicitly pitched to reduce dependence on government funding, the organization raised a magnificent $7,800 for its coffers from the (apparently few) "friends of NAC" (Vickers *et al.* 1993: 108).

Today NAC boasts greater financial independence, claiming that only a quarter of its own $1 million annual revenue is provided by government. In fact many of NAC's affiliates are also government funded, meeting their NAC dues from the public purse. Others, like the YWCA, are affiliate members who have little knowledge of or involvement in the decision to use their dues to support NAC. Feminist groups are now well established, fertilized by generous federal, provincial, and municipal funding. In 1995–96 Canadian Heritage alone dispensed some $8.6 million to a variety of women's groups. Such groups also access a wide range of other federal sources (Canada 1996: 3–33). In Ontario, the Rae government was particularly energetic in shovelling public funds to groups purporting to represent a variety of constituencies of grievance (see chapter 10).

NAC's position on employment equity was summarized by Avvy Go, a prominent NAC activist, appearing before the House of Commons Human Rights Committee in support of yet more draconian legislation[7]: "We know for years … businesses *are not voluntarily going to hire more racial minorities or people with disabilities or women or aboriginal people* and so on. They have to be told to do so" (Minutes of the Standing Committee on Human Rights and the Rights of the Disabled, 1995: 42:8, emphasis added). It is worth pausing to consider this claim. In the view of an organization that has been front and centre in the battle for legislation, employers will not hire, without legislative coercion, groups who comprise more than 60 per cent of the Canadian labour force.

RADICAL ILLUSIONS

Advocates of preferential hiring policies often present themselves as radical crusaders, yet few envisage any personal sacrifice, and many foresee a direct benefit. Frequently the advocates are members of groups who will benefit from the policies. Some are employed in the equity industry, which profits from an ever more stringent regulatory framework. Where no direct benefit is envisaged, there is certainly no direct sacrifice made. When organized labour lends its voice to employment equity, it does so while insisting there be no challenge to the principle of seniority. In other words, no current union member will be adversely affected, as any changes in the composition of the workforce will be achieved at the expense of job applicants, not existing incumbents. Any change to representation in senior positions must be achieved without impact on the sacred union principle of "Buggins' turn."

Equity advocates like to present their opponents as obdurate defenders of white male privilege, but there have in fact been very significant changes in gender roles with remarkably little resistance, given the magnitude of the transformation. The pervasive "systemic" barriers portrayed by advocates do not appear to conform to common labour market experience; hence the lack of widespread support for equity legislation, even amongst its beneficiary groups.

Earlier generations of immigrants to Canada experienced far more marked discrimination than is apparent today but voiced no demands that on arrival they were immediately entitled to a proportionate share of all jobs, at all levels, in all sectors of the economy. This is the demand now posed by the advocates who claim to represent more recent immigrants. The generous tax-funded support that ensures these advocates a platform might be thought to give the lie to their claims of pervasive discrimination.

In Ontario, a Gallup poll in December 1993 found only one in five supported the Rae government's equity legislation; among women, a key beneficiary group, one in four supported the legislation. The absence of widespread public support has been noted by preferential hiring advocates. Reflecting on the absence of support "after fifteen years of fighting ... among women and communities of people of colour" [sic], Judy Rebick notes: "When the Harris government announced they were going to get rid of Bill 79, the NDP employment equity bill, there was very little response. It appeared that nobody cared" (Rebick and Roach 1996: 65). Could it be that the only "communities of colour" which exist are those in receipt of one or other government grant? Could the voice of Canadian feminism actually represent only a well-funded minority?

2

Orthodoxy

Asserting Race and Gender Inequality

For women as a group, progress is glacial ... for Aboriginal
women, disabled women and visible minority women there
was no progress at all or negative progress.

Office of the Employment Equity Counsellor,
Opening Doors, 1992.

Liberal political discourse has been predicated on a univer-
salistic notion of citizenship. This notion has been challenged
by a number of "excluded" groups, such as women, people
of colour, gays and lesbians and people with disabilities. Each
of these groups is contesting its marginality.

Christina Gabriel, former policy analyst,
Ontario Women's Directorate, 1996[1]

Orthodoxy is so deeply entrenched in debates over employment equity
that it is not uncommon to find the existence of gross discrimination
simply asserted, as though it is so self-evident as to excuse the tiresome
necessity of examining and presenting statistical data. Andrew Cardozo, former head of the tax-funded Canadian Ethnocultural Council,
a founding member of the National Employment Equity Network, and
president of the Pearson Shoyama Institute, another beneficiary of
government patronage, illustrates the approach. Cardozo, writing in
the journal of the Institute for Research in Public Policy, claims that
an examination of the first four annual reports on the operation of
the federal Employment Equity Act indicates that progress has been
"terribly slow and in some cases non-existent" (Cardozo 1993: 27).
He presents no evidence to support this conclusion, which is far from
self-evident to anybody familiar with the data in the reports.

From the particular case of federally regulated industries Cardozo moves to a sweeping indictment: "The failure of employment equity has meant that the workforce is becoming less and less reflective of Canadian society" (ibid.). Again no evidence is offered and, as we will see, the statement is absurd, of interest only because it evidences the willingness of apparently serious policy journals, funded by taxpayers, to publish unsubstantiated assertions, so long as they conform to orthodoxy.[2]

WOMEN'S ILLUSORY DISADVANTAGE

Statements about the disadvantages of women frequently rely on claims that are self-evidently absurd but regularly repeated. In a recent book on women and work, journalist Judith Finlayson reports that women with families work an average of fifteen hours more a week than their male counterparts (Finlayson 1995: 14).[3] The figure could only be believed by those ready to give credence to any claim that portrays men as insensitive parasites and women as eternal victims. The growth of dual income families has significantly increased pressures on the household. What kind of men sit around while their partners do their share of the work, benefiting from some sixty hours of additional leisure time each month?

Statistics tell a very different story. Statistics Canada surveys the total productive activity of Canadians. The 1992 General Social Survey found that in intact families, with one or more children under five, where both parents were in employment, women engaged in a daily average of 10.6 hours of productive activity, men in 10.2 hours. The weekly difference is less than three hours (Statistics Canada 1995: 83). What the data indicate is that while women continue to do more "housework," men do more paid work.

Curiously, the largest gap in productive activity occurred in couples without children, households which would ordinarily be under less time pressure; here a full one-hour average daily difference was reported. This is, however, still less than half the figure cited by Finlayson.

Maureen O'Neil, a bureaucrat who played a major role in the evolution of preferential hiring policies federally and in Ontario, serving as the first coordinator of Status of Women Canada, general secretary of the Canadian Human Rights Commission, and later as deputy minister of Citizenship in Ontario, gives voice to a similar myth. In a 1993 article, O'Neil advised her readers: "women have *far less* leisure time than men" (O'Neil 1993: 317, emphasis added). No source is offered for this observation, since it is obviously self-evident.

Indeed who, familiar with the pretexts of orthodoxy, would think to challenge such a claim? Who could doubt that those social engineers who spent millions transforming the face of Canada had their facts right?

Statistics Canada is not the only source to which Finlayson and O'Neil might have turned. The International Labour Organization in 1992 issued a report on women's wages that pointed to the international prevalence of women's hours of work exceeding men's. For those who might not have had a chance to see the report, the *Globe and Mail* editorialists quoted from the press release: "The analysis shows that women put in more hours of labour every week than men when housework is combined with other work in every area of the world *except North America and Australia* (where men worked 49 hours, versus 47.5 for women)" (10 September 1992, emphasis added).

Facts are irrelevant. When I challenged Finlayson's claim, in the letters columns in the *Globe and Mail* following a glowing review of her book, she responded with an appeal to gender-based sympathy. "As a wife, mother and wage earner," Finlayson replied, she had been too busy to read the recent Statistics Canada study to which she (incorrectly) attributed the figures that refuted her claim. In any case such figures were obviously wrong. Apparently unaware of the canons of survey research, Finlayson concluded that the data would inevitably be flawed by the fact that "the busiest women are not likely to have time to respond to surveys" ("Letters," *Globe and Mail*, 30 December 1995).

University of Winnipeg economists Derek Hum and Wayne Simpson solemnly advise their clients at Statistics Canada that since "women earn roughly one half the amounts of their male counterparts ... it is clear that women are disadvantaged" (1994: 10). To reach this figure Hum and Simpson take the average of all labour market incomes, though women are far more likely than men to work part-time. Does a woman's decision to take a part-time position in retail sales rather than a full-time position in a more highly paid occupation, such as mining, reflect disadvantage? Are the wage differences between predominantly male and female occupations invariably, or even commonly, attributable to gender bias? If women disproportionately choose to place greater emphasis on child care rather than their careers and in consequence earn less, is that disadvantage? Do families in which men earn more than their partners divide their expenditures accordingly?

Those who wish to portray women as victims eschew statistics that show a rapid closing of the gender gap for younger workers in favour of comparisons which compare all female labour force participants to all males.[4] This ensures that the lower earnings of earlier generations of women with a less extensive commitment to the labour force can be used to buttress claims that income differentials remain large, and change glacial. What is offered is not scholarship but politically correct posturing. To reach the conclusion that gender wage differences are necessarily a function of discrimination requires an uncritical acceptance of radical feminist ideology. This would see men and women legislated into equal participation in every area of the labour force.

The data generated by feminist ideologues is broadcast widely as evidence of discrimination. The Saskatchewan Government Employees Union, advertising in support of "pay equity" demands, which will see Saskatchewan taxpayers contribute to higher salaries for female public servants with no reduction in the pay of the presumably relatively overpaid, male public servants, offers an unequivocal conclusion: "The pay system discriminates against women. The extent of this discrimination can be measured. It's called the wage gap. Women still make about 64 cents for every dollar that men make" ("We Can't Afford It," SGEU advertisement *Briarpatch*, October 1995).

The union's position is not extreme. Advertising for a national conference to be held in Saskatchewan in 1996, Towards Workplace Equity, funded by the Government of Canada's Labour-Management Partnership program at Human Resources and Development, assures would-be delegates: "In 1911, women earned on average just over half of what men earned. Now women are making about 61 percent of men's wages. The difference in earnings is called the wage gap. *It's also called discrimination*" (Pay Equity Coalition of Saskatchewan 1996, emphasis added). Obviously whatever figure the SGEU can come up with can be bettered, a characteristic of escalating claims of victimization. The implication of the historical reference is clear: women's position is little changed since 1911, before women had the franchise.

The Saskatchewan Federation of Labour, one of the sponsors of the tax-funded conference, offered its own unique way of capturing the enormity of women's oppression, in an advertisement supporting the Women's March Against Poverty earlier in the year: "For a woman to make as much in a day as a man, she'd have to work until 10:30 at night. Then who'd make supper?" (*Briarpatch*, April 1996). This succeeded in combining misleading information about the labour market with misleading information about housework.

To celebrate 1997 International Women's Day the Canadian Labour Congress brought together a wide array of meretricious statistics intended to persuade the reader that, contrary to the dramatic change in women's labour market position and the continued actual and relative growth in female earnings and share of more desirable labour market positions, women faced a direct and increasing attack on their position in the labour market (CLC 1997). This project, like the Saskatchewan conference, was financed by taxpayers, through the federal government's Labour-Management Partnerships Program. The CLC report eschewed any coherent attempt to compare the experience of men and women in the labour market in favour of a search for evidence that might suggest, to a casual reader, that women and an array of "equity seeking" groups faced dire hardship. It is a curious approach that reduces the effects of major economic changes, with adverse consequences for many Canadians, to more fodder for the politics of group grievance. The reality for large numbers of Canadians is that disparate factors including globalization, the effects of mounting public sector debt, the increasing labour force participation of women, high immigration levels, and new technology have created a much more precarious labour market. This combined with rising taxes has produced a significant decline in after-tax income, which fell by some 9 per cent from 1989 to 1997 (*Globe and Mail's Report on Business*, 3 June 1997). Instead of confronting these changes, which would raise some difficult questions about the congress's policies on public sector deficits, immigration, and the belief that women should be equally represented in every area of the labour market, the CLC pursue the eclectic collection of data and opinion designed to persuade readers of women's increasing victimization.

It is not always easy to establish where the CLC's tax-funded researchers obtain their figures, but what is striking is the selectivity of the data provided. Readers learn that in 1995 women had an official unemployment rate of 9.2 per cent, women under 25 a rate of 15.6 per cent (CLC 1997: 5) – evidence, we are to assume, for women's increasing marginalization. For those who failed to recognize the significance of this the first time, it is repeated above a table that provides more detail on gross, and genderized, unemployment totals (ibid.: 46). What this reveals, to those who look beyond the text, is that male unemployment levels are significantly *higher*.[5]

Readers are further advised that the rate of industrial injury for women is rising while that for men is declining, with an increase in the rate of injury for women on the job from 19.1 per cent in 1984 to 26 per cent in 1992 (CLC 1997: 41). The report's authors might have added that Statistics Canada data indicate that 96 per cent of those killed on the job are male and that men suffer three time as many non-fatal injuries as women (Laframboise 1996: 108). Readers instead are advised that occupational health and safety studies do not have sufficient "gender impact analysis. Studies do not take into account the double or endless work day for women" (CLC 1997: 41).

The implication is that this onerous burden is contributing to female injury rates – but how do we reconcile this with the continuing dramatic difference between male and female rates? The CLC's answer is simply to eschew comparison in favour of claims of increasing female oppression.

CBC Radio reported the CLC's claims on its eight a.m. news (some three hours before the CLC embargo ended) and led with the story on the national news at six p.m., interviewing a number of women who offered unequivocal support to the CLC's claims (CBC Radio, 5 March 1997).[6] In effect, CBC treated the CLC's report as a straightforward statement of fact; no critical voices were aired. Listeners told that the study "shows women are losing ground" could only assume that women were indeed having to re-fight the battles of thirty years ago. The CLC press release highlighted an OECD statistic indicating that Canada had a higher incidence of low paid female employment than any other country apart from Japan. This was dutifully emphasized in CBC coverage, but the same OECD report also showed that Canada had a higher level of low paid male employment than any other country but the United States, suggesting that what may be the driving factor is not gender but a labour market that generates profoundly unequal outcomes.

The CLC was simply repeating the orthodoxy of the Canadian left. Confronted by a questioner in the NAC women's issues debate in the 1997 election campaign, NDP leader Alexa McDonough had no doubt that "women are losing ground, losing the battle for equality (CPAC, 26 May 1997).[7]

The *Globe and Mail*'s "Amazing Facts" columnist Bruce Little surveyed a range of labour force data to address a claim, made by a caller, that "Canada's dreadful job market in the 1990s has been especially hard on women." Little's conclusion was that women had actually fared far better than men, obtaining, for example, 69 per cent of the 510,000 new jobs created between 1990 and 1996. Many of these were part-time, but women got 84 per cent of the net new full-time jobs. Little reported that of 203,000 new management and administrative jobs created, women got 85 per cent; of the 68,000 new teaching jobs, women got 84 per cent. In natural sciences (including math and engineering) women make up only some 20 per cent of all job holders but secured 38 per cent of the 54,000 new jobs created (*Globe and Mail*, 14 April 1997).

Discrimination against women is frequently claimed on the basis that they remain substantially under-represented in the most senior positions. The possibility that many women may have consciously decided to combine family and work place responsibilities in a way which maximizes the benefits from both is discounted or attributed to nothing more than the effect of patriarchy. Senior positions are overwhelmingly filled by those with long labour market service. Female participation levels have risen rapidly, but in many areas the relevant pool of older workers remains overwhelmingly male. Such factors are so transparently central to any analysis that their regular omission can only highlight the substitution of polemic for scholarship.

It is not only in employment and at home that women are said to face discrimination. Canadians are regularly reminded that the CPP fails women, since the average annual payments to females are lower than those to males (Cohen 1993, Townson 1995). Is this further evidence of pervasive gender discrimination? Again what is offered is not scholarly analysis but ideological demagogy in which facts are selected to fit a conclusion predating any objective examination.

As CPP payments are, in fact, a direct function of contributions, lower payments to married women can only be assumed to evidence inequality in the myopic view of those who assume retired couples squirrel their money away in separate accounts and perhaps keep their food in separate cupboards. Curiously lacking from the discussion is the fact that on a contributory basis women fare far better from the plan than men. The reason is simple: women live on average some six years longer than men, and in consequence they collect longer and therefore, in total, larger CPP payments relative to their contributions. Married women who will typically outlive their spouses will also collect survivor benefits based on their husbands' contributions.

I have never encountered any male writer or advocate who has suggested that female CPP contribution rates should increase, but there are many feminists quick to highlight aspects of the plan perceived to favour males.[8] There are of course no groups whose continued receipt of tax dollars requires them to highlight the many and varied ways in which males, or more particularly white males, might be portrayed as victims, as Status of Women Canada and a variety of other groups do for women. There would, in any case, be remarkably few men who would wish to demand genderized contributions to the CPP, in contrast to what might be assumed by those familiar with some feminist caricatures.

THE MYTH OF RACIAL DISADVANTAGE

Much of the disadvantage detected by equity activists is artificial. Claims are driven by ideological assumptions about appropriate male and female roles or an apparent assumption that each new immigrant group has a charter claim on a proportionate share of the nation's resources, including proportionate representation in employment at every level. How else can there be any merit to the repeated claims that visible minorities are not equally represented in every sphere and at every level in the labour force? Eighty-three per cent of Canada's visible minority population, according to 1991 census data, are first generation immigrants (Canadian Heritage 1994b: 1). Yet the evidence for racial disadvantage frequently seems to depend on nothing more than the observation that visible minorities make lower average earnings than other Canadians.

The depth of discrimination might be illuminated by statistical analysis, but the multi-million dollar equity industry has been remarkably coy in pursuing rigorous analysis. If discrimination is claimed, it should at a minimum result in similarly qualified males and females, with similar lengths of time in the Canadian labour market and similar English/French language capacities, achieving markedly dissimilar outcomes. In contrast, claims of discrimination frequently depend on gross comparisons of markedly dissimilar populations. Groups that disproportionately include recent arrivals, fluent in neither of Canada's official languages, are compared to long-term residents. If prejudice against non-whites has a pervasive influence on labour market outcomes, it will affect all visible minority groups, irrespective of educational levels and cultural and social characteristics. The unchallenged statistical evidence that the labour force position of different visible minority groups is highly diverse might cast doubt on the claim that racial discrimination constitutes a central issue in labour market outcomes (Kelly 1995).

Nonetheless the operation of preferential hiring policies ensures that in a growing number of fields, particularly in the public sector, recent immigrants endowed with the desirable group "disadvantages" will secure more favourable treatment in applications for positions or promotion than white males born in Canada. The impoverished son of a white single parent family may struggle to achieve the standard of excellence demanded by the police or the fire service, only to find that lower scoring candidates, with far more advantageous family backgrounds, will secure preferment. There are, no doubt, white Canadians (as well as Canadians of other racial backgrounds) with prejudiced attitudes, but their influence has to be set in context. The barriers of poverty are much more formidable than any that may result from ethnic background. Ethnicity has always cut two ways, as a barrier to progress in some settings and as an aid in others. Compensating benefits will be small, at least in economic terms, where visible minorities are overwhelmingly poor, but this is rarely the case in contemporary Canada.

Employment equity advocates make great play of small differences in group outcomes, but a variety of factors may affect success, including the vagaries of height and perceived attractiveness. An array of studies have documented the link between height and success or, conversely, the penalty paid by those of below average stature. Surveying the evidence *The Economist* concludes: "Surely the notion of SHRIMPS (Severely Height Restricted Individuals of the Male Persuasion) as an oppressed group is silly and the idea of special protections or compensatory benefits for short men preposterous? Actually no – unless all such group benefits are equally dubious" (23 December 1995). *The Economist* notes that in contrast to many of those who benefit from preferential hiring programs, SHRIMPS actually share a common recognizable characteristic: "American Hispanics have nothing in common except the "Hispanic" label itself ... At least SHRIMPS are all detectably short." In Canada many of the visible minorities embraced by preferential hiring are "visible" only in the eyes of the government bureaucrats whose job descriptions include racial classification.

A number of studies have also shown the advantages of physical attractiveness in labour market success. An investigation by ABC News compared the experience of job seekers: "Employers gushed over the Adonis and Cindy Crawford lookalikes, and hired them five times out of five. Their plainer rivals were treated coldly the minute they walked through the door" (Freedland 1996).

THE LANGUAGE OF ORTHODOXY: EMPLOYMENT EQUITY DOUBLESPEAK

All animals are equal but some animals are more equal than others.

George Orwell, 1945

Many Canadians are unaware how far legislated preferential hiring has gone. The *Globe and Mail*'s highly regarded columnist Jeffrey Simpson attacks a draft manifesto proposing a merger between the Conservatives and Reform as no more than Canadian conservatives "hawking American snake oil" (10 April 1996). Simpson specifically skewers the proposed abolition of "ethnic and sex hiring quotas" in Canada as "pure rhetoric for something that does not exist." Simpson's difficulty in recognizing what does in fact exist is in no small measure a tribute to the duplicity that has characterized debate on preferential hiring policies in Canada.

The 1984 Abella report noted the resistance to American-style affirmative action programs in Canada and proposed to overcome this by calling its preferential hiring proposals "employment equity." This term was quickly adopted and may have led many to assume that Canada had shunned the reverse discrimination and explicit quota setting characterizing American programs. For Abella the issue was cosmetic, a way of defusing opposition: "it matters little whether in Canada we call this process employment equity or affirmative action" (Abella 1984: 7).

The City of Toronto had already recognized the merits of careful attention to language when it renamed its own affirmative action program the "Equal Opportunity Program" almost as soon as it was launched. The city had established numerical goals for some positions by 1982, for all external positions in 1985, and for all vacant positions in 1992 – an example of the escalating reach of preferential hiring advocates (City of Toronto 1995). It continued to dress its policies in the language of "merit," but in a situation in which increasing attention was paid to the possession of desirable designated group characteristics, being an able-bodied white male was not helpful. In 1996 the controversy over the appointment of new firefighters brought the issue into the open. The news that all twenty-four successful candidates in a highly competitive recruitment process were able-bodied white males resulted in calls for changes in recruitment.

The Toronto Fire Department, overseen by the City of Toronto Equal Opportunities Division and the Personnel Committee, chaired by preferential hiring advocate Kyle Rae, had engaged in extensive outreach activities to encourage more applications from designated group members and a rigorous review of its testing procedures. This resulted, among other changes, in the passing mark on the fitness test being reduced to 16 from 18 and the removal of any bonus point from that element of the selection procedure. The department, which had made no new appointments in over two years and received 1,386 applications when hirings were announced, employs two full-time recruiting officers who target designated groups. The department also engages in extensive advertising, much of it directed at designated groups.

The report from Toronto's Management Services Department (1996) indicated that a total of 189 candidates passed the four-stage selection process, which included, in the first stage, possession of a number of basic qualifications, including first aid training and a relevant driving licence. Those who possessed such qualifications had to pass three further hurdles: a fitness and strength test, a minimum of 75 per cent on an aptitude test, and a minimum of 75 per cent on an interview and skill assessment. Candidates who scored over 87 on the aptitude test received a bonus point, as did those who scored over 87 on the interview. The candidates were then ranked; those with two bonus points were placed in band 1, those with one bonus point in band 2. Thirteen candidates who placed in band 1 were automatically recruited, and eleven further candidates were selected by lottery from the 83 in band 2. Only three designated group members were in band 2; a further nine were in the next band. No evidence was presented that the testing was inherently discriminatory, beyond claims that the pass level required on the fitness test was too high and in consequence discriminated against women (*Toronto Star*, 16 May 1996). The results were, nonetheless, held to provide evidence of "hard-line antagonism to change" in the department (Kashmeri 1996). The Ontario Human Rights Commission promised an investigation, and Kyle Rae announced that the selection process had "failed" (*Toronto Star*, 16 May 1996).

Ceta Ramkhalawansingh, head of the city's Equal Opportunity Division, suggested the result indicated that "ranking" did not work. This had been a "fast track" procedure; in future the pre-qualification requirements, or the first stage, would be omitted to ensure there were no barriers to designated group applicants (personal communication, 26 May 1996). Margaret Hageman, speaking for the Alliance for Employment Equity, took a similar position, suggesting candidates could be selected from any who had achieved a minimum pass level (CBC, *Face Off*, 7 May 1996). Kyle Rae indicated that he too would favour an end to ranking. Referring to opposition from the firefighters to recruitment of lower scoring candidates in preference to higher scoring ones, Rae endorsed establishing a simple qualification threshold that would facilitate measures to favour recruits from target groups: "Members of council are bound and determined not to allow in what the firefighters union tells them are unqualified candidates. In fact, they are qualified candidates" (*Toronto Star*, 16 May 1996).

The problem revealed by the outcome to the recruitment process was not that it could be shown that equally meritorious candidates had been discriminated against because of race or gender, or that less able candidates had succeeded over more able. The problem was simply that the results failed to reflect the desired group representation. The proposed solution was to sharply reduce the importance of merit in recruitment, in favour of a system that would permit the Equal Opportunity Division, and Kyle Rae's personnel committee, to insist on appropriate selection on the basis of race and gender from those who passed a minimum qualification threshold. In the name of equity a merit-driven system would be replaced by one that would overtly discriminate on the basis of race and gender in order to attain numerical targets (quotas) set by Rae and the city's preferential hiring bureaucrats. This would not only result in a reduction in the quality of new recruits: it would also serve to create the very animosity preferential hiring advocates claimed to detect in the Fire Department.

The City of Ottawa, which announced the recruitment of twelve new firefighters shortly after the controversy over Toronto's recruitment, escaped significant media attention. The Ottawa appointments, unlike those in Toronto, were not merit driven but dictated by the city council, which instructed the fire department to establish separate pools for women, visible minorities, aboriginals, and white males. Seventy-five per cent of recruits were to be drawn from the designated groups, taking the highest ranked member in each of the groups until the target was filled.[9]

The preferential recruitment policy had been established in February 1994, after the city council had been advised that outreach and recruitment would result in only a small number of designated group candidates entering the qualified pool: "For this reason, it is critical that these few candidates be identified and targeted for preferential selection" (Ottawa 1994). The suggestion is not that designated group candidates faced discrimination: preferential hiring was rather justified by the very few who would enter the qualified pool. The unanimous adoption of the policy by the council is indicative of the rapidly extending parameters of preferential programs. Once justified to address perceived historic or contemporary discrimination, preferential hiring was now justified simply because few qualified candidates had the desired group characteristics.

The city ran an extensive outreach program and provided special training courses to assist candidates in exam preparation. The courses were ostensibly open to all candidates, though the city conceded that "99 per cent" of the places had been taken by designated group members (personal communication, 24 July 1996). A spokesman for the firefighters association reported that many white male candidates had failed to obtain a place on the courses (pers. com. 24 July 1996). More than 1,400 applications were received and 202 applicants passed the three stage test, including 15 designated group members, none of whom was a woman. The recruitment rate for successful designated group members was 60 per cent, for successful white males less than 2 per cent. The city claimed that many of the designated group candidates scored in the highest band and would have been recruited without the reliance on separate pools, but there was no dispute that the recruitment saw lower-scoring designated group members hired in preference to higher-scoring white males. A request by the firefighters association to see the distribution of scores was refused.

It is unclear why recruitment on merit would have resulted in discrimination. The city had undertaken extensive revisions to the testing program to eliminate elements perceived to discriminate on grounds irrelevant to job performance. This resulted in a number of changes, including the abolition of the benchpress in the fitness test.

Ironically, women, the one group which might have been placed at a relative disadvantage through tests which placed great emphasis on physical strength, remained unrepresented in new recruits.

Historically firefighter recruitment came under attack from those who claimed that an old-boys network favoured recruitment of those with friends and relatives already on the force. Such nepotism may well have been common before the introduction of increasingly competitive testing. Under the guise of employment equity, however, the City of Ottawa introduced discriminatory practices far in excess of any alleged in the past. White male recruits had never been provided with special coaching at the city's expense to improve their competitive edge in qualification tests. There is no evidence to suggest that at any time more than 98 per cent of qualifying applicants from designated groups had been turned down (as were white males in 1996); indeed, by the city's own account, the problem was rather the small number entering the qualified pool.

The City of Toronto, which recruited strictly on merit, was charged with discriminatory practices and is under investigation by the Ontario Human Rights Commission. Ottawa, which overtly discriminated against one group, white males, saw little controversy.

If Jeffrey Simpson wants explicit evidence of race and gender hiring quotas he might turn to the RCMP, frequently cited as one of the country's most important historical and contemporary institutions. It is covered by federal equity legislation. In February 1995 RCMP Assistant Commissioner C.G. Allen appeared before the House of Commons Human Rights Committee as it considered the new federal employment equity legislation. Allen confirmed that the force had established clear racial and gender set-asides for the majority of new recruits: visible minorities 112, aboriginals 112, women 95 (excluding visible minorities and aboriginals) (Minutes of the Standing Committee on Human Rights and the Rights of the Disabled, 1995: 29:10).[10] The assistant commissioner did not dispute that the recruitment policy resulted in higher-ranked white males being passed over in favour of lower-scoring target group candidates. Simpson's confusion is perhaps understandable, as prior to confirming details of the RCMP's precise numerical targets (or quotas), Allen stressed the need to provide the right public relations spin: "We must not create a perception that quotas are part of employment equity in the RCMP. Both the public and the membership will respond negatively to that" (ibid.: 29:6).[11]

The CBC lays claim to considerable tax revenue on the grounds that it plays an essential role in shaping Canada's national identity. While it does not appear to have established precise quotas, its pursuit of preferential hiring policies is explicit: "Staffing policies have been altered to give preference when external candidates are being considered for a position, to qualified candidates from an ethnocultural community [sic]" (Canadian Heritage 1996: 63).[12] This appears to go some way further than setting quotas. Candidates unable to claim relevant group membership qualifications are marginalized in competition for every post, though nepotism may secure continued access for those with compensatory ties of family or friendship. In the fiscal year ended March 1995, forty-seven internship proposals were funded through the CBC Help Fund; "almost half" went to members of a visible minority (Canadian Heritage 1996: 63). This outcome is difficult to reconcile with the merit principle.

Where employers do not establish explicit quotas it is not uncommon to find positions exclusively reserved for those who have the desired racial (and often gender) characteristics. In the fall of 1995 the University of Windsor proudly announced no less than four academic appointments which had been filled outside the normal process of advertising and open competition by visible minorities. Windsor has in fact long-established "targets" for gender recruitment to each faculty. The pace is slow since there are few new appointments, but resource pressures have not interfered with the university's ability to appoint an "equity assessor" to monitor the equity issues in any appointment.

Carleton University has explicitly waived the normal requirement that candidates for professorial posts hold a PHD in the case of aboriginal and racial minority applicants. In February 1996 Dalhousie University announced the appointment of the first successful applicant for a series of planned academic appointments, to which eligibility is limited to those who are black. The James Robinson Johnston Chair in Canadian Black Studies institutionalizes race as the qualification (or barrier) to appointment. It is a measure of how far race-based policies have progressed that the Canadian government, through Canadian Heritage, should be prepared to finance such segregationist provision.

The University of British Columbia has been the subject of considerable scrutiny in the race and gender wars currently infecting Canadian universities. An advertisement for the law faculty at UBC announced a new opening: any candidate was eligible for a junior appointment, although only designated group members could be appointed at a senior level (*Globe and Mail*, 26 August 1996). Responding to the controversy provoked by its notice of recruitment for a new president, which indicated that applications from designated groups would be "especially" welcome, Associate Dean Judith Myers reported the existence of gender targets for science faculty recruitment.

The Faculty of Science "equity plan" established goals for female recruitment "based on their proportion among the pool of potential candidates" (Letters, *Globe and Mail*, 1 October 1996). This would appear to be a clear quota policy.

The claim that recruitment of academic staff should parallel the numbers in the qualified pool raises many questions, not least the way in which the size of the pool is to be measured. Certainly Myers's report that in 1995 women comprised 25 per cent of successful applicants suggests a generous interpretation. In 1991, for example, a year that would include many doctoral graduates still seeking academic appointment, women comprised 32 per cent of those granted doctorates but much lower proportions in most of the sciences, ranging from a high of 29 per cent in agriculture and biological sciences to a low of 9 per cent in engineering and applied sciences (HRD 1994b: 19).

Preferential hiring advocates were quick to defend UBC's "especial" welcome for those who were not able-bodied white males. A similar "especial" welcome directed to able-bodied white males would have resulted in immediate action by the provincial human rights council.

In the advertising of positions, the ritualistic embrace of diversity and the emphasis on the welcome that awaits each and every designated group candidate is no doubt grist to the mills and coffers of newspaper publishers, requiring the addition of the relevant phrasing to each and every notice of recruitment. It is a testimony to the zeal of preferential hiring advocates that great attention is devoted to the particularities of the wording; but can there really be those eligible for university appointment who are unaware that to be anything other than an able-bodied white male is a positive godsend for any applicant?

Quotas, formal or otherwise, are an almost certain outcome of employment equity legislation. There are a wide range of factors affecting the representation of different groups in various labour market categories. Employers who are under pressure to make their workforce "representative," particularly those with a high profile like the RCMP or the CBC, will be driven to move from hiring on merit to hiring by group characteristic. If women, racial minorities, the disabled, or aboriginals had really been excluded and large numbers of qualified candidates were eagerly seeking appointment, the changes that could be achieved by simply removing discrimination would still be relatively slow. In contrast, the rapid changes in the labour force composition in Canada, combined with the failure of women and visible minorities to seek the predicted proportionate representation in each and every occupation, make the achievement of some targets highly problematic. The failure of the labour market to conform to the unrealistic picture offered by preferential hiring advocates results in ever greater degrees of discriminatory intervention to engineer the proportional outcomes that are believed, without evidence, to be the natural result of the operation of a non-discriminatory labour market.

Not everyone shares Simpson's conviction that quotas are irrelevant to understanding the Canadian legislative framework. NAC activist Avvy Go gave the House of Commons committee some insight into fashionable semantics: "The reason people stopped using the term 'quota' is the backlash out there. Every time we talk about employment equity, the business sector or people who are not interested in employment equity say, oh, this is quota-setting; we don't like quota. That's why people started to use another term, 'numerical goals.'" (Minutes of the Standing Committee on Human Rights and the Rights of the Disabled, 1995: 42:8).

SKIN POLITICS

The result of the well-funded chorus of escalating demands for "equity" is not the removal of race and gender as dominating criteria for appointment but their insertion. Martin Luther King's vision was of a society in which individuals would be judged by the content of their character, not the colour of their skin. In Canada skin colour is increasingly the test of qualification. Rosemary Brown, a former NDP member of the Legislative in British Columbia, was appointed by fellow New Democrat Bob Rae to head Ontario's fractious Human Rights Commission. When Brown, a first generation Jamaican immigrant, was asked if she thought her race and gender had played any part in her appointment, she replied that she hoped so.

Judy Rebick, denouncing UBC political science professor Philip Resnick's attack on the implicit preferential policies in his university's search for a new president, sneered that Resnick was once left wing.[13] This Orwellian rewriting of history suggested that the Canadian new left born in the struggles of the 1960s favoured hiring on the basis of group characteristics. The reality is, of course, the reverse. The principles espoused called on people to be treated as individuals. Rebick, in contrast, was clear that being a woman or a minority was indeed a particular qualification for appointment to the UBC position (CBC Radio, *Morningside*, 13 September 1996). Resnick was true to the historical legacy; Rebick, whose career prospered under government sponsorship in NAC, gave voice to the very claim the left, prior to the birth of grievance politics, had always opposed – that race or gender should provide privileged entitlement.

Sunera Thobani, not even a landed immigrant by the time she decided she had the prerequisite biological qualifications to lead NAC, constantly emphasized the entitlement she believed flowed from skin colour. Before Thobani formally assumed office she was already broadcasting the "progressive" changes she had instituted in her short time in British Columbia. Thobani, a member of the "coordinating collective" of the tax-funded Vancouver Status of Women organization, was the principal author of what was called, in the Orwellian vocabulary popular in such discussions, an "anti-racist" policy. This resulted not in the elimination of racial bias but in its introduction. White staff were replaced, and 75 per cent of the staff became "women of colour" (*Globe and Mail*, 10 May 1993).

Three days before her anointment Thobani advised the readers of the *Ottawa Citizen* that the women's movement had benefited middle class white women and could only "forge ahead under the leadership of the women most marginalized in society"; the movement had to address those who faced the "harshest discrimination" (Thobani 1993). Prior to taking over NAC Thobani was a sociology PHD student at Simon Fraser University. Normally those pursuing PHDs might be thought privileged – certainly their career prospects are superior to those of the vast majority of their contemporaries. Many of those pursuing a PHD in sociology hope to obtain academic employment. In the current climate of cutbacks this is difficult, but, as we have noted, a number of universities have implicit or explicit preferential hiring policies that afford particularly favoured treatment to those who offer a combination of race and gender "disadvantage." In these circumstances it would be more than reasonable to conclude that, far from representing some marginalized constituency, Thobani was in a highly privileged position. Certainly the fact that she had gained such ready access to postgraduate doctoral studies in a country in which she was not even a landed immigrant scarcely suggests massive discrimination. Nonetheless, there was little overt challenge to her remarks. For the most part Canadians seemed ready to accept that skin colour did indeed result in social marginalization, or at least they kept a polite silence.

Those who failed to accept the egregious claims of the self-styled women of colour risked denunciation as racists. Suggestions that Thobani's exceptionally few years in the country constituted scant qualification to lead a movement that purported to represent Canadian women, or that her obsession with skin colour was divisive, were dismissed "as part of the backlash against feminists, particularly feminists of colour who challenge white domination" (Thobani 1993).

Subsequent events confirmed the benefits that could accrue to the "disadvantage" of colour. Thobani resigned from the NAC presidency to take up the Ruth Wynn Woodward Chair at her alma mater, Simon

Fraser University. Thobani is, to my knowledge, the only Canadian chair holder who is simultaneously still studying for a PHD at the university at which the chair is held. The previous holder of the chair, Vanaja Dhruvarajan, was also South Asian (Simon Fraser University 1995). Consistent with the requirements of identity politics, Dhruvarajan offered "entirely unique" [sic] courses: Women of Colour and Indo Canadian Women (ibid.). Other holders of the chair included Rosemary Brown and Hilda Chong. There seems little evidence that racial minorities have been marginalized in these appointments. In common with much of the Canadian feminist movement, the Wynn Woodward Chair had its origins in the former department of the Secretary of State, which in the mid-eighties contributed $500,000 to the creation of an endowed chair, one of five regional endowed chairs initiated at the time. In effect Thobani moved from one government-funded position to another, making a career out of her proclaimed marginalization.

Marginalization is not simply a psychological condition, to be claimed at will. It is also a measurable social phenomenon, marked by such factors as high levels of unemployment, low educational levels, exclusion from more prestigious occupational categories, low pay, and political powerlessness. The widely proclaimed double disadvantage of visible minority women is, as we will see, a chimera, justifying demands for preferential treatment. As John Fekete has acutely observed, biopolitics transforms an illusory disadvantage into a real advantage: "The new piety is organised around abstractions like equity and inclusion – very broad terms, dripping with the pathos of injustice and exclusion, and open to changing definition by those who claim the authority to speak for 'disadvantage' ... biopolitics is Calvinist, and links disadvantage to the 'disadvantaged,' that is, to elite groups, assigned privileged standing by virtue of their putatively oppressed condition" (Fekete 1994: 203).

Interviewed on CBC Radio's *As It Happens* after she announced her resignation as NAC president, Thobani not only repeatedly confirmed that race was central to her mission but expressed the hope (soon to be fulfilled) that it would continue to be the determining qualification to lead NAC. Thobani was unequivocal when asked about a successor: "I certainly hope it's going to be a woman of colour" (16 March 1996).

The most striking aspect of the interview, which was characterized by a degree of deferential sycophancy which CBC Radio reserves for those it knows to be on the cutting edge of progressive thinking, was the assumption that Thobani's agenda was commendably advanced. When Thobani boasted that the changes introduced under her mandate would endure, changes such as the introduction of "women of colour co-chairs" to every NAC committee across the country, interviewer Joey

Slinger refrained from asking why 10 per cent of the female population should merit such power, or, more seditiously, why "women of colour" might be assumed to share some skin-colour determined agenda. The tone of the interview was most aptly illustrated when Thobani observed that she had confronted an "anti-immigrant agenda" and a "tremendous shift to the right," referring, apparently, to the replacement of Mulroney's Conservatives by Chrétien's Liberals. Slinger offered no challenge and solemnly asked Thobani if she thought anyone other than a "woman of colour" could have led resistance to such a shift. Thobani's answer was predictable.

There are some transparent contradictions in Thobani's perspective, reflected in the simultaneous claim that the growing power of women of colour in NAC reflects the need to ensure that the concerns of the most marginal women are met, and the claim that the problems NAC confronts are continually worse. If white feminists are incapable of providing relevant leadership, then surely under the leadership of those with higher melanin content progress will be rapid. Yet even as Thobani takes office she is already warning of the increase in racism and homophobia (Thobani 1993). Three years later these problems appear even more intense. At root the questions that she faces, but her CBC interviewer failed to ask, are why, if society is indeed so profoundly racist, is she able to secure her position as head of NAC, and why, if NAC represents so many Canadian women, do the same women keep electing governments that represent a "tremendous shift to the right"? Finally, why, if NAC can only make progress under "women of colour," has Canada apparently become less and less receptive to the NAC agenda unveiled by Thobani?

Thobani, and those who share her racial vision, might be excused for their growing perception of deeply entrenched racism since their views are regularly reinforced by other disciples of orthodoxy. CBC Radio's *The House* (17 June 1995) covered the 1995 NAC convention that voted to ensure that a "woman of colour" co-chair would serve on each NAC committee. Two "experts" were interviewed, former NAC president Judy Rebick, who enjoys a close relationship with Canada's public broadcaster, and Carleton academic Jill Vickers, co-author of a hagiographic account of NAC's history. The program addressed the organization's decline in support and impact, but given those selected for interview, the obvious explanations were not canvassed. The problem the experts identified was Canadian racism. Vickers suggested: "What has changed is the colour of NAC and that explains a lot of what has happened." Judy Rebick saw NAC's problems as a result of the depth of racism in the women's movement: "The fundamental division we face in our movement is racism ... We didn't understand ourselves how hard it would be to overcome years of conditioning."

Beyond the flamboyant rhetoric of NAC's tax-funded politicians and the CBC's credulous commentators there is no evidence to point to the growth of racism. Thobani's constant emphasis on the prerogatives of skin colour does, nonetheless, reflect the growth in some quarters of racialized politics. Canadian author Neil Bissoondath highlights the parallels: "To be 'racialized' is to have acquired a racial vision of life, to have learnt to see oneself, one's past, present and future, through the colour of one's own skin. It is not new – *Mein Kampf* hinges on a racial vision; apartheid could not have existed without a racial vision – but it is, in certain circles, acquiring a new respectability as old enemies grow to resemble each other" (1994: 103).

Skin colour is not only seen as a prerequisite for access to certain jobs: it has also become an acceptable principle of social organization. Canadians have been quick to condemn clubs that discriminate on the basis of race and gender, but in Calgary the Women of Colour Collective invites no censure and is one of a consortium of groups directing part of an $8 million research program into immigrant settlement, funded by a number of government agencies, including Citizenship and Immigration and the Social Science Research Council (Citizenship and Immigration, News Release, 22 March 1996).

In 1997, not yet a Canadian citizen, Thobani appeared at an invitation-only event to mark the fiftieth anniversary of Canadian citizenship (as distinct from what was previously British Commonwealth citizenship). Thobani took the opportunity to speak on behalf of Canadians who happened to be members of a visible minority. She claimed that being Canadian was an elusive goal for many visible minority immigrants and their descendants. She reported that she continually had to explain "my presence and my legitimacy" (*Ottawa Citizen*, 16 February 1997). Could this perhaps refer to those who might have wondered why a woman with so little time in the country could have attained so many publicly subsidized rewards and yet have complained so vehemently about the grotesque treatment of "women of colour"? Apparently not: Thobani assured her audience that "no matter how many generations you have been here, you continue to be labelled."

What is striking about such nonsense is that it is not simply laughed out of court as an egregious claim for victim status meriting yet more preferential treatment. Does anybody really imagine that second, third, fourth, and fifth generation visible minority Canadians spend their time explaining their legitimacy? No doubt, like Canadians of Irish, Ukrainian, Italian, or many other ethnic groups, the question of an individual's family history in Canada may be discussed, but does Professor Thobani really believe Canadians think the presence of black or Asian Canadians is all a ghastly mistake? Before she was able to offer her insights into the plight of the suppressed and the "illegitimate" presence of visible minorities, a Canadian of Chinese ethnic background had already been appointed lieutenant-governor of British Columbia. Did he spend his time explaining how he came to be in the province?

BIOLOGY AS DESTINY

The position of those who claim entitlement on the basis of skin colour is curious. Apparently it is acceptable to discriminate in favour of particular groups by virtue of gender or skin colour, unless they happen to be able-bodied white males. It was allegedly discrimination in favour of this group that first gave rise to the burgeoning grievance industry.

The emphasis on the determining nature of the biologically given characteristics of gender and melanin content is in sharp discord with libertarian values. One of the more ironic legacies of a movement that can trace much of its ancestry back to the radical activists of the 1960s who, railing against the tyranny of conformity, urged people to "do your own thing," is the development of a style of politics that imprisons its practitioners in the ever-tighter confines of proliferating group identities. The hedonistic politics of self-fulfilment, leavened with a genuine commitment to social and economic equality, gave way to the cultivation of group grievance.

Anthony Appiah, a professor of African American studies and philosophy at Harvard University, probes the circumscribed freedom afforded to those, like himself, whose life-scripts are supposedly determined by their group memberships:

Demanding respect for people as blacks and gays requires that there are some scripts that go with being an African-American or having same-sex desires ... there will be expectations to be met, demands will be made ... the politics of recognition requires that one's skin colour, one's sexual body should be acknowledged politically in ways that make it hard for those who want to treat their skin and their sexual body as personal dimensions of the self. And personal means not secret but not too tightly scripted ... Between the politics of recognition and the politics of compulsion, there is no bright line (Appiah 1994: 162–3).

Robert Fulford, in a critical review of Canada's official multiculturalism, notes that many of the putative beneficiaries do not share the bureaucrat's enthusiasm: "many among us are more interested in escaping than embracing the various forms of culture imposed by heritage" (*Globe and Mail*, 19 February 1997).

One of the pernicious consequences of Canada's contemporary pre-occupation with identity politics is that it moves us further from the goal of creating a society in which such matters are of ever-diminishing importance. The focus on group grievance and group entitlement makes issues of race, gender, and sexual preference increasingly divisive. Preferential hiring policies inevitably increase the importance that attaches to group membership: "Individuals find subtle pressures to make use of their group affiliation not necessarily because of any desire to be associated with a group but because groups become the basis for rights ... New lines of conflict are created by government action" (Glazer 1987: 75).

Feminism advanced from a concern with the interests of one gender to a celebration of its often warring constituents – heterosexuals and lesbians, "women of colour" and their (implicitly) colourless sisters, the ableist and the disabled. Canadian South Asians must account for the position of "privilege" of South Asians in Africa, heterosexual women must critically examine their "sexual privilege" (Sheth and Handa 1993: 43). The further divisions are apparently limitless: if white women's dominance oppresses their sisters "of colour," why not also Jewish women or (colourless) immigrant women? If the disabled are oppressed by the abled, why not vegetarians by meat eaters? If heterosexuals oppress lesbians, what of the plight of bisexuals or transsexuals? Where do the fat and the thin, the tall and the short, the beautiful and the aesthetically challenged stand on the hierarchy of grievance? Where legitimacy is conferred by the celebration of grievance, only a fool would be without one.

In women's studies courses, where the claims for special status of "women of colour" are loud, white women respond by claiming the privileges of those raised in single parent families, those whose parents are on welfare or are blue collar workers. In this world of ever more defined group identities, stability and unity are rare. Christina Hoff Sommers, in her acerbic account of feminist excesses, *Who Stole Feminism*, provides the example of the lesbian support group that split between black and white members; tension then developed between black lesbians with white lovers and those with black lovers (Sommers 1995: 30).

A POLITICS OF INCLUSION

The image of visible minorities as powerless victims that is favoured by those who like to portray Canada as a deeply racist society fails to reflect the reality that among visible minorities are rich and poor, highly educated professionals and illiterates. Visible minorities are employers and employees, managers and subordinates. In Vancouver, where a rapidly increasing proportion of the population is now of Asian descent, the Chinese community includes many extremely wealthy entrepreneurs with substantial investments in the province. The *Globe and Mail* described a fundraising event organized by a Chinese immigrant organization, SUCCESS, which intended to raise a modest $5 million for a new community building. The Cantopop show, which also attracted many of B.C.'s non-Chinese Canadian elite, notwithstanding the fact that they would for the most part not understand the Mandarin or Cantonese lyrics, aimed to raise $1 million towards the target. The goal was easily passed when one entrepreneur kicked in a $500,000 donation (9 January 1996).

The result of the strident denunciations of alleged discrimination and the concomitant demands for increasingly vigourous remedy is the creation of a fundamentally distorted picture of Canadian society. In contrast to the proposition that race constitutes a defining barrier to acceptance is the remarkably little impact it appears to have on such factors as electoral fortune. The nomination of a black Conservative candidate to the safe Conservative seat in Cheltenham in the south of England led to the seat's loss. In the United States race has been seen as a virtually insurmountable barrier to the White House; Colin Powell's potential candidacy was widely hailed as opening the door to a black American for the first time. Yet in British Columbia, Moe Sihota, the first Sikh elected to a Canadian parliament and a former minister of Constitutional Affairs, was forced to resign from Cabinet after being disciplined by the Law Society. He returned as Environment minister and was widely canvassed as a leadership candidate to replace Mike Harcourt as NDP premier. Sihota decided not to run, but there was no suggestion that his ethnic background would have been an insurmountable barrier.

In Ontario, Dave Tsubouchi, the Harris government's first and much reviled minister of Community and Social Services who advised social assistance recipients to respond to swinging cuts by looking for discount cans of tuna, is of Japanese ethnic background. This is of no more obvious relevance to his politics or his electability than the fact that veteran Liberal MPP Alvin Curling, who led the sit-in to force debate on the Conservative's controversial omnibus bill, is black. City of York councillor Rob Davis represents an area with a significant black population. Davis, who is black, is not averse to playing the race card. Alas, for those who suppose there is some broader rising of the racially oppressed, Davis is also an enthusiastic Ontario Tory, who ran unsuccessfully in the by-election caused by Bob Rae's resignation.

Lincoln Alexander, Ontario's first black lieutenant-governor, is also a Tory. Born in Toronto, Alexander was elected to the House of Commons in 1968 to represent blue-collar Hamilton. Alexander served in Joe Clark's cabinet in 1979 and as Ontario's lieutenant governor from 1985 to 1991. Alexander was not the first Canadian-born black to enter legislative politics from Ontario; he was preceded by Leonard Braithwaite, who was elected to the Ontario legislature by the well-heeled Liberal voters of Etobicoke in 1963.

In Prince Edward Island, Joe Ghiz became Canada's first visible minority premier. Ghiz, in common with the P.E.I. electorate, may have been forgiven for failing to recognize the historical significance of this. Ghiz made little secret of his admiration for a country that allowed the son of a small grocery store owner to reach the highest levels. The Canadian government, however, is in no doubt that Canadians of Lebanese descent are among the growing constituency of those who require the benefit of legislated preferential hiring.

Canada has a debilitating preoccupation with identity politics, most obviously displayed in the perennial debates over national unity. Yet this country has not witnessed the racial conflicts that have created profound schisms in many societies in the developed and developing world. Any international comparison would suggest that Canada is characterized by remarkably low levels of racial conflict. More curiously, governments that preside over profound racial divisions make great efforts to portray their countries as models of racial harmony. In Canada governments devote their resources not to the promotion of a common, colour-blind Canadian identity but to funding those whose primary justification for support is the claim that discrimination and bigotry are the daily fate of the country's racial minorities. For the promoters of the politics of identity, what Canadians have in common is much less important than the divisive grievances that may be claimed by an apparently limitless number of groups.

This focus masks other issues that cry out for attention but remain marginalized by the myopic agenda of those who see race and gender conflict everywhere. *Globe and Mail* columnist Jeffrey Simpson highlights one consequence: "Very few people, alas, speak of income disparities and economic injustices in these neo-conservative days, in part because the 'politics of recognition' now dominate the public square" (28 June 1995).

The feminist movement has claimed to embrace the concerns of all women, but its activists have been overwhelmingly drawn from the ranks of the single, the professionals well able to pay others to perform domestic tasks, and the paid advocates. The NAC leadership is dominated by those who draw their income from the public purse. Women in the professional middle classes have found in feminism a powerful ally. It has legitimized demands for preferential hiring and promotion to the marked benefit of a generation of university professors, teachers, and aspirant public sector bureaucrats. Feminism has justified an explosion in government programming intended to redress a range of alleged injustices, with consequent enhancement of the career opportunities of those hired to deliver the new programs, litigate the court challenges, and evaluate the program's delivery. The beneficial effect on the life circumstances of poorer Canadians is questionable, though they have paid generously through taxes to support the measures.

Public funding has been made widely available to those who would make a career in the fostering of group grievance. Concerns over broad social injustice or the widening gap between the incomes of corporate and professional elites and ordinary Canadians are out of fashion, but those who can dress their case in the mantle of race and gender are assured not just a sympathetic ear but a generous public subsidy. The effect of fragmenting the efforts of would-be social reformers and focusing attention on such vague but classless generalities as the alleged privileges of white males is little considered by those whose careers have been founded on a willing pursuit of the government's cheque. The plethora of Ottawa-based lobby groups, who owe their existence to subvention from their bureaucratic sponsors, have shown themselves adept in shifting their measured concerns to meet the latest priorities of their paymasters.

Ironically, as more and more resources and policy interventions have been directed to women and racial minorities and particularly to those who can lay claim to both "disadvantages," social changes have been particularly adverse for men. The loss of large numbers of blue-collar jobs and the downward pressure on the earnings of manual workers have been widely documented. There are other signs that all is not well. *The Economist*, in a provocatively entitled article, "Men: Tomorrow's Second Sex" (28 September 1996), noted a range of factors affecting contemporary males, including their relatively poorer performance in the education system and the fact that while women are disproportionately located in economic sectors where employment is expanding, men, particularly the less skilled, are in declining areas. The consequences, *The Economist* argued, include increasing social stress as unemployed men fail to form stable families, single parent families proliferate, and crime increases.

While Canadians are regularly urged to recognize the injustices done to women in the universities, there is a stunning silence on the implications of current graduation levels, which show males securing only 42 per cent of undergraduate degrees. Real income for Canadian males has been declining for twenty years, women's income steadily increasing. It is the apparent plight of the latter that commands government attention.

The marked increase in female labour-force participation has been driven not simply by a shift in women's objectives but by the real economic pressures on Canadian families. The consequence of the growth of dual earner families is not simply the release of women from some, frequently exaggerated, second class status: it is also a dramatic increase in pressure on the viability of the family as a unit for socializing the young.

Canadian tax policies, in contrast to those of many other countries, eschew taxing the family unit in favour of individual taxation. This is consistent with feminist claims that families do not share income equally and with the feminist agenda that taxation policies should maximize female labour force participation. Granting greater tax recognition for a dependent spouse would, it is argued, provide a disincentive for women to enter the labour force, since any increase in income would be partially offset by increases in the husband's tax liability. The impact of the feminist agenda is to reduce individual choice. Taxation on the basis of household income could assist families with young children where one parent wishes to stay home, particularly if combined with greater tax recognition of the presence of young children. Such policies, in Canada, encounter a feminist veto.[14]

The effect of tax policies is compounded by the extensive public subsidy available to day care. In Ontario, for example, low-income parents may receive up to $12,000 a year, and extensive subsidies are also provided direct to day care centres. Parents who would prefer that one spouse stay home to provide child care receive no similar support. In contrast, their income is reduced by taxes imposed to finance a panoply of public provision. The challenge is not in the difficulty of designing redistributive social policies that would enable more parents to provide care for their own young children but in the formidable alliance of bureaucrats, day care providers, feminists, and public sector unions who support and benefit from the present policies.

There is a striking convergence between the agenda of government-funded feminists, who believe they are on the cutting edge of progressive thinking, and the changing dynamics of a market place increasingly driven by global economic forces leading to growing income disparities. A continual downward pressure on real earnings, particularly at the lower end of the labour market, has compelled families who could previously depend on one wage earner to require a second income (Osberg 1988). The entry of growing numbers of women into the labour market, in turn, is one of the factors causing a decline in wage levels (Economic Council of Canada 1990: 15). The effects on working class family life and the destruction of community have been dramatic, though little explored. A plethora of resources have been made available to those advocating public child care; no similar resources are offered to those who might wish to document the negative effects of the relentlessly increasing pressures on the nuclear family.

Claims that women or other designated groups experience discrimination can serve not only to legitimate the demand for preferential consideration but also to deflect criticism from arrangements that might otherwise invite condemnation. Issues that once would have attracted the attention of advocates of greater social and economic equality may now be framed in terms of the grievances and rights of competing identity groups. This was illustrated in the controversy surrounding the terms of appointment of Canada's first female police chief, Christine Silverberg. In addition to her $125,000 a year salary Silverberg also negotiated with the Calgary police commission for a $115,000 pension top-up, over a five year period, and $115,000 to cover relocation and any losses sustained on the sale of her Hamilton house. Normally the city provides $8,000 in relocation expenses. When city council balked at these terms it was suggested that Silverberg's gender was a major factor in the criticisms. University of Toronto criminologist Philip Stenning, described as Canada's foremost expert on police issues, suggested rank and file officers were behind the difficulties: there was "a strong preference for a man over a woman." How Stenning knew this is unclear. University of Ottawa criminologist Julian Roberts also suggested gender was the critical issue: "The subtext here will be: Here was a women who was promoted out of her depth and here's what happens. The first female police chief has to be a success" (*Globe and Mail*, 29 July 1996).

This focus on gender was no doubt convenient, deflecting attention from the substantive question of the merit of Silverberg's unusually generous treatment. Many Canadians have experienced declines in property values without calling on taxpayers to fund their losses. It is unclear why the police commission thought it necessary to add $23,000 a year to the chief's pension entitlement, a sum exceeding the annual income of many Canadians. The controversy in Calgary, far from reflecting some gender-driven witch hunt, closely paralleled the furore that greeted the news that Ottawa police chief Brian Ford had used the opportunity provided by the reorganization of police services to collect a $311,000 settlement as he relinquished his contract with the City of Ottawa and took office the next day as regional police chief (Loney 1995b).

The tidal waves of political correctness, the sanctimonious commitment of politicians to equity, the flood of legislation, and the media focus have turned our attention endlessly to the issues of identity politics. Meanwhile Canada has become a significantly more unequal country with growing income polarization. One measure is the increase in child poverty which, according to calculations by the National Welfare Council, rose by more than a third from 14.9 per cent of all children in 1980 to 20.5 per cent in 1995 (*Globe and Mail*, 5 April 1997).

But when the question of poverty in Canada is raised it is almost invariably a subtext of some new airing of a feminist or ethnic grievance, as though to be poor is somehow less ignominious or less worthy of concern if the poor are male and white. In 1996 the Canadian Labour Congress, most of whose dues-paying members are male, joined together with the National Action Committee on the Status of Women to announce a cross-country "Bread and Roses" march against not poverty itself but the presumably more pernicious variant that afflicts women and children.

3

Canadian Feminists and the Cultivation of Racial Grievance

Racism continues to ravage the multicultural fabric of Canadian society.

Evelyn Kallen, 1995

The rhetoric of victimhood will continue as long as there are benefits to be derived from it, which is to say as long as whites seek absolution.

R.H. Bork, 1996

All societies that include diverse religious and ethnic groups have the potential for conflict and discriminatory behaviour that pits those groups against one another. Claims that in Canada there is pervasive discrimination based on skin colour are widespread. Generally absent from the discussion is any sense of historical or international perspective. Researchers who list particular racial incidents or document the antics of overtly racist groups convey an image of Canada as racist, but the image has more to do with a myopic search for confirmation than with the rigours of social investigation.

The question is not whether Canada includes racial bigots. It does, though not all of them are white. Some may occasionally be found in positions of power, most damagingly in police uniforms. The issues are whether racism is common, whether it is sanctioned by institutional support, reflected in voting patterns, approved by powerful interests in society, endemic to a very understanding of contemporary Canada, central to an individual's life chances. These indeed are the claims made by those who call on white Canadians to acknowledge their culpability and who advocate a range of preferential provisions for the alleged victims. A number of Canadian academics have been eager to offer

sweeping indictments of Canadian society, providing an aura of legitimacy to the champions of grievance politics.

York University emeritus professor Evelyn Kallen, in her study *Ethnicity and Human Rights in Canada*, provides a long list of racial
incidents in support of the contention that there is "mounting evidence" of racism in Canada. Kallen's evidence covers a twenty-year
period and ranges over violent incidents on the Toronto subway,
conflict between white and black taxi drivers in Montreal, activities
of the Klu Klux Klan and Aryan Nations Church, police shootings in
Toronto, the views of Dudley Laws and the Black Action Committee,
and Stephen Lewis's report on the Yonge Street mini-riots (Kallen
1995: 35–8).

Kallen's description suggests a society in which racism is everywhere;
yet visitors from Europe and many parts of the United States to cities
such as Toronto, Montreal, or Vancouver would be struck not by the
presence of racial tension but its absence. What Kallen offers is not a
scholarly inquiry into Canadian race relations but a conclusion in
search of evidence – a pattern common in Canadian academic writing
on the subject. Kallen's list of incidents reflects a striking common
thread: the issues cited are all conflicts between whites and members
of a visible minority.

Nowhere does she cite the many instances of conflicts occurring
between different visible minority groups or members of groups which
at first glance might be thought to share a common identity. The
growing violence that threatened the future of intercollegiate high-
school basketball in Toronto in 1995 was fuelled by rival black groups
with different ethnic backgrounds. In Ottawa racial conflicts in schools
occur between Kuwaitis and Somalis, Asians and Caribbeans, as well
as black and white. Such conflicts are rightly a matter of public concern
but are unlikely to be effectively addressed by school board policies
driven by the simplistic understandings offered by fashion-conscious
academics, which reduce ethnic conflict to the alleged racism of white
Canadians. Many conflicts which are framed in racial terms may in
fact occur for reasons having little to do with any underlying racially
driven antagonism, including drugs, rivalries over girl (or boy) friends,
and sports.

Kallen's search for evidence of increasing racial conflict leads her
not simply to give disproportionate attention to clearly racist incidents
and behaviour but to seek further support for her argument by embracing a much wider constituency in her indictment. Kallen claims the
emergence of the "new racism" expressed by those who oppose affirmative action on the grounds that it is unfair to white Canadians. This
becomes "a covert expression of the new racism ... a strategy to

maintain racial inequality" (Kallen 1995: 32). Other evidence of the new racism is exhibited by those who reject multiculturalism, believe immigration levels are too high, or oppose special treatment for ethnic minorities. Is it reasonable to conclude that those who reject the politically correct attitudes on these issues are racist? The evidence suggests that an obsession with race is rather a characteristic of the race industry; many Canadians wish to do nothing more than have people judged and treated on merit and have immigration linked to labour market demand.

Opposition to affirmative action is entirely consistent with a belief that all individuals warrant equal treatment. In support of the wide-spread existence of "new racism," Kallen cites the finding by Gallup that 74 per cent of respondents to a survey believed that government should hire for management positions solely on the qualifications of candidates (Kallen 1995: 33). Concern might more usefully be directed to those who failed to share the view.

York University anthropology professor Frances Henry, in a volume sponsored by Citizenship and Immigration, reported that funding for race relations and anti-racism programs in Canada has been "severely cut" (Collins and Henry 1994: 548). No evidence is provided for a claim that seems dramatically at odds with the emphasis placed on these matters at the time she was writing, not least by the Rae government in Ontario. This included extensive financial support for organizations that claimed to be addressing racial issues, and to aca-demics who supplemented their professorial salaries advising the pol-iticians and bureaucrats mandated to deal with race relations.[1] Henry is, however, in no doubt of the urgency of the situation: "Recent events across Canada demonstrate the sense of frustration, powerlessness and marginalisation among racial minorities, especially the young (many of whom are second- or third-generation Canadians), who appear to have lost hope in the future" (Henry 1994: 548). Henry offers no empirical evidence that might support this apocalyptic vision. Is this perhaps true of the large number of racial minority students who attend York University? Are the one in five PHD students who are members of a racial minority marginalized, powerless, and frustrated (Wannell and Caron 1994a: 4)?

Kallen and Henry are reflective of a wide range of academics who, supported by extensive public funding, have found the encouragement of grievance easier than the presentation of a careful investigation of race relations. In common with many others, Kallen finds it unneces-sary to provide empirical demonstration of the "racial inequality" she claims as pervasive (Kallen 1995: 32).

There are certain self-fulfilling consequences to the tireless cultivation of the image of Canada as a profoundly racist society. For some this can serve to explain and legitimize failure or justify actions intended to pay back those perceived to be responsible. Others will be encouraged to resituate everyday setbacks in racial terms. *Globe and Mail* staff writer Jan Wong, returning from the Atlanta Olympics, ran afoul of Canadian customs and immigration, who appeared to doubt the authenticity of her Canadian passport. Wong was understandably irritated at being kept waiting for an hour to gain admission to the country of which she is a citizen. The resulting article in the *Globe and Mail* recounting the experience left no doubt as to the explanation. The reason she had been stopped, she concluded, was her skin colour. The only evidence presented in support of the claim is the fact that she was the only Canadian passport holder held up. The article indicated that a summer student had made the decision to attach a blue slip to her customs declaration occasioning the delay and that one officer said there appeared to be "bubbles" under the passport photo and differences in coloration in the lettering.

Wong may have been the victim of an ill-trained, over-zealous summer student and a tardy response from his superiors, but she presents no reason to believe the same fate could not have fallen any traveller, including the direct descendants of Sir John A. Macdonald.[2] None of the many thousands of other visible minority Canadians who must have passed through the airport that day appear to have been delayed along with Wong. The reader is left in no doubt, however, as to the conclusion to be drawn in Wong's report of her exchange with an immigration supervisor:

"My colleagues warned me it would be really racist in Atlanta. Well it wasn't."

"I hope you don't feel that way about here," he said.

Some people cry when they leave their homeland. I cried as I walked through the gates into Canada (Wong 1996a).

Two months later after much investigation, a letter from Minister of National Revenue Jane Stewart, who is responsible for Canada Customs, and a behind-the-scenes tour at Pearson Airport, Wong presented plenty of evidence to question the competence of the customs and immigration procedures, but none that pointed to racism. She was nonetheless hopeful that "some good may have resulted." The minister had ordered all student officers in Canada to take "cultural awareness classes" (Wong 1996b). This was no doubt welcome news to the burgeoning diversity training industry, companies like Manitoba Liberal leader Ginny Hasselfield's Cross Cultural Communications International, which had received a $3 million untendered contract from Human Resources and Development for immigrant job placement training (*Globe and Mail*, 16 October 1996). The response was indicative of official sensitivity to allegations of racism, and the embrace by many members of the Canadian elite of the view that less estimable Canadians are bigots. Instead of confronting such charges and investigating their authenticity, the government's response gave a credence to Wong's claims that was not merited by the results of her own further investigations.

The proposition that "cultural awareness" training for students of widely differing backgrounds, recruited in one of the most ethnically diverse cities in the world, is a useful expenditure of tax dollars is not self-evident. Since Wong, a widely travelled journalist and best-selling author, was born and educated in Canada, it is unclear what "cultural awareness" would have brought to a handling of the particular case. It is equally doubtful that exposure to "trainers," whose competence is frequently assumed to flow from their skin colour and gender, and whose factual grasp of such basic issues as the number of visible minorities in Canada is parlous (Loney 1996), will do much to reduce any bigotry which may actually exist.

THE COLOUR OF GUILT:
RACE IN THE CANADIAN WOMEN'S MOVEMENT

> Knowing that their doctrine was incubated in a racist environment, feminists chose to address only the issue of sex oppression, the implied decision being that other oppressions were irrelevant to a discussion of the oppression of women. Feminism and its theories are by definition racist.
>
> M. McKenzie, 1987

> Unless I am to die from this violence of daily social relations of being a non-white, South Asian woman in a white Ontario, Canada classroom [sic] – I have to dissociate.
>
> York University sociology professor Himani Bannerji, 1995

The growing acceptance of the image of Canada as a pervasively racist society has owed much to the activities of Canadian feminists in endorsing and promoting the pre-eminence of race as the basis for grievance and, consequently, entitlement.

The embrace of racism as a pervasive contemporary Canadian plague required two sets of players: on the one side, a group largely made up of recent immigrants, who found that claims of racism buttressed a politics of entitlement; on the other, a group of feminists, who suddenly found the culture of grievance, which had once been their exclusive preserve, invaded and hijacked. The funding for the interchange was generously provided by Canadian taxpayers.

Many of the early battles were fought out at NAC, an organization whose influence has depended more on its ability to access and influence elite networks than on any grass-roots base. NAC claims to speak for three million Canadian women, yet its existence is almost entirely dependent on government funding. The organization may continue to capture the headlines, particularly from the CBC, as when in early 1996 it put the newly elected government of Ontario on a four-month notice to cease its "war on women"; but NAC's troops don't send many cheques, beyond those drawn on the public purse.

In retrospect the success of a handful of people, with very few years in the country, to hijack the Canadian agenda was remarkable; the level of sheer gall astonishing. Previous immigrant groups arrived in North America eager to succeed and gain a share in the growing economic prosperity. Ethnic groups served as important bases for political and commercial ventures; parents scraped and saved, hopeful that their children would gain the benefits. Obviously there had to be a better way. The approach taken by those who claimed to speak for Canada's growing visible minorities was to assert, on arrival, a charter claim to a pro rata share. Jeffrey Simpson contrasts the enthusiasm with which earlier generations embraced Canada and the desire to become "Canadian" with the demands for special provision and recognition of victim status of those who claim to speak for contemporary immigrant groups. Earlier European immigrants "saw Canada as a land of opportunity to which they owed obligations, not the other way round" (Simpson 1993: 246).

The politics of entitlement might have been less successful if Canadians had been more willing to call the bluff of those who saw every example of racial disproportion in outcomes as evidence that Canada was "systemically" racist. There were remarkably few takers; for the most part those who engaged in these debates were only too eager to grasp the opportunity for self- and wider flagellation. Susan Findlay, former head of the women's program at the Secretary of State, expresses the muddled, ahistorical guilt that pervaded the women's movement as they confronted the same allegations of privilege they had once cheerfully levelled against men:

Some feminist organizations have, since the mid-1980s, made serious attempts to tackle the issue of white women's privilege in feminist organizations, and to increase the participation of women of Colour in their organizations. At the time of writing, the executive director of NAC is a woman of Colour. The executive director of the Legal Education and Action Fund (LEAF) is also a woman of Colour. In 1992, the annual meeting of the Canadian Research Institute for the Advancement of Women – "Making the Links" – was organized for, and primarily by, women of Colour. In 1993, Sunera Thobani became the first woman of Colour to be elected as president of the National Action Committee on the Status of Women (Findlay 1993: 159–60; the confusing but deeply symbolic interchange of upper and lower case is common to this discourse).

Thobani was not actually elected but acclaimed, in a proceeding in which race was central to her coronation. Findlay might also have added to her list Glenda Simms, the Jamaican-born head of the Canadian Advisory Council on the Status of Women. Some might have thought that this reflected quite extraordinary progress for members of ethnic groups which are overwhelmingly made up of first generation immigrants. Nonetheless the guilt of their white sisters was not assuaged. Reviewing the changes Findlay concludes "the task of undoing privilege is slow" (Findlay 1993: 160). The suggestion that the historical domination of mainstream feminist movements by white feminists reflects privilege is curious, as they remain the overwhelming numerical majority.

Findlay was doing no more than expressing a prevailing orthodoxy. Concepts such as the privilege of white women had ceased to have any clear, empirically verifiable meaning. Racism had become an epithet to be used by racial minority women in pursuit of grants, elected office, preferential employment, or simple appeasement. Racism was everywhere, and offence easily taken. One Canadian participant in the government-funded delegation to the UN women's conference in Nairobi in 1985 reports that she was "aghast" at the questions white women asked: "How do you say sisterhood in Swahili?" or, "How do I know when a Kenyan man is coming on to me?" (Pierson et al. 1993: 252–3). The woman who was aghast was born in Nairobi.

Judy Rebick, who played a singular role in fostering the growth of skin politics and propagating the image of Canada and white Canadians as pervasively racist, illustrates the eagerness to extend the charge of racism so far as to render it devoid of meaning. She finds it evident in the media's treatment of Arnold Minors, a high-profile member of the Toronto police services board, whose comments that many blacks viewed the police as an army of occupation led to much comment. For

Rebick the media response was "racism pure and simple ... because he is Black and on the police board, the media are looking for Arnold Minors to be biased. They accept and even expect a pro-police bias on the part of most members of the police commission, but they are looking for a Black person on the police board to be biased in favour of the Black community and against the police" (Rebick and Roach 1996: 43).

Rebick's comment, as a summary description of expectations, is unexceptionable: the media apparently suspect that most board members have biases but that black members' bias may not be pro-police. In the context of the regular notorious conflicts occurring between the police and those who claim to speak on behalf of the black community, such a presumption would not be unreasonable. The only problem lies in the bizarre assertion that this is "racism pure and simple." Criticism might no doubt be levelled against the sensational coverage of black/police relations by some media, but that is not Rebick's charge. Apparently to avoid racism the media would have to assume that black board members in general, and Arnold Minors in particular, would be as likely to have a pro-police bias as the white board members. The only people likely to start from such an assumption would have lacked the elementary understanding of contemporary Toronto required of even a rookie reporter.

Many allegations of racial discrimination rest on no more than the claim that visible minorities lack proportional representation. Problems of appropriate numerical representation for visible minorities have been compounded by pervasive confusion over the numbers involved. It might be thought that those who were obsessed with issues of race would have apprised themselves of basic factual data but this was frequently not the case. Kiké Roach, whose conversations with Rebick in their book, *Politically Speaking*, were modestly intended to point the way forward for Canadian progressives, railed against the under-representation of racial minorities in Canadian newsrooms. Roach was convinced that "at least" 15 per cent of Canada's population are visible minorities (ibid.: 41); therefore 15 per cent of journalists should be too.

In fact visible minority adults, fifteen and over, comprised 9 per cent of the Canadian population in 1991, double the 1981 proportion (Kelly 1995: 3). This includes those in the country on a temporary basis with no right to work. The figure is based on the "one drop" rule, which includes any individual with any visible minority origin in the count, as well as groups of questionable "visibility" such as Lebanese Canadians and some Latin Americans. Many of those in the count do not share Statistics Canada's view that they are members of a visible minority and are unlikely to be picked up on any self-report questionnaire. Others are fluent in neither English or French, which may afford some limitation to their contributions to a mainstream Canadian newsroom.

Rebick expressed her concern over the representation of visible minority and aboriginal women in NAC prior to her presidency. In 1990 she notes that they comprised only five of the twenty-five member executive (Rebick and Roach 1996: 107). That groups which made up less than 12 per cent of the contemporary population should comprise 20 per cent of the executive would not suggest an urgent need for the "affirmative action" measures that soon followed. There was a strong element of the politics of the cultural revolution in the cacophony of demands that the women's movement address its racism. Red Guards, largely characterized by melanin content but sometimes joined by melanin-deficient volunteers who sought salvation by denouncing other colourless feminists, demanded not simply an acknowledgment of the force of racism but of an individual's own complicity in it. What was demanded was apology, recantation, and re-education: "White middle-class feminists, who developed original feminist discourse, started to say out loud that racism existed ... They were, needless to say, very reluctant to say that they as white women were racist. Yet if the theorists of the movement did not make eradicating their own prejudices a priority, then they themselves were being the oppressors of women" (McKenzie 1987).

The charges made were sweeping. Himani Bannerji, who has spent twenty-five years teaching sociology at York University, describes her experience: "The social relations of teaching and learning are relations of violence for us, who are not white, who teach courses on 'Gender,' 'Race' and 'Class', to a 'white' body of students in a 'white' university" (Bannerji 1995: 224). York University is one of the most racially and ethnically diverse in the country. It is unclear what real "violence" Bannerji has encountered there, but she does offer as an example of her concerns a female student who was a police officer, married to a police officer, who failed to share Bannerji's (no doubt carefully researched) view about police culpability in the shooting of a black teenager: "I want to shout at her, just plain scream – 'you fucking racist idiot', 'you killer' ... my anger seeking the release of name-calling, a slap across the face, not this mediated rage." Perhaps aware that even York University's indulgence might be stretched by this response, Bannerji tries a different approach, though one that raises other ethical questions about what standards highly paid university professors should be held to: "Carefully, cunningly, smoothly I create with comments and statements and debates an ambush for her racism."

The failure to follow through on her first reaction is not without its costs: "My work and I part company. I am aware of doing violence to myself by choosing this pedagogic path" (ibid.: 225–6).

Bannerji reserves a particular fury for white academic feminists: "To this day I have never, with one solid exception, heard a white woman academic speak honestly about her own work, problems of change with respect to inner and outer racism" (Bannerji 1995: 230). With no apparent deliberate irony Bannerji observes that she finds it "very hard to remember names and faces of white women" she meets at gatherings intended to design courses or discuss a curriculum (ibid.). It would be tempting to dismiss such writing as so patently absurd as to merit no serious comment. Yet the article, originally published in the tax-funded journal *Resources for Feminist Research*, on whose editorial board Bannerji sits, was reprinted in a series of essays intended to map out the next steps for the academic advocates of grievance politics: *Beyond Political Correctness: Toward the Inclusive University*. The edited collection was put together with financial support from Carleton University and published by the University of Toronto Press.

Faced with accusations of pervasive racism, many white feminists, contrary to Bannerji's diatribe, were quick to agree, both on their own account and that of others. Jill Vickers (former president of the Canadian Association of University Teachers) and her fellow academics give voice in their history of NAC to prevailing orthodoxy. Describing developments in the mid-'80s, they claim "women of colour had begun to force white women in NAC to face up to their racism" (Vickers *et al.* 1993: 144). The racism is simply asserted: if a small number of ambitious racial minority women found this a useful and increasingly fashionable charge, it is enough evidence for our learned academics to know it as truth and to dispense with the need for scientific investigation. We know racism exists and is a pervasive and dominating fact in Canada because "women of colour" have said so. Presumably we can only wait until they decide whether it has got better or worse, since it is apparently not a measurable social phenomenon but a question of personal perception. To deny pervasive racism is simply to give evidence of a desire to maintain white privilege.

This approach is consistent with the general style of radical feminism, which displays a preference for attacking the character of opponents rather than addressing complex arguments. Those who dispute preferential hiring policies, for example, may frame such opposition in terms of universal values, insisting on individual merit, but feminists know better. Responding to political science professor Philip Resnick's attack on the University of British Columbia's preferential hiring policies,

Sunera Thobani wrote from her chair at Simon Fraser University to warn readers of the *Globe and Mail*. Resnick's argument, she maintained, was no more than "an attempt to preserve the privileges enjoyed by a certain sector of our society" ("Letters," 23 September 1996).

White Canadian feminists' eagerness to endorse the views of visible minority militants was evident in the response to a 1988 report from the Canadian Advisory Council on the Status of Women. *Immigrant Women in Canada: A Policy Perspective* failed to find the requisite degree of hardship and racial discrimination and was quickly condemned by visible minority activists. Leaping into the fray, Susan Findlay condemned the council and noted "the protests which *erupted throughout* the immigrant and visible minority community" over the failure to recognize racism and systemic discrimination (in Pierson *et al.* 1993: 88, emphasis added). There is of course no such community. Rather, there was an orchestrated chorus of outrage from those whose careers depend on such outrage. Findlay's endorsement was, however, illustrative of the eagerness of white feminists to move beyond a confession of their own racism to a condemnation of others.

The willingness to atone for racism was limitless. Jennifer Dale Tiller, an Ottawa-based "equity communications consultant," describes her encounter with Afrocentric academic bell hooks (sic), in words reminiscent of a teenager's account of a meeting with a rock star: "Now was my chance. She was sitting alone. I timidly asked her if she would sign my book. She smiled, said yes, and talked with me about the conference. I was proud to tell her that I was one of the organizers. I was so excited that bell hooks was showing an interest in me" (Moriba-Meadows and Dale Tiller 1995: 237).

Dale Tiller joins a black colleague in a group assembled around hooks: "I felt as comfortable as a puppy by the fireplace at bell's feet. I probably looked like a little puppy sitting there because I felt so much admiration for this woman I idolized her" (ibid.: 240). The group is otherwise comprised of black women, and Dale Tiller is quickly put in her place: as hooks asks other group members about their plans, Dale Tiller realises she is not going to be asked. On the way back to her car she finds the pain of this rejection too much: "I can't hold back the tears any longer. I cry uncontrollably in my car." Later, reading a passage in *Talking Back*, where hooks explains that she is more comfortable speaking directly to black women, Dale Tiller has a cathartic insight: "Again you have reduced me to tears, bell. This time I cry for joy. I knew that you had consciously skipped me in the discussion ... Now I know that it wasn't me ... I thought I personally had done something wrong, but I hadn't ... By putting Black women

at the speaking centre you gave them voice and power and confidence"
(ibid. 247).

The most remarkable aspect of these outpourings is that the essay
in which they appeared, co-authored with black student Geraldine
Moriba-Meadows, won the Women's Studies Essay Award from the
Department of Women's Studies and Feminist Research (sic) at the
University of Western Ontario. Moriba-Meadows dispenses with the
imprisoning conventions of grammar in her contribution to these
reflections on the meeting with the great American feminist: "i didn't
want to care how jennifer felt but because i am sensitive to how one
feels silenced / i did care * shit * if she hadn't come over here with
me this wouldn't even be a dilemma * 'jennifer why don't you go away
* give us a chance to rejoice in our sisterhood/and our BLACKNESS'"
(ibid. 243). The prize-winning essay not only dispenses with grammat-
ical convention: it also shuns such androgynous requirements as scholarly reference. This proved no barrier to its subsequent inclusion in
Beyond Political Correctness (Richer and Weir 1995), charting the
future for Canada's race and gender driven professoriate.

One white feminist who took the call for re-education seriously is
barbara findlay (who has, like bell hooks, carried the obsession with
upper and lower case one step further). She earnestly recounts her own
efforts: "I went to my first unlearning racism workshop ... in 1987 ...
Suddenly whole aspects of the world made immediate, and different,
sense to me. Of course I had absorbed the racism of the society, along
with its sexism, homophobia and so on ... I would need systematically
to re-learn the world again ... the scrutiny of myself in the world as
a white person was both, painful and shameful" (findlay 1992).

The advocates of skin politics, for their part, have embraced some
curious notions. Kiké Roach, law student at Queen's University, one
of Ontario's most prestigious universities, daughter of Charles Roach,
a prominent Toronto lawyer, might not appear to be an overwhelmingly convincing illustration of oppression. Nonetheless Roach is in no
doubt of the need for racially segregated organizations. In her "conversations" with Judy Rebick she boasts of her success in convincing
other students of the merits of such apartheid practices as an undergraduate at McGill. Roach was a founder of SHAKTI, whose race-based
membership requirements, not surprisingly, aroused the ire of other
students: "One South Asian woman in particular kept coming back to
the meetings and insisting that whites should be included. Finally
someone talked to the woman separately. We discovered that she had
grown up surrounded by white people, and she had always tried to
gain their approval. She came to the realization for the first time

through the discussion, and later on became a big SHAKTI supporter"
(Rebick and Roach 1996: 159).

THE CRUSADE OF THE RIGHTEOUS

Patronizing (or rather "matronizing") attitudes towards Black
Women, as well as the language and concepts that White
feminists use, effectively exclude us.

> Dalhousie law professor Esmeralda Thornhill, 1989

The fervour of the self-proclaimed victims, with their appeals
to sex, race and ethnicity, rivals that found in any fundamentalist religious movement and has, indeed, replaced religious
faith for a number of its proponents.

> D. Cook, 1996

A number of milestones in the growth of racial politics in Canada have
attracted wider attention. These include the controversy at the Royal
Ontario Museum over the "Into the Heart of Africa" exhibition, which
resulted in anthropologist Jeanne Cannizzo being driven from her
position at the University of Toronto, and the racially exclusive Writing
Thru Race conference organized by the Writers' Union, with (inevitably) support from the Canada Council. One of the earlier confrontations between those who espoused traditional colour-blind liberal
principles and those who asserted the pre-eminence of skin politics
occurred at the 1988 international PEN conference in Toronto. This
would have continuing reverberations and provided an illustration of
the inflated claims made by activists, the egregious nature of the
demands, and the high price that could be exacted from white Canadians who refused to engage in the required self-abasement. The fallout
from the PEN conference would ultimately include the well-publicized
resignation of social activist and writer June Callwood from the board
of Nellie's, a Toronto hostel providing services to battered women. A
review of this history illustrates the bizarre claims made by the protagonists of racial grievance, the length to which some white commentators were prepared to go in publicly professing the depth of white
guilt, and the sacrifice of the interests of clients to the fractious politics
of race and gender.

Callwood's first run-in with the self-appointed guardians of visible
minority Canadians occurred when the PEN conference was picketed
by a group calling itself Vision 21, who were protesting the "silencing"
of so-called writers of colour. The clamour of the "silenced" attracted
considerable media attention. The protesters objected to the lack of

Asian, African, and Native Canadians in the PEN delegation – though according to their own figures 14 per cent of the delegates fell into this category, somewhat higher than the proportion in the Canadian population.[3]

PEN conference participants, reading the protesters' leaflet, might have wondered if they had inadvertently arrived in Durban. African, Asian, and Native Canadian writers, they were told, "continue to face the implacable face of racism in writing and publishing here in Canada." Warming to the theme, the protesters linked their plight to that of PEN's imprisoned writers: "There is often, in fact, a direct link between the power structure that supports the privileged position of white writers in countries like Canada, the circumstances of their own writers of colour, and the existence of regimes which imprison writers in other countries" (Philip 1992: 151). Surprisingly, given the dire circumstances described, only twelve protesters were involved, half of whom were white.

The confrontation between Callwood and one of the protest organizers, Marlene Nourbese Philip, has become one of the more celebrated face-offs between those who claim to find racism everywhere and their detractors. Callwood, exasperated at the failure to engage the demonstrators in rational dialogue, allegedly suggested they "fuck off." Philip, who claims that her purpose is "to disturb the peace of those invested in [sic] maintaining the status quo," seems nonetheless to have led a sheltered life. She immediately interpreted the incident in racial terms: linking the confrontation with Callwood to a telephone caller who, she claimed, had called her a nigger, Philip went on to compare her situation with that of Chinese dissidents: "Ms. Callwood was the only one who became verbally abusive ... This sort of irrational response to legitimate protest comes close to being the verbal equivalent of actions of governments such as the Chinese government towards its dissenters" (ibid.: 153).

The charge that writers were discriminated against on the basis of their colour may have lacked evidence, but it served as part of a wider campaign to demand preferred access to public funding to racial minority writers and artists. Nourbese Philip's book *Frontiers*, which includes much of the indigestible and repetitive prose elicited by this incident, received tax-funded support from no less than four different sources: the Canada Council, the Ontario Arts Council, the Government of Ontario through the Ontario Publishing Centre, and the Multiculturalism Directorate, Canadian Heritage.

In addition to inchoate ruminations on the perceived injustices sustained at the hands of PEN, *Frontiers* includes other tirades against cultural organizations that fail to share Philip's less than original views on the central relationship between race and cultural expression. Philip is not content to restrict her denunciations to those whites who have been insufficiently swift in making an apology. She reserves a particularly vitriolic stream of abuse for Trinidadian-born author Neil Bissoondath, a critic of Canada's "cult of multiculturalism" (Bissoondath 1994). Inevitably, Bissoondath, in common with Philip's other victims, is also a racist.

So far as I am aware, *Globe and Mail* books columnist Margaret Cannon was not among the protesters standing outside the PEN conference, but in *The Invisible Empire: Racism in Canada*, she makes clear her sympathies for the claims of Philip and her handful of fellow protesters. Cannon traces the link between the incident at the PEN conference and Callwood's subsequent departure from the board of Nellie's, a social service agency offering a range of services to women and children in Toronto. Nellie's became the scene of one of the many conflicts that developed between different factions in the women's movement. Such conflicts originated in significant part from the conflicting agendas of competing identity groups. The willingness of governments and groups like the United Way to fund "feminist collectives" running service delivery agencies allowed such agencies to eschew conventional management structures. Some became increasingly embroiled in the divisive personal politics of service providers, to the growing neglect of client needs.

Callwood's resignation from the board of Nellie's followed a prolonged campaign by visible minority staff who, having been recruited in an effort to ensure that Nellie's "represented" the community it served, insisted on denouncing their colleagues as racist. Callwood's refusal to condone this destructive activity led to the addition of the call for her resignation to a long list of demands laid by the Women of Colour Caucus. What is remarkable about Cannon's account is that, having described what to most people with voluntary sector experience appeared to be a breakdown of effective service delivery, she concludes that the accusers were after all right – a conclusion that appears to be driven by a willingness to engage in whatever self-abasement is required in order to appease those who shout racism. Referring to the *Globe and Mail*'s comment, "If racist can be attached to Ms. Callwood, what are we to call those who do believe and act on those principles with which the word has traditionally been associated?" Cannon concludes, "Maybe we have to call them us" (1995: 163).[4]

Cannon is not the only writer to seek expiation. Author Stan Persky, reviewing Philip's *Frontiers* for the *Globe*, was quick to assert his own claim to victim status. Persky noted that Jews and gays "have in recent historical memory been as much the object of literal slaughter as

Philip's African forebears." He advised *Globe and Mail* readers that he could not imagine how anyone "in good faith" could challenge Philip's description of the "character of racism" in Canada (30 January 1993).

Philip has since found a generous platform in such publications as *Fuse*, which receives support from the Ontario Arts Council, the Canada Council, and the Ontario Ministry of Culture and Communications. Under the pretext of cultural commentary, *Fuse* affords space to those whose ideas might not otherwise find a market. The provision of such tax subsidy might seem to give the lie to the claim that writers are denied publication because of their race. Not so, in the 1990 summer issue of *Fuse* Philip waxed indignant. Informed by a grasp of Marxist concepts that might be generously described as mechanical, she explained to *Fuse*'s readers, without any sense of contradiction, why it is that minority writers (like Philip) are not published: "The only audience that matters in Canada is the white audience and how members of the 'ideological superstructure' – reviewers, critics and publishers alike – ... sees the Canadian audience as narrow-minded, provincial and unable to read and enjoy anything but work written by white writers ... The reason why African, Asian and Native writers have difficulty getting published has little to do with audience and markets and much more to do with racism and power" (Philip 1990: 42).

It is useless, as PEN discovered, to confront such claims with facts. Rohinton Mistry, a first-generation Indian immigrant, saw his first novel nominated for the prestigious Booker award. *Such A Long Journey* (1991), the story of the tribulations of a Bombay bank worker in the 1960s, scarcely situated itself in some pantheon of white Canadian concerns. His second novel, *A Fine Balance*, again set in Bombay, won the Governor General's prize, the 1996 Commonwealth Writers Award, and was also nominated for the Booker. The 1995 Commonwealth Best First Novelist prize for the North American region went to Hiromi Goto, a Japanese-born first generation Canadian; the overall prize for best first novel was awarded to Adib Khan, an Australian writer.

In 1996, the first novel of a female Indian writer, Arundhati Roy, secured advances of more than $1 million. In 1997 it won the Booker award, and is a bestseller in Canada. *The God of Small Things*, set in the Indian state of Kerala, tells the story of the death of a little girl as witnessed by her cousins, over a twenty-four hour period. This Indian novelist scarcely evidences the narrow literary concerns proclaimed by Philip. The list of published and acclaimed visible minority writers is long but irrelevant to what is, at root, a demand for recognition of

victim status and consequent preferential access to writing and publishing resources, irrespective of merit or its absence.

The magazine in which Philip's piece first appeared, funded by
Philip's "ideological superstructure," featured three other visible
minority writers. One, Rozeena Maart, is succinctly described as "a
black South African feminist scholar-cum-activist in the areas of Black
Consciousness and violence against women, and [who] advocates a
feminist agenda for anti-apartheid and anti-capitalist politics in South
Africa." Maart, who reviews the (silenced?) poetry of co-contributor
Nourbese Philip, displays a concern with racial difference and implicit
superiority that would have invited censure in any white writer: "In
'Dream-skins,' we experience the Elements of Earth as they shape the
identity of the black female: the mentioning of the Earth, the Sea,
Blood, the thought that it brings memories of the experience of menstruation unlike the silence of it in Canada where its flow is prevented,
tamponized, thinly rolled and tucked away, made invisible like the
people who reproduce the wealth of this nation. The blood-cloths ring
with reminiscence of presence, of belonging, of the assertion that
menstruation, that blood and the way we bleed are different" (Maart
1990: 47).

Other articles in the same issue comment (favourably) on the decision of the Ontario College of Art to discriminate in hiring against
men; on the alleged marginalization of lesbian women, elegantly
expressed as "their singularized positioning, which only perpetuates a
disempowering discourse of absence"; Guatemala; lesbian art; AIDS;
and abortion clinics. Reading *Fuse*, it is difficult to conclude that arts
funding discriminates against minorities; it is also hard to see why
taxpayers are on the hook to fund a magazine that boasts less than
four hundred paid subscribers.

There are striking commonalities between the ideas of those who
condemn what they claim is pervasive racism in Canada and the views
of those who believe race is indeed a decisive predictor of ability,
character, and talent. Philip maintains that the extraordinary progress
made by "Africans" in the New World since "the earliest emancipation
date, 1838 – beggars the imagination." She suggests that the "overwhelming impediments" put in the way of "Africans" are "partially
an acknowledgement of fear on the part of the dominant white culture
– the fear, *as they perceive it*, that, given half a chance, we will replace
them in all fields" (Philip 1992: 21, emphasis in original). There is no
mistaking the suggestion of black superiority or white psychosis but
Philip's history, so far as Canada is concerned, is misleading. The
proclamation of emancipation is of little relevance to an understanding

of Canadian history; slavery had largely ended in British North America by the end of the eighteenth century.

Fellow Trinidadian Canadian Dionne Brand shares with Philip a visceral sense of racial oppression and the marginalization of "writers of colour." Brand has also accessed generous public support to publish her views. *Bread out of Stone*, a collection of essays, received financial support from Canadian Heritage, the Ontario Arts Council, the Canada Council, and the Ontario Publishing Centre. Brand sees the pre-eminence of race everywhere, attributing opposition to multiculturalism to the ease with which whites assimilate, "the elasticity of 'whiteness,'" which swallows and within a generation "cleanses" Italians, Portuguese, Eastern Europeans, and others (Brand 1994: 174). In contrast "a deeply racialized and racist culture ... represses the life possibilities of people of colour" (ibid.). Brand offers little empirical evidence that might allow the reader to judge the accuracy of this characterization but suggests that Canadian culture is organized around "whiteness": "Assumptions of white racial superiority inform the designation of formal culture in this country and the assigning of public funds" (ibid: 158–9). It is difficult to know what measures would satisfy Brand. Appointed to a jury for the Governor General's award for poetry, she immediately makes clear to her fellow panellists her own racialized vision and the impossibility of searching for any consensus: "I want to state from the beginning that we are unlikely to agree" (ibid.: 167).

Elsewhere in the collection she attempts to capture what she claims is the sense of rejection faced by young blacks: "The newspapers said immigrants were taking away white people's jobs, the newspapers said Black youths were running amok, the newspapers said before Black people came here there was no racism, the newspapers said before Black people came here there was no crime ... the newspapers said soon there'll be more people of colour than white here, the newspapers said you had to be white to be Canadian" (ibid.: 103). Brand finds it unnecessary to provide any references for of the statements she alleges or evidence that any newspaper has offered its readers such simple-minded coverage. What is offered, funded by Canadian taxpayers, is not research or even careful reflection but the repetition of fashionable orthodoxy – equally evident when Brand turns her attention to education.

By Brand's account young blacks face a city that "could barely acknowledge their existence and fought hard against giving them an equal education" (ibid.: 103). Yet the Toronto Board of Education has been recognized as a world leader in responding to a multicultural,

multi-ethnic constituency; indeed, its efforts might be faulted for placing undue emphasis on such issues as home language instruction to
the detriment of the core curriculum.

While the fracas at Nellie's featured in *Toronto Life*, the article failed
to reflect the required acknowledgment of white guilt. The limits of
tolerable debate on the subject were spelled out by Linda Carty, in her
foreword to another tax-subsidized feminist anthology. Carty describes
the *Toronto Life* article: "It is chilling reading, clearly racist in under-
tone and often homophobic in its references to women being attacked.
It is all the more chilling to know that something so vile was deemed
worthy of publication by one of the city's major magazines" (Carty
1993: 12).[5]

Carolann Wright, a central protagonist in the Nellie's imbroglio,
made clear her own racialized perspective in response to a suggestion
that she might owe something to those who, like Callwood, had
marched for women's equality: "She actually believed that I, a seventh
generation African Canadian, could owe anything to anyone other
than the Africans that came before me" (Wright 1993). In a world in
which the combination of traditional barbarism and modern weaponry
create a lethal mix, it is useful to have as a benchmark the magnitude
of the persecution of feminist "women of colour" revealed by the
coverage of Nellie's: "No truer horror is experienced than the one of
meeting the face of the halo-laden victim (June Callwood) on the cover
of a magazine looking beleaguered and worn out from the daily task
of fighting off Women of Colour" (ibid.).

Nellie's was not unique. In Ottawa, Interval House, a women's
shelter that receives $600,000 a year in public funding, suffered similar
racial divisions and a breakdown in effective service delivery. Three
consultants' reports highlighted the failings in the centre, the last
recommending closure, and documented the internal feuding. As in
Toronto, the absence of any management structure left "the collective"
to wrestle, unsuccessfully, with a resolution. Consultants reported that
some staff slept through their night shifts, defective plumbing leaked
through light fixtures, children were inadequately provided for, some
staff refused to talk to other staff, telephone messages from lawyers
and doctors were often not passed on. The staff language at the House
was not what most taxpayers would expect to find at a facility
provided for vulnerable women and children: "Several women felt they
had 'progressed' or 'advanced' along some undefined path to acceptance, as measured to the degree to which they had changed their
habitual pattern of speech and original sensibilities, and began to use
swear words" (Gentium Consulting 1994). Interval House gained more
unwelcome public attention when black staff member Sylmadel Coke

was alleged to have criminally harassed several staff members and charged under the new anti-stalking law. Coke also featured in an unsuccessful prosecution of board member Carol McLeod, whom she claimed karate chopped her after a dispute over a time-sheet (*Ottawa Citizen*, 4 June 1995). The shelter remained open, in spite of recommendations for its closure.

A former Ontario shelter employee, Rita Kohli, who describes herself as a "South Asian lesbian educator and activist," has added further groups to the growing catalogue of victims, documenting the alleged plight not only of "women of colour" working in shelters but also of immigrant and Jewish women (Kohli 1993: 393).[6] Kohli starts from the proposition that Canada is a "white supremacist society" in which minority races and cultures are oppressed (ibid.: 395).

Kohli does not name the shelters in which such oppression occurs but in 1994 the Shirley Samaroo House, which annually received $900,000 in public funding, closed down, riddled with a variety of conflicts including those between different factions of black workers – Jamaicans and Canadians on the one side, those born in Africa on the other. According to one report, "Many people were more concerned with their own victim status than with their clients. They focused a great deal of attention on extracting admissions from the less oppressed, and practising the politics of confrontation" (Wente 1994).

Kohli's interviews with ex-shelter workers raise a cacophony of identity demands from those who believe that their sexuality, ethnicity, race, class, and religion demand urgent attention. The reader might be excused for forgetting that the purpose of tax funded shelters is to provide emergency care for victimized women and children, not to provide ongoing therapy for feminists on staff. Certainly the description of the levels of staff conflict, frequently mobilized around competing identity politics, suggests the merits of placing provision in the hands of professionally managed and directed service providers.

Reading the accounts of feminists wrestling with the alleged pandemic of racism is reminiscent of the accounts of those called upon to re-educate themselves in China's cultural revolution. Charges are vague but crimes are detected everywhere. In the end, as Cannon has told us, the only safe route is confession. Those who have confessed to their own guilt are then encouraged to join in the denunciation of others.

OISE professor Ruth Pierson offers a hand-wringing account of the struggles of white feminists to come to terms with their "participation in other women's oppression" (Pierson *et al.* 1993: 190). In *Strong Voices*, a volume produced by four academics, there is a disturbing lack of careful analysis but a great enthusiasm for embracing guilt.

White feminists, for the most part, found it impossible to contradict the claims of those who detected racism everywhere. If racism were claimed, so the logic seemed to flow, it could only be because it was there. Visible minority feminists who wished to assert their credentials and perhaps further their claim for advancement found little reason to refute the fashionable position; to challenge orthodoxy would have been at some personal cost.

Pierson embraces the vision of Canadian delegate Ravinda Din, who attended the 1985 Nairobi conference to mark the end of the United Nations Decade for Women. Din, an Asian, born in Nairobi and raised in Kenya, found the experience of being surrounded by other "women of colour" crystallized her recognition of racism in the Canadian women's movement. It may have done so, but it was a curious awakening. The naive assumption that racism is an attribute peculiar to or even disproportionately present in the Canadian or western women's movement might have given pause to those familiar with the acute racial tension in East Africa, frequently spilling over into overt discrimination, violence, and expulsion of indigenous Asians. It would be interesting to know how many Asian women were included in the delegations of Uganda, Kenya, Tanzania, and Zambia. Had Din no experience of racism at the hands of those diverse ethnic groups with whom she felt such immediate racial solidarity?

Judy Rebick summarizes what appears to be the dominant view among white feminists for whom racism is a pervasive, if ill-defined, Canadian scourge. Those who resist the claims of the advocates of racial politics are simply guilty of wishing to preserve racial privileges while denying their racism. The opposition of some writers to the racially exclusive Writing Thru Race conference was "part of the struggle of the Canadian cultural elite to deny the reality of racism in the country" (Rebick 1996: 34). Such denial, warns Rebick, can only lead to further "polarization." Obviously those who dispute the politics of racial grievance must be held responsible for its continuance. We must recognize the "shocking" impact of racism "on all of our behaviour" (ibid.: 38).

The use of the charge of "racism" to silence or intimidate those who might wish to demur in the face of this or that demand or to question the claim that race is the defining issue is widespread. Esmeralda Thornhill, who was appointed to the racially exclusive James Robinson Johnston Endowed Chair in Black Canadian Studies at Dalhousie University in 1996, illustrates the approach in her 1982 paper to the First International Conference on Research and Teaching Related to Women: "Women's Studies must break with traditional approach, traditional content, and traditional values, and go beyond the proverbial cosmetic cover-up or lip service, in order to become more relevant to Black Women and not merely appear as a fight in which white women are fighting for the right to oppress Black Women equally with white men" (Pierson and Cohen 1995: 242). Those who would reject Thornhill's perspective are simply dismissed as fighting for the right to oppress black women "equally with white men." Thornhill offers no explana tion of the way in which in contemporary Canada white men, individ- ually or as a group, engage in such oppression.

WOMEN'S PRESS: PLAYING THE RACE CARD

> Intransigence, a fear of being "coopted" that amounted to paranoia, fanaticism of a dour and unbending kind, and an ideological rancour against "male, white, Western, monied culture" possessed many individuals and gradually sapped the cultural nationalism of the sixties and seventies. ("Fanaticism consists in redoubling your effort when you have forgotten your aim," George Santayana once wrote.)
>
> T. Henigan, 1996

> Although recent feminist writing does not explicitly advance positions of white domination, much of it reflects and thus helps to reinforce the racism that characterizes our society.
>
> UBC law professor Marlee Kline, 1989

The issue of the unique perspectives and problems of that large pro- portion of the world's population who are embraced by the rubric "women of colour" occupied hundreds of hours of time at the Toronto- based Women's Press. The press, in common with other centres of feminist struggle, owed its existence to tax funding, in this case the Canada Council and the endlessly accommodating Ontario taxpayers, through their Arts Council. Again the demand which was made was that the press give attention, space, resources, and uncritical obeisance to those women able to speak with confidence for the vast constituency of the colour-defined oppressed. Again, to read the accounts of the leading figures is to embrace a vision of a society riven with the grossest racial oppression. Indeed it is remarkable that women of colour failed to take urgent steps to warn their sisters overseas of the horrors they would face should they ever arrive in Canada.

The demands posed by the "front of the bus caucus" were for both preferential treatment for "writers of colour" and a recognition by white women of their "privilege" (Findlay 1995: 379). Opposition to feminist demands was regularly denounced as nothing more than a backlash driven by men's desire to maintain male privilege. Visible minority activists simply transferred the charge to their white counterparts. The white feminists were at something of a disadvantage since racial minority women "had the exclusive right to define the way that racism worked" (Findlay 1995: 380). This parallelled the claim of feminists to an exclusive right to say how sexism worked.

Some white members of Women's Press were sufficiently cognisant of their guilt to recognize the failings of the press: "Feminist publishing was marginal to women of Colour, for example because feminist theory and practise did not speak to these women nor address *the centrality of racism in their lives*" (Gabriel and Scott 1993: 42, emphasis added).

The press was in fact marginal to the overwhelming majority of women, its survival guaranteed not through the sale of books but regular transfusions of public money. Its a priori assertions of pervasive racism cannot, as we will see, be supported by any reference to educational or labour market statistics. If racism were such a central issue in the lives of visible minority Canadians it could be expected to lead to widespread social mobilization. In contrast, the overwhelming number of those mobilized are in receipt of one or other government grant.

The struggle at Women's Press had little to do with equality of access. The "front of the bus caucus" triumphed, while those who had opposed them left voluntarily or were dismissed. A group of white feminists were driven out of the organization and resources directed to visible minority writers. Some 50 per cent of the press members who remained were so-called women of colour, the rest, women whose sense of guilt was assuaged by taking part in an organization in which they were destined to be second-class citizens. The press's Writers Reserve Program, generously funded by the Ontario Arts Council, limited support for white writers to 25 per cent of all grants. The further fracturing of identity politics was not limited to the differences presumed to flow from melanin content; the press also boasted of its success in "dramatically" increasing the number of books it published by "white lesbians and lesbians of Colour" (ibid.: 47).

Imbued with the zeal of all true believers, Women's Press quickly moved from debate to dictat with the publication of its anti-racist guidelines. These made clear who would be eligible for assistance from the tax dollars it administered and what ideas were permissible. Naturally women of colour were particularly welcome; such writers had carte blanche: "We will publish fiction and non-fiction work by

Women of Colour on issues determined by their concerns" (in Pierson *et al.* 1993: 448). Writers without colour faced a more circumscribed welcome. Restrictions included fiction in which "the protagonist's experience in the world, by virtue of race and ethnicity, is substantially removed from that of the writer" (ibid.: 449). If this were not a sufficient barrier, excluding much of the world's great fiction, seven further restrictions were identified including those against the writer's appropriation of "the form and substance of a culture which is oppressed by her own," travel writing that failed to recognize "the limits of the perspective within the writing itself," and finally, "a manuscript whose analysis includes women of colour as a supplement to a text, rather than incorporating Women of Colour into the overall content and structure." Those who might fail to grasp the difference would perhaps miss the shift in the sentence from small case to large case.

It may be tempting to dismiss the Women's Press as an unrepresentative excrescence, a development driven by those whose racial obsessions, combined with an ignorance of literature and culture, led to comic conclusions. This was not the view of many feminists: Women's Press was thought to be at the cutting edge of the transformation of "white middle class" feminism. Its anti-racist statement appears as the final extract in a volume devoted to reproducing some of the key texts of the Canadian women's movement, funded by the Ontario Ministry of Education, the federal Secretary of State, the Canadian Employment and Immigration Commission, and the Social Sciences and Humanities Research Council (Pierson *et al.* 1993).

Sister Vision Press, also supported by the Canada Council and the Ontario Arts Council, had an even more restrictive policy than Women's Press, describing itself bluntly in smaller print as "Black Women and Women of Colour Press" (Bannerji 1993a). It seems unlikely that Canada's cultural bureaucrats would have been quite so free with subsidies to other kinds of racially exclusive publishing ventures.

The issue of the appropriate representation of aboriginal and visible minority Canadians within the feminist movement has had a pervasive impact. At root this is an argument about power and resources, dressed up as a debate over equity. The debate is premised on an assertion that ethnicity is central. When those who have deployed ethnicity to assert entitlement are confronted by claims that ethnicity does not establish competence, they profess outrage. The demand is not simply for proportional representation but for those favoured with victim status to be privileged in selection for office and allocation of resources.

RACIAL STEREOTYPES
ON THE FRONTIERS OF PROGRESS

To accuse the women's movement of antimale hostility, intolerance and extremism is an outrage.
Judy Rebick, "Letters," *Globe and Mail*, 2 August 1997

The guilt so readily professed by many white feminists and their male
supporters rests on an implicitly patronizing view of visible minorities
as victims. Susan Findlay, reviewing the progress of pay equity, argues
that bureaucratic decision-making is constrained by the priority given
to the "economic interests that dominate society rather than the interests of women, the working class *and racial minorities*" (Findlay 1991:
84, emphasis added). The proposition that women and racial minorities somehow stand outside the class system is, to say the least, bizarre.
What are we to make of women like Kim Campbell who hold office
in Conservative regimes; who, like Maureen Kempston Darkes, president of GM Canada, head corporations; who, like Pauline Jewett,
became the first female president of a major Canadian university in
1974 at Simon Fraser; or who, like former NAC activist Lorna Marsden, president first of Wilfred Laurier University and then of York, the
highest-paid university president in Ontario, hold prestigious professional positions? What of those who, according to this theology, are
doubly disadvantaged, being both female and members of a racial
minority? Women like Liberal Ida Chong, who unseated NDP finance
minister Elizabeth Cull in Oak Bay-Gordon Head in the 1996 provincial elections? Is Chong a victim of patriarchal confusion and racial
false consciousness?

Globe and Mail columnist Rick Salutin, dismissing the claim that
the entry of businessmen into the campaign against separatism represented a change, asks, rhetorically: "'The CEOs have taken over.' From
whom – themselves? Who else has been calling the shots for the past
15 years? The United Church? The communists? The jobless youth
and visible minorities?" (*Globe and Mail*, 2 February 1996). This
grouping of visible minorities with groups that are demonstrably marginal is a caricature that speaks directly to the myopic vision of well-
heeled progressives.

Visible minorities do not fall neatly into some oppressed category
whose sympathies can be automatically assumed. Calgary Reform MP
Jim Silye decided to leave federal politics to run for the provincial
Conservatives. Silye, a former football hero with the Calgary Stamped-
ers, lost the nomination for the seat of Calgary Fort when he secured
fifty-nine votes to the 441 of the winner, Wayne Cao. Cao who was

expected to win the seat for Ralph Klein's Conservatives, had arrived in Canada from Vietnam some twenty years earlier. His victory could scarcely be viewed as an aberration; in large measure it depended on his recruitment of other visible minority supporters into a party regularly vilified by Salutin (*Globe and Mail*, 29 November 1996).

Bronwyn Drainie, one of Salutin's colleagues on the *Globe*'s arts pages, offered a similarly patronizing view of Japanese Canadians, like so many others apparently imprisoned in the legacy of their ancestry. Attacking Toronto Harbourfront's cultural exhibit Today's Japan, Drainie suggested that the show was too "avant-garde" for Japanese Canadians. Unfortunately the representatives of one of the most highly educated and successful ethnic groups in Canada to whom Drainie spoke found it impossible "to voice their criticisms to a forum as public as the *Globe and Mail*" (2 May 1996). The problem, Drainie concluded, was that since Japanese Canadians came from "farming and fishing stock," the show was simply over their heads. This genealogy-as-destiny view fails to note that Japanese men and women are, on an age-standardized basis, more likely to have a degree than other Canadians (28 per cent for men, 20 per cent for women) (Kelly 1995: 6).

OISE professor Ruth Pierson goes further, arguing, in all seriousness, that a number of groups, including blacks and Asians, are "colonized within our own country" (Pierson *et al.* 1993: 190). This is an astonishing statement, applied to groups that are fully enfranchised, represented in provincial and federal parliaments, and include some of the wealthiest individuals and families in Canada. Do OISE graduates "learn" about such colonization from Professor Pierson as part of OISE's curriculum? In an attempt to further hone the boundaries of those who might claim victim status, Pierson offers her own stereotypes. She suggests that the term "immigrant" masks the difference between whites from middle-class anglophone and francophone backgrounds and "'non-whites' from poor, so-called 'Third World' countries" (ibid.: 206). Contrary to Pierson's imagery, there are many poor white immigrants, just as there are many affluent "non-whites."

The eagerness of white feminists to embrace the claims of racial minority women for special status in the hierarchy of oppression has resulted in some improbable putative alliances, in which racial minorities have been portrayed as standing shoulder to shoulder with others in the vanguard for social change. Yet the cultural mores of some visible minorities place women in a markedly subordinate position, reflected in terms of the daily division of labour and sanctified by an egregious religious interpretation. Most contemporary Canadian males have mastered at least some minimum level of domestic competence. In contrast, in many South Asian Canadian families roles remain

rigidly divided, the domestic competence of men an oxymoron. Reporting on the problem of arranged marriages in Canada, the *Globe and
Mail*'s multiculturalism reporter, Isabel Vincent, noted the views of
informed analysts: "Many men of South Asian origin have been soci-
alised to be dominant and are not taught basic survival skills, such as
cooking and cleaning, when they are growing up" (9 April 1996). In
Canada arranged marriages remain common while in India child marriages, though illegal, persist in some areas (Andrew 1996).

Interpretations of Islam vary widely but include, for many, an
emphasis on the second-class status of women who must, at all times,
be sensitive to the need for modesty and decorum. In a number of
countries Muslims practise polygamy. Moshod Abiola, for example,
imprisoned claimant to the Nigerian presidency, a wealthy Muslim
businessman, had, before the murder of his "senior" wife, three wives,
numerous mistresses and some sixty children (*Globe and Mail*, 6 June
1996). Nigerian pop superstar Fela Anikulapo-Kuti, a progressive critic
of the country's military dictatorship, had accumulated twenty-seven
wives by the time of his death from an AIDS-related illness in 1997,
leaving questions as to how many of his wives had contracted the
disease (ibid., 5 August 1997).

In Egypt, government attempts to ban female genital mutilation have
been largely unsuccessful. One study suggests as many as 97 per cent
of Egyptian women are victims of the practice (*Guardian Weekly*,
6 July 1997). In sub-Saharan Africa, wife abuse is endemic, and few
legal sanctions exist. The regional coordinator for the East African
group Women and the Law explained to one reporter: "A lot of men
– and women – think beating your wife is something you do if you
really care about her" (ibid., 12 May 1996).

The cultural attitudes prized by some Caribbean males may also be
thought to contrast with the feminist ethos, not least an aggressive
sexual machismo and an unwillingness to accept equal parental responsibility. Yasmin Alibhai-Brown, in a critical review of the tensions this
has created between black men and women in the U.K., and the growth
of "baby mothers – women who have children with short term boy
friends," cites the views of Darcus Howe, a prominent late middle-
aged, black media figure and former editor of *Race Today*: "I am a
West Indian. That means I make children all the time." In the U.K.
51 per cent of Afro-Caribbean babies are born to single parents
(Alibhai-Brown 1994). In Canada such macho attitudes are reported
to be particularly pronounced among black gang members. Detective
Sergeant David McLeod, an expert on black organized crime with the
Metro Toronto police, giving evidence in the trial of those accused of
the Ottawa murder of Sylvain Leduc, noted the importance to gang

culture of dominance over women and told the court of one gang member who had received a trophy for having twenty-two "baby mothers" (*Ottawa Citizen*, 2 November 1996).

Obviously such issues have been of secondary concern to Canadian feminists. Reflecting on her high-profile involvement in the campaign to defeat the Charlottetown Accord, NAC president Judy Rebick offered her own anecdotal evidence, framed by a stereotypical view of racial minority roles: "But what's more visible to me is the support we have from racial minority men and gay men. I don't get into a taxi cab or get served in a restaurant without a racial minority man saying how great NAC was in the referendum, and how much they think that the struggles of women and the struggle against racism are linked" (Gotlieb 1993: 383).

There is more than a little irony in the fact that those who make a public display of their concern seem incapable of recognizing that racial minorities in Canada are not a homogeneous, powerless group. Perhaps caught in the historic image of the Chinese laundry, the radical patrons of Canada's visible minorities find it difficult to comprehend the significance of the fact that Chinese and South Asian Canadians are increasingly important players among the groups who "dominate society." Internationally the imagery conjured up is, if anything, more ludicrous: imprisoned in an image of nineteenth-century colonialism, the feminist racial vision eagerly embraced by fashion-conscious male camp followers accounts for neither the burgeoning Asian economies of the late twentieth century or the contemporary Ghanaian village chief who, with twenty wives to wait on him, insists that those of his subjects who are female approach him on their knees (Stackhouse 1996b). In the real world, skin colour is no predictor of moral behaviour, politically correct views, or wealth. Five of the world's ten richest billionaires are non-white (Pool 1996).

4

Beyond Orthodoxy

Canadian Race Relations
in International and Historical Perspective

Out of the seemingly separate pieces of history ... we come
to see racism and sexism as the very foundation of Canadian
nationhood.

OISE sociology professor Roxanna Ng, 1989

DESPERATELY SEEKING RACISM

There are good reasons to view claims of pervasive Canadian racism with
scepticism. The supporting empirical evidence relies on selective presentation of racial incidents, data on outcomes that highlight failure and ignore
success, and the redefinition of racism to embrace those who fail to accept
the arguments offered. Remarkably little evidence exists, outside the constituencies ploughing the rich field of government grants and public sector
employment, that race or racial discrimination are issues dominating the
concerns of Canadians. Where are the political parties that perceive the
advantages to be gained by appealing to the alleged racists among us?
Where are the mass movements of the kind seen south of the border,
campaigning against racial injustice? More than one million black American men rallied in 1995 in Washington, mobilized by Louis Farrakhan,
the head of the Nation of Islam, a politician who preaches black superiority, and an unremitting anti-Semite. In Toronto an attempt to mimic the
rally drew a mere forty people, to hear the ubiquitous Dudley Laws speak
at Queen's Park (*Globe and Mail*, 17 October 1995).[1]

THE POLITICS OF RACE

Canada has not only been spared its own Louis Farrakhan: it has also
produced no David Dukes. In the United States the exploitation of race

has not been the exclusive prerogative of politicians on the margin. In 1988, running well behind Michael Dukakis in the presidential campaign, George Bush turned to racial concerns, most notably in the TV ad featuring the case of Willie Horton, a black rapist who committed rape and murder after being released by Governor Dukakis. In contrast, there are no electorally successful Canadian politicians who owe their position to racist appeals, no signs that significant numbers of Canadian voters are seeking a political movement that will pursue a racial agenda.

Much smaller demographic changes in Europe than those in Canada in the past two decades have given rise to a virulent political backlash. In France the overtly racist National Front became a significant political force, securing 15 per cent of the vote in the first round of the 1995 presidential elections. Some weeks later, in municipal elections, the Front captured Toulon, Marignane, and Orange and showed itself to be a powerful force in local politics in other cities. One poll found that two-thirds of respondents believed there are "too many Arabs" in France (*The Economist*, 27 April 1996). In early 1996 UN investigator Maurice Glele-Ahanhanzo reported that the country was in the grip of "a wave of xenophobia and racism" (*Guardian Weekly*, 21 April 1996). Allowing for hyperbole, this is still a transparently more fraught situation than that which any investigator might report in Canada. The xenophobia and racism observed by the United Nations was said to have been fuelled by laws introduced three years earlier by then Interior Minister Charles Pasqua to tighten immigration controls. A parliamentary committee in early 1996 urged a series of further harsh measures, including the right to deport delinquent minors, even if born in France, to their parents' country of origin, if relatives were available to look after them (*The Economist*, 27 April 1996).

In Germany a number of vicious assaults on immigrants and refugees and organized arson attacks on hostels providing them with accommodation resulted in weak police action and an ineffectual response from the ruling Christian Democrats. More forceful than the response to the racial fanatics were the government's moves to further restrict access by refugees. In Austria Jorg Haider's Freedom Party is overtly anti-immigrant; many Austrians claim that it is national socialist in its philosophy. Haider denies these charges, but there is no question that he has praised Hitler's employment policies and addressed Wehrmacht and Waffen ss veterans' rallies. In the 1995 parliamentary elections, running on a strong anti-immigrant platform, the Freedom Party gained 22 per cent of the popular vote (*Guardian Weekly*, 17 December 1995). In 1996, running in the Vienna state elections, the party raised its share of the vote to 28 per cent, finishing second behind the Social

Democrats with 39 per cent (*Globe and Mail*, 14 October 1995). The party secured a similar share of the vote in the nation-wide elections to the parliament of the European Union. In Belgium the right-wing, anti-immigrant Vlaams Blok is the leading party in Antwerp, the country's second-largest city.

In Russia, the 1996 presidential elections saw General Alexander Lebed emerge as Yeltsin's chief security adviser and potential successor. In his own nationalistic, presidential campaign one of Lebed's themes, in the words of the British *Guardian*, was "the need to maintain the sacred 'genetic fund' of Russian blood" (*Guardian Weekly*, 7 July 1996).

In Hungary, often described as one of the more liberal and successful of the former Soviet bloc countries, foreigners of any kind are at risk of violent assault from local xenophobes. A Budapest English-language newspaper runs a regular warning to visible minorities to take care when out at night, but all foreigners are vulnerable. In 1995 the British magazine *Holiday* published a survey ranking Budapest one of the most dangerous holiday destinations in the world (LeBor 1996).

Margaret Thatcher's initial electoral victory in the U.K. may have owed something to her willingness to reach out to voters with racial concerns, most noticeably in a television interview in 1978. This followed a number of racial disturbances and elicited the comment from the would-be prime minister that she recognized that people felt "swamped" by immigrants and that firm action must be taken to reduce immigration. Subsequent polling suggested this and other linked policy announcements significantly increased electoral support for the Conservative opposition (Loney 1986: 52). Overtly racist parties which frequently flaunt their neo-Nazi credentials remain confined to the margins of British politics but in some areas, notably parts of London's inner city, they have at times garnered significant electoral support.

Race remains an emotive electoral issue in the U.K. There is little primary immigration, and the country runs an extremely restrictive refugee policy, but with the Labour Party 30 per cent or more ahead in the polls in 1995, the Conservatives again played the race card. The government proposed to further tighten controls on refugees, creating a so-called "white list" of nations from which claims of applicants would be assumed to be unfounded. The government also proposed new checks to identify illegal immigrants using public services (*Guardian Weekly*, 5 November 1995). The home secretary announced that employers would be required to check the status of all new employees. The change was expected to cost business some $50 million annually and involve investigation of the estimated two million of the fourteen million annual job changers who do not have a national insurance number. The majority of these, the Home Office believed, were British citizens or European Union citizens entitled to work anywhere in the E.U. A smaller number, estimated at 200,000, would be from other countries, including illegal immigrants. The purpose of the changes was simple: in the words of *London Financial Times* journalist Joe Rogaly, the government's intent was "to exploit racial fears" (*Globe and Mail*, 16 November 1995).

In New Zealand, where recent immigration changes have increased Asian immigration, the New Zealand First Party increased its support to 22 per cent in opinion polls, running an overtly anti-immigrant campaign (*The Economist*, 27 April 1996). Support subsequently declined, but in parliamentary elections the party gained 13 per cent of the vote and emerged as the key player in negotiations over the formation of a new government with the National Party and the opposition Labour Party, neither of whom emerged with a clear majority (*Globe and Mail*, 14 October 1996). Unfortunately for those for whom politics can be readily reduced to good guys versus bad guys, the leader of the New Zealand First Party, Winston Peters, now the country's deputy prime minister, is a Maori.

Australia has also experienced increasingly overt electoral hostility to visible minority, predominantly Asian, immigrants. Independent Queensland MP Pauline Hanson caused a storm of protest when she called for a ban on further Asian immigration, but a poll in the *Sidney Morning Herald* showed 48 per cent in agreement with her views compared to only 38 per cent opposed (*Globe and Mail*, 30 October 1996). A subsequent poll suggested a party led by Hanson would secure 18 per cent of the vote. Sixty-six per cent of those questioned agreed with the call for a short-term halt to immigration (ibid., 13 November 1996).

Racial and ethnic tension are not the prerogative of the advanced capitalist societies. In India vicious intercaste rivalry is accompanied by outbreaks of overt conflict between Hindus and Muslims and Hindus and Punjabis. Overtly xenophobic political parties vie for power in some states, promising the persecution of religious and ethnic minorities. The Bharatiya Janata Party is committed to Hindu supremacism and makes an explicit appeal to caste prejudice and anti-Muslim sentiment. Its support is overwhelmingly drawn from upper-caste Hindus who oppose affirmative action programs for Dalit and low-caste Hindus (*Guardian Weekly*, 12 May 1996). The party promises to deport Bangladeshi immigrants. The BJP is linked to the Hindu supremacist RSS, the Rashtriya Swayamsevak Sangh, a corps of Hindu fanatics with over a million members. The corps is committed to expelling Muslims from India and is believed to have been responsible for the deaths in Bombay of some 1,400 in attacks on Muslim neigh-bourhoods in May 1993. The RSS is linked to the Bombay municipal government, and police were ordered not to intervene in the massacres (Stackhouse 1997a). Any Canadian political party promoting the big-otry that lies at the core of the BJP would rightfully be condemned to the margins. In India the BJP, together with its allies, is the largest block in Lok Sabha, India's lower house of parliament, with 195 seats (*Globe and Mail*, 14 May 1996). In May 1996, it briefly formed the government.

The film *Borders*, which offers a xenophobic view of the 1971 war with Pakistan, was described by one Indian critic as "dangerously fanatical." The film, released in 1997, broke every box-office record (Stackhouse 1997b).

In Pakistan, non-Muslims are only permitted to vote for candidates in so-called reserved seats. In Sindh province 246 people, including 148 women, were reported killed in a recent fifteen-month period, under the tribal custom of *karo kari*, which encourages relatives to deal with alleged sinners. Tribal punishment of those transgressing sexual mores was a particular risk for women. The Human Rights Commission of Pakistan reported that "often mere imputation or faintest suspicion ... was enough provocation" (*Globe and Mail*, 26 March 1996). In the same province slavery continues to flourish. The description offered by a *Guardian* correspondent of one of the thousands of plantation slaves bears repeating, as there is a curious silence about such issues among those who believe melanin content dictates virtue[2]: "Like his grandfather before him, Rupo Koli was born a slave, and all his days were the same: long hard hours in sugar cane fields, with a coil of rope hissing through the air to his shoulders when he faltered under the burning sun" (*Guardian Weekly*, 31 March 1996).

Koli, his wife, and eight children were sold to a new owner in 1991 for $1,500. The family wore leg irons in the field, were chained to wooden posts at night, and were regularly beaten before being freed by human rights activists. Bonded labour in Pakistan was outlawed in 1992, but in a society dominated by landlords who rely on such labour for profit margins, much as the slave owners of the American South did more than one hundred years earlier, enforcement is weak: "Although his story is horrifying, Mr Koli recounts it as if it were completely normal – and in this part of Pakistan it is ... feudal landlords rule as they have always done: with casual brutality."

In Nepal in early 1996 violent outbreaks rocked the western districts of the normally peaceful kingdom. The majority of the area's inhabit-ants are of Tibeto-Burmese origin but are dominated by "Indo-Nepalese high castes, absentee landlords and government officials"

(*Guardian Weekly*, 17 March 1996). The violence was attributed to the work of Maoist agitators and a crackdown by law enforcement agencies.

The widespread incidence of prostitution in Asia, including extensive child prostitution, is a result not only of the corrosive effect of poverty; it is sanctioned by social mores that accord women and girls a subordinate status. Frequently the condition of those entrapped in the industry, which, in India, includes many girls of Nepalese origin, is akin to slavery (Langellier 1996).

In Africa, the tensions between rival ethnic groups have erupted into full-scale wars and systematic ethnic cleansing. Racial tension between blacks and Asians born on the continent has resulted in frequent and sometimes vicious conflicts. Laws have been passed intended to curb Asian commercial activity and favour blacks and outright property expropriation has occurred. In 1971 Tanzania passed the Acquisition of Buildings Act, restricting individuals to the ownership of one residence; additional residential buildings would pass into government ownership. The primary target of the legislation was Tanzanian Asians. African Ugandan dictator Idi Amin expelled seventy thousand Asians and seized their property. In Kenya, Tanzania, and Zambia, tensions between Asians, who are disproportionately involved in commerce, and the African majority continue to be evident. In October 1995 rioting and looting broke out in Livingstone in Zambia. Virtually every one of the eighty Asian families was affected and a number of businesses destroyed. Similar tensions between blacks and Asians are to be found in other countries including Guyana and Trinidad.

The tension between blacks and Asians in multiracial countries formed the backdrop to a Canadian controversy that originated in the publication of Neil Bissoondath's eloquent attack on Canada's cult of multiculturalism (1994). The attack produced outrage among those who had made a career denouncing Canadian racism. The most subversive implication of Bissoondath's book was the suggestion that government policy and the burgeoning race relations and multicultural industry it had spawned were exacerbating racism rather than addressing the problem of forging a common, colour-blind Canadian identity. Concern was particularly evident at Canadian Heritage, the department responsible for multicultural programs. The department responded in part by funding a special issue of *Border/Lines*, which purports to be an arts magazine.[3] The issue focused on the question of multiculturalism in a manner more acceptable to Canadian Heritage bureaucrats.

The principal article was a vitriolic attack on Bissoondath by writer Marlene Nourbese Philip, like Bissoondath, born in Trinidad. Philip suggested that Bissoondath's intellectual position stemmed from his racial origins. Asians, Philip claimed, have played a problematic role "in African societies such as Guyana, Trinidad, Kenya, South Africa and Uganda, and more recently in the United States with the tensions between Koreans and African Americans" (Philip 1995: 4). Asians, wrote Philip, were placed higher in the colonial hierarchy: "the colonialist construction of South Asian qualities placed them above Africans." According to this race-as-destiny view, Bissoondath's argument and his failure to share Philip's views about Canada's extreme racism are a result of this racial history. Philip maintains that this background is important in "explaining the creation of the colonial psyche and mentality in writers like Bissoondath, and the role he plays in yet another colonial society, Canada" (ibid.).

The suggestion that Bissoondath's ideas are the result of the compromised history of the ethnic group to which he belongs is a view not dissimilar to other attempts to attribute negative characteristics to individuals on the basis of group membership, whether greed, lack of patriotism, deviousness, or low intelligence. It is an apt commentary on Canada's muddled multicultural program that in the name of fostering racial harmony it provides funding for the promotion of such nonsense.[4]

DESPERATELY SEEKING RACISTS

Contemporary Canadian experience stands in marked contrast to both the experience of Western Europe and the intensity of ethnic, religious, and racial conflict that has plagued some developing countries. In contrast to Nourbese Philip's view of ethnicity as destiny, Canada has allowed the possibility of rebirth and transformation.

In Canada, as we have noted, no significant political party (outside, arguably, Quebec) rests its appeal on racial policies. The Reform party is the favourite target for charges of racism, but such accusations reflect an ignorance of the party's philosophical base and its actual practices. The party's primary appeal rests in its successful construction of a populist vehicle to articulate western Canadian alienation. The focus of this alienation is on federal fiscal incompetence and constitutional arrangements resulting in the proliferation of government. In the immigration area Reform policies advocate nothing more than a restoration of the historic link between immigration flows and labour market demands. Reform's success owes much to its ability to capitalize on issues where the left has fled the field. This may be distressing for those who hold more progressive views, but it scarcely merits attempts to impute to the party views which it explicitly rejects.

Progressives in Canada have failed to present any credible policies on spiralling federal and provincial deficits and the growing debt. The legacy includes the continuing erosion of social programs, a loss of national autonomy in directing economic policy, and a diminished confidence in the ability of government to ameliorate social problems. Held hostage by the public sector unions and hindered by a degree of economic illiteracy which is as astonishing as it is pervasive, many in the NDP and the coalition of social groups that cluster round the CLC and the union-funded Centre for Policy Alternatives spent years labelling the deficit and the debt as a right-wing chimera.[5] Such myopia not only ignored the inevitable reduction in social spending that would be triggered by the pre-emption of an ever increasing proportion of government revenue by debt interest payments but also failed to learn from the experience of the Reagan presidency.

The pursuit of so-called supply side economics by the Reagan administration led to an explosion of public debt. What should have been of particular interest to Canadian progressives were the distributional consequences of high government debt, which played a significant role in growing income polarization (Phillips 1990). Soaring government deficits and rising debt exercise an upward pressure on interest rates, with negative consequences for economic growth and for those borrowing money. It requires no great economic grasp to appreciate that high interest rates benefit lenders, who, in general, are significantly more affluent than borrowers. Those who failed to identify the devastating social consequences of rising debt levels prefer to respond to program cutbacks with the charge that these are driven not by a gathering fiscal crisis but by some nefarious right-wing conspiracy and the malignant interest rate policies of the Bank of Canada. Meanwhile much of their support has marched to the right.

A parallel history occurred in the left's response to the unhinging of immigration from the requirements of the labour market. The NDP, the CLC, and their allies failed to give voice to labour's traditional response, that increases in immigration without any increase in employment could only weaken the bargaining power of labour and result in further downward pressure on wages and rises in rent levels. Instead fashion dictated that any attempt to restrict immigration, to focus attention on the employability of would-be immigrants, or to examine the social costs be decried as racist. But while there is extensive evidence which points to increasing concern over immigration levels, there is little support for a racially based immigration policy. The 1994 year-end Environics poll Focus Canada found that 68 per cent "strongly disagreed" and 22 per cent disagreed with the statement that "non-whites" should not be allowed to immigrate to Canada (Canadian Heritage 1995). By contrast, elaborate changes to immigration law in the U.K. contained clear racial intentions, notably the introduction of "patriality" and "grand patriality" in determining eligibility for claims of U.K. nationality. This was intended to facilitate continuing immigration from the "white commonwealth" of those of British descent, while closing the door on further non-white immigration.

It is impossible to find any remotely parallel element in Reform policies. The party's response to the suggestion by soon-to-be-ex-party whip Bob Ringma that a store owner who found that black or homosexual employees upset his customers could fire them or send them to the back of the store provoked a rebuttal by the party leadership. Deputy party leader Deborah Grey suggested: "the right answer is to show the customer the door" (*Globe and Mail*, 3 May 1996). When MP David Chatters rekindled the controversy by suggesting discrimination against gays could in some circumstances be justified, Reform leader Preston Manning announced that the next MP to go against the party policy of equal treatment for all Canadians would be expelled from caucus.

If Canada is indeed a deeply racist society with "mounting evidence" of racism (Kallen 1995: 35), Ringma's ill-considered comments might have been expected to strike a resonant chord. Certainly politicians comfortable with racial appeals would have had little difficulty with the comments. In contrast, Reform's strategists suggested that such remarks were doing the party enormous damage. In an article setting out the party's position, Manning insisted that the party "stands for the fundamental equality of all Canadians ... The party supports affirming the equality of all Canadians before the law rather than ... the creation of special categories of Canadians with group rights." Manning suggested that those who did not understand what this meant should leave the party: "Most Reformers are simply not interested in defending their views, and most Canadians are not interested in electing a party that harbours them" (*Ottawa Citizen*, 7 May 1996).

This failed to stop the attempt to reconstruct Reform as the authentic voice of Canadian racism. In October 1966, as they sought to lay the ground for the next election, the federal Liberals joined the fray calling the party the voice of the "extreme right." B'nai Brith, an organization not usually loathe to detect bigotry and prejudice, was moved to respond. Vice-president Stephen Scheinberg commented: "to call the Reform Party as a whole extreme right is to stretch the meaning of this term beyond recognition ... It will be difficult to recognize real extremists if we apply this term to everyone on the right of centre" (B'nai Brith News Release, 30 October 1996).

The Liberals' attempt to portray what was then the third largest party in the House of Commons as the voice of the extreme right provided an implicit comment on those Canadians who had elected it.

An academic at the University of Guelph, Stanley Barrett, with funding from the Canadian Secretary of State, precursor to Canadian Heritage, took the argument one step further. In an analysis of extreme right groups such as the Western Guard and the even more obscure Nationalist Party, groups whose racism is visceral and overt, Barrett argued that what was important about his endeavour was what it revealed about Canada as a whole: "The basic assumption of this paper is that the radical right publicly expresses to a considerable degree what the majority of people think and feel privately, albeit often unconsciously ... the value of investigating the extreme right is not solely or even mainly for what we learn about it, but instead what it tells us about the society in which it exists" (Barrett 1991: 87).

In this analysis it matters not that such neo-fascist organizations invite almost universal loathing, that thousands of Canadians died fighting fascism in the Second World War, or that Canada played a leading and widely supported role in bringing pressure to bear on apartheid South Africa. It is clear from the ivory towers of Guelph and the offices of the well-paid civil servants who generously supported this research that unconsciously, in our heart of hearts, most of us feel "to a considerable degree" that the neo-fascist, lunatic fringe expresses our thoughts.

In the U.K. a number of Conservative politicians have been quite willing to pander to racist elements in the electorate. In France the appeals of the National Front have resulted in a move by Chirac and other conservative politicians to mine the same electoral vein. In Canada the Reform party eschewed such policies, responding, for example, to the decision to ban turbans from the Canadian Legion with an unequivocal statement from the party leader regretting the decision. Charles Strahl, who served as the party's critic on the government's employment equity legislation, attracted enough hostility from the improbably named Aryan Nation Church that he was honoured with a message on one of the "Nation's" hate propaganda lines.

Vancouver journalist Murray Dobbin, who has made something of a career demonizing Reform, charged that the party's infiltration by CSIS informant Grant Bristow reflected the party's racism (CBC Radio, *The House*, 24 Sept. 1994). Dobbin's argument appeared to rest on the claim that since the party's immigration policies attracted support from racists, the party was racist. This has a curious ring of familiarity. McCarthy and his allies at the height of the cold war accused liberals engaged in progressive causes of being communist sympathizers, since communists joined the same organizations. Obviously undeterred by the vilification which the party's alleged policies on race had incurred, a number of visible minority candidates stood for Reform in the 1997 election, three of whom were elected. Transparently neither Reform's members who selected the candidates or Reform's voters were greatly moved by the question of race.

Hedy Fry, Canada's minister of Multiculturalism, has sought to dismiss all opposition to official multiculturalism as the voice of reaction: "The criticisms levelled by a few political opponents of multiculturalism are really just the proof of its success. It's because multiculturalism has gone mainstream, it's because ethnocultural groups are making progress that we hear from the far right wing" (Fry 1996). One problem with Fry's attempt to silence her critics by imputing extreme ideas is empirical. Bissoondath, one of the better-known critics, is a writer whose views readily fall into the social democratic tradition; this places him to the left of Fry, who made her political debut as head of the British Columbia Medical Association. It is unclear what "progressive" agenda Fry's government is pursuing.

Robert Martin, professor of law at the University of Western Ontario, has also been a vociferous critic of the politics of identity. Martin is a committed socialist who rejects the "notion of market supremacy," calling for more progressive taxation and much greater control over corporations. He dismisses the obsessive focus on interest group politics and the "celebration of self" inherent in the demands of groups for whom biology and sexual preference is indeed destiny: "The politics of social radicalism is the politics of middle-class dinner party chatter. But it has managed to take this harmless, if vacuous, activity a step further than had hitherto been managed. Its practitioners have persuaded themselves, and many others, that they are not merely chattering, but bravely creating a new and better world" (Martin 1996: 163).

Christopher Lasch provides an acerbic account of the American progressive elite's betrayal of popular concerns and their fascination with the "politics of radical gestures." He cites with approval the call for a politics that emphasizes class rather than racial divisions but notes that this might lead to real change – "always an unwelcome prospect for those (including many self-styled radicals and cultural revolutionaries) with a heavy investment in the existing arrangements" (Lasch 1995: 140).

The portrayal of Reform and other opponents of the politics of identity as racist serves to maintain the progressive credentials of those who embrace the politics of identity. The reality is that the fascination with such politics has gone hand in hand with the decline in the popular appeal of the Canadian left. For white low- and middle-income earners, the effect of such politics is to label them as bigots, while offering nothing that might address the concerns of those who see their own incomes falling and job security decreasing. Indeed, preferential hiring will place such groups at a further disadvantage.

In Canada those at the forefront of the politics of grievance have not only been able to rely on generous public funding from governments that have no apparent progressive agenda but they have also frequently occupied positions affording considerable personal privilege. The tenured university "radicals" who have been so eager to rally behind the fractious demands of identity groups hold views that suggest many less worthy Canadians are bigots from whom the vulnerable must be protected; hence the need for societal legislation and an array of institutional codes and resources to enforce "zero tolerance" and protect academia from contamination. The professoriate occupy positions of enviable social and economic power. Salaries for senior academics, normally accessed by nothing more demanding than longevity, are in the $80,000–$110,000 range, higher still for the burgeoning army of deans and vice-presidents; pensions and benefits are equally generous. Not surprisingly the politics of race and gender may appear more attractive than the pursuit of Lasch's vision of greater social equality.

ORTHODOXY AND HISTORICAL REVISIONISM

Fortunate indeed was Canada to have set in motion in 1793, the year of Eli Whitney's invention of the cotton gin and the passage of the first Fugitive Slave Act, the extinction of slavery within its borders.

Robin Winks, 1971

The vilification of the Reform party is consistent with a broader current of opinion that perversely ignores Canada's enormous success in building a multi-racial society, in favour of a myopic search for evidence of Canadian guilt. Canada has plenty of historic moments that scarcely invite modern celebration. The existence of slavery in Canadian history demands recognition; however, to focus on slavery in Canada without any recognition of the presence of slavery in a wide range of societies over thousands of years is to invite not understanding but guilt. The transatlantic slave trade of the seventeenth and eighteenth centuries was a horrific and barbarous historical occurrence, but slavery was widespread in African and Arabic societies before and after that trade (Ferro 1997). Canada's treatment of early Chinese immigrants and the actions against Canadians of Japanese origin in the Second World War are less than glorious moments in history, but these are neither the nation's defining characteristics nor a reflection on current attitudes.

The evidence suggests that ethnic groups that have experienced historic injustices in Canada have displayed a remarkable resilience. Japanese Canadians faced property confiscation and internment in the Second World War and, for some, deportation as well. Today they are among the most successful ethnic groups in the country. While this does not absolve Canadians from acknowledging the enormity of their historic treatment, it does suggest its limited contemporary relevance. If there is a need to find a group whose historic treatment has produced a legacy requiring urgent redress, Canadians might more usefully turn to the social and economic problems faced by many aboriginal Canadians. There is no parallel obligation in regard to Canada's visible minorities, the overwhelming majority of whom are here by direct personal choice.

One of the more remarkable achievements of the race industry has been the creation of an image of Canadian history in which ethnic harmony is usurped by the arrival of immigrants with "visibly" different characteristics. Trevor Wilson, head of Omnibus Consulting, which does extensive business in the "diversity training" industry, illustrates the historical view of the orthodox: "For many years, Canada's society was relatively homogeneous, but as the Canadian population became more diverse, issues of unfair treatment became more evident" (Wilson 1996: 5).[6] This observation is a travesty of Canadian history, which is replete with examples of the grossest prejudice and discrimination against immigrants – without regard to skin colour. Canadian historian Donald Avery notes the mounting concern of Anglo-Canadians as more than a million immigrants arrived between 1911 and 1913, an increasing proportion from central and southern Europe: "In the minds of many Anglo-Canadians the arrival of these 'hordes' of foreigners stirred deep suspicion" (Avery 1995: 42).

During the First World War eighty thousand enemy aliens were registered and 8,579 interned, becoming "the object of intense Anglo-Canadian hostility" (ibid.: 71). The majority of these aliens were of German or Austro-Hungarian origin. Many of those interned were leased out to employers at minimal pay rates. When a group of thirty-two Austrian internees went on strike in North Bay protesting dangerous and unsanitary conditions, they were jailed for six months for "breach of contract" (ibid.: 74). At the end of war many of those who had faced registration and sometimes internment now faced demands that they be fired from their jobs to make way for returning soldiers; calls for enemy aliens to be deported were commonplace. In Winnipeg, on 28 January 1919, demobilized soldiers attacked foreigners, wrecked the German club, the offices of the Socialist Party of Canada, and the business of a prominent Jewish socialist. The police made no attempt to intervene, while the *Winnipeg Telegram* commented on the cowardice of those assaulted (ibid.: 77).

Immigrants in the early decades of the twentieth century continued to face bigotry long after their arrival. Many years later an immigrant would still be viewed as "a Jew or an Italian by the Anglo-Canadians that he encountered in his daily business" (Harney and Troper 1975: 181). Ethnic segregation was evident in residential settlements, a function of income, prejudice against immigrants, and the desire of immigrant groups to preserve a common culture. In Winnipeg, at the end of the First World War, Anglo-Saxons lived in the South End; continental Europeans lived in the North End, an area where infant mortality was twice as high (ibid.). There were marked discrepancies in income and opportunity between different ethnic groups. Analysis of 1931 census data, for example, indicated that those of Central European origin had average annual periods of unemployment twice as long as those of British origin (ibid.: 111).

Opposition to immigrants from the "wrong" European countries was fuelled by beliefs that such "races" were inferior to those of Anglo-Saxon stock and by concerns that they would spread the seeds of radical dissent in Canada. In the period before the Second World War deportation of those who were thought to be a drain on the system, because of poverty and unemployment, and of radical agitators, was widespread: "Deportation, both formal and informal, helped to create a hidden system of migrant labour that functioned more like a 'guest worker' system ... It was a concealed but necessary regulator of the balance between labour demand and labour supply" (Roberts 1988: 9). Between 1930 and 1935 some 26,000 were deported, whether because they were deemed indigent or subversive (Whitaker 1987: 14). Deportation was more commonly deployed against non-Anglo-Saxons. Even British-born radicals fared much better than their "foreign" counterparts: leaders of the Winnipeg General Strike who were of British origin appear to have escaped deportation (Roberts 1988: 85).

In the Depression the efforts of Canadian authorities to suppress radical politics intensified. In Toronto in 1929 regulations were passed "against non-English language public meetings and disorderly or seditious utterances" (ibid.: 126). The association of subversion with "foreign" influences needs to be understood in the context of the wider xenophobia of WASP Toronto (Levitt and Shaffir 1987). Canada's refusal to accept many Jewish refugees, even as the threat which they faced mounted, was driven by wider anti-Semitism. The *Globe and*

Mail illustrated the link between such anti-Semitism and wider political concerns in a 1937 editorial: "Although it cannot be said that a majority of Jews are Communists, the indications are that a large percentage, and probably the majority of Communists are Jews" (Avery 1995: 122–3).

Prejudice against Jewish immigrants and others of non-Anglo-Saxon stock persisted after the Second World War and was reflected in disproportionately low admission rates for Jewish refugees compared to others (Abella and Troper 1982: 274). Jewish immigrants continued to face significant obstacles: no visa applications were accepted in the new state of Israel, and anti-Semitism among immigration officers appeared commonplace. As late as 1957, when Canada was admitting Hungarian refugees, those who were identified as Jewish were the subject of particular suspicion (Whitaker 1987: 67 and *passim*). In the post-war period Canada continued to operate an immigration policy that reflected a de facto hierarchy. Commenting on the relatively small number of Greeks admitted in spite of the number fleeing a repressive right-wing regime in the aftermath of the civil war, Whitaker notes: "Canadian immigration officials showed little enthusiasm for Greeks; southern Europeans were not much favoured in this era" (ibid.: 69).

The contemporary reinterpretation of history by the diversity training industry and the advocates of skin politics omits the depth of interethnic conflict and leads to gross simplification. Canada's history is replete with examples of ethnic competition and attempts to restrict access to jobs or resources to privileged, more powerful groups. Such measures were not exclusively directed against racial minorities nor can the explanation be simply reduced to racism.

Earlier opposition to Asian and, more particularly, Chinese immigration in British Columbia, for example, was rooted in concerns by white workers that they would face reduced wages and conditions and possibly total displacement as employers sought out and imported cheap Asiatic labour. The contractors for the western section of the Canadian Pacific Railway, for example, imported thousands of Chinese workers. The argument over Asian immigration in B.C. was in many ways a class conflict, pitting employers against labour (Avery 1995: 46). In this conflict Asian workers were the victims of persistent discrimination and sometimes violent assault by white workers. Employers took advantage of their vulnerable position: many Chinese labourers had borrowed money to come to Canada and were, in consequence, indentured labourers, forced to take any kind of work and hand over a large part of their meagre earnings to pay off the debt. Asians not only provided a source of cheap and pliable labour to employers but could also be used as strike breakers, as in 1913 during the Vancouver Island coal strikes (ibid.: 57). This further inflamed racial tensions.

But in her history of early Japanese and Chinese immigration to British Columbia, Patricia Roy notes the positive change of attitude after the Second World War and suggests that this was "relatively easy" since race, in the sense of physical appearance and beliefs of innate white superiority, had never been the "sole source" of antipathy. Roy notes other historic concerns, including the apparent willingness of Asians to work for lower wages and worries that the potentially large numbers of Asian immigrants would turn the province into a place where "Asian rather than western standards prevailed." She concludes: "The campaign for a 'white man's province,' though blatantly racist in appearance, was, in fact, a catch phrase that covered a wide variety of concerns and transcended particular economic interests" (Roy 1989: 267).

If earlier generations of immigrants, including many of European origin, experienced far greater discrimination and overt hostility without requiring a vast panoply of interventions to secure their subsequent success, the case for continued funding of the contemporary race industry is weakened. The politics of grievance depend on the claim that recent "visible" immigrants face novel and more intense barriers than previous immigrant groups. In reality those who immigrated to Canada in the last twenty-five years encountered a society vastly more tolerant and receptive than that found by many earlier immigrants. In the 1930s Canada, to its shame, refused Jewish immigrants even as they faced death. In the 1980s Canada's refugee policy, the most generous in the world, resulted in the admission of many thousands of refugees from Africa and Asia whose primary motivation was not the fear of individual persecution but escape from countries ravaged by ethnic and communal violence and consequent economic breakdown.

CANADA'S BLACK POPULATION: HISTORICAL AND CONTEMPORARY DIVERSITY

The reconstruction of Canada's racial history suggests that Canada is fundamentally no different from the United States, most notably in its treatment of and attitude towards blacks and their consequent disadvantaged position. This historical myth fits conveniently with the fashionable view among black militants that "Babylon" is all the same and blacks everywhere united in the struggle against injustice.

But slavery was never a major social institution in Canada, nor, historically, was Canada's black population proportionately large.

Today's black population is characterized by enormous diversity. Canadian-born blacks are not primarily the descendants of Canadian slaves; prior to more recent immigration from the Caribbean, Africa, and elsewhere, they were far more likely to be the descendants of those who entered Canada on the underground railroad, fleeing American slave-owners long after slavery was abolished in Upper Canada. A conservative estimate suggests that by the late 1960s approximately half of the black population of Canada could trace its roots back to fugitive American slaves (Winks 1971: 241). Far fewer would be able to trace their roots back to slave owners in the area that became Canada. Today Canada's black population is overwhelmingly composed of first generation immigrants and their descendants; more than 200,000 immigrated between 1971 and 1991 (Torczyner 1997: 25).[7] The proposition that as a group they are victims of some historic disadvantage which obliges redress from contemporary Canadians is self-evidently absurd. The myth does, however, fulfil a function: it legitimates a wider claim of victimization which, as D'Souza argues in his seminal study *The End of Racism*, is essential to the survival of the race industry (1995: 481).

Thirty years ago Canadians were sometimes accused of having a rather mawkish attitude to the country's history of black and white relations. Canadians, it was suggested, overlooked the existence of slavery in New France, the Maritime provinces, and Upper Canada and ignored segregated schools and a litany of racial conflicts in favour of a myth that placed *Uncle Tom's Cabin* at the heart of the country's history. This reflected not only the popularity of the novel, the story of a heroic fugitive slave making a new life in Canada, but also confusion as to whether, as was sometimes (incorrectly) claimed, the novel was actually inspired by real-life experiences of James Henson. A fugitive slave from Maryland, Henson played a prominent role in Upper Canada, notably in the black community of Dawn (Winks 1971: 178 and *passim*).

Today, it would seem, the pendulum has swung to the other extreme: Canadian history simply mirrors that of the United States. Indeed, according to former Ontario Human Rights Commissioner Rosemary Brown, slavery in Canada persists: "A look at the life of the women domestics from the West Indies and the Philippines will show *poor nonwhite women are still, in many instances, enslaved* in those jobs. The word 'slavery' may have disappeared from our vocabulary, but the treatment of domestics, as designated by our immigration laws, ensures that the practice can continue" (Brown 1991: 173, emphasis added). There are, no doubt, exploitative employers and even instances of gross abuse, but the allegation of slavery is reflective not of

Canadian institutions but of the bizarre views of those who built Canada's grievance industry.[8]

The first lieutenant-governor of Upper Canada, John Graves Simcoe, a supporter of anti-slavery campaigner William Wilberforce, pledged, when he arrived in the capital of Niagara in 1791, to oppose any law that "discriminates by dishonest policy between the Natives of Africa, America or Europe" (Hill 1981: 15). Simcoe was as good as his word, and two years later in 1793 the first Legislative Assembly of Upper Canada outlawed the importing of slaves into the colony. The law was nonetheless a "bitter disappointment" to Simcoe, who had wanted an outright ban on slavery (ibid.: 17). In 1803 Lower Canada freed its estimated three hundred slaves (Gillmoor 1995). Following the war of 1812, John Beverley Robinson, Upper Canada's attorney general, said that courts would uphold the freedom of blacks who arrived in Canada (Hill 1981: 25) at the same time the courts were handing down decisions against local slave-owners.

Although there are no accurate figures on the number of blacks who entered Canada fleeing American slavery, Hill offers a "conservative guess" of thirty thousand (1981: 39). The influx of blacks fleeing slavery and the increasingly strong anti-slavery movement in Canada West created a climate hostile to the remaining slave-owners. Winks, in his authoritative history, notes the absence of any provision for compensation to slave owners in British North America in the Imperial Act of 1833 abolishing slavery throughout the Empire, and the fact that the provinces were not mentioned in the Act; he concludes that "for the purposes of emancipation, the British government did not consider slavery to exist in those provinces" (Winks 1971: 111). Hill, a black Canadian whose career included serving as research director of the Metropolitan Toronto Social Planning Council in the late 1950s, and subsequently as chair of the Ontario Human Rights Commission, noted in his history of blacks in early Canada: "After the turn of the 19th century most Canadian blacks were free" (1981: 18). In 1851 the Northern Convention of Coloured Freemen met in Toronto, with hundreds coming from across the northern United States, Canada, and England. The convention resolved that slaves fleeing America should come to Canada rather than go to Africa, since Canada was better placed to direct action against slavery (ibid.: 59).

Great play is made of white culpability for the slave trade, ignoring the ubiquity of slavery, the active involvement of Africans, and the central role played by the Royal Navy in finally suppressing the trade. These complexities fail to fit the simple picture of white persecution offered by Afrocentrists. Nation of Islam leader Louis Farrakhan denounced as myth claims that slavery persists in modern Africa. In response the *Boston Globe* sent two reporters to southern Sudan where they purchased two young slaves for $500 each and returned them to their families (*Globe and Mail* 19 August 1996).

Glenda Simms, the Jamaican-born president of the now disbanded Canadian Advisory Council on the Status of Women, eloquently if unintentionally illustrates the extent to which the search for historical grievance results in historical reinterpretation. In a volume of essays exploring the meaning and future of Canadian citizenship, she argues that Canada now has "three components: 'Canadians' (white Canadians), 'Canadian citizens' (non-white Canadians) and Aboriginals ... the concept 'Canadian' has been steeped in a tradition of racism and exclusion" (Simms 1993: 334). Since Simms is doing no more than provide orthodoxy with some rhetorical embellishment, she finds it unnecessary to provide evidence that such categories have any real world existence. Do Canadians really believe that their fellow citizens are defined by such a hierarchy? A 1993 Gallup poll found that no less than 76 per cent of Canadians agreed with the statement that "cultural and racial diversity is a *fundamental* characteristic of Canadian society" (Canadian Heritage 1994a: 2, emphasis added) – a marked contrast to the exclusionary ideas many Anglo-Saxon Canadians expressed towards a whole range of ethnic groups in earlier decades.

In her search for evidence of racist culpability Simms unearthed a document from Longford School in Saskatchewan, which records some impressions of the "negro" population who had arrived in the area in 1908. The archival excerpts recount: "These Negroes were musical and fun loving. One young man was especially fond of fried chickens which caused his neighbours to keep locks on their chicken coops and blame the poor fellow every time a hen was missing" (Simms 1993: 343). The extracts make reference to a black death from what appeared to be flu in 1918, which resulted in a visit from a white neighbour, Mr MacLaughlin, who initially was refused entry to the house. No reason is given for this.

Simms is in no doubt as to the significance of these dusty extracts: "It is almost frightening to recognize that the stereotype of the fun-loving, fried-chicken eating Black male is recorded in such an obscure Canadian settlement ... One cannot help but wonder why Mr MacLaughlin was not a welcome neighbour. Did the Black community recognize the level of racism that affected their lives?" (Simms 1993: 344).

In contrast to Simms's search for evidence of historic culpability, Winks, in his scholarly history, records the presence of a number of blacks in western Canada, including Alfred Shadd who practised medicine in Kinistino and Melfort, Saskatchewan, "and encountered no prejudice" (Winks 1971: 303). Shadd also edited the *Melfort Journal* and ran for office for the Conservatives. It is entirely possible to read the extract offered by Simms as evidence of no more than a friendly interest in neighbours who were culturally distinctive. The visit by Mr MacLaughlin appears to have resulted from nothing more than a concern to help. In the extract included by Simms, it is noted that MacLaughlin "wrapped the dead boy in a blanket and brought him to Mr Charles Warren. He was later buried in the Mount Pleasant Cemetery."

Frances Henry, an anthropologist at York University, who has done much to foster the culture of grievance in her portrayal of Canada as a grossly racist society (Henry 1994, Henry *et al.* 1995), gives little credit to Canada's role in the underground railroad but is in no doubt as to the views of those who sought freedom in Canada: "After the abolition of slavery in the USA many Canadian blacks chose to return to the USA, recognizing that the value attributed to the colour of one's skin would continue to mark and marginalize them within Canadian society" (Collins and Henry 1994: 527).

This marginalization appears not to have been a problem for William P. Hubbard. The son of black Americans, Hubbard was born in Toronto in 1842. Elected as a Toronto alderman in 1894, he went on to serve as city comptroller from 1904–07, in which capacity he filled in for the city's mayor during his absence (Winks 1971: 331).

It is difficult to know at what point the received view of Canadian racial history changed, but much of the revisionist approach was driven by the multicultural industry. Government funding of a range of ethnic organizations with little grass-roots membership provided voice and a platform to those whose careers and continued funding depended on the successful articulation of grievances, historical and contemporary. In the educational field a lucrative trade developed in rewriting the past to appease contemporary concerns. In this process the real historic grievances of specific groups of black Canadians, notably in Nova Scotia, were transformed into the racially defined legacy of disparate cultural groups who shared little beyond the accident of colour.

Winks, in contrast, notes the difficulty of drawing definitive conclusions about the black experience from so much contradictory information. Canadian history certainly provides abundant evidence of bigotry, but it also offers many examples of Canadians who transcended conventional racial thinking. Winks observes the "formlessness of the racial barrier" in the first decades of the twentieth century. In Dresden, Ontario, blacks could not eat with whites; in London, Ontario, the mayor supported a suit brought by local blacks against a restaurant that refused them service. Blacks could join the YMCA and boy scouts in Toronto but not in Windsor. Blacks could be buried in Anglican churchyards in Toronto and Windsor but not in Halifax or Fredericton. The Knox Presbyterian Church in Toronto invited a black Arkansan to minister for a month in 1923; in Presbyterian churches in Halifax and Saint John blacks were barred as parishioners (ibid.: 325).

A MADE-IN-CANADA HISTORY CURRICULUM

The Canadian Civil Liberties Association, which lists among its backers such luminaries as Robert Stanfield, Allan Blakeney, Edward Broadbent, and the late Joe Ghiz, proffered its own vision for the history curriculum in September 1995. Pitching its agenda in the context of "disquiet" over unfortunate manifestations of racial and ethnic tension in Ontario, the association deplored the ignorance of students concerning major occurrences in Canadian racial and ethnic history (Canadian Civil Liberties Association 1995).

Before turning to the association's proposals for the school curriculum it is worth considering the events that had caused its disquiet. The deputy mayor of Markham, Ontario, had expressed reservations about the rapid growth and planned future expansion of exclusive Chinese shopping malls. Her comments had won support from some Chinese Canadians who rejected the apparent ghettoization implicit in such developments. Other critics argued that the malls represented the worst kind of speculative development, inadequately planned and with little concern for their impact on the character of the bedroom communities of Markham and Richmond Hill. To label such debates as evidence of rising tension seems indicative of a desire in the race industry to drum up business in slack times. The suggestion also serves to curtail the opportunities for citizens of a multi-ethnic society to discuss any matter that may have an ethnic character.

The Civil Liberties Association also expressed concern about unwarranted generalizations about Somali abuse of the welfare system and the targeting of the Jamaican community regarding the disproportionate amount of violent crime "allegedly" perpetrated by young people from that country. It is unclear why the Civil Liberties Association believes discussion of such matters should be avoided or why an organization ostensibly concerned with civil liberties believes that it should police the boundaries of permissible discussion. There is good reason to query the high dependency level in the Somali community. The relationships between recipients in a culture where one man may have a number of wives and the channelling of funds back from Canada to support the activities of Somali warlords are matters of legitimate concern to those whose taxes provide benefits. The high level of Jamaican involvement in crime may be difficult to quantify, since as a matter of policy relevant data are not collected, but there is no shortage of press reports and expert comments attesting to the real existence of the problem.

In Toronto a special police unit has been established to tackle black (predominantly Jamaican) organized crime. The black leadership of the Harriet Tubman Community Organization[9] called a press conference in late 1994 to highlight the growth of black crime in Toronto, warning that if action was not taken, Toronto could follow the route to urban deterioration seen in the United States (*Globe and Mail*, 9 November 1994). There has been a large number of well-publicized crimes in which the assailant was black. In March 1996 Linda Delellis, a young mother of two, was shot and killed in her driveway in the City of York in Metro Toronto, the unintended victim of a drive-by shooting. The intended victim of the shooting, which was believed to be connected with the area's thriving drug trade, was black, as was the shooter. *Globe and Mail* columnist John Barber observed: "in the case of almost all of the city's most notorious murders of this decade, the perpetrator or alleged perpetrator has been a young, black male" (14 March 1996). An article on Montreal's gang wars, prompted by the gang-related killing of a Jamaican-born gang leader, drew attention to the high propensity for violence of that city's Jamaican gangs. Although only 15,000 Montrealers are of Jamaican origin, "almost one in every seven murders committed in the Montreal Urban Community since 1990 involves a Jamaican-born resident as either the suspected killer or the victim" (*Ottawa Citizen*, 26 July 1994).

The *Globe and Mail* had reported on the existence of a Jamaican crime wave in a series of articles in July 1992. In contrast to the frequent assertion that high levels of crime are a response to some perceived failure of Canadian society, the *Globe and Mail* coverage noted the extraordinarily high rates of crime in Jamaica itself. In 1991, Kingston, the country's capital, had a per capita homicide rate twelve times that of Toronto. In the first eight months of 1996 the country, with a population of 2.3 million, recorded 739 murders (*Globe and Mail*, 11 November 1996). The roots of this high level of crime lie in the reliance of the island's political parties on armed gangs to advance their cause and intimidate their opponents, and in the island's extensive role in the international drug trade.

Crime levels in Jamaica are noted in the "Travel Information Report," issued by the Department of Foreign Affairs, which advises Canadian visitors "to exercise caution and prudence in urban areas such as Kingston." To reduce the risk posed by the "relatively high incidence of street crime," travellers are advised to avoid economically depressed areas and "visiting unknown places after dark." The report notes that "drug trafficking is a serious problem" (11 October 1995). The problem is now exacerbated by the increasing number of Jamaicans who are being deported after committing crimes abroad. In the first eight months of 1996, 1,066 were returned to the island (*Globe and Mail*, 11 November 1996). In 1996 the United States Bureau for International Narcotics named Jamaica as one of thirty "major narcotics-producing and transit countries" (*Economist*, 4 January 1997).

In the United Kingdom organized criminals from Jamaica, the Yardies, have created a massive influx of crack cocaine and been involved in a number of extremely savage attacks. A 1996 report for the Canadian Criminal Intelligence Service spoke of "the enormity of the problem within London" and described an extending pattern of gang penetration into other cities, concluding, "by the very nature of their stranglehold on the crack cocaine market, they are a threat to the security and stability of the nation" (Davies 1997). An investigation by a senior Scotland Yard detective, Roy Clark (now deputy assistant commissioner), reported corruption in the Jamaican police, links with senior Jamaican politicians, and Yardies making regular trips through U.K. airports, often with false papers. Clark warned: "It has been made abundantly clear by all I have spoken to that unless there is a consistent, aggressive and long-term strategy to deal with Jamaican criminals in London, there will be ever and sharply increasing incidents of murder, violence, drug related crime and crack availability" (Davies 1997).

It was suggested that Scotland Yard's failure to take effective action lay in part in the fact that many of the Yardies' victims were black and attracted little press attention, while senior officers were "apparently nervous that they would be accused of racism if they continued to target the black gangsters" (ibid.). The limited action that was taken led to the government being "bombarded with complaints that Jamaicans were being targeted in a racist way" (ibid.). In Canada, when the *Globe and Mail* series reported at length on the disproportionate involvement of Jamaicans in so-called black crime (police sources were quoted to the effect that 40 per cent of Metro robberies involved blacks of whom 90 to 95 per cent were Jamaicans), a number of those approached for the story refused comment. One Metro officer referred to the taboo on the subject: "We can't say it because we're not allowed to. You can't print the truth, and I don't see how the hell you're going to write this story" (*Globe and Mail*, 10 July 1992).[10] The Canadian Civil Liberties Association would like the taboo strengthened, though the effect will certainly be to reduce pressure for action.

Black crime is now a major problem in Montreal and Toronto, and Jamaicans and Canadians of Jamaican background are the principal protagonists. What is remarkable is how little this is the subject of public discussion; if it were, the politicians and bureaucrats who bequeathed Canada this problem might be held to account.[11] The purpose of vigorous public debate is to provide an opportunity for citizens to form opinions based on the best information and analysis available. The Civil Liberties Association apparently believes this should take second place to the need to avoid any offence that may be caused by focusing attention on sensitive topics.

The final example of rising racial tension cited by the association in its letter to the Ontario government is remarkable chiefly for its triviality: "Most recently, there are claims that radio broadcasters attributed the province's legal aid deficits to a supposed excess of Jewish lawyers." In fact there was only one such claim, which scarcely invited the orchestrated outrage which followed. In retrospect the incident tells us more about the absence of substantive issues of concern, for surely if racial and ethnic tension were as widespread as the association supposes, this minor affair would have gone unremarked. The incident originated in a comment by a Toronto radio commentator, Brian Henderson, regarding the well-publicized financial difficulties of the province's legal aid plan: "Rightly or wrongly Jewish mothers are infamous for advising their offspring to become doctors, dentists or lawyers ... The result is that we have too many of all three in this province, especially lawyers." The subsequent furore resulted in CHUM issuing an apology and agreeing to run a series of anti-racist public service announcements, provide its employees with anti-racism seminars, and co-sponsor a student human-rights award with B'nai Brith. This failed to appease the Canadian Jewish Congress who called for disciplinary action. Curiously absent from the debate was any concern about the re-education sessions agreed to by CHUM, or the apparent acceptance of some notion of collective guilt, which would lead all CHUM employees to be re-educated to atone for the ill-considered remark of a colleague.

The response to Henderson's faux pas was consistent with the broader thrust of zero-tolerance approaches to comments perceived to cause group offence – a response that inevitably places increasing restrictions on free speech. Jonathan Rauch, in his powerful critique of growing censorious trends, cites the fate of CBS commentator Andy Roony, compelled to apologize and suspended from his job after making a comment that, it was claimed, was offensive to blacks: "What was disturbing was not the legality of CBS's action but the mentality which seemed to impel it: the activists' belief that they had a right not to be offended, and the network's readiness to concede that right" (Rauch 1993: 23). It was, as Rauch points out, precisely the notion that people had a right not to be offended that underpinned the Iranian mullahs' fatwa against Salman Rushdie: "America is full of people who deplored Khomeini's attack on Rushdie but launched similar if less deadly attacks on 'offensive' persons here at home" (Rauch 1993: 22). It was equally open to Henderson's critics to refute his arguments rather than to seek to punish and silence him.

The Civil Liberties submission to Ontario's minister of Education used as a springboard the findings of a questionnaire distributed to two hundred Toronto students in their final year of high school. The questionnaire probed student knowledge of a number of historical questions, including slavery, Japanese internment and property confiscation during the Second World War, and the existence of policies intended to deter immigration of blacks, Chinese, and East Indians. The responses indicated low levels of awareness, but it is difficult to know what significance can be attributed to this. History has been marginalized in the school curriculum, and the survey failed to establish any relevant benchmarks. In the jargon-laden world of education in Ontario the "learning outcomes" approach ushered in by the Rae government explicitly de-emphasized a content-oriented, subject-driven curriculum in favour of "cross-curricular learnings." In the words of the province's educrats: "Facts change; information expands; concepts are the constant" (Emberley and Newell 1994: 39). Not surprisingly, in this increasingly contentless world, many students have tuned out.

Is student ignorance of the history of Canadian race relations any more pronounced than ignorance regarding other facets of Canadian history? The association reports that only 25 per cent "knew that blacks were once slaves in this land," only 16 per cent knew that aboriginals were once slaves,[12] and only 27 per cent knew about the wartime internment of the Japanese. This needs to be placed in context before any conclusions are drawn regarding the history curriculum. How many of those tested could name the Fathers of Confederation or the place at which the historic meeting was held? How many could name the political party led by John A. Macdonald? How many could accurately estimate Canadian losses in the First or Second World War? A test administered to a select group of university students, all of whom had taken at least Grade 10 history and were pursuing first year Canadian Studies in Glendon College's "demanding bilingual program" at York University, is indicative. Only 10 per cent of the students could name Canada's four founding provinces (Canada East (Quebec), Canada West (Ontario) Nova Scotia, and New Brunswick). Sixty-one per cent failed to name Sir John A. Macdonald as Canada's first English-speaking prime minister, and only 17 per cent named Sir Wilfrid Laurier as the first French-speaking prime minister (Burgess 1997).

Many of those who responded to the Civil Liberties Association questionnaire will have been first generation Canadians who would be disproportionately dependent on the schools to gain an understanding of Canadian history. There are powerful civic arguments for imbuing students with a sense of history, including the social conflicts and conflicting interpretations inherent in any such study. The Civil Liberties Association might more usefully have directed its attention to the threat to an informed democratic culture posed by the erosion of history teaching in the schools. But the curriculum advocated by the Civil Liberties Association is not, in fact, concerned with providing a broad historical grasp of the conflicts and changing values that have forged a young country. The association prefers an emphasis on white guilt and racial grievance. Students are to be alerted to the history of slavery in Canada, but the association's curriculum review makes no reference to the ubiquitous practice of slavery at that time and earlier in a large number of societies embracing all racial groups, to the far larger number of blacks who entered Canada on the underground railroad, or to Canada's effective abolition of slavery far earlier than most other countries.

Aboriginals too were enslaved; some Indians, predominantly Pawnees, were enslaved by the colonists of New France in the 1700s. But the history of minorities as victims provides an inevitably limited view. Aboriginals were not simply passive spectators or victims. Indian nations played a critical role in the shifting military and political alliances which preceded the birth of Canada, and Indians were themselves involved in the slave trade. Many slaves in the early eighteenth century were Sioux captured by the Ottawa and Cree (Eccles 1969: 149). During the Revolutionary War, Indians in the Detroit area captured and traded slaves. Winks reports that black captives were more fortunate than white, since they would be sold rather than killed (Winks 1971: 31). Indians were also slave owners. Joseph Brant, principal chief of the Six Nations, kept slaves, including a number apparently taken prisoner during the war (Winks 1971: 34). Brant also allowed escaped slaves to settle on his lands and intermarry with the Mohawks (Hill 1981: 13).

The institution of slavery existed in some West Coast Indian societies as it did elsewhere in the pre-conquest Americas. By the standards of later North American slave owners, some of the practices were especially brutal, with large numbers of slaves killed in potlatch ceremonies as testimony to the wealth of their owners, to mark events such as the construction of a long house or the funerals of their masters. D'Souza suggests that it was precisely the savagery of the practices of the some indigenous groups that turned an initially positive image of the Indian population into an "entirely justified revulsion" (D'Souza 1995: 350). Slavery in some North West aboriginal societies continued until late in the nineteenth century, when it was finally ended by American and Canadian authorities (Donald 1997). The historical perspective of those who would transform the curriculum into a litany of the crimes of western white males is necessarily selective.

Civil Liberties General Counsel Alan Borovoy, commending curriculum reform to Ontario's minister of Education, argued: "people's grievances are better understood when there is knowledge of the background that produced them." This sentiment is unexceptional, but few students have any claim on a group grievance. In effect, visible minority students, who are overwhelmingly first or second generation Canadians, are to be encouraged to perceive themselves as victims, heirs to some historic grievance regarding the policies and practices of earlier generations, rather than welcome beneficiaries of the contemporary policies to which they owe their presence in Canada. Students are to be offered a highly partial view of history in which whites are portrayed as the persecutors of others. It is not easy to see the educational merits of such an approach or to detect any evidence that race relations might be improved through this.

The curriculum implicit in the Civil Liberties proposal fails to situate conflict having a racial aspect within the wider context of the ethnic conflict which has been a pervasive factor in Canadian history. This fits with contemporary orthodoxy that portrays a world in which good guys ("people of colour") are perennially beset by bad guys (whites). Canadian history, in contrast, suggests that bigotry was not preserved for those of a different colour. Situating racial conflict within this broader framework of inter-ethnic and class conflict usefully disrupts the agenda of those who would transform history into the allocation of grievance and guilt. Unfortunately, the history taught to many students will be all too reflective of the agenda of the Civil Liberties Association. A recent text, *Towards Freedom: The African-Canadian Experience*, intended for schools, offers numerous examples of the search for grievance. The treatment of the Maryland-born black, Matthew Henson, is illustrative. In Winks's scholarly history, Henson "was to be hailed as the codiscoverer of the North Pole" (Winks 1971: 297). In the school text we learn "the glory for discovering the North Pole has gone to Admiral Peary, not Matthew Henson or the Canadian aboriginals who were part of the expedition" (Alexander and Glaze

1996: 101).[13] This, students are assured, is typical of Eurocentric media, just as Sir Edmund Hillary not Sherpa guide "Tenzing Norkay" was praised for the conquest of Everest. In fact Hillary and Tenzing Norgay's names were invariably linked together, with Hillary regularly emphasizing the latter's contribution. Standard reference books maintain the linkage to this day. An article in the *Ottawa Citizen* under the headline "Grandson of Hillary's co-climber tops Everest" reported the recent success of Tashi Tenzing in reaching the summit (24 May 1997). Typifying the text's concern to ensure that students learn the depth of Canadian bigotry, the authors suggest the electoral success of the Conservatives under Joe Clark in 1979 reflected, in part, that "Canadians were at odds about the 'darkening complexion' of their society" (ibid.: 230). Inevitably, the book that offers this myopic account was published with financial support from Canadian Heritage.

So-called civil libertarians and assorted politicians are not alone in pursuing the theme of history as guilt. CBC Radio's current affairs program *As It Happens* chose to mark 21 March 1996, the United Nations' International Day for the Elimination of Racial Discrimination, with the repeat of a program first broadcast in 1949, about racial segregation in Dresden, Ontario. The broadcast portrayed a town in which blacks were segregated in employment, accommodation, and services, which was indeed the case. Dresden had a black population of some 17 per cent and claimed to be the site of Uncle Tom's cabin – but was it representative of the plight of blacks in Canada or Canadian attitudes? Dresden was under the glare of publicity precisely because of the extent of discrimination, and it remained a focus of attention by the media and the Ontario Human Rights Commission for many years. CBC Radio offered no context but left listeners to assume that this was reflective of a larger historical legacy. There is no doubt merit in the exploration of historical themes in order to gain greater insight into contemporary debates, but the conclusion which follows from any careful analysis is not that we are living on some continuum of guilt but rather that we have broken free from the bigotry of the past.

Levitt and Shaffir, in their history of the savage rioting that occurred between Jews and swastika-waving gentiles in Toronto in 1933, make the point eloquently. Those waving the swastika were not fully formed Nazis, though the symbol was designed to provoke; they were, however, full-blooded xenophobes protesting what they saw as the threat to WASP cultural traditions by Jews and other more recent immigrants. The riots took place in a context in which ethnic segregation was deeply entrenched: "The trouble at the eastern beaches and the riot in Christie Pits are as understandable in the Toronto of 1933 as they are inconceivable in Toronto today. The 'Belfast of Canada' has become a multicultural mosaic, one of the great cities of the world, liberal in outlook and tolerant of diversity" (1987: 265). Orthodoxy is not, however, easily rebutted. In contrast to Levitt and Shaffir's view, a review of the Global TV program "The Riot at Christie Pits" concludes: "scenes of today's Toronto *prove race relations haven't improved*" (Nazareth 1996, emphasis added).

5

Rebutting Orthodoxy

The Myth of Racial Discrimination in the Canadian Labour Market

Most immigrant women and women of colour are employed in the labour-intensive, low-wage sector, utilized as a reserve labour force, subject to intense exploitation, and often denied the most basic labour rights.

> Queen's University sociology professor Ronnie Leah, 1989

We recognize that relations among women are hierarchical: in a white dominated social order, white women enjoy positions of privilege as part of the dominant culture, and women of colour exist in positions of subordination because of their race.

> University of British Columbia law professor Marlee Kline, 1989

ETHNICITY AND STATISTICAL DATA: A CAUTIONARY NOTE

The proponents of preferential hiring policies claim that discrimination against visible minorities in Canada is pervasive. The previous chapters present a range of statistics that cast some doubt on this claim. In later chapters other statistical evidence is deployed to confront the claims of preferential hiring advocates.

As statistics are readily used in support of a variety of positions, it is perhaps useful to preface with some cautionary comment a review of the conclusions that might be drawn from 1991 census data. Labour market earnings offer a useful measure of economic success; however, such earnings are affected by various factors including qualifications, hours worked, length of labour market service, area of geographic residence, and age. Ethnic groups disproportionately concentrated in areas characterized by high paying labour markets will, all other factors being equal, earn more than groups located in low earning markets. Age is a central factor; ethnic groups on average significantly younger than the population as a whole might have a lower median income than another group while still out-performing that group in each age category. The reason is easily identified: the median income for those born in Canada, in full-time employment, aged 15–24 in 1990, calculated from 1991 census data, was $18,890, while for those 45–64 the income was $32,018. If group A has 60 per cent of its members in the first group and group B has 60 per cent of its members in the second group, the age differences alone may overwhelm any other influence.

In a society characterized by profound inequalities of income and wealth, groups with a low median socio-economic status will do less well than groups with a high status. Ethnic groups that are long established may have advantages over more recent arrivals. The descendants of immigrants who arrived with few resources and occupied low paying jobs will be disadvantaged relative to the descendants of more affluent and occupationally successful immigrants. Cultural characteristics, including the value placed on education and the importance attached to material success, will also affect outcomes. In some cases such factors may result in very rapid upward mobility; in others, attitudes that legitimate failure by attributing responsibility to external adverse factors may compound the disadvantages arising from the low socio-economic status of a group. The continual focus on the way in which schools allegedly fail black students and on claims of pervasive racism, often apparently endorsed by "experts," affords a convenient excuse for black failure or the pursuit of economic success through less legitimate channels.

The prevailing assumption among preferential hiring advocates is that in the absence of discrimination ethnic groups will all experience similar success. More sophisticated analyses take into account such variables as educational attainment, arguing that groups with equivalent educational levels should experience similar outcomes. In fact the wide variety of factors that influence labour-market success make it unlikely that different ethnic groups will achieve similar outcomes. Cultural differences, including the importance attached to education, the value placed on material as distinct from other rewards, occupational preferences, and a host of other influences will be at play. Ethnic occupational concentration cannot be simply attributed to the effects of discrimination; in making career choices, children will be influenced by role models and the encouragement or potential assistance offered by parents, relatives, and friends.

Nowhere has it been demonstrated that in the absence of discrimination different groups would be equally represented in all areas of the labour market. Thomas Sowell, reviewing a range of evidence that indicates a prevalent international pattern, notes the success of preferential hiring advocates in creating the widespread belief that in the absence of discrimination, groups would be evenly represented: "That what exists widely across the planet is regarded as an anomaly, while what exists virtually nowhere is regarded as a norm, is a tribute to the effectiveness of sheer reiteration in establishing a vision – and of the difficulties of dispelling a prevailing vision by facts" (Sowell 1990: 135). Orthodoxy asserts that in the absence of discrimination outcomes would be uniform. Careful investigation suggests otherwise.

In Canada ethnic groups are not randomly distributed in different economic sectors; considerable variations are evident. In agriculture, for example, the proportions range from 8 per cent for those of Dutch origin aged 15–64 reporting an occupation, to close to 0 per cent for many other ethnic groups including Greek, Portuguese, Jewish, and Chinese. Twenty-three per cent of those of Greek origin report working in the accommodation/food/beverage services sector, compared to 5 per cent of those of Polish, Dutch, and German background and 4 per cent of those of Italian background. Eleven per cent of those with Italian origins report occupations in the construction sector, while only 6 per cent of those of Greek origins and 3 per cent of those of Jewish origin report such occupations. Fourteen per cent of those of black origins report occupations in the health and social services, compared to 7 per cent of those of Chinese origins (Canadian Heritage 1994b: 8). Figures for self-employment reveal similar wide variations, from a high of 19 per cent for those of Jewish origin and 13 per cent for those of West Asian and Arab origins to a low of 5 per cent for those of Portuguese origins and 4 per cent for those of black origins (ibid.: 4). The disproportionate number of Jews who are self-employed is often attributed to the response of Jews to WASP exclusionary practices, particularly prior to the Second World War, but no similar pattern is evident for many of the groups alleged to experience discrimination today.

The evidence of disparate ethnic outcomes in labour market income is not hard to find – it simply requires reference to census data. Marked discrepancies in earnings occur across all ethnic groups, vary between different geographic areas, and are not reducible to skin colour. Those who seek to document labour market discrimination have designed more sophisticated models that introduce a range of variables including educational attainment. That similarly qualified groups fail to attain similar outcomes is held to provide evidence of discrimination. Generally such comparisons lack sufficient detail to ensure that like is being compared with like. Different ethnic groups may be concentrated in different disciplinary areas, in more or less prestigious universities. The relative numbers with different qualifications may tell us nothing about median graduating averages that would show some groups far higher than others. The ethnic breakdown for doctoral degrees in the United States, for example, indicates that of the 1,100 doctoral degrees granted to blacks in 1992, nearly one half were gained in education. In other areas blacks were correspondingly under-represented. Only four gained PHDs in mathematics, compared to 423 whites and 51 Asians (D'Souza 1995: 304). Such differences must inevitably affect outcomes.

THE HISTORICAL CONTEXT

> For Jews and other minorities, the Canada of the 1930s and
> '40s was a world of quotas and restrictions. Banks, insurance
> companies and large industrial and commercial interests did
> not hire Jews. Few of the country's teachers and none of its
> principals were Jewish. Department stores barred Jews as
> salespeople. Jewish doctors could not get hospital appoint-
> ments. There were no Jewish judges, and Jewish lawyers were
> excluded from most firms. Universities imposed quotas on
> Jewish students ...
>
> Irving Abella, *Globe and Mail*, November 1996

Proponents of preferential hiring argue that some groups are victims of historic disadvantage requiring contemporary redress. The Abella report, which preceded Canada's federal legislation, was firmly based on that proposition (see chapter 6). A large number of ethnic groups can claim to have experienced historic discrimination. Prior to the Second World War, Canada had no shortage of bigots and a long list of likely targets (see chapter 4). Jews were subject to extensive discrimination, as were other non-WASP white immigrants; South Asians, black Canadians, Chinese Canadians, and above all, in the 1940s, Japanese Canadians, experienced discriminatory treatment.

The legacy of such treatment and the attitudes that legitimized it should, if preferential hiring advocates are correct, be evident today. More particularly, if Canada is indeed a pervasively racist society, racial minorities might, as a group, be expected to be paying a penalty. They might be expected to experience discrimination at every point, in education, professional or technical qualification, hiring, retention, and promotion. Groups that experience such discrimination are unlikely to be passive victims; they will seek to adapt and respond.

Jewish immigrants, for example, have responded to occupational closure by pursuing educational and professional qualification in areas where they might succeed, notably through professional self-employment. Overall, however, a markedly discriminatory society should result in sharp contrasts between favoured groups and those targeted for discriminatory treatment.

ETHNICITY AND THE CANADIAN LABOUR MARKET

The argument voiced by preferential hiring advocates is that discrimination is racially driven, and if this is the case it should be evident in comparing the experience of ethnic groups born in Canada with similar language capacities and access to the same range of educational, cultural, and social resources. (Comparison of groups that include Canadian born and foreign born raises questions about equivalence of qualifications, language capacity, and a range of other issues.)

The favoured ethnic group in Canada might be thought to be those of British origins. The median income for this group, over 15, born in Canada, and in full-time work, based on 1991 census data, was $30,234 (figures are calculated from Statistics Canada, Custom Tables, based on the 1991 census). The highest median income, $38,797, was gained by those of Jewish ethnic origin, the second highest, $34,257, by those of Japanese ethnic origin. The Canadian-born of Chinese ethnic origin had a median income of $30,449, those of West Asian origins $30,105, Arab origins $30,011, Sikh origins $29,537. The presence of a number of ethnic groups regarded as subject to historic or contemporary labour market discrimination in the higher earning groups is parallelled by the presence of "non-visible" ethnic groups in the lower ranges. Those of Dutch origin had a median income of $28,354, those of Portuguese origin $24,869. Canadians of black origin had a median income of $25,143. The lowest median income, $20,791, was found among Canadians of Korean ethnic origin.

Striking differences between Canadian-born visible minority groups are difficult to account for on the basis of discrimination. Nationally the mean income of Japanese Canadians, with full-time income, the second highest in the country at $39,473, is nearly 20 per cent higher than for Chinese Canadians, reflecting a much larger number of highly paid individuals in the Japanese group. If such outcomes reflect greater discrimination against Chinese Canadians the mechanisms through which this occurs are not readily apparent.

These broad labour market figures are useful in raising questions about the assumptions on which preferential policies are based and in suggesting the wide variety of ethnic experience in the labour market. A more careful measure might be found in the comparison of ethnic groups in the same age bands in the same labour market. The caveat to be noted here is that as the area of comparison is narrowed down, the size of the populations become smaller.

Vancouver has a significant number of Canadian-born of Chinese, Japanese, black, Sikh, and South Asian ethnic origin. The age group 45–64, in full-time employment, will be less sensitive to age variations than the age group 25–44, where a disproportionate number of younger workers could have a substantial effect on median earnings. A further advantage of the selection of the older age group for comparison is that if discrimination is a significant factor, it might be expected to be most evident here, since those targeted for discriminatory treatment will, during their working careers, be disproportionately denied relevant training and promotion opportunities, and confined to less well-remunerated positions.

The highest median income in the Canadian-born 45–64 group in the Vancouver census metropolitan area (CMA), $53,894, was gained by those of Arab ethnic origins, though this is a small population group. The next highest earners, again a small group, were those of Greek origin, with a median income of $52,108. Those of Swiss ethnic origin had a median income of $43,588, followed by Jewish Canadians with a median income of $40,594. Among visible minorities, those of Japanese origin in the same group had a median income of $36,666, those of Chinese origin $33,468, Sikh origin $34,680, other South Asians $36,536, and black origin $31,524. Although these earnings are not at the top end of the median range, neither are they confined to visible minority groups. Earnings for the same groups of Hungarian, Ukrainian, Italian, and Dutch ethnic origin were respectively: $32,906, $36,339, $36,786, and $35,391.

In the Montreal CMA, comparing similar groups we again find no pattern of visible minority concentration in the lower income ranges. Those of Chinese ethnic origin, 45–64, born in Canada, in full-time employment, had a median income of $32,179 – close to the median for all full-time Canadian-born workers in that age range of $32,941. Those of Arab origin had median earnings of $36,884, those of French origin $32,214, Italian origin $30,970, black origin $29,225, Greek origin $31,521, Japanese origin $41,383, Portuguese origin $23,325.

In the Toronto CMA those of Jewish ethnic origin, 45–64, born in Canada, in full-time employment, had the highest median income at $49,682, followed by the small group of those of West Asian ethnic origin at $45,702. Those of British origin had a median income of

$38,344, those of Japanese origin $38,237, Italian origin $36,349, Chinese origin $35,940, black origin $30,452, and Spanish origin $30,266.

What is clear from any review of census data is the wide variation in ethnic outcomes and the absence of any consistent link between visibility and outcomes. The burgeoning employment equity industry is built on a veritable stack of cards, founded, from Abella on, not on any careful examination of statistical data but either on the assertion of discrimination without supporting evidence, or the deliberate cherry picking of data that purports to support a conclusion already reached. Where research does produce evidence that refutes the case for preferential hiring, it is, as we will see, ignored. Sceptics need of course look no further than the 1991 census.

Although various government agencies, provincial, federal, and municipal, employ a plethora of employment equity bureaucrats, curiously the 1991 figures on outcomes for the Canadian-born of different ethnic backgrounds have received little official attention. One exception was a short, unrefereed paper, "Earnings Differentials among Ethnic Groups in Canada" (Pendakur and Pendakur 1995), produced by Canadian Heritage. The paper led to some extravagant claims in the press, apparently endorsed by the paper's authors. Simon Fraser University economist Krishna Pendakur, who co-authored the paper with his brother, Canadian Heritage analyst Ravi Pendakur, had no doubt that the study demonstrated the labour market was not "very fair" and that "some kind of equalization policy was necessary" (*Globe and Mail*, 6 October 1995). The *Globe and Mail* reported that the study "challenges any remaining assumption that the country is a model of tolerance" (ibid.).

Among its more surprising findings, based on 1991 census data, were that males of Chinese, black, Portuguese, and Greek ethnic origin, born in Canada, paid a similar earnings penalty from discrimination compared to (other) white, Canadian-born males. Blacks born in Canada experienced a 16.3 per cent penalty, Chinese 12.7 per cent, Greek 16.2 per cent and Portuguese 14.7 per cent. This conclusion is inconsistent with claims that racial discrimination is the key factor and might have suggested a more cautious approach, including questions as to the adequacy of the methodology. If a claim is to be made that these results evidence discrimination, it is surely incumbent on the researchers to offer some explanations. What have Canadians of Greek origin done to merit such unwelcome attention? What are the sociological factors that result in Canadians of Greek ethnic origin experiencing a higher penalty than Canadians of Chinese ethnic origin? Do such results provide support for claims of pervasive *race-based* discrimination? Could something other than discrimination account for the apparent divergence in outcomes?

And why was this "discrimination" against racial minority men born in Canada totally absent in the figures for racial minority women born in Canada?

These issues might have merited comment or suggested the need for peer review, but Canadian Heritage proceeded to publication. In spite of expressions of surprise at the findings by others in Canadian Heritage and elsewhere, it seems the ministry organized no discussion forum before or after publication. Any such publication appearing under the imprimatur of the government of Canada inevitably attracted far more notice than a paper in an academic journal, though the latter would at least have been refereed.

Two months later the paper had entered the historical lexicon: "A Simon Fraser University study released earlier this year by the federal Heritage Department found that for (other) visible minorities in Canada *there was little doubt* that discrimination plays a *significant* role in their lower rate of pay and *slower advancement in the labour force*" (ibid., 27 December 1995, emphasis added).

The brothers produced a second paper offering more detailed analysis in June 1996. Again this was presented in the media as evidence that Canada was a profoundly discriminatory country. *Maclean's* suggested the need for "some national soul-searching" (2 September 1996: 10). The conclusions were indeed startling: in the Montreal area, for example, it was reported that when such factors as length of service, qualification, industry of employment, and type of occupation were taken into account, Canadian-born visible minority men experienced an "earnings penalty" of 17 per cent compared to similar white Canadian-born men. As discrimination in societies characterized by deep racial or ethnic division occurs at many different levels, stigmatized groups will have less access to educational and training opportunities and will be concentrated in less desirable, usually lower paying, occupations. What the Pendakurs' statistics suggest is that in addition to such barriers, a significant *further* penalty remains. Teachers, for example, or assembly line workers, with similar qualifications and lengths of service apparently receive markedly different incomes depending on their racial origin.

It is difficult to understand how such mechanisms might work. In many occupations pay scales are closely tied to qualification and seniority. Once an individual is hired as a hospital porter, for example, the opportunities for racial differentiation in payment are limited. It could be argued that such differentiation takes place in less regulated areas of the labour market, but this would need to be much more significant than the 17 per cent penalty suggested, to compensate for areas in which such discrimination does not occur. More remarkably, the 17 per cent penalty observed in Montreal, a city with a cosmopolitan reputation, was not present in Vancouver, where an "insignificant" 4 per cent gap was observed (Pendakur and Pendakur 1996: 21–2).

Nationally the picture is equally confusing. Not only is there no evidence of discrimination against visible minority women born in Canada, but while the Canadian-born of Chinese ethnic origin pay a "penalty" of 12.5 per cent, the group of "other visible," which in these calculations includes a high proportion of Canadians of Japanese ethnic origin, pays no penalty (ibid.: table 5). Equally surprising is the finding that among the white Canadian-born, Greeks pay a 14.5 per cent penalty and Balkans a 10.5 per cent penalty. The penalty paid by the Canadian-born of Portuguese ethnic origin observed in the first paper was no longer evident in the tabular presentation in the second (Pendakur and Pendakur 1995: 15 (table 6), 1996: 19 (table 5)). There is some confusion, insofar as the authors advise us "Greek and *Balkan* men born in Canada appear to suffer statistically significant earnings penalties of over 10%" on one page, only to write two pages later, "Among men we find that Canadian-born Greek, *Portuguese*, Black and Chinese men face large and significant earnings penalties" (1996: 19, 21, emphasis added). The table, however, indicates no penalty for the Canadian-born of Portuguese origin.

The Pendakurs claim much larger penalties for visible minority immigrant men, but here again the findings are surprising. Chinese immigrants pay only a 1 per cent penalty, compared to 18 per cent for Vietnamese and 17 per cent for Greek immigrants. The authors give little attention to these issues but suggest the need for more aggressive preferential legislation: "If these earnings differentials are due to discrimination, it may be an argument for some kind of equalizing policy, such as quotas, comparable worth policy or hiring policy ... a hiring policy can only eliminate discrimination due to allocation across industries and occupation ... even after controlling for such differences, substantial earnings gaps between ethnic groups remain" (Pendakur and Pendakur 1996: 25).

A subsequent draft paper by two Canadian Heritage analysts, which examined the Pendakurs' paper and a number of other similar studies, argued that the measurement of the key determinants was insufficiently precise to permit sweeping conclusions about discrimination, omitting some factors which might be relevant to outcomes, providing insufficiently detailed information on others, and attributing statistical significance to differences too small to merit it: "Our conclusion is that these studies are of little policy relevance, especially if social justice issues such as labour market discrimination or unfairness are the object of study" (Adsett and Kralt 1997: 3). This paper was not published by Canadian Heritage.

In contrast to the publicity given to the Pendakur paper, an analysis by Arnold de Silva, author of an earlier Economic Council of Canada study *Earnings of Immigrants*, received no coverage. The new study by de Silva appeared in a working paper published by the Applied Research Branch Strategic Policy of Human Resources and development. De Silva found that after taking account of quality differences in education, language, and work experience, discrimination in native-born male earnings was reduced to about 1 per cent: "Thus, the main finding of this study is that a large portion of what is often believed to be discrimination turns out to be a reflection of differences in the quality of education and experience between visible minority men and their white counterparts" (1996: 1). Examining the native-born, de Silva found an earnings gap of only 3.5 per cent of which he attributed 62 per cent to productivity differences and 38 per cent to discrimination (ibid.: vi).

The extensive attention given to the Pendakur claims and the failure to afford coverage to de Silva's findings can not be attributed simply to the proselytizing zeal of the former. The Pendakur claims fed directly into grievance politics, affording "proof" of the claims of orthodoxy. In contrast, if de Silva is right, Canada has embraced a costly folly, sanctioned by most of the country's elite.

The McGill Consortium for Ethnicity and Strategic Planning, which is located not in the Department of Statistics or Economics but in the School of Social Work, also entered the fray, releasing an interim report on its analysis of 1991 census data on Canada's black population with considerable attention to maximizing media coverage. The press release made a number of claims that might appear to offer unambiguous evidence of disadvantage, including the reports that "Black men are better educated than men in general in Canada" and "Black persons in Canada have substantially lower incomes" (McGill 1997). Evidence in support of these claims could indeed be found in the report, but a closer examination indicated that the authors had not undertaken any age standardization. This is a matter of considerable significance, as younger groups in the Canadian population have significantly higher education levels but markedly lower average earnings. Might this affect the reports findings?

The press release referred to the younger age structure but failed to offer any comment on its potential relationship to the other findings: "The Canadian Black community is considerably younger than the

Canadian population as a whole. Almost two out of three Black persons in Canada are under the age of 35 (64.2%); only slightly more than half of the total Canadian population (53.2%) falls into this age group ... One in ten of Black persons in Canada is over the age of 55. The corresponding figure for the total population is twice as high" (Torczyner 1997: 22).[1]

The group's analysis of 1991 census data indicated a disproportionate number of single parent families in the black community: "persons in single parent households accounted for almost three times as many persons in the black community as in the total population (24% and 9% respectively)" (Torczyner 1997: 28). The figures for black children are even more striking. Four out of ten of black children aged 0–14 lived in single parent families, in extended families, or with non-relatives, compared to one in seven such children in the Canadian population as a whole (ibid.)[2]. Among husband and wife black families, 19.6 per cent earned more than $75,000 a year, compared to 21.3 per cent of the broader population. In contrast 55 per cent of blacks living in single parent families lived below the poverty line (ibid.: 29–39).

The high level of black single parent families is a major contributor to the high level of child poverty, and to a range of other social problems.[3] The McGill Consortium's analysis offers a remarkable explanation for the disproportionate number of black single parent families, focusing not on cultural mores but Canada's immigration policy, which, historically, has resulted in the admission of more black women than men: "It is also *quite clear* that the significantly higher levels of single parent families among Canadian Blacks can be attributed *largely* to this gender imbalance – given the 6% fewer adult Black men than women in Canada" (ibid.: 28, emphasis added). It requires some intellectual dexterity to conclude that parents fail to stay together because of a gender imbalance, but it is reflective of grievance politics that responsibility should be attributed to factors beyond the control of the individuals involved.

Torczyner told the *Globe and Mail*: "Clearly, the number of marriages in a community is predicated on the availability of suitable partners. Given the gender imbalance resulting from Canadian immigration processes, it is not surprising to find a smaller percentage of currently married persons in the black population" (8 February 1997). Surprisingly this "imbalance" had had little observable effect on the availability of temporary reproductive partners.[4] It is reflective of the fashionable preoccupation with racial thinking among Canadians who believe they have captured the progressive high ground that it should be assumed that "suitable partners" are racially determined. In the real world there are a wide range of potentially "suitable" partners.[5]

The McGill study was financed by Canadian Heritage, and its report was released at a press conference attended by the minister of state for Multiculturalism, Hedy Fry. CBC Radio's national news (7 February 1997) left listeners in no doubt as to the causes of the black disadvantage found by McGill, interviewing Windsor law dean Juanita Westmoreland Traoré, Ontario's former employment equity commissioner, who provided an entirely predictable response.

Other analysis of the experience of visible minorities, including those born abroad, provides little support to those who claim pervasive discrimination. Visible minority members are not, as a group, excluded from more prestigious labour market categories. A Statistics Canada analysis of adults in visible minority populations, based on those who worked in the eighteen months prior to the 1991 census, found them "as likely as others to be in professional occupations" (Kelly 1995: 7). These figures stand in stark contrast to the claims of orthodoxy. In a tract dedicated to proving that "Canada is a racist country and always has been," Barbadian-born writer Cecil Foster offers the unequivocal but characteristically unreferenced assertion: "Racism is still encountered in the professions where minorities have become so disillusioned about breaking in they have given up trying" (Foster 1991: 1, 9).

Kelly reported that visible minorities were less likely to be employed in managerial positions (8 per cent) than other adults (10 per cent). Given the importance of length of service in accessing managerial jobs, this is not surprising. If racial discrimination were the critical variable, we might expect a degree of uniformity, but again the defining characteristic is diversity. Seventeen per cent of Koreans are in the managerial group but only 3 per cent of Filipinos (Kelly 1995: 7).

A 1993 study undertaken for the Interdepartmental Working Group on Employment Equity Data used a different data base, examining the Statistics Canada Labour Market Activity Survey for 1988 and 1989. The data revealed no pattern of discrimination in the employment of visible minorities. In total in 1988 10.2 per cent of male employees and 7.8 per cent of females fell in the category "middle level and other" managers, compared to 12.1 per cent of visible minority males and 6.5 per cent of females. There was a larger proportion of visible minority male employees (16 per cent) in the professional category than males as a whole (11 per cent). A slightly smaller proportion of visible minority females (16.2 per cent) was in the professional category compared to all females (16.9 per cent). Visible minority males were more likely to be supervisors than their white counterparts but less likely to be foremen (IWGEED 1993: 9).

A key factor in the relative success of different ethnic groups with a large immigrant composition may be a lack of knowledge of one of

Canada's official languages. Two University of Alberta economists who studied immigrant experience in that province in the 1980s concluded that immigrants who arrived in the province with a knowledge of English had earnings 1.78 times greater than those who arrived with no knowledge; the difference in earnings between the two groups declined only slightly over the six years studied (Waldron and Chambers 1995: 4). This is a far larger difference than any which has been attributed to the alleged effects of racial discrimination. The disadvantage is not necessarily driven by discrimination: as many jobs require language fluency, employers might reasonably conclude that those who lack understanding of the language of the work place will be less productive.

The Alberta study, like other studies of immigrant experience in the Canadian labour market, noted the marked difference in earnings between the different immigrant classes: independent, family, refugee, or assisted. These again were far larger than any impact attributed to discrimination. Immigrants in the independent class received higher average incomes than labour market participants who had immigrated in the family, refugee, or assisted relative classes. Those in the independent class had incomes 87 per cent higher than the immigrant group as a whole, while those in the family class were 32 per cent lower. Ethnic groups contain very different proportions of those in the different immigrant classes, with consequent implications for relative earnings.

A study for Citizenship and Immigration observed a similar sharp disparity in the earnings of independent and family class immigrants. When linguistic capacities and education were taken into account the difference was smaller but remained marked. Independent class immigrants who arrived in 1985 reported earning an average of $45,324 in 1988, compared to a Canadian average of $21,569 and a family class average of $14,495 (Citizenship and Immigration 1994: 4). The greatest differences, when skill levels were taken into account, occurred among the most skilled group. Independent class immigrants earned some three times the average of similarly skilled family class immigrants (ibid.: 8).

The argument that labour market outcomes for racial minorities in Canada are not primarily driven by discrimination is not new; indeed, what is striking is how far Canadian legislation has proceeded in the face of contradictory evidence. Writing in 1985, before the passage of the federal employment equity legislation, Conrad Winn noted: "The fact that first generation immigrants are often low income earners is not primarily, if at all, a matter of racism ... Immigrants arrive with different language abilities, job skills, and capital. Non-

British immigrants often arrive with fewer of the requisites for occupational achievement than become available to their Canadian-born children. Thus, Asian Montrealers earn 56 per cent more if they are native born rather than foreign born" (Winn 1985: 689).

THE MYTH OF DOUBLE DISADVANTAGE

> There's general acceptance now within the women's movement that issues of doubly-disadvantaged women are central. If we don't fight racism, if we don't fight concerns of the most disadvantaged women, then we're not fighting for women.
>
> NAC President Judy Rebick, *Ottawa Citizen*, 10 August 1992

Some Canadians will be members of more than one designated group, and significant attention has been given to the additional "disadvantages" faced by these groups. Yet evidence for such additional disadvantage is remarkably slim, the acceptance of its existence a reflection of the power of orthodoxy. A report to Ontario's Ministry of Citizenship, the lead agency in developing the province's employment equity legislation, captures the driving assumptions: "Being a woman may be more detrimental to one's income than being a visible minority. Being a woman and a member of a visible minority has the greatest negative effect on income" (Abt Associates 1988: 6).

The conclusion is unambiguous – that race and gender determine differential labour market outcomes – although no convincing evidence is provided. It is not a lack of command of one of Canada's official languages, discontinuous labour market service, lower qualification levels, shorter hours worked, preference for one kind of work over another, greater commitment to child care responsibilities, or any of a host of factors that affect outcomes: rather, labour force participants are prisoners of their race and gender.

Demographer Monica Boyd (a supporter of preferential hiring policies) in her review of 1986 census data found scant evidence of discrimination against racial minorities born in Canada. Visible minority Canadian-born women aged 25–64 actually had a mean employment income some 13 per cent higher in 1985 than their white female counterparts. After adjusting for age, region of residence, CMA residence, marital status, education, occupation, full-time/part-time status, and weeks worked, visible minority women still enjoyed a slight income advantage. Canadian born visible minority men, in contrast, earned a mean income some 2 per cent less than their white male counterparts, or 4 per cent less, on an adjusted basis.

Boyd did not address the implications of the findings for Canadian-born visible minorities. Certainly the data are hard to reconcile with claims of widespread labour market discrimination on the basis of "race." Instead Boyd preferred to turn her attention to a group that might afford more comfort to preferential hiring advocates: visible minority immigrants. Boyd provides evidence of significant income disparities between Canadian- and foreign born non-visible minorities and foreign-born visible minorities and concludes that this is evidence "consistent with the rationales underlying Canada's employment equity policy ... [of] a pattern of disadvantage" (Boyd 1991: 307). The problem with this is that it is extremely difficult to establish that similar groups are being compared. If racial discrimination is the cause of this outcome, why does it not have a similar impact on Canadian-born racial minorities? This question is so obvious that its absence in Boyd's analysis attests to the prior claim of orthodoxy over scholarship.

Boyd omits consideration of the conclusions that might be drawn from her data on Canadian-born racial minorities, but in the hands of University of Toronto sociology professor Jeffrey Reitz, Boyd's findings are simply transformed. Far from challenging the proposition that discrimination is widespread, in Reitz's review this becomes evidence that "although the disadvantages experienced by these native born Canadians are not as great as those experienced by immigrants they are nonetheless *significant and substantial*" (Reitz 1993: 35, emphasis added). This is a remarkable statement, given that Canadian-born racial minority females experienced no disadvantage; indeed, to the (doubtful) extent that such small differences convey any significance, and that labour market outcomes are racially determined, it would make as much sense to conclude that racial minority females benefited from positive discrimination insofar as even their *adjusted* earnings remained slightly higher.

Boyd extends the purview of equity legislation to those whose "disadvantage" is to have been born abroad. The endorsement of the idea that those who immigrate to Canada acquire, in contrast to previous generations, a right to an immediate "fair share" is not as far-fetched as it might seem. Supreme Court Justice Bertha Wilson gave judicial endorsement to the concept of immigrant disadvantage in a case involving the British Columbia Law Society's claim that citizenship was a requirement for practising the profession. The erudite judge argued that immigrants should be treated as disadvantaged, "an analogous category to those enumerated [in the Charter]." In this particular case the face of disadvantage was an Oxford-educated, American lawyer (Gwyn 1995: 226–7).

A 1992 study commissioned by Statistics Canada was premised on the assumption that double disadvantage exists: "Employment equity research typically examines the employment characteristics of four designated groups ... for people who belong to more than one designated group, this approach fails to measure the additional employment disadvantage they experience" (Mohan 1992: 1). There is no question of inserting any cautionary "if," no testing of any hypothesis. Research is intended instead to garner evidence to support a conclusion already reached.

If significant discrimination against visible minority women exists, it will presumably have an effect across the board, yet the study commissioned by Statistics Canada, notwithstanding its *parti pris* assumptions, provided remarkably little evidence of such double disadvantage. The study was based on an analysis of data from the 1988 Labour Market Activity Survey. Feminists characteristically view women's increasing involvement in the labour force as evidence of progress, and by this measure visible minority women were actually advantaged: 74.6 per cent were in the labour force at some time compared to 71.2 per cent of other women.

The study compares the level of satisfaction of visible minority women in part-time employment regarding the number of hours they were able to work with that of other part-time women workers. The rationale for the comparison is that visible minority women would be disadvantaged if they were less likely to find the hours of work they wanted. In fact visible minority women were as satisfied on this score as other women. When similar comparison was made regarding satisfaction with the number of weeks worked during the year, again there was no significant difference. In case the reader should forget that we are comparing groups who are already disadvantaged, the author reminds us that although the overwhelming majority are satisfied with the number of weeks worked, "if a considerable portion of these women are also doing a full-time unpaid job at home, they may be 'satisfied' with the number of weeks of paid work because they could not contemplate doing more work." This stereotype of women being called on to do two full-time jobs bears witness to the feminist credentials of the researcher but not to the empirical evidence afforded by Statistics Canada's own surveys.

The study compares the unemployment experience of visible minority and other women. One comparison was of the average length of time of the most recent period of unemployment. Visible minority women were unemployed for a significantly shorter period of time, sixteen weeks in the 25–64 group compared to 21.6 weeks for other women who had experienced unemployment. In contrast visible minority women were slightly more likely to be unemployed at some time during the year – 21.6 per cent compared to 18.8 per cent. The most significant difference between visible minority and other women which the researcher was able to identify was the average length of job tenure. The most recent full-time job held by visible minority women had lasted 4.1 years compared to 5.4 years for other women; for part-time workers the figures were 2.3 years and 3.1 years. These are significant differences which might have merited comment. Could the difference be explained by the fact that the overwhelming majority of visible minority women are first generation immigrants, many of them relatively recent arrivals? The researcher offers no clue.

In contrast the data on relative earnings is replete with commentary and complex further calculations, driven, it would seem, by the need to confirm the existence of disadvantage. The problem for the researcher is that at first brush the data not only fail to provide substantive evidence of the widely proclaimed "double disadvantage," they suggest that on some measures visible minority women are significantly ahead. In the managerial/professional, clerical, sales, and service categories visible minority women have higher average weekly earnings than other women, $487 compared to $453 in the managerial/professional group. Only in processing are the weekly earnings lower, $275 compared to $310. The researcher then asks whether these earnings may be the result of longer hours of work. Previously the researcher compared hours of work with a view to seeing if visible minority women might be disadvantaged by having too few; now the reader is advised, as though it is no more than a statement of fact: "Of course there would be no advantage to visible minority women if these higher wage rates were gained by working longer hours per week." It would seem more reasonable to assume that in the labour market workers in fact take account of both wage rates and the number of hours of work available.

The introduction of the variable hours worked still left visible minority women in the managerial/professional, clerical, and sales categories paid more, on an hourly basis, with service and processing paid less. These figures scarcely provide evidence of systemic discrimination. Rather, they support a conclusion that visible minority women face no *generalized* discrimination in earnings. The study in contrast chose to emphasize the lower hourly earnings of women in service and processing jobs, categories in which visible minority women are overrepresented. The earnings and hours worked by women in all categories are then combined to produce a global average. This enables the study to conclude: "Overall, the jobs held by visible minority women have a lower average wage rate ($9.46 versus $9.90), require longer hours of work (33.8 hours versus 32.5 hours), and pay about the same average weekly earnings ($329 versus $326)" (Mohan 1992: 17).

The data which the study reviews raise substantive doubts about the existence of any double disadvantage. In some areas visible minority women are somewhat ahead of other women, while in other areas they are behind. Given the disparity between the two groups in such matters as length of experience in the Canadian labour market and fluency in one of Canada's official languages, matters not even referenced in the study, the conclusion that should reasonably be drawn is that visible minority women have been very successful in achieving equality of treatment with other women in the labour market. In contrast the four points highlighted in the conclusion are:

- Visible minority women are more likely to be unemployed at some time during the year.
- The jobs they hold have a lower average wage rate.
- The jobs they hold have longer hours of work per week.
- A higher proportion of the jobs they hold are in Service or Processing occupations, and jobs held by visible minority women in these two areas pay less an hour than jobs held by other women (ibid.: 22).

In this way Canada's leading data analysis agency marshals facts in support of a conclusion that had demonstrably preceded any analysis.

Another study, again commissioned by Statistics Canada, examined job movements, comparing women and men and, with more limited data, the experience of visible minorities. The study was prefaced by a chapter on models of discrimination drawing heavily on American research. The casual reader might have assumed that this had equal application to Canada; certainly there was no suggestion to the contrary.

The research, however, found no support for the view that the labour market is characterized by discriminatory behaviour in the areas examined: "There is very little evidence to be found in this study of different treatment of minorities in job movements within and between firms. Women seem to be somewhat more favoured in that they are less likely to lose their jobs and are more likely to be promoted" (Boothby 1992: 51). Might this cast doubt on the extent of labour market discrimination in Canada? One of the characteristics of discriminatory labour markets is that some groups experience more unfavourable treatment in layoffs and promotions. Feminists, for example, argue that in periods of contraction women are disproportionately expelled from the labour force. If groups are discriminated against, logic suggests that such discrimination will be generalized. If on the other hand research finds no evidence of discrimination in job movements and promotions, this raises questions about other claims of discrimination. It suggests that the hypothesis underpinning the research may be wrong. But this is not the conclusion suggested: rather, the author proposes that the search for evidence of discrimination should simply shift: "the focus of employment equity research on the labour market should be on the process of assignment of jobs when workers first enter or re-enter the labour market" (Boothby 1992: 51).

The assertion that visible minority women face "intentional or systemic discrimination" often depends on statistical evidence showing that racial minority women earn less than other women, who in turn earn less than men. The alleged gap depends on the particular statistics cited. It need not be large for it to be adduced as conclusive evidence.

A lengthy report to Metro Toronto, issued under the imprint of the Chief Administrator's Office, documents the gap between the earnings of various visible minority groups and the Metro average. The report concludes that all visible minorities are disadvantaged but visible minority women are more disadvantaged: "Strategies to address barriers ... should focus on racial minority women who are more disadvantaged" (Turner 1995: 70). In fact the evidence presented in the report indicates that racial minority men gained a lower proportion of average comparable salaries than their female counterparts. In reviewing the figures it should be borne in mind that the racial minority groups contain a much higher proportion of immigrants than the larger Metro Toronto population. Black men earned 70.8 per cent of male average earnings, South Asian men 72.5 per cent. In contrast black women earned 80.8 per cent of the female average, South Asian women 81.7 per cent (ibid.: 69).

The Ontario Women's Directorate, in a pamphlet intended for wide distribution published under the authority of the Ontario government, cited earnings for female visible minorities of $19,187 and other women of $20,550 as evidence of the particular disadvantage faced by racial minority women (Ontario Women's Directorate 1993). This is a difference of 6.6 per cent, scarcely, one might conclude, damning evidence of gross discrimination. The Women's Directorate failed to ask whether such a difference might be attributable to non-discriminatory factors and simply used the discrepancy in earnings as part of the "evidence" used to propagandize the case for intentional and systemic discrimination. The directorate made no effort to identify the influence of age, language capacity, or seniority – factors which have a major impact on outcomes and which would all result in lower average earnings for visible minority labour force participants, insofar as, on average, they are younger, with less seniority, and have proportionately larger numbers who are fluent in neither of Canada's official languages.

The directorate's shoddy analysis is evident elsewhere. The report cites as further evidence of discrimination the fact that 14 per cent of visible minority women clerical workers have university degrees compared with 4 per cent of other female clerical workers in Ontario. Speaking for the Ontario government, the directorate concludes without any hesitation: "This shows how systemic discrimination in employment can present barriers to opportunity for racial minority women." There are many possible explanations for the disproportionately large number of degree holders among visible minority women employed in clerical positions. Such explanations include the lack of English language fluency among some of the degree holders; degrees obtained at foreign institutions which would not be regarded as equivalent to Canadian universities by reasonable employers; and the disproportionate number of visible minority degree holders who are recent labour market entrants and less likely than their counterparts to have moved into higher paid jobs.[6] None of these are considered. Recent university graduates have faced a much more difficult labour market than previous generations, a fact which will also impact on many foreign graduates moving to Canada.

The directorate defines systemic barriers: "Essentially, these policies and practises operate to exclude racial minorities and other groups for reasons that are not job related. Examples of systemic discrimination include credentialism, the requirement for 'Canadian experience,' or excessive employment or academic qualifications that are not required for the job."

The claim that credentialism – the insistence that candidates for particular positions or promotions hold formal qualifications – leads to systemic discrimination legitimizes the removal of qualifying requirements from favoured designated groups. In fact the examples mentioned impact on a variety of groups. Visible minorities born in Canada will encounter no particular problem offering Canadian experience; first-generation Greek, Ukrainian, or Portuguese immigrants will be as vulnerable as visible minority immigrants and less likely to have English language proficiency than some included in the visible minority group. The question of whether academic qualifications are excessive might be thought a matter for employers. The reality, in the Canadian labour market, is a sharp decline in the availability of employment for those lacking a degree or other post-secondary qualification, particularly for younger workers (Little 1996). Employment equity activists propose that for designated groups such qualification requirements be waived, affording preferential access to those with the right group membership. Surprisingly, this demand has met with some success. The Office of the Employment Equity Commissioner, for example, established in Ontario by the Rae government, never stipulated formal qualifications even for such positions as senior policy adviser, with a salary in excess of $66,000.

ASSERTING DOUBLE DISADVANTAGE

The absence of any convincing data underpinning claims of labour market disadvantage might seem to raise a challenge to those who proclaim that the concerns of the "doubly disadvantaged" are the most pressing matter for feminist ideologues. In practice such arguments are based not on evidence but belief. One of the more striking aspects of the contemporary debate, even where participants speak from an apparent basis of scholarly inquiry, is the absence of concern to ground even the most outrageous claims in any kind of empirical evidence. Transparently for believers, and presumably for their students, some truths are self-evident.

Linda Carty, editor of a recent Canadian feminist anthology, argues that white feminists directly benefit from discrimination in employment: "As white women are able to move up into the higher paying and more prestigious jobs in larger numbers, they are being replaced by racial-ethnic women who find themselves with no opportunity to get out" (Carty 1993: 15). Carty, who holds a PHD from the Ontario Institute for Studies in Education, found it unnecessary to offer any empirical evidence in support of her claim that in effect Canada has a segregated labour market. Again the repetition of the precepts of orthodoxy substitutes for social analysis; victims are identified not by investigation but group membership. The concept "racial-ethnic" is a novel if meaningless one, embracing everyone but here no doubt serving as a code for whatever groups Carty deems worthy of sympathy and preference.

Ronnie Leah, formerly a Queen's University sociology professor, in an academic paper prepared with financial support from the university's Advisory Research Committee, makes a number of apparently factual statements for which there seems to be scant evidence. Black women are "segregated into the lowest status service jobs"; the "extreme form of exploitation" experienced by black and immigrant women is maintained by "discriminatory government policies." Leah eschews the tiresome business of offering statistical evidence in favour of sweeping historical assertion: "Historical patterns of systemic discrimination have led to the development of a labour force that is *segregated* by gender, race and ethnicity" (Leah 1989: 168, emphasis added).

It has become commonplace for white feminists, seeking to exculpate their guilt, to acknowledge the privileged position they hold. Sue

Findlay, former head of the Secretary of State's Women's Program and veteran of the wars at Toronto Women's Press, illustrates the muddled reasoning that purportedly provides evidence of mainstream feminism's failure to reflect the concerns of visible minority women. Findlay (1993a) offers as an example Ontario's equal pay legislation which, she rightly notes, was particularly advantageous for women in the Ontario Public Service. More contentiously, she argues that pay equity was primarily beneficial to "privileged" white women. Since the primary beneficiaries of equal pay legislation would be OPS members, Findlay claims visible minorities would not share in the gains as much as their white counterparts.

Visible minorities, in Findlay's view, are disproportionately represented in small social service organizations which would not enjoy the same benefits from pay equity, since budgets would not be automatically increased to meet equity increases. Findlay offers no empirical evidence in support of her argument but buttresses it with the observation that the majority of women in the Equal Pay Coalition were white. Given the demographics of Ontario, this is less than remarkable. But in fact visible minorities were and are over-represented in the Ontario Public Service, in comparison to their numbers in the population. In 1992 racial minorities constituted 12.7 per cent of OPS employees, which compares to the 8.6 per cent equity benchmark for visible minority representation in Ontario, suggested by the 1986 census (1991 data were not yet available). Not only were racial minorities over-represented but 57.8 per cent of the racial minority employees were women (Management Board Secretariat 1993: 29). Far from pay equity privileging white women, to the extent that it primarily benefited OPS members it disproportionately "privileged" racial minority women.

Findlay bemoans the slow rate of progress: "Some of the limits of anti-racist practices are undoubtedly related to resistance by white feminists to loss of their privileges. These privileges are deeply rooted. White feminists must continue to focus on understanding how everyday practices as white feminists reproduce our privileges" (Findlay 1993a: 211). If such privileges are illusory, eradication may be challenging.

6

Government by Race and Gender

If NAC has become firmly established in the public's mind as the organizational voice of women, and if it has been able to articulate a feminist perspective that purports to represent the majority of Canadian women and their needs, it is in large part thanks to the SOS [secretary of State] and its Women's Program.

Leslie Pal, 1993

The more a ruling class is able to assimilate the most prominent men of the dominated classes, the more dangerous and stable its rule.

Karl Marx

THE MARCH OF THE FEMOCRATS

Today [NAC] *represents* over five hundred groups, with a membership of over three million.

A. Gotlieb 1993, emphasis added

To understand the development of the politics of grievance in Canada it is necessary to step back and examine the role of the federal government, which played a key part in the creation of the National Action Committee on the Status of Women and in sponsoring a range of other gender and racially based groups. The government through direct funding, and through the Canada Council and the Social Sciences and Humanities Research Council, also played a central role in sponsoring the growth of women's studies in Canadian universities. This provided an important base through which the politics of grievance came to dominate intellectual discourse on many campuses.

Provincial funding, particularly in Ontario, also facilitated the growth of organizations purporting to speak for different identity groups. Federal and provincial funding ensured the publication of many books, magazines, and journals that appeared to lack scholarly, cultural, or commercial appeal. Writers and publishers found the propagation of grievance provided access to a rich array of government grants.

The multicultural left make great use of the notion of "community," casually assigning whole groups into some common fraternity or sorority on the basis of race, gender, disability, sexual preference, or some other characteristic presumed to provide a unifying force. It is a curious stance for those who once embraced the centrality of social class. Michael Lind, writing on the American experience, observes:

Each community is a classless society, in which the black businessman and black beggar, the gay movie mogul and the gay truck driver, experience a mystical fraternity. The irony is that the major beneficiary of this kind of thinking is the white overclass, the white power structure itself. Class consciousness, weak enough in the United States to begin with, has been almost obliterated by the multiplication of particularistic communal mysticisms subsidized by the very government and white overclass that they purportedly threaten. Far from being revolutionary, identity politics is merely America's version of the oldest oligarchic trick in the book: divide and rule (Lind 1995: 141).

Lind's description provides an apt summary of the legacy of thirty years of Canadian government policies, and its eager embrace by those who imagine they are on the frontiers of radical thought.

The development of employment equity policies and their implementation were crucially affected by the constituencies created by federal largesse. Many of those who became involved in the groups that depended on government sponsorship played a key role in first designing, then administering the new equity programs. Federal and later provincial sponsorship, particularly in Ontario, became an effective midwife for many careers in the booming grievance industry, while the burgeoning field of women's studies trained many of the new cadre. When Ontario's Office of the Employment Equity Commissioner came to recruit, it did not advertise in provincial newspapers but targeted recruitment to graduates of women's studies courses and such organizations as the Coalition for Visible Minority Women, Access for New Canadians, the Riverdale Immigrant Women's Centre, and the Jamaican-Canadian Association. The ostensible purpose of the Office of the Commissioner was to break down labour market barriers, but few Ontarians would have ever learned of the job openings at the Commission. Those who were recruited were to be partisans, not bureaucrats.

CBC Radio and Television provide privileged platforms to those who claim to represent the growing cast of victims, a relationship epitomized in the transformation of Judy Rebick from NAC president to CBC personality. At one moment a partisan co-host of *Face-Off*, the next the guest "moderator" of *Cross-Country Check-Up*, appearing regularly as a pundit on *Morningside*'s Friday political panel, Rebick also appeared on CBC TV's *The National* to speak for the protesters who sought to close down Toronto (25 October 1996). Her ubiquitous presence was evident in the 1997 election campaign, when she was heard on *As It Happens* (22 May 1997) offering a partisan account of the failure of the party leaders, other than McDonough, to agree to attend a NAC sponsored debate (which Rebick was to chair) and showed up the next day yet again on *Morningside*'s Friday political panel. It is impossible to find any conservative figure who fills so many varied public roles for the corporation.[1]

Those who portray Canada as a racist society will find willing endorsement from CBC personalities, a cultural elite happy to show their own enlightenment by condemning their fellow Canadians as bigots. Peter Gzowski on CBC's *Morningside* (28 November 1996) interviewed Cecil Foster, whose account of the black experience in Canada, *A Place Called Heaven: The Meaning of Being Black in Canada*, stands as a classic of grievance politics. If Rosemary Brown is defeated for the NDP leadership by Ed Broadbent, Foster maintains, it is not because she is a neophyte MLA from British Columbia running on a radical platform that discomforts the party establishment while Broadbent is a well-respected federal MP, but because this is "an example of how integration does not work, of how the best often doesn't win when race becomes the ultimate factor" (Foster 1996: 148).

Foster, whose book received financial support from the Canada Council, the Ontario Arts Council, and, inevitably, Canadian Heritage, found no challenge to these or any of his other claims.[2] When Foster attributed a traffic ticket to racism rather than speeding, Gzowski apparently accepted it as an example of DWBB – Driving While Being Black. The original story of this outrage fills no less than nine pages, its significance in no doubt: "it is because of experiences like this" that Foster wrote the book. It is an interesting observation that at no point does Foster provide any evidence that in his apprehension or his successful attempt to "plea bargain" a reduction in the fine, race was ever a factor. It is unclear how the officer issuing the ticket could be aware of Foster's colour, as the ticket was issued in the evening while Foster was travelling at 120 km an hour down a crowded freeway (ibid.: 2–9). There are undoubtedly real issues to be addressed in the relationship between the police and Toronto's black residents, but these cannot be simply reduced to the discriminatory behaviour of police.

The relationship needs to be understood in the context of the disproportionate involvement of *some* blacks in crime as well as the lamen-
table record of the Toronto police in a wide range of law enforcement
and community relations areas. If blacks faced routine persecution in
driving offences, this would be evident in statistical data, but in the
category of drinking and driving offences, for example, in 1992–93
black remand rates were half of the white rate (Commission on Systemic Racism 1995: 90).

However, at the end of the thirty-minute interview Gzowski and
Foster were in agreement about Canada's "benign racism." Foster
maintained that he doesn't see "much difference" between the blatant
racism of the southern United States and that of Canada – one may
be more subtle, but "you still don't get the job." Warming to his theme
Foster claimed that whether you look in politics, the arts, radio, and
television, in "any aspect of mainstream life you see very little representation of minorities." Gzowski offered, "Let's you and I start by
agreeing that CBC is generally too white."

The media's role in the growth of grievance politics and the increasing fracturing of political debate should not be under-estimated. "The
media is the mirror in which all the narcissists of identity politics seek
their reflection," says Michael Ignatieff. "The question to ask of all
ethnic or gender extremists is whom, exactly, do they represent?"
(Ignatieff 1996: 52–3). He warns that the continuing attention to the
voice of extremists has significant consequences for the views of readers and listeners: "If they hear only extremists, if they hear only the
autistic monologue of the convinced, they slowly but surely lose contact with their own inner voices, their own inner doubts. They begin
to stop thinking. They begin to be 'spoken' for, 'thought' for by
prejudice" (ibid.).

FEMINISM'S MIDWIFE

The establishment in 1967 of the Royal Commission on the Status of
Women and the commission's report three years later marked a major
increase in the federal government's involvement in defining and
orchestrating a feminist agenda. In 1973 the government responded to
a commission recommendation and established the Canadian Advisory
Council on the Status of Women. The council was intended to give
independent advice to the government on issues believed to be of
concern to women. However, since members were appointed by the
government, which provided all the council's funding, its claims to
independence were as dubious as its claims to representation. More
important than the council were the plethora of apparently independent women's groups and programs which the government began to

fund, a process that would have a decisive influence on the emergence of a "progressive" agenda dominated by the politics of identity, in place of what had once been the inclusive politics of poverty and social inequality.

The response to the Royal Commission played a major role in shaping the relationship between government and those who claimed to speak for Canadian women. The researchers and policy analysts seconded to the commission re-emerged as members of the interdepartmental committee advising government on how to respond to the commission, or as departmental advisers on the status of women (Findlay 1995: 78). In essence this group became the catalyst for the creation of a growing constituency of self-defined feminists on the federal payroll. The commission also cemented relations between key federal bureaucrats and women's groups.

The late 1960s and early '70s were characterized by a significant increase in government activity that sought to promote "citizen participation." The rhetoric of Trudeau's "Just Society," combined with concerns to promote national unity, resulted in an enhanced role for the Department of the Secretary of State, which dramatically increased funds to a variety of voluntary sector groups. Funding for the Citizenship Branch, driven primarily by national unity concerns, rose from $4.6 million in 1969–70 to $44 million in 1971–72 (Pal 1993: 112). The effect of this funding was to increase the government's control over the political direction and activities of recipient groups. The program was presented as a major platform of a progressive agenda which promised to empower groups previously excluded from influence and to promote a more active democracy. In reality the program gave government increasing leverage over the agenda and resources available to citizens' groups (Loney 1977). The program found enthusiastic support among bureaucrats, whose domain extended rapidly, and among those who found publicly funded employment in groups that had previously been authentically voluntary or that sprang into existence to access the new funds.

The increased taxes required to finance the growing army of Secretary of State dependents resulted in a situation in which individual citizens had less discretion over spending in order that government bureaucrats would have more. The logic of government funding of so-called voluntary organizations is the concentration of power in the hands of bureaucrats and politicians. The irony of the history of growing state intervention in funding voluntary organizations is that those who advocated such intervention believed themselves progressives. In fact their views might be more accurately described as elitist, believing governments could be more easily persuaded to fund progressive causes than individuals.

FEMOCRATS AND SOCIAL CHANGE

I think government funding is one of the reasons why the
women's movement in Canada is so strong.

                                             Judy Rebick, 1996

Feminists complained loudly about the difficulties they encountered in
pursuing their agenda in a public service that at senior levels remained
overwhelmingly male. Sue Findlay, one of the more prominent activists,
who headed the Secretary of State's women's program in the 1970s,
has described in some detail the resistance they experienced (1995). In
retrospect what is striking is not the frustrations but the pervasive
nature of the impact.

The problem that has perennially dogged the feminist mission is the
issue of whether gender in and of itself is the key determinant in
interest group politics. Not surprisingly, activists claimed to speak for
broad if not universal constituencies. Among those dispensing federal
largesse in the Secretary of State's women's program it was fashionable
to distinguish between the mainstream national groups, dominated by
the affluent and the articulate, and the "community." The feminist
bureaucrats placed great emphasis on ensuring close links with the
community. Some clearly saw themselves as agents of sweeping social
change, albeit from the comfort of a government office and a generous
salary: "they [feminist bureaucrats] can establish feminist alternatives
to the bureaucratic mode of operating that reinforces patterns of
inequality, or advocate policies that challenge the ideology of capitalism and patriarchy" (Findlay 1987: 48).

Community is a much abused term, and its use in the Secretary of
State's women's program in the 1970s foreshadowed similarly egregious uses by bureaucrats in the Rae government. When senior officials
in the Ministry of Citizenship actively promoted efforts to block the
production of Garth Drabinsky's *Show Boat*, for example, they purported to be doing no more than assist concerned communities.[3] In
fact what the Secretary of State bureaucrats sought was to direct funds
to radical feminist groups that shared their agenda. These groups
represented the opinions of a relatively small number of activists, not
least those who not only perceived men as their opponents but coupled
this with an inchoate anti-capitalist critique.

Findlay, reviewing her own experience within the government, suggested that she faced senior managers who acted as "gatekeepers to
maintain the interests of a ruling class of white men." This created a
"'chilly climate' for women who wanted a career in the public service"
(1995: 112). In fact, in the 1970s and '80s, women progressed rapidly
in the federal public service, a point discussed at greater length below.

The difficulties referred to by Findlay were a function not of gender conflict but of the resistance of the bureaucracy and its political masters to radical change. The willingness of mainstream politicians to embrace feminist demands led to a number of policy changes in areas compatible with other political priorities. The muddled politics of radical feminists emphasized issues of identity; the resistance they faced they described as white and male, yet many of those who might have been persuaded to share some of the egalitarian demands they put forward were also white and male. The alliances they sought were also mediated by race and gender, but there were many women of a variety of racial backgrounds who shared none of these radical objectives and who would have emphatically supported the "gatekeepers" identified by Findlay.

Resistance to change there may have been, but there can be no disputing the success of feminist activists, inside and outside government, in using federal funds to create a national organization claiming to speak for Canadian women. Two points stand out from the meeting of feminists and the federal bureaucracy. The first is the enormous success feminists had in accessing well-paid jobs, resources, and substantive policy changes. The second point is the apparently limitless naiveté of those who imagined they could combine prestigious government jobs with radical social transformation. Findlay, reflecting on the experience of state sponsorship, suggests that between 1966 and 1979 the state's response to women's demands "validated the faith of liberal feminists in the strategy of reform by the state." By 1980, however, it was clear to her that "the state and the political strategies of liberal feminism had failed to produce substantive changes in the everyday lives of women or in the relations of power between women and men at the societal level" (Findlay 1987: 31). The proposition that the "state" might achieve such broad social transformation, in a liberal democracy, reflects a notable degree of faith in the power of government action.[4] Those with less trust in the motives and competence of politicians and bureaucrats might take comfort that the realization of this agenda remained attenuated.

A MADE-IN-OTTAWA WOMEN'S MOVEMENT

> Democracy works best when men and women do things for
> themselves, with the help of their friends and neighbours,
> instead of depending on the state.
>
>   Christopher Lasch, 1995

The practice of using general tax revenues to finance groups
with particular axes to grind has created a multi-million-

dollar system of bureaucratic patronage that operates with
little accountability to ministers, members of parliament, the
media or to taxpayers.

John Bryden, Liberal MP, 1994

The NAC is a democratically constituted feminist organization
with 704 member groups *representing more than three million
women*. We speak on behalf of our membership and the
coalition partners who are in solidarity with us.

Joan Grant-Cummings, "Letters," *Ottawa Citizen*,
12 May 1997, emphasis added

The 1972 Strategy for Change conference in Toronto, which brought
together a range of women's groups, was organized by the Committee
for the Equality of Women which had played a central role in shaping
the recommendations of the Royal Commission on the Status of
Women. Financing for the conference was provided by the federal
government. The conference established the National Action Committee on the Status of Women, an organization whose growing prominence was critically dependent on federal funding which increased to
$600,000 annually before cutbacks in the late 1980s. In contrast to
the normal course of organizational development from local to regional
to national, NAC depended on increasing government funding to build
an organization from the top down. NAC was provided with direct
funding for regional organizing, and this was accompanied by a rapid
growth in funding to a range of women's groups, which met the criteria
established by the burgeoning number of femocrats in Ottawa. These
groups would in turn affiliate to NAC, providing further income to the
organization.[5]

The critical role that the federal government played in financing
groups claiming to speak for Canadian women is illustrated by the
disparity between NAC's success in leveraging money from government
and from its members – who, as noted earlier, provided minimal
support from their own pockets. The Canadian Congress for Learning
Opportunities for Women, a NAC affiliate, was another beneficiary of
the Secretary of State's Women's Program. The congress pursued an
avowedly feminist political agenda but faced with reductions in government support from a peak of $293,000 in 1987–88, was able to
raise only $8,200 in a special appeal to members (Pal 1993: 236).

The issue of dependence on government financing was a source of
some tension in NAC. Many members were aware of the seeming
contradiction in being overwhelmingly dependent on a government the
organization sought to influence. Concerns came to a head in 1981

when, after a number of acrimonious debates and motions, the conference voted 87 to 46 in favour of a motion calling for NAC to decrease its dependence on government funding. In the next year the funding committee, led by Chaviva Hosek, lobbied for increased government funding for women's groups and accepted NAC's share.[6]

In 1986, the Secretary of State funded a conference that established the National Organization of Immigrant and Visible Minority Women, a reflection of the increasing fracturing of identity politics. Some visible minority activists would have preferred separate organizations for visible minorities and for non-visible minority immigrants, but here as elsewhere, the federal piper called the tune. According to one account, delegates felt they had no choice: "there will be funds for only one not two groups" (Pierson *et al.* 1993: 206). Others might wonder what philosophy informed the top-down creation of groups of dubious representation, who would then be legitimized in speaking on behalf of vast constituencies to the same bureaucrats who had recently signed their cheques.

The financing of ostensibly representative groups of activists was not, of course, confined to feminists. Journalist Elaine Dewar has detailed the complex links tying environmental groups to government and sometimes to the same multi-national interests that, at first glance, they might appear to oppose (Dewar 1995). Pollution Probe, for example, had headquarters in Toronto owned until 1988 by the federal government; in that year the government sold the building, valued at $660,000, to Pollution Probe for $175,000. In 1989 the organization received $209,000 from various levels of government, while other funds were raised by door-to-door sollicitation. This was done not by members or volunteers but by unionized CUPE members who were paid a commission in addition to their regular wage. In the period September 1990 to September 1991, more than half of the organization's revenues were spent on fund-raising. The organization had even fewer claims to represent any grass-roots movement than NAC; its membership was comprised by its board of directors (Dewar 1995: 339–45).

Again such sponsorship creates incestuous relationships between politicians and bureaucrats and the ostensibly independent groups who enjoy government largesse. Government-funded human rights groups can play a crucial role in meeting government objectives in countries such as Indonesia where opposition to Canadian trade can be defused by apparent efforts to support human rights.[7] Environmental or human rights groups, like those active on women's and ethnic issues, create the illusion of vigorous democracy while assisting governments in managing their agenda. The close relations between government bureaucrats and the groups they fund increase the power of bureaucrats to shape the political agenda. Groups that share their perspective are funded and, in turn, are able to lobby politicians apparently speaking in the name of public constituencies. This was the tactic NAC used, as we will see, when the Mulroney government took office.

The early 1980s saw significant increases to funding of the women's program. The government also provided financing for a major increase in feminist influence in the universities with funding for the creation of five chairs in women's studies at Canadian universities, including the Wynn Woodward chair at Simon Fraser University which Sunera Thobani, a graduate student at the university, was later to resign from NAC's presidency to occupy.[8]

NAC was and remains a curious organization. It is formally constituted by other organizations, many of whose members would have had no knowledge of the fact that they had been affiliated. Access to government funding has freed NAC from dependence on membership dues, and many affiliates are themselves publicly funded. The Canadian Research Institute for the Advancement of Women, a group of salaried academics, for example, was funded by the Women's Program in the Secretary of State, and in turn it affiliated with NAC. The York University Women's Centre, the Women's Resource Centre at Memorial University, the Wilfrid Laurier Faculty of Social Work and many others concluded that their tax-funded mandate included support for NAC, as did a host of other tax-funded refuges, ethnic groups, and social service organizations (Vickers *et al.* 1993: 305–19). What is notable is how little the whole movement depended on those who might be willing to put their hands in their own pockets.

Today NAC boasts that only 25 per cent of its revenue comes from government and seeks to claim a more authentically popular mandate. In fact much of the other revenue continues to flow from groups like the National Organization of Immigrant and Visible Minority Women, which in turn secure their funding from the public purse or from organizations funded to provide social services, which in turn divert funds to NAC. Other affiliates like the 380,000 strong YWCA have no relevant mandate from their membership, many of whom would be astonished to learn that their joining the local YWCA might have political significance or meaning. Under Thobani's leadership NAC increased its affiliated membership, particularly targeting labour and visible minority groups. There is no evidence that rank and file union members share NAC's divisive agenda; in Oshawa it was precisely the pursuit of such an agenda by the Rae government that caused the UAW to disaffiliate from the NDP. Many of the new visible minority affiliates simply continue the practice of using public funding rather than depending on contributions from grass-roots members.

The dependence on spending somebody else's money may also account for the survival of one of NAC's more curious characteristics. Affiliated organizations vote not on the basis of the size of their membership but on one vote per organization. The lack of any coherent connection between affiliated groups' membership, level of financial contribution, and voting strength at NAC AGMs contributed to what one highly sympathetic study described as a vulnerability "to co-optation by an organized subset of groups bent on a particular course" (Vickers *et al.* 1993: 227).

NAC's political dynamics have been strongly influenced by government funding. In the early years, when dependence on direct funding was overwhelming, the executive was caught between the demands of the members and the expectations of NAC's political and bureaucratic sponsors. The fact that financial viability was ultimately dependent on pleasing government funders initially diluted the control of the AGM. Speakers' views and the content of motions carried less weight, since participants were not putting their money where their mouths were or "paying the freight" when it came to implementing policy (ibid.). There were also elements of elitism that fitted comfortably with NAC's financial dependence. Lorna Marsden, a well-connected Liberal, was an early NAC president. Marsden was an active advocate of equal pay for equal work legislation but sceptical of the ability of ordinary Canadians to grasp the issue, preferring to seek accommodation with political and bureaucratic elites (Marsden 1980).[9]

The lack of a clear democratic structure of accountability, the dependence on tax funds to support the organization, the unrepresentative nature of the groups funded and affiliated, the explicit exclusion of pro-life women's groups, and the growing evidence that many women rejected NAC's policies did little to diminish the organization's claims to speak for Canadian women. The 1987 orientation package for new executive members provided information that might have surprised those unfamiliar with NAC's ambitions or informed by more traditional notions of democracy. New members were informed: "Essentially you are an unpaid MP for women in your region of Canada" (Vickers *et al.* 1993: 161).

HANDLING THE TORIES

NAC's ability to work with its bureaucratic sponsors to help shape the political agenda was illustrated by the way in which it orchestrated the presentation of evidence to the Parliamentary Committee on Equality Rights, set up in 1985 by the new Conservative government. The election of the Conservatives had threatened to disrupt NAC's influence in Ottawa; many Conservative MPs were unsympathetic to interest group politics, particularly where those interests owed their representation not to grass-roots activity but tax funding. The new Conservative majority also included many who did not share NAC's radical feminist agenda. The challenge for NAC and its bureaucratic patrons was to ensure that the organization continued to dominate the way in which women's issues were defined. In particular NAC's challenge before the Equality Rights committee was to persuade the committee to accept that equality meant not equality of opportunity but equality of outcome, which in turn might require treating some groups more favourably than others. Equality demanded not gender-neutral legislation but action to achieve the radical feminist vision of men and women equally represented in every facet of life – a view that, among other assumptions, rested on the belief that it was a proper function of government to legislate women into equal labour force participation.

NAC's success with the Committee on Equality Rights rested on the organization's ability to act in collaboration with its government funders to ensure that one view dominated the committee's proceedings. NAC received funding to establish its own equality rights project, which was used to ensure that constituent groups developed a common position. The majority of all the briefs presented to the committee by women's groups came from NAC affiliates (Vickers *et al.* 1993: 239).

But though NAC was successful with the Committee on Equality Rights, its relationship with the federal government was increasingly hostile. The reduction in public funding, reflecting broader fiscal pressures on government, paralleled the increasing dominance in the organization of those who eschewed mainstream feminism, demanding greater attention to the issues of race, disability, and sexual orientation. These issues came to the fore under Judy Rebick, NAC's first full-time president. The most influential group, who quickly came to dominate NAC's agenda, were the self-styled "women of colour" who demanded a unique position within NAC and special representation at every level. The rapid dominance of NAC's agenda by the advocates of skin politics reflected the corrosive consequences of state sponsorship; if NAC had been dependent on fund-raising from its members, it would have been deterred from such divisive adventures.

THE COLOUR OF GRIEVANCE

A key factor in the success of vocal activists around the world
is their ability to strike a responsive chord in the "trendy
middle classes" in the name of a group which has not elected

them and which often has views radically different from
theirs.

Thomas Sowell, 1990

Strong feminist representation is crucial if multicultural policy
is to address the marginalization of women of colour.

Christina Gabriel, former analyst,
Ontario Women's Directorate, 1996

For a generation, the [American] multicultural left has claimed
to be leading a radical assault on "the white power structure."
The white power structure has responded by granting the
multicultural left practically every one of its demands, consistently expanding racial preference policies and adopting the
language of diversity and multiculturalism from classrooms
to newsrooms to congressional and judicial chambers.

Michael Lind, 1995

The Canadian women's movement is unique in its preoccupation with
the issue of skin colour. No parallel can be found in the large and
more successful National Organization of Women in the United States.
Dependent on its own fund-raising, NOW is much less vulnerable to
capture by particular interest groups or to a myopic preoccupation
with particular constituencies of grievance. NAC's emphasis on skin
colour as a basis for entitlement to elected office is equally unusual.
When the black leader of Britain's largest trade union ran for re-
election, it was on the basis of his record, his character, and his policies.
Bill Morris made no claim that his colour gave him entitlement to
special consideration.

The demands of those who claimed to speak for Canadian women
who are visible minorities were not for equal treatment in NAC but for
recognition of their right to have disproportionate influence at every
level in the organization and a preferential claim on the senior positions. The issue emerged prominently in NAC's criticism of the Canadian Panel on Violence Against Women, established by the Mulroney
government with a $10 million budget. The panel owed its existence
to demands by feminists for federal action. Once established, it became
the focus of increasingly destructive attacks, primarily driven by the
charge that the panel did not adequately represent racial minorities.

Mobina Jaffer,[10] a regional vice-president of the National Organization of Immigrant and Visible Minority Women (NOIVMW), was one
of the nine panel members, but NAC demanded at least three further

seats to represent the 9 per cent of Canada's population classified as members of a visible minority. NAC's position was that only then could the particular concerns of "women of colour" be addressed. The demand was not simply for unequal representation but for the right of the groups to appoint their representatives (Levan 1996: 345). NOIVMW, it will be recalled, owed its origins not to any grass-roots organization but to sponsorship by bureaucrats in the Secretary of State; but it had no doubt that it, not the elected government, had the right to appoint two members to the national panel.

Jestina Blakehill, president of the National Congress of Black Women, which demanded the right to appoint one of the additional members, gave voice to the racial vision that underlay the complaints: "As an African woman, I would not go in front of a white group and tell them what is happening to me" (*Ottawa Citizen*, 10 August 1992). The government's refusal to meet the demand led to a number of women's organizations including NAC and NOIVMW boycotting the panel.

Judy Rebick played a singular role in propelling the growth of a racial agenda in NAC and paved the way for Sunera Thobani to succeed her as president. Rebick explained NAC's attacks on the panel: "There's a general acceptance now within the women's movement that issues of doubly-disadvantaged women are central" (*Ottawa Citizen*, 10 August 1992). Rebick remains a determined advocate of the centrality of racial identity to social and political life, finding comfort even in the O.J. Simpson trial: "One of the positive outcomes of the O.J. Simpson trial was the realization by both the prosecution and the defence that, for the verdict to have credibility, they needed a predominantly female jury. An acquittal would be credible only if the jury was predominantly female; a conviction, only if the jury was predominantly black" (Rebick 1996:32).

The centrality of race is understandable, suggests the CBC commentator, "with one in three black American men in prison" (ibid.: 33). Orthodoxy, as we have noted, depends not on evidence but assertion – the incarceration level for black Americans is disturbingly high but does not include one third of the adult male population.[11] Simpson was acquitted but was the verdict credible? Closer to home Rebick displays an equally puzzling racial vision: even the Bernardo case is evidence of Canada's racism. Rebick's views of the case are offered in her conversations with Queen's law student Kiké Roach in *Politically Speaking*. The Bernardo issue is first raised by Rebick, who is obviously concerned at the opprobrium heaped on Karla Homolka, a product we are to understand "of the same patriarchal power relations that create violent men." Roach quickly steps in to assure her co-conversationalist that the police failed to apprehend the murderous duo not because, on the evidence of this investigation, they would be hard pressed to organize a booze-up in a brewery but because the Bernardos "look like a nice, white, middle-class couple, which translates into 'normal.'" Roach contrasts this with the fact that "police routinely stop Black men on the street because they fit the description 'Black male.'"

Rebick in turn draws on the authority of no lesser expert than *Toronto Star* columnist Michele Landsberg: "Michele said to me, "If that guy had been Black, they would have been on it in a flash. Racism helped kill those girls" (Rebick and Roach 1996: 128).

Thobani, Rebick's chosen successor, had spent four years in Canada on a student visa when she laid claim to the post on the grounds that only the most "marginalized" could lead the woman's movement forward. An obsession with skin colour characterized her term in office, during which one of the major "achievements" was the appointment of a "woman of colour" co-chair to every committee. The centrality of race to NAC politics was confirmed with the overwhelming victory won by Thobani's replacement, Jamaican-born Joan Grant-Cummings, following her statement "for me it's not a role to woo disaffected white women" (*Globe and Mail*, 13 June 1996). The election that put Grant-Cummings in office highlighted the way in which a small number of people effectively control NAC, many of them delegates for tax-funded organizations such as women's shelters, which have a mandate for service delivery not political activism. NAC boasted some 670 affiliates in 1996, but in the election only 176 votes were cast, 90 per cent of them for Grant-Cummings. NAC does not allow proxy voting, believing that delegates have to experience the sense and mood of the meeting.

Grant-Cummings, who graduated with a Bachelor of Science degree from the University of Ottawa in 1983, was formerly the head of Canada's largest women's health centre. Prior to her election as president she had served as NAC treasurer. In common with many NAC activists, her working life has been largely spent in organizations funded by taxpayers. The small number of women who participated in her selection did nothing to diminish the new president's claims to represent a massive constituency: "The NAC is a democratically constituted feminist organization, with 704 member groups representing more than three million women. *We speak on behalf of our membership and the coalition partners who are in solidarity with us*" ("Letters," *Ottawa Citizen*, 12 May 1997, emphasis added).

The 1996 annual conference coincided with the culmination of the women's march against poverty. Much was made of the significance of this event, which saw some five thousand people from across

Canada assemble on Parliament Hill. In retrospect what is striking is how few were mobilized, given that the Canadian Labour Congress placed its considerable organizational resources at NAC's disposal. In contrast, for example, the Ontario Federation of Labour put 100,000 people on the streets of Hamilton and even more on the streets of Toronto in a demonstration against the Ontario government. Equally notable, for an organization that claimed to have been pursuing an "inclusive" agenda which prioritized the concerns of "women of colour," was how few racial minority women could be seen in the crowd. Unlike NAC's leaders those assembled were overwhelmingly white.

The tax-funded Canadian Research Institute for the Advancement of Women is another feminist organization that experienced conflict over race and ethnicity. A 1992 conference, Making the Links, was organized by and dominated by "women of colour," but few links were apparently made. The few white women who attended were largely silent, resulting in demands that they contribute more fully. The workshop on "white supremacy" focused on an exploration of white privilege, and white participants were called upon to explain how it worked, though many apparently found the experience uncomfortable (Findlay 1995: 395).

The CRIAW conference illustrated the narcissistic preoccupation with white privilege and Canadian racial persecution which was increasingly infecting feminist activities. Many of the conference speakers were first-generation immigrants who had left countries with degrees of racial and ethnic conflict far greater than any found in Canada, attitudes towards women that would be an anathema to most Canadians, and human rights records that ranged from grotesque to indifferent. Occupying well-paid positions, largely in the public sector, they used the opportunity provided by CRIAW and its federal sponsors to berate the privilege and covert racism they claimed to detect among their white sisters. In a world in which there is no shortage of real problems there could scarcely have been a more eloquent demonstration of feminist irrelevance than the egregious laments of CRIAW's speakers or the confused responses of those white feminists who sought redemption and re-education. In these debates racism and privilege ceased to have any defined meaning, whether in overt acts of discrimination in the fields of employment, housing, and education or the profession of beliefs that placed groups in some perceived racial hierarchy. Instead, well-heeled racial minority women found in the cultivation of grievance an opportunity to portray themselves as oppressed while using the charge as justification for claims for preferential treatment.

CRIAW's success in "making the links" remained limited. In 1994, its president, Monica Goulet, resigned, claiming the institute failed to address the concerns of racial minority and aboriginal women. Goulet had previously commented that the CRIAW board did not afford "full representation" to racial minority or aboriginal women (Pierson and Cohen 1995: 262). Together these groups held one-third of the seats on the eighteen-person board, more than double their proportion in the general population.

Goulet, an aboriginal, reports that her own initial election to the board was "primarily because the board was trying to become more multicultural ... I did not know the person who nominated me" (Pierson and Cohen 1995: 260). She was nonetheless outraged when her suitability was questioned, comparing herself to NAC president Thobani, whose own "acclamation" owed much to NAC's preoccupation with race. Thobani's coronation invited some adverse comments from those who thought other criteria may have been more important. Goulet commiserated: "When I tell you that my heart went out to Sunera, it did so because I had experienced similar racism" (ibid.: 261). In Goulet's case the "racism" was apparently exhibited when her nomination became the subject of "hot controversy." After less than a year in office she resigned as president, claiming that CRIAW was not a "comfortable" place to be for aboriginal women and that the same was probably true for other racial and ethnic minority women (ibid.: 262).

IN PRAISE OF ETHNICITY

They have different languages like us and they have different people and they have managed to keep the country together, so we share this notion that it is possible to have different languages and be united at the same time.

Jean Chrétien on the common links between the Indonesian military regime's multicultural policies and Canada's (in Stackhouse 1996a)

In eleven years of illegal occupation, Indonesia has brought about the deaths of about 200,000 East Timorese, and seeded the Catholic country with about 100,000 settlers, mostly Islamic and often forced from Java. Its military government has starved the people and tried to break their language and culture.

Hugo Young, 1996

> The forgotten freedom fighters of East Timor ... are emblem-
> atic of the struggle by Oceanic civilisations to prevent them-
> selves from being "pacified" (for which read "assimilated")
> and to defend the extraordinary cultural diversity that is their
> great hallmark.
>
> Le Monde, 27 March 1997[12]

The department of the Secretary of State not only served as a midwife to the women's movement but also suckled a host of ethnic organizations that came to dominate the discussion of rights, entitlements, and the very concept of Canadian nationality and character. The legacy of this initiative reached its nadir when Jean Chrétien's first secretary of state for Women and Multiculturalism, Sheila Finestone, told CTV's W-5 in January 1995 that there was no single Canadian identity and that "Canada has no national culture." It was to be another year before an appropriate epitaph was written. Finestone was dropped from the government in a reshuffle that saw (bilingual) anglophones from Quebec pushed aside to make way for (bilingual) francophones. Not for the first time the politics of identity devoured one of its architects.

The enthusiasm for funding groups that purport to represent ethnic constituencies can be traced to the fallout from the Royal Commission on Bilingualism and Biculturalism, and the reaction of some Canadians of a variety of ethnic backgrounds to what appeared to be a very narrow vision of the country's history and make-up. In a critical review of government sponsorship of groups that claim, with little evidence, to speak for large constituencies, Leslie Pal notes that ethnic concerns were neither well organized or focused; the voices raised were those of ethnic elites, not those of a grass-roots movement. One reason for the weakness of the response was the "small size and hence limited resources of most ethnic groups and their associations" (Pal 1993: 114).

Trudeau announced the birth of multicultural Canada on 8 October 1971, claiming that the policy would "help break down discriminatory attitudes and cultural jealousies" (ibid.: 115). Trudeau articulated the confusion that lies at the heart of multiculturalism: "National unity if it is to mean anything in the deeply personal sense, must be founded on confidence in one's own individual identity; out of this can grow respect for others and a willingness to share ideas, attitudes and assumptions. A vigorous policy of multiculturalism will help create the initial confidence" (ibid.). The characteristically mellifluous phrasing concealed some thorny questions. Why was ethnicity held to play such a central part in identity? Why should a constant emphasis on ethnic difference create a sense of national unity?

The policy, devised as an afterthought to the reaction of a few self-appointed ethnic spokespersons to the vision of the Royal Commission on Bilingualism and Biculturalism, was opportunist rather than rooted in any coherent philosophy. Two years earlier the government's Indian policy paper had announced a process of rapid assimilation. The paper, far from celebrating cultural diversity, ignored the distinctive heritage of the country's aboriginal population and the strongly expressed desires for a continuing distinctive lifestyle in favour of policies that would abolish the Indian Act and treat Indians in exactly the same way as other Canadians. The new proposals invited swift condemnation from aboriginal leaders but even as the government back-pedalled, the minister of Indian Affairs and Northern Development, Jean Chrétien, moved ahead with plans to encourage industrial development in the north.

Peter Usher, a social scientist in the department, who had examined the implications of oil development for the Banks Island Inuit, publicly cautioned against the threat to the traditional harvesting economy posed by the department's pro-development approach. Chrétien's response was a personal attack on Usher, "the typical white man who knows what is best for the Eskimos" (L. Martin 1995: 231). He gave directions that the department "get that guy under control." Usher, who had spent many years in the North, was relieved of any responsibilities and left workless until he resigned. Was Usher the typical white man out of touch with aboriginal concerns, or should that label have been applied to Chrétien? Usher's subsequent career included a term as research director of the national Inuit Tapirisat. His views were subsequently endorsed by the Berger Commission, established to identify the best route for the construction of a natural gas pipeline in the Mackenzie River Valley. The commission, in a landmark report, argued that construction was incompatible with aboriginal goals which were far removed from the growth-oriented concerns of southern Canadians. In particular, construction threatened the harvesting economy and the survival of a distinctive and viable aboriginal culture which that economy underpinned (Berger 1977).

The assimilationist aboriginal policy backed by Trudeau stood in marked contrast to the soon-to-be-announced multicultural policy. Those who chose to immigrate to Canada might be expected to have some obligation to adapt themselves to the country's culture and values; those who found the ties of ethnicity too powerful could, for the most part, choose to return to their native countries. Canada's aboriginals, in contrast, had nowhere to return, an unchallenged claim to have been here first and, in many northern communities, an identifiably distinctive lifestyle rooted in the harvesting economy.

The multicultural policy provided direction to the expanding role of the Citizenship Branch, which initiated core funding of a range of organizations purporting to represent particular ethnic constituencies. The dubiousness of claims to representation was highlighted by the finding of a 1976 evaluation that the typical group funded had from twenty to eighty-five members, and 83 per cent had less than three hundred members (Pal 1993: 190). The small size of the groups funded did not inhibit those who claimed to speak for ethnic or racial constituencies. The appointment of a minister of state for Multiculturalism in 1972 and the creation of the 101-member Consultative Council on Multiculturalism reflected the recognition by the Liberals, now in a minority government following the election, that ethnic politics could be used to rebuild party support.

The Conservatives under Brian Mulroney also saw the electoral advantages to be gained by promoting links with ethnic groups and promoting multicultural policies. Funding was increased, and in 1988 the Canadian Multiculturalism Act provided a legislative framework for the promotion of multiculturalism and further entrenched the right of groups claiming to speak for ethnic constituencies to demand funding and consultation. The ethnic groups which the policies had fostered demanded more, calling for a full Ministry of Multiculturalism.

The official endorsement and, more importantly, funding of organizations whose purpose was to celebrate ethnic differentiation resulted in the acceleration of demands that Canada be seen simply as the sum of its ethnic constituencies. The changing demographics of Canada, resulting from changes in immigration policy and immigrant flows, created an increasingly racial dynamic. The traditional ethnic organizations had sought to assert their place in Canadian history in the face of the overweening demands of anglophone and francophone constituencies and the often-neglected prior claims of Canada's aboriginal peoples. The government-funded organizations, which claimed to speak for visible minority ethnic groups, had a much more ambitious agenda: in essence their demand was for legislative action to secure for newly arriving immigrants the economic benefits and political gains that previous immigrant groups had depended on time and effort to secure. The absence of a proportional share or the refusal to promote the requisite legislation would simply confirm the depth of systemic racism.

The Canada Council, which is accountable to Canadian Heritage, was also the site of demands for special consideration and for the privileging of those who claimed to speak on behalf of allegedly suppressed constituencies. Thomas Henigan, a close observer of the Canadian cultural world, notes the council's increasingly compromised response: "the Council, in the familiar manner of a semiofficial government organization vulnerable to the criticism of zealous minorities, was mightily concerned to be as proactive as possible on behalf of ethnic artists. Yet one of the cornerstones of Council policy, that artistic quality alone should decide who gets the grants, was clearly incompatible with such politically motivated rule making" (Henigan 1996: 64).

Alberto Manguel, addressing the "voice appropriation" controversy, was blunter: "the Canada Council, whose function is to serve the artistic community, actually defends the limiting of the imagination and pretends to instruct the artist on a 'more appropriate way to work'" ("Letters," *Globe and Mail*, 28 March 1992).

The council began to respond to demands that it accommodate the "cultural differences" of allegedly disadvantaged groups by moving away from the merit principle to a recognition of group entitlement. In 1992 the council embraced the idea that culture itself might have to acknowledge some prior group proprietary rights, expressing concern about "voice appropriation" by writers who might speak in a voice other than their own. The uproar at the cultural illiteracy of policies that would have spelled the death of most fiction forced a retreat, but not before the same nonsense had begun to affect publishers, wary of undertaking any project unlikely to receive council backing. Meanwhile the Concordia University Women's Centre joined the debate, banning a work by artist Lyn Robichaud because its subject matter, an African woman carrying a bunch of bananas on her head, was "racist."

The voice appropriation fiasco saw council director Joyce Zemans lecturing Canadian writers on the "need for authenticity" and commending *Madame Bovary*, because Flaubert "authenticated his writing" by living "with these women," a comment which lead Alberto Manguel to add "presumably meaning he shared his life with a bevy of Bovarys" (Letters, *Globe and Mail*, 28 March 1992). Quick to see the centrality of this concept to a reinterpretation of the world's great literature, Patrick McFadden suggested "the uncanny cultural authenticity" of George Orwell's *Animal Farm* resulted from "Orwell's dutifully heroic practice (alas, these days too often misunderstood!) of bestiality" ("Letters," *Globe and Mail*, 28 March 1992).

The council learned little from this debacle and proceeded to provide grant support to the racially exclusive Writing Thru Race conference held in Vancouver in 1994. The conference was organized by the Writers Union, which, in turn, received substantial annual grant support from the Canada Council. The council, like its sponsors at Canadian Heritage, continues to afford a generous reception to those whose claim on the public purse is based on the principle of group entitlement.[13]

The importance of government funding to the emerging shape of ethnic politics in Canada and the marginality of grass-roots contribution mirrors the history of the women's movement. The Canadian Ethnocultural Council (CEC), which claims through its affiliated members to speak for millions of Canadian, is overwhelmingly dependent on government funding. In 1989–90, Pal reports, only 2 per cent of the organization's revenue came from non-governmental sources (Pal 1993: 204). Liberal MP John Bryden notes that although the council is an umbrella organization with thirty-eight ethnic organizations listed as members, they contribute only $8,250 in membership dues. This compares to more than $320,000 in government grants in 1989, an election year in which the council received particularly favourable treatment. What of other sources of income, from those who think the council's work merits support? In 1993 the council collected $770 in donations, in 1992, nothing (Bryden 1994: 24).[14] Financing is also extended to many of the groups which comprise the CEC. The National Association of Canadians of Origins in India claims to speak for 750,000 Canadians, but in 1993 it raised only $4,881 through memberships, donations, and other revenue, relying on a $68,000 operating grant from Multiculturalism (Bryden 1994: 43).

However dubious its claims to representation, the CEC has played a significant role in advancing ethnic politics, lobbying for the establishment of the Department of Multiculturalism and Citizenship and for preferential hiring programs. In evidence to the 1983 House of Commons Special Committee on Participation of Visible Minorities in Canadian Society, for example, the CEC demanded not only preferential hiring and training programs but that the federal government consult with ethnic organizations before making any order-in-council or Senate appointments (Pal 1993: 206).

The activities of those who purport to speak for ethnic constituencies in Canada are paralleled in other countries, though the extent of public subsidy appears to be unique to Canada: "Unelected 'spokesmen' who speak boldly to the media in the name of groups seeking preferential policies are a common social phenomenon from New Zealand to Britain to North America ... Any fundamental re-examination of the assumptions behind preferential policies – and still more so any resulting change of policies – can expect to encounter their vocal, bitter and determined opposition, including inevitable charges of racism against outsiders, labels of 'traitor' put on any members of their own group who disagree publicly with them, and whatever other claims or charges seem likely to be politically effective" (Sowell 1990: 174).

It is ironic that the legacy of the Trudeau government should be the entrenchment of those who claim special rights for ethnic groups and emphasize the entitlements that should be presumed to flow from group membership. Trudeau's own philosophy, frequently articulated in the debates over constitutional revision, asserted the equality of all Canadians: "You can't have a nation of people with different rights in front of the state," he said during an interview on CBC Radio's *Morningside* on 21 October 1996. But this is, of course, exactly the situation created by preferential hiring policies and legislated in Trudeau's Charter of Rights and Freedoms.

Other Liberals have been guided less by philosophy than expediency. Multiculturalism minister Hedy Fry gave voice to contemporary policy at a meeting of ethnic elites, funded by Canadian Heritage and sponsored by the Pearson Shoyama Institute, whose president, Andrew Cardozo, is former head of the Canadian Ethnocultural Council. Responding to criticism of Canada's multicultural program and policies based on group preferences, the minister suggested that just as in Confederation smaller provinces received special protection, including greater representation, so some contemporary ethnic groups might merit privileged arrangements beyond simple guarantees of equal treatment (Juliette Cuenco Seminar, Ottawa, 27 May 1996). The minister's view appeared to echo George Orwell's observation that "all animals are equal but some are more equal than others" – the very antithesis of the philosophy argued with such consistency by Trudeau in addressing Canada's constitution and opposing the demands of Quebec nationalists.

The multicultural program created a powerful constituency of support among those who were beneficiaries of government largesse. Critics of the program could command no similar support. When multiculturalism minister Fry announced the $24 million endowment for the Canadian Race Relations Foundation, destined to be another centre for ethnic patronage, it was swiftly welcomed in the *Toronto Star* by none other than Andrew Cardozo, who in a column attacking the Ontario Conservatives was pleased to inform his readers that in spite of federal cutbacks "in Ottawa ... there are still quality of life ideas. Hedy Fry the junior minister for multiculturalism and the status of women, introduced the new multiculturalism policy and established the long-promised Canadian Race Relations Foundation" (*Toronto Star*, 18 November 1996). Cardozo was identified as president of the Pearson Shoyama Institute, but few readers would be aware of the institute's intimate ties to Canadian Heritage.

Cardozo played a similar role in defending the changes to multicultural programs proposed in the Brighton Research report (1996). When he was interviewed on Ottawa's CBC Radio before the department had actually released the report to the public (CBO *Morning*, 15 October 1996),[15] Cardozo was presented as an expert on public policy. CBC, which is responsible to the Canadian Heritage minister, made no mention of Cardozo's close ties to Canadian Heritage or the generous funding the Pearson Shoyama Institute receives from the department.

The incestuous link between Canadian Heritage and its beneficiaries was again illustrated in an exchange of letters in the *Globe and Mail* occasioned by the resignation of Harjot Oberoi, the Sikh holder of the Canadian Heritage-funded chair of Sikh studies at UBC, following repeated protests at his views by Sikh fundamentalists. Reg Whitaker, a York University political science professor, suggested this afforded evidence of the "futility" of the government's multicultural program (19 July 1996). The response came not from Canadian Heritage's politicians or bureaucrats but from Cardozo, who accused Whitaker of borrowing neo-conservative ideas and picking on the Sikhs, linking Whitaker's defence of a Sikh scholar to the turban controversies at the RCMP and the Canadian legion (26 July 1996).[16]

Cardozo's attempt to tarnish Whitaker with the charge of racism was indicative of the way in which such debates are carried on. The purpose of Whitaker's intervention was simply to insist on the application of the principle of academic freedom. The intervention of UBC's dean of arts, Shirley Neuman, gave some indication of the constraints placed on such chairs, of which the federal government has endowed twenty-six (HRD 1995b: 17). The problem, said the dean, was that Oberoi "wishes to pursue research interests beyond those mandated by the chair in Sikh and Punjabi studies" (Letters, *Globe and Mail*, 19 July 1996). Neuman noted that "such a broadening and expansion of interests frequently characterizes the best scholars." UBC's dean failed to add that only in the case of Professor Oberoi had this required resignation from a university chair.

Cardozo made a similar attempt to conjure up the spectre of racism in an attack on *Globe and Mail* columnist Robert Fulford, who had been unwise enough to criticize multiculturalism. "Official multiculturalism, the automatic classification of citizens according to race and ancestry, was a bad idea in the beginning," Fulford wrote, "and in time will probably be seen as one of the gigantic mistakes of recent public policy in Canada" (*Globe and Mail*, 19 February 1997). Cardozo's response commenced with the suggestion that lurking not far from the surface was something altogether less pleasant than simple dismissal of race-based policies. The imagery is worth considering, as an attempt to direct debate away from substantive issues by imputing xenophobia to those who reject the enduring claims of race and ethnicity in favour of a common Canadian citizenship: "Robert Fulford has once again launched one of his tirades against multiculturalism in a manner reminiscent of the British Raj fighting to keep Canada British against the invading hordes" ("Letters," *Globe and Mail,* 24 February 1997).[17] Six months later Cardozo was appointed to the CRTC. The members of the commission, who draw six-figure salaries, are appointed by the minister of Canadian Heritage.

Cardozo is not, of course, the only beneficiary of multicultural funding to be active in its defence. A lengthy article by Gina Mallet, "Has Diversity Gone Too Far?" in the *Globe* (15 March 1997) invited a swift response from UBC professor Charles Ungerleider who, in addition to his full-time university position, has received generous patronage from Canadian Heritage, most recently as author of the Brighton Research report. Ungerleider was quick to suggest that the attack on multiculturalism had some more nefarious purpose: "The flaws in Ms. Mallett's article are numerous. She invokes the authority of University of Calgary political scientist Thomas Flanagan without properly identifying him as the one-time architect of the Reform Party's ideology and strategy" (*Globe and Mail,* "Letters," 26 March 1997). It is unclear why Ungerleider believes involvement in a political party which has widespread support in Alberta either qualifies or disqualifies Flanagan to express a view on the issue, but such intervention is consistent with a wider attempt to silence critics of official multiculturalism by suggesting that they are reactionaries or worse.

The proliferation of federally funded chairs in ethnic studies and the provision of research grants and post-graduate support, like the parallel provision of federal support to women's studies, provides federal bureaucrats with the financial means to foster a constituency of academics and students who share their vision. The funding of a conference organized by the Canadian Committee on Women's History, held at the University of Toronto, is suggestive of the way in which such bureaucratic sponsorship works to entrench identity politics at the centre of any discourse. The committee was funded to organize a conference "for women's historians to discuss the integration of race and ethnicity into courses on women's history" (HRD 1995b: 26). In the process of the endless fracturing of Canadian identity it is no doubt only a matter of time before we have government-funded conferences for gay and lesbian historians to discuss the integration of Asian gay and lesbian history into courses on gay and lesbian history.

There is, in the growing fascination with identity group history, a perhaps understandable loss of focus on some of the central facets of Canadian history. In a recent volume of feminist discourse we learn that Chinese Canadians were first brought to Canada "in the early 1800s" to work on the railroads (Rebick and Roach 1996: 83). This was some seventy years before British Columbia joined Confederation and apparently preceded the development of the requisite technology.

Funding for ethnic organizations is not confined to Canadian Heritage; provincial and municipal governments have also seen the benefits to be gained from such patronage. Once established, ethnic organizations quickly learned of other potential sources of financial sponsorship, creating in the process a further fracturing of Canadian society as services are delivered not to generic constituencies defined by need or some common condition but to groups bound by ethnicity or frequently colour. The award for the most imaginative initiative might go to the Ethno-Cultural Association of Newfoundland and Labrador, which secured $59,500 from Health Canada to develop a "culturally sensitive" program of smoking cessation for ethnic minorities (Corcoran 1996). However, the Edmonton Chinese Community Service Centre promised an even narrower focus, securing a modest $27,656 to "lay a groundwork" for an initiative to reduce "harm from tobacco use" among Chinese in Edmonton (ibid.). What expertise either organization might claim in countering tobacco use or why citizens might not access common programs is apparently not of concern to Health Canada.

In Ottawa the city council together with the province provided some $1 million in funding to a multicultural centre, urged on by the council's Advisory Committee on Visible Minorities. In an area already served by a plethora of community centres, the case for the new centre appeared to rest on the odd notion that a separate centre, directed to so-called multicultural communities, would promote multiculturalism, racial harmony, and cross-cultural understanding. The latter two goals might have been more obviously achieved by assuring relevant program provision and outreach at the six centres already serving the area. The Multicultural Centre ran for more than four years before the city council were finally unable to resist the overwhelming evidence that it served little purpose and had few users. In 1995, for example, ten programs were offered, eight of which were only one-time activities, "for a total of 3,950 attendances." In 1996 when the centre closed, it had amassed twenty-five individual memberships and seven group memberships. In 1994 and 1995 it failed to raise a single dollar in donations (City of Ottawa 1996). As one councillor observed when taxpayers were relieved from further obligations, the centre "served to segregate the multicultural community [sic] instead of integrating them into existing centres," though that may have been a rather generous estimate of the centre's influence (*Ottawa Citizen*, 25 January 1997).

Undeterred by this costly venture into the politics of identity, in the spring of 1997 the council moved to consider expanding the mandate of its unelected Advisory Committee on Visible Minorities and rename it the Advisory Committee on Equity and Diversity. The renamed committee would have a mandate to speak on behalf of an expanding cast of alleged victims, characterized by gender, sexual orientation, religion, or poverty (*Ottawa Citizen*, 2 May 1997). As the committee moved to speak for an ever-larger proportion of the electorate, the question which remained to be addressed was· why bother with the troublesome business of electing a city council?

The proliferation of funding for projects purporting to address the agenda of particular identity groups inevitably tempted others to join the bandwagon. The Canadian Council on Social Development historically focused its concerns on socio-economic questions of particular concern to lower income Canadians. Faced with declining support from its traditional patrons in the federal government, the council moved to address more politically fashionable questions. In 1997 it secured a $225,000 grant from Ontario's lottery-funded Trillium Foundation to "build knowledge on the changing socio-economic status of women in Canada with respect to disability and literacy issues" (Trillium 1997). The council has no obvious expertise in the area of literacy and the summary description of the project provides little insight into what hypotheses are to be tested, appearing to embrace a universe of concerns: "The gender and literacy stream will examine the influence of gender on the relationship between literacy levels and economic security issues such as income, source of income, employment status, occupation, education, parents' education, and employment as well as literacy practices at work and outside the workplace" (ibid.). The gender focus reflects current fashion but contrasts with a wide range of evidence suggesting that Canadian women are more successful than men in secondary education and in securing access to colleges and universities.

THE ILLUSION OF UNITY

The political driving force behind many of the federal government's minority initiatives was, ironically, the national unity issue (Pal 1993). It was hoped, for example, that NAC would play an important role in uniting women in Quebec and the rest of Canada on gender lines. Funds were provided to NAC specifically to assist this objective, but after a number of confrontations NAC and the Federation des Femmes du Québec parted ways. NAC, in common with many other self-styled progressives, ceased to take any stand on keeping Canada together. The organization, which prided itself on what it believed was its central role in defeating the Charlottetown Accord, sat out the 1995 referendum. The politics of identity make an insistence on the indivis-ibility of Canada difficult. When hundreds of thousands of Canadians gathered in Montreal in a last-moment appeal for unity, NAC, like its allies in the Canadian Labour Congress, stayed in Ottawa. Judy Rebick did offer a "feminist" analysis of the Montreal rally: "'Please stay', was like the last-ditch effort of a neglectful husband who respects his wife's announcement that she's leaving him by bringing home flowers and saying, 'I'm going to be good and I'm going to come home every night and take care of the kids'" (Rebick and Roach 1996: 139).

The government's generous support for ethnic organizations was also driven by the belief that it might forge a stronger sense of unity, while appeasing ethnic voters upset by the suggestions that there were merely two languages and two cultures to consider. Again the strategy failed. Quebec pursued an overt goal of integrating Quebec newcomers into the dominant francophone milieu, though the visceral ethno-centrism of many *pur laine* Quebecers created some difficulties in delivering the promised unity. Ottawa, in contrast, embraced multicul-turalism, a policy premised on the assumption that groups wished to maintain a distinct cultural identity. To the traditional cultural con-cerns of long-established ethnic groups were added the growing demands of those claiming to represent newer groups of immigrants, for increased government action to afford their groups special rights and protections against what they claimed was a dominant privileged white majority.

The result of federal policies was the further institutionalization of identity politics and the legitimation of an ever more disparate chorus of grievance and consequent demand for special treatment. The fos-tering of multiculturalism did not make it easier to resolve ongoing conflicts with Quebec nationalists but harder: "The reality is a politics over-determined by division and difference. The Meech Lake process reveals this quite well: group after group appeared before committees, conferences and the media first to applaud cautiously the possibility of constitutional reconciliation with Quebec and then to demand equal status and full protection of their rights" (Pal 1993: 257).

The gurus of identity politics offer a different analysis, maintaining that those who complain of the fracturing of Canadian identity are simply mourning the demise of Anglo white male domination. Rebick cites Robert Fulford and Richard Gwyn: "Of course the common identity was *their* identity as white Anglo males. Things were much more defined when white Anglo males defined reality and everyone else had to fit into that" (Rebick and Roach: 1996: 74, emphasis in original). This provides a curiously hegemonic view of Canadian history from a one-time Marxist and self-styled socialist. Was the Canadian identity of the earlier decades of the twentieth century so easily adduced? What of the white Anglo males – radicals who sought to overthrow governments, not secure increased grants – who played a leading role in political movements whose vision far exceeded the banalities proffered today? Where do the vibrant cultures of other ethnic groups fit in this myopic reconstruction?

Quebec nationalists, for their part, seemed intent on denying the significance of demographic changes, preferring to portray Canada in ways suggesting little had changed since Confederation. Lucien Bouchard, assuming the mantle of Quebec premier, spelled out the implications of this nineteenth-century world view: "Canada is divisible because Canada is not a real country. There are two people, two nations and two territories. This one is ours" (*Globe and Mail*, 29 January 1996). The idea that there is a Quebec "people" is not confined to separatists. Treasury Board Minister Marcel Massé declared: "There exists a Quebec people as there exists an Abénaki people, a Cree people, an Inuit people" (ibid., 14 May 1995). This emphasis on the enduring claims of ethnicity is consistent with the dictates of identity politics, but it highlights the difficulty of forming any over-arching sense of national identity that transcends the claims of historic entitlement or contemporary special treatment. It is consistent with a broader, if disturbing, thrust in politics at the end of the millennium, eloquently captured by Eric Hobsbawm, "the amalgam of slogans and emotions – it can hardly be called an ideology – which flourished on the ruins of the old institutions and ideologies, much in the same way weeds had colonized the bombed ruins of ... European cities after the Second World War bombs fell. This was xenophobia and identity politics" (Hobsbawm 1994: 566).

Contemporary multicultural policy has travelled a considerable distance from its first tentative steps, when it was offered as a balance to official bilingualism and biculturalism. Today the vision which is offered is of Canada as the world's first consciously "polyethnic" state (Brighton Research 1996: 5). Canadians who think the government is simply offering a helping hand to ethnic newcomers may be surprised to learn that the intent is to assist individual Canadians to retain their distinct cultural heritage in perpetuity. This is a goal embraced by no other government anywhere in the world: "Canada had charted a unique course among nations in pursuit of a sometimes elusive, and controversial vision of a society in which people retain their heritage languages and their cultural identification while enjoying the full benefits of a citizenship founded on shared rights, freedoms and obligations" (Brighton Research 1996: 5). Those shared rights are somewhat compromised by the preferential policies adopted to meet the demands of a range of identity groups.

Multiculturalism has been embraced by groups that are not normally allied. The most vocal defenders are those who benefit from direct sponsorship, who frequently present multiculturalism as a progressive program concerned to combat racial persecution and afford recognition to minority cultures. Multiculturalism has also been defended as the ideal complement to globalization, an expression of polyethnicity that fits well with the diminished role of the nation state in the new economy.[18] There is, indeed, some merit to this claim: Michael Lind, analysing the American experience, highlights the fit between multiculturalism and corporate marketing strategies (Lind 1995: 139–80). The contradiction, as Lind notes, is that others claim a radical victory in securing such policy responses.

The policy, and the consequent involvement of politicians and bureaucrats in sponsoring ethnic organizations, results in an emphasis on ethnicity or group identity rather than social class. It has assisted in the transformation of the concept of social justice into an agenda for intra-group equality rather than broad social equality. This was evidenced in the evaluation of multiculturalism programs by Brighton Research, where, in the context of a discussion of the evolution of multicultural programming, we are advised: "The gradual development of an infrastructure that promotes social justice for all Canadians should, in time, create the one condition most central to democratic citizenship: equality among all Canadians" (Brighton Research 1996: 39). In a recent volume on multiculturalism, Carleton political scientist Elliot Tepper offers an equally uncritical, utopian vision of multiculturalism as "the policy response to the search for equality in a plural society" (Tepper 1997: 196). The fact that income polarization is increasing, and that more than one in five Canadian children are raised in poverty, should not detract from the immanence of this multicultural nirvana.

Multicultural funding provides the opportunity for pork-barrelling in which favoured ethnic groups or individuals can be rewarded with financial support. There is little coherent monitoring or evaluation of program expenditures. A recent report noted that many files regarding funded projects were incomplete and that while project reports were required, many grant recipients simply forwarded posters and advertisements. In the words of one commentator, the impact of project expenditures is "unknown and unknowable" (Brighton Research 1996: 62). Liberal MP John Bryden, who has actively campaigned against continued government funding to special interest groups, was blunter in his assessment: "Because government grants enable organizations to exist without active memberships, they are not troubled by internal accountability. This might be all right if the government money came with some strings attached, with a requirement to show how well the money was spent. Alas, this is not the case" (Bryden 1994: 5).

Responding to the strategic review of multicultural programs, of which the Brighton Report was a part, Canadian Heritage offered little insight into any measures it intended to take to ensure more effective controls over program spending but took the opportunity to provide multiculturalism with a renewed ideological message: "The renewed Multiculturalism Program will help build a more inclusive and cohesive society by addressing three objectives: *Social Justice, Identity and Civic Participation*" (Canadian Heritage, Backgrounder, October 1996, emphasis in original).[19]

The identity to be promoted was that of a Canada of hyphenated-Canadians. Traditionally social justice and civic participation have been facilitated by programs directed to the alleviation of poverty. The late Christopher Lasch provided a cogent account of the links: "Social and civic equality presupposes at least a rough approximation of economic equality" (Lasch 1995: 22). In the contemporary Liberal account, billionaire Canadians with intimate ties to the government may transfer their wealth outside the country tax free; family trusts abound, and social justice and civic participation are achieved by fostering a patronage-driven culture of fractious identity politics. Those who might fail to recognize that a government cutting social programs, unable to combat high levels of unemployment, and apparently indifferent to growing income polarization was actually pursuing a progressive agenda have obviously missed the point.

7

Endorsing Orthodoxy

The Abella Report and
Federal Employment Equity Legislation

> No society can long survive that cannot find useful work for
> its people and that mortgages its future with crushing debt.
> When this happens, a nation becomes fragmented and tribal-
> ized, and particularities of gender, ethnicity, and language
> explode.
>
> Eric Kierans, 1994

> Preferential policies allow intellectuals as well as politicians
> to be on the side of the angels (as locally defined at the time)
> at low cost – or rather, at low down payment, for the real
> costs come later, and have sometimes been paid in blood.
>
> Thomas Sowell, 1990

TRUDEAU'S FLAWED LEGACY:
LEGISLATING INEQUALITY

The 1982 Canadian Charter of Rights and Freedoms includes an
"Equality Rights" section affording legal protection to affirmative
action programs. Originally Section 15 was to be called "Non-
Discrimination"; the change in name and the extensive reach of the
section was attributable to feminist lobbying.

Mary Eberts, a lawyer with the elite firm Tory, Tory, Deslauriers and
Binnington, a firm which includes former Conservative premier Bill
Davis, was one of those who played a key role in defining the charter's
equality provisions. For Eberts, who lived in Toronto's exclusive
Rosedale area and was married to a prominent Ontario Liberal, now
a provincial judge, equality had little to do with its traditional meaning.
What Eberts and her colleagues were seeking was the introduction of

preferential rights for designated groups, based on a radical feminist view at some variance with the way many Canadians view equality.

The charter's Section 15 permits "any law, program or activity" where the object is "the amelioration of conditions of disadvantaged individuals or groups." If some Canadians are to have more rights, others must have less. These contradictions are central to Section 15, resolved in the real world at the expense of groups unable to seek the benefits of special measures. The charter identifies a range of groups meriting affirmative action, while the explanatory text makes it clear that this list is not "exhaustive." The courts are expected to develop new grounds for "non-discrimination," permitting yet more affirmative action programs "for other groups of people who may have suffered as a result of past discriminatory laws or practises" (Canada 1982: 15). The expanding list of those who may merit preferential treatment places increasing onus on the ever smaller group of those able to make no such claim, who must, in consequence, bear the burden of redressing the alleged historical wrongs.

The charter, according to those who secured the equality rights provisions, should be interpreted to provide not for equality of treatment but "equality of results." Interviewed by Jeffrey Simpson, Eberts gave voice to her view of women's persecution, complete with the meretricious use of statistics which seems to inevitably accompany such debates:

> Even women who appear prosperous and successful experience a different reality from that experienced by men *who seem to be in the same social and economic class.* They seldom achieve parity with their male partners in the labour market and in the division of household tasks. Women who work outside the home must work harder than men for recognition promotion and pay. Women's wages are only 62 percent of men's wages ... In the home the workplace and the community, women are often "fair game" for sexual harassment, violence, insult and pornography, which men rarely experience and seldom notice happening to women (Simpson 1993: 90, emphasis added).

The courts in interpreting the equality provisions must, according to Eberts, be educated to these realities and interpret the law accordingly. It requires no great sociological grasp to appreciate that in this egregious vision the concerns of blue collar white males or males who are unemployed count for little against the persecution faced by those, however rich and influential, who daily confront the disadvantages of their gender.[1]

Michael Lind comments on a similar American claim for the prior entitlement of gender disadvantage: "The vertical divisions between biological identities as whites or blacks, males or females, are far more important than class differences. Women on Park Avenue are thought to be suffering the same oppression as women in trailer parks – dressed in fur or polyester, they are sisters" (1995: 142).

The identification and priorization of group rights is a curious feature in a charter that stands in many ways as the principal intellectual legacy of the Trudeau era. Trudeau, in opposing any entrenched special status for Quebec, repeatedly articulated the view that all individuals must be equal before the state and decried claims for special group rights: "Because I am a liberal I believe the individual is the ultimate carrier of worth" (CBC *Morningside*, 21 October 1996). Trudeau may profess the belief that "in a democratic country everyone is equal" (ibid.) but his Charter of Rights and Freedoms denied equal treatment to able-bodied white males in access to employment and other goods and services where putatively disadvantaged groups could establish preferred entitlement.

The expansive nature of preferential programs is inherent not only in the wording of the charter but in the operation of the courts. A variety of programs exist to assist groups which claim disadvantage, and the lawyers whose careers depend on assisting them, including the Legal Education and Action Fund (LEAF) and the Court Challenges Program, but an able-bodied white male challenging the validity of any preferential hiring or training program would find no similar assistance. Human Rights Commissions have shown little sympathy for challengers to affirmative action programs. Any designated group member who reported that a demonstrably less qualified able-bodied white male had been appointed to a position for which he or she had applied would have a prima facie case. An able-bodied white male, faced with the appointment of a less qualified designated group member, would certainly be advised that this was consistent with the special measures required to redress historic disadvantage or "systemic discrimination."

Groups gaining from affirmative action may not, in fact, have experienced any relevant historic discrimination – they may simply benefit from currently fashionable trends which priorize group membership over merit. There is no evidence that Canadian universities, for example, have discriminated against racial minorities in academic employment over the period of time in which current employees have been recruited. A number of universities have, nonetheless, established preferential hiring programs that result in better qualified candidates outside the preferred racial target groups being passed over for appointment. In some cases the normal requirement that candidates for a professorial post hold a PHD has been waived for those able to offer compensatory racial and gender "disadvantages."[2] Many of the beneficiaries of these programs will be recent immigrants into Canada or the children of such immigrants – groups that would not have experienced historic discrimination even if such discrimination had existed.

The Charter of Rights occasioned considerable hoopla on the part of the Trudeau Liberals, much of it driven by the idea that the charter gave new and more enforceable rights to Canadian citizens. Subsequent events suggested that the charter was more influential in shifting decision-making in controversial areas away from elected politicians to appointed judges or members of human rights tribunals. The charter and the generous funding of intervenor groups ensured the prospect of significant legal changes without the messy business of securing popular consent.[3]

LEGISLATING EQUITY

It is unnecessary, incidentally, to seek much further for an explanation of feminism's appeal to the professional and managerial class. Female careerism provides the indispensable basis for their prosperous, glamorous, gaudy, sometimes indecently lavish way of life.

Christopher Lasch, 1995

The federal government's interest in the employment equity field started in the 1960s. The degree to which men dominated the public service is illustrated by the fact that until the Public Service Act was amended in 1964 married women were ineligible for permanent employment status. Not until 1974 were women allowed into the RCMP. In 1967 the Public Service Employment Act outlawed sex discrimination in the federal civil service. In the same year the Royal Commission on the Status of Women was established. Its report three years later gave a significant impetus to women in the public service, recommending a number of measures to promote their advancement.

The government responded in 1971 by establishing the Office of Equal Opportunity in the Public Service Commission. In early 1972 a cabinet directive was issued to deputy ministers to increase the number of women at the higher levels of the public service. In 1983 Treasury Board introduced an Affirmative Action Policy intended to provide for the "equitable representation and distribution" in the public service of women, aboriginals, and the disabled. The policy was amended in 1986 to include visible minorities.

The Royal Commission on Equality in Employment was announced by Employment and Immigration Minister Lloyd Axworthy in 1983.

Axworthy obtained his graduate education in the United States at the height of the American civil rights movement and was an admirer of the Kennedys. The Canadian legislation and judicial interpretations of equality rights were to be strongly influenced by the American experience, notwithstanding the profound differences in the two countries' histories. Twelve years later, as Chrétien's first Human Resources minister, Axworthy brought in new, more comprehensive federal employment equity legislation.

The Royal Commission had its origins in continuing demands by feminists for government action to secure higher pay for women and a greater share of more prestigious labour market positions. The Liberal government had already responded to pressure to increase the representation of women in senior positions in the public service with a range of programs, including the establishment of coordinators in each ministry to oversee women's recruitment and promotion. When the Liberals returned to power in 1980 following the defeat of Joe Clark's government, the throne speech promised further action to address feminist demands. The government promised the establishment of an affirmative action program in a number of departments including Treasury Board. This was extended to all departments in 1983. The establishment of the Royal Commission signalled the government's interest in extending its reach beyond the direct public sector into "crown corporations and corporations wholly owned by the government of Canada" (Abella 1984: ii).

Employment equity appeared to mesh well with the Liberals' "Just Society" rhetoric, apparently promising a more egalitarian society with government action helping the less powerful. It appeared to offer a low-cost way of continuing to emphasize a progressive agenda in an environment in which the Liberals' failure to match revenues with expenditures was creating a growing fiscal crisis which discouraged continuing increases in social program spending. Judge Rosalie Abella's appointment reflected this ideological chimera; her report consistently portrayed preferential hiring in terms redolent of a commitment to greater social equality. In fact the increasing number of women in the work-force was significantly driven by the growing pressure on low and middle income Canadian families. Families which could once survive on one wage increasingly required two. Osberg, reviewing the changing labour market, noted the marked decline in the income of one earner families: "in real terms the average traditional 'family' was about $1,400 poorer in 1984 than in 1973" (Osberg 1988: 15).

The attempt to present preferential hiring as part of a strategy to achieve social justice is evident on the first page of Abella's report, which is headed with the well-known quote from Anatole France: "The law, in its majestic equality, forbids the rich as well as the poor to sleep under bridges, to beg in the streets, and to steal bread" (Abella 1984: 1). The thrust of Anatole France's argument is directed at gross social and economic inequality, a matter which had little to do with Abella's mandate. The commission was to be concerned not with the question of the allocation of resources between rich and poor or the question of what degree of social inequality was desirable but with the entirely different task of establishing mechanisms that would provide for equality in outcomes between particular identity groups. It mattered not, from this perspective, if the richest 25 per cent should have 80 per cent of the nation's income and wealth, providing the demographic composition of the group mirrored that of the Canadian population or, more particularly, that women, the disabled, aboriginals, and visible minorities were at least equally represented in every desirable economic category.

The increase in the representation of women in the top earning group might in fact increase the concentration of income and wealth, since employment equity would primarily benefit more affluent members of designated groups. Those obtaining preferred appointments in universities, government departments, or corporations were frequently partnered with high earning men. The ideological commitment to treating members of a family unit as independent, with each spouse "responsible for his or her own support" (ibid.: 27), legitimated tax policies that favoured upper income households where there were two high earners. Tax policies are not based on the Carter Commission's "ability to pay"; in the feminist vision supported by Abella and successive Canadian governments, a family with a $90,000 a year income from one earner pays a much higher tax than a family with the same income from two sources. The beneficiaries include upper income feminists and their partners, who escaped the tax impact that would have followed the application of higher marginal tax rates to total family income.

The groups which were to receive preferential hiring benefits from "employment equity" included rich and poor, but as Abella recognized, every member of a "disadvantaged" group would be assumed to be disadvantaged (ibid.: 15). This would inevitably result in the rich "disadvantaged" being treated more favourably than genuinely deprived individuals who were not included in beneficiary groups.

Abella's sentiments about women's position in the labour market are expressed in sweeping terms. Women's progress was largely "chimerical." Women's access to employment necessitated participation in a full range of educational opportunities, requiring "dramatic changes in the school system" (ibid.: 24–5). In contrast to this apocalyptic rhetoric, women were rapidly increasing their representation in more prestigious labour market positions and constituted 51 per cent of university graduates and 58 per cent of community college graduates by 1982 (Wannell and Caron 1994b).

Many of the supposed disadvantages faced by women in the labour market stem not from discrimination in employment but from child-care responsibilities (Fox-Genovese 1996). These are a function of (changing) social values and the broader (changing) organization of the economy. There is, as we have noted, little difference between the earnings of single men and single women. The suggestion that society owes some duty to women to equalize their earnings, to compensate for the outcome of decisions taken by individuals and families about the priorization of labour market versus domestic activities, appears to rest on assumptions that find no wider application. There is, for example, no suggestion that governments have an obligation to compensate high school drop-outs for their lower average earnings or to compensate men who choose relatively low paid clerical work over those who pursue high paying, arguably more onerous jobs in mining.

Men who decide to prioritize child raising over the pursuit of a career, or to sacrifice their own career prospects in following a partner to a new city where she has a better career prospect, invite no parallel consideration. In contrast, under employment equity legislation, they will be treated less favourably than female competitors who are single or whose spouses have placed their own careers in a subordinate position. A woman who has no family responsibilities will, under employment equity, secure preference over a white male single parent.

As women characteristically marry older men, with less labour market experience their earnings will tend on average to be lower. If one partner withdraws from the labour market or moves to part-time work to facilitate child care, economic factors will encourage the lower paid partner to make that choice (Crowley 1994: 50). Employment equity cannot address this dynamic; it can only provide hiring and promotion preferences to women as a group, whether or not they have been affected by any "systemic" disadvantage.

Social policy provision in a liberal democracy might reasonably seek to maximize the individual's opportunity to make informed choices. Employment equity, as conceived by Abella, rests on the assumption not of extending choice but of creating a fiscal, social, and occupational environment in which women will be encouraged to pursue full-time work. Women who chose to stay home and raise their children would find no assistance from any measures proposed by Abella.

The provision of programs that assist families in which both parents work has an uneven impact. Generous maternity benefits and workplace day-care facilities are the prerogative of secure workers, particularly those in the public sector. Feminists have frequently railed against the "chilly climate" on Canadian campuses, but a 1991–92 survey found that of 176 workplace day-care centres, more than half were provided by universities (Frank 1996). Women academics find an array of scholarships and other programs specifically designed to assist them, while a battery of status of women officers and anti-harassment units are ready to respond to any perceived slight. These facilities will be absent in the workplaces of low income women whose taxes help fund such provisions.

The disproportionate benefits that employment equity programs afford to the more affluent and successful members of target groups is an international phenomenon. Thomas Sowell notes the attraction of preferential policies to governments seeking to respond to popular grievances: such policies offer a "quick fix" at relatively low cost. The demand for preferential policies is articulated by elites claiming to give voice to the demands of the masses, but the evidence suggests that such policies respond not to lower class needs but middle class aspirations (Sowell 1990: 167).

VISIBLE MINORITIES

> The paradox of affirmative action is that, in the name of eliminating racism, it institutionalizes race.
>
> Robert Martin, 1993

The inclusion of visible minorities in preferential hiring legislation owes much to the American experience. Affirmative action to address perceived racial discrimination was pioneered in the United States in the 1964 Civil Rights Act, where the clear target of concern was black Americans, a group which, in contrast to other visible minorities, did not owe its presence in the United States to free migration but to the compulsion of slavery. Nathan Glazer, a prominent critic of American policies, leaves no doubt as to the "severe deprivation, rooted in racist prejudice and expressing itself in formal or informal discrimination and segregation" experienced by black Americans (Glazer 1987: ix). In contrast, Glazer argues, other minority groups exercised no similar claim: "it is not their fate nor their power nor their claim on the conscience that motivates this massive machinery" (ibid.: xviii).

Other groups did become embraced within the programs but on the basis of rather weaker claims, which would not have been sufficient to mobilize the legislative majority required to push through the program, since their experience mirrored that of previous immigrants, "each in turn, overcoming some degree of discrimination to become integrated into American society. What this process did not seem to need was the active involvement of government, determining the proper degree of participation of each group in employment and education" (ibid.: xii).

The experience of other visible minority groups in the United States parallels that of most immigrant groups. There is no evidence of pervasive exclusionary policies although, like earlier immigrant groups, they are sometimes the focus of prejudice and resentment. The striking division in the United States on a wide range of measures is not between white and non-white but between black Americans and others (Hacker 1992: 3–17).

Glazer argued that the civil rights movement and vigorous enforcement of strong anti-discrimination laws would, without specific affirmative action programs, have had a major impact on the position of black Americans. Once established, however, affirmative action programs created their own impetus, bringing into play constituencies that sought an ever wider mandate and more onerous enforcement apparatus. This is evident in the spirited resistance in California to the implementation of Proposition 209 which bans race and gender preferences in state employment, contracting, and education: "The proposition's opponents are well placed to fight a guerilla war, too. Every college campus in the state has dozens of affirmative-action officers, diversity counsellors and the like, who are unlikely to take early retirement or retrain as nuclear physicists" (*The Economist*, 16 November 1996).[4]

Canadian blacks, in contrast to their American counterparts, are overwhelmingly "free immigrants." Census data for 1991 indicate that 44 per cent of black Canadians immigrated in the past twenty years (Torczyner 1997: 25). Eight out of ten blacks in the Canadian labour force are immigrants (Torczyner: 26). There is evidence of discrimination in the treatment of some Canadian-born blacks, most notably in Nova Scotia, but not only was the group as a whole far smaller than their American counterparts but their historical experience was quite different. While Canada followed America's lead in introducing preferential hiring, it lacked its southern neighbour's reasons. Any analysis of the American experience points to the central importance of the presence of a large ethnic group whose social condition was closely tied to the legacy of slavery; without such a group, the evidence suggests that America would not have introduced race-based preferential hiring.

Ironically, as Canada has moved to entrench such hiring policies more deeply, affirmative action in America has come under growing attack, with the Republican platform in 1996 committed to its abolition. The legal consequences of the approval given by 54 per cent of Californian voters to Proposition 209 remain uncertain, but "judges and politicians will hardly fail to note that the only time the people at large have been consulted on affirmative action they have voted resoundingly against it" (*The Economist*, 16 November 1996). The proposition went into force on 28 August 1997 with reports that a further twenty-four states were considering rescinding affirmative action programs (CBC *Radio News*, 28 August 1997).[5]

The American program, with its considerable resources, proved singularly ineffective in remedying the perceived problem. Bussing and preferential training, hiring and promotion programs precipitated increased racial conflict. The inclusion of Asians and Hispanics in the target groups diluted program impacts while benefiting many who had no reasonable claim on such special assistance. The proliferation of beneficiary groups resulted in growing conflict; the imposition of quotas, as in the California state university system, could lead to a situation in which the child of a South-east Asian refugee required higher marks than the child of a black millionaire to gain acceptance. Such conflicts no doubt contributed to growing opposition to affirmative action among minority groups.

Canada learned little from the American experience and failed to ask whether the measures deemed necessary to address the legacy of slavery and institutionalized discrimination were an appropriate response to the adjustment difficulties of visible minority immigrants, some of whom had cultural, economic, and educational characteristics that promised to afford considerable labour market success.

Judge Abella acknowledged the apparently diverse labour market experience of visible minorities and the difficulty of identifying those groups in greatest need. Statistics Canada data was not, she noted, sufficiently refined "to make determinative judgements as to which visible minorities appear not to be in need of employment equity programs" (Abella 1984: 46). This raises the obvious question as to how discriminatory behaviour based on "visibility" can effect some visible groups but not others. Abella ignores this difficulty, preferring, even in the absence of data, to assert what she knows to be true, even where it appears to contradict the evidence she cites. Racism, she assures her readers, "though sometimes inadvertent is nevertheless pervasive" (ibid.: 4).

Abella reports that while crown corporations lacked reliable data on visible minority employment, "it was clear from information learned from meetings" that visible minorities "were not employed in significant numbers by any of the corporations" (ibid.: 103). It is difficult to know what conclusion should be drawn from this. Visible minorities made up 4.3 per cent of the Canadian labour force in 1981 (CHRC 1997a: 14): what would "significant" employment look like? The data collected under the first survey, conducted under the new legislation in 1987, will have under-reported actual visible minority employment, since many of those officially defined as visible minorities fail to self-identify; but the results showed that in the range of industries covered, including crown corporations, visible minorities comprised 5 per cent of all employees, 5.24 per cent of full-time hirings, and 6.92 percent of promotions (HRD 1994a: B-7–B-9). Not surprisingly, there was wide variation; visible minorities constituted 9.47 per cent of employees in the banking sector but only 1.03 per cent of those in metal mines (ibid.: B7). Should this lead to the conclusion that systemic barriers existed in metal mining? Visible minorities are overwhelmingly located in CMAs where opportunities for careers in metal mining appear small.

Perhaps evidence of discrimination might be found in the lower salaries earned. Given that many visible minorities would have been first-generation immigrants, and given the importance of seniority in accessing higher earnings, some significant difference might have been expected. Visible minority men in the regulated industries had average salaries of 98.16 per cent of all male employees, visible minority women 96.22 per cent (ibid.: 58).

It is not immediately clear how racism, which suggests a belief in not only the existence of "races" but also of a hierarchy and implies consequent action, could be "inadvertent." Presumably Abella is simply echoing fashionable claims that such issues as the requirement for Canadian experience or qualification thresholds, which may disproportionately impact on some visible minority groups, should be included under the expansive and increasingly meaningless rubric of "racism."

Monica Townson, in a commissioned research paper, noted the lack of relevant information regarding racial minorities, including a lack of agreement on who should be categorized as such: "Once an acceptable definition of 'visible minority' has been established, data on labour force activity and incomes would have to be classified in the same way. Lack of information in this form prevents any assessment of the 'social indicators of discrimination' for Canada's population of 'visible minorities'" (Townson 1985: 349). Logically, in the absence of evidence, a researcher might be expected to question how we know of the existence of a particular social problem; but Townson did not pursue this issue.

The discussion of visible minorities in the report is notable for the confusion over what is to be addressed. Much of the discussion concerns the difficulties immigrants face in securing adequate language training, recognition of their qualifications, and access to better paid jobs, particularly where Canadian experience is a requirement. These are no doubt significant issues, but they have nothing to do with skin colour. They are a function of immigration and will in some cases pose greater barriers to white immigrants than visible minority immigrants, depending on fluency in one of Canada's official languages and the comparability of the educational system in the country of origin.

This confusion of the problems faced by some immigrants and the supposed discrimination faced by visible minorities was to remain a persistent theme. A report to the Ontario minister of Citizenship, the lead ministry in developing Ontario's employment equity policies, claimed that "visible minority women" tended to be more disadvantaged than visible minority men. The report acknowledged "wide variations." The next sentence in the paragraph noted: "Immigrant women are located in both the highest and lowest status occupations." There was no explanation as to why a claim about visible minority experience might be illuminated by a discussion of those whose defining characteristic was not "visibility" but immigration status (Abt Associates 1988: 3).

Abella cites the views of those who attribute their failure to progress to racial discrimination, but commissions of this nature do not constitute random samples. The commission will inevitably have acted as a magnet for those with a grievance. There are a wide range of reasons why individuals fail to secure the promotion they believe they merit. Jag Bhaduria, who moved from Liberal to independent MP when his intemperate comments to school board officials became known, believed that many of his difficulties in securing the promotions he knew he merited flowed from his skin colour. Others may not have agreed. The commission provided a privileged forum for groups whose purpose is to advance particular ethnic interests and secure continued public funding by claiming to speak for allegedly disadvantaged constituencies.

Some of those who have immigrated to Canada, particularly from the Third World, have been members of indigenous elites. In moving to Canada they seek to improve their economic status in an environment apparently offering better prospects. In common with other immigrants, they may have experienced some loss of status in moving into a society that fails to accord the same value to the educational, family, and social connections as in the country of origin. In common with other immigrants, newly arriving visible minorities may have found Canadian insider networks relatively inaccessible. In an intellectual and social climate in which it has become fashionable to attribute lack of desired social mobility to discrimination, it is tempting for those for whom immigration has meant upward economic mobility but reduced social status to attribute this to prejudice. Important figures in their own countries, such elite immigrants quickly moved into ethnic leadership roles, articulating demands that would grant them fast-track access to the same status in Canada.

Abella's claim that racial minorities were "unjustifiably excluded from the opportunity to compete as equals" (Abella 1984: 29) did not find universal support. Alexander pointed out that the commission's own data failed to make the case, with visible minorities exhibiting below average levels of unemployment and Japanese and Indo-Pakistani males having similar proportions in the managerial class to Canadians of British ethnic origin; Japanese males also had, together with males of British origin, the highest proportion earning in excess of $30,000 a year (Alexander 1985). Bricker (1985) pointed to the fluid nature of ethnic group status with evidence that the groups who experienced the highest degree of negative mobility were of white ethnic background.

Abella's failure to root her recommendations for preferential hiring measures for visible minorities in empirical data did not deter others from hailing the report as yet further evidence of discrimination. York University anthropology professor Frances Henry, who has undertaken extensive consultancy work for provincial and federal governments, reported in a volume sponsored by Citizenship and Immigration: "The Commission *revealed evidence* that racial minorities experience lower participation rates, high unemployment and underemployment rates, occupational segregation and low income levels" (Collins and Henry 1994: 537, emphasis added).

The legislation that followed the Abella report covered some 350 employers including crown corporations and federally regulated industries. In all, some 600,000 employees were covered. Employers were required to prepare programs ensuring that their work-forces are representative of the available workers. Employers who failed to provide an annual report were liable to a $50,000 fine. In addition the Federal Contractors Program required companies with more than one hundred employees, who wished to compete on federal contracts of $200,000 or more, to sign a certificate committing the company to various employment equity measures. This was backed by powers for on-site compliance reviews. Some 880 companies with 891,000 employees were covered by 1992. The program provided an important aid to feminists in the universities, seeking to introduce hiring programs which provided overt preference to female candidates (see chapter 11). The federal public service was exempted from the Employment Equity Act, since it was already covered by the Treasury Board Affirmative Action Policy, but the exemption was a continuing focus of agitation by equity activists and was remedied in 1996.

The Canadian employment equity industry has been notably loathe to undertake studies that might seek to measure precise program impacts or to disaggregate the experience of particular target groups. One reason may be that the resulting disparity would cast doubt on the central proposition that "visibility" or gender determines outcomes. If, for example, analysis were to show that some visible minority groups out-perform some white groups, how far could visibility be said to determine labour market success or failure? However, it is a reasonable hypothesis that more careful targeting of groups which might genuinely lay claim to a historical disadvantage that has continuing implications for labour market status would have secured more cost effective results.

Canadian employment equity legislation targets the recent affluent Hong Kong immigrant equally with the impoverished seventh-generation black Canadian in Nova Scotia. The legislation has not created the same inter-ethnic conflict as has occurred among beneficiary groups in the United States, as all those designated as visible minorities are placed in the same group. It may well be that in the future there will be calls to target more precisely when it becomes apparent that not all beneficiary ethnic groups have been equally successful. The Canadian legislation is certainly equally vulnerable to the conflicting claims of natural justice, creating a situation in which the son of an unemployed Cape Breton miner might be passed over in favour of the daughter of a Chinese Canadian brain surgeon.

Meanwhile, aboriginal Canadians, a group whose contemporary position owes much to a historic legacy of settler aboriginal relations, have secured few benefits from employment equity, which has arguably served to direct attention away from policies more relevant to their situation.

THE QUESTION OF DEFINITION

There are pressures to include in the visible minority sub population, groups which are neither non-white in colour nor non-caucasian in race but the members of which may be economically disadvantaged for reasons of language, recent immigration etc.

Statistics Canada, 1990

The creation of employment equity programs that confer benefits on designated groups necessarily involves defining who is to be included in the beneficiary groups. Given the competitive advantages conferred by preferential programs, there is pressure to include additional groups. The 1992 parliamentary review of the Employment Equity Act heard calls for the addition of a range of new beneficiaries, including "immigrants who experience language and cultural barriers to employment ... older workers ... persons disadvantaged because of national or ethnic origin, religion or sexual orientation" (Redway 1992: 7).

Definition, with the usual exception of gender, is not straightforward, and the problem of racial categorization proved particularly intractable. Following Abella's anthropological insights, the act defined as a visible minority those who "are non-white in colour or non-caucasian in race." The world proved to be more complex than the learned judge had envisaged: races do not exist as discrete groupings, except in the fevered imaginings of racial theorists. The question of how to determine whether a caucasian is white or non-white is one that Abella failed to address. In practice, people from a common ethnic and geographic background might vary considerably in the degree of "whiteness"; understandably they might find attempts to categorize on the basis of melanin content not just offensive but antithetical to the very notion of a liberal, inclusive society. Ultimately the problem of classification is irresolvable. Race has no biological base, only a shifting social base. Government attempts to define such "racial" social boundaries will inevitably serve to entrench them, fostering the racial consciousness that preferential hiring advocates claim to oppose.[6]

Statistics Canada has wrestled with the issues of definition, inclusion, and exclusion for many years, at some considerable public expense. The problems are not of course unique to Canada: any country that seeks to base policies and practices on racial characteristics faces similar difficulties, as the architects of apartheid quickly discovered. In Canada there have been attempts to add some groups to the list of "visible minorities" and to exclude others. Ethnic groups have shifted between categories from one census year to the next. In 1986 the North African countries were excluded from the places of birth used to assign respondents to the black group and assigned to the Arab group. Cubans, Puerto Ricans, and those from the Dominican Republic were also excluded and reassigned to the Latin American group. Counted as "black" in analysis of the 1981 census, by 1986 they had been miraculously transformed.

Some groups are largely unaware of the government's attempt to categorize them. At focus-group sessions in Montreal and Toronto conducted on behalf of Statistics Canada, West Asians expressed surprise that Statistics Canada included them as part of Canada's visible minority population (White 1988: 11). In a survey intended to verify the 1986 census responses, less than a third of those who identified West Asian parental origins considered themselves to belong to Canada's racial or visible minority population (ibid.). This rejection suggests that the experience or perception of this group is at marked variance with the determination of Statistics Canada, though this group exhibit many of the same characteristics in areas such as unemployment and income levels as other beneficiary groups with large numbers of recent immigrants.

There is some evidence that Japanese Canadians are also unenthusiastic about being deemed a visible minority. only half of the Japanese respondents identified themselves as belonging to a racial or visible minority. In the Chinese group 96 had paternal Chinese origins but only 56 self-identified as being a visible minority in Canada. In all, in the follow-up study, one third of those who Statistics Canada allocated to a visible minority group on the basis of their paternal origins did not self-identify as members of a visible minority (White 1988: 10). To add further confusion, a significant number of those who stated that they were in a visible or racial minority (37.5 per cent) failed to meet the Statistics Canada definition. The largest group were aboriginals, who are identified separately; however, a range of other ethnic backgrounds were also identified, including francophones, Acadians, Mennonites, Ukrainians, and Jews.

A survey of Chinese Canadian students at York University found that a majority of those who spoke Chinese at home did not consider themselves to be members of a visible minority (*Globe and Mail*, 6 October 1994).

Many Canadians have a mixed heritage. Should those who are of European and aboriginal, Chinese, and Ukrainian, white and black heritage welcome the government's persistent concern to categorize them? Why should they share the identity definitions developed by Statistics Canada analysts? Unfortunately for Statistics Canada, even when respondents are advised that the data is needed to implement federal employment equity goals, many fail to share the government's enthusiasm. One report on focus groups noted "many respondents (even those in visible minorities) aren't sure they approve of job equity legislation" (Breedon 1988: 8). Elsewhere, a Statistics Canada report notes the (heretical) view expressed by many visible minorities at the focus groups that "they wanted to obtain their employment on the basis of merit not quota" (White 1988: 14).

On the other hand the provision of significant preferences which flowed from membership in the designated group could encourage others to want to join. The argument became confusing when groups such as the Portuguese, which failed to meet Abella's standards of "visibility," demanded entrance on the grounds that they were anyway failing relative to other ethnic groups. To admit such groups would be to admit the possibility that race was not after all the defining experience, but that would be to throw into question the whole multi-million dollar enterprise which Abella's report had unleashed.

The problem of defining group membership for employment equity purposes is in some ways insuperable, resulting in a series of decisions that can only be described as arbitrary. Argentineans and Chileans are not included in the employment equity count for Latin Americans, while Costa Ricans and Venezuelans are. Palestinians are counted in the West Asian group, yet Israelis are not, though the latter group includes many members of the former.

Wally Boxhill, a federal employee who has devoted considerable time to the vexing question of racial categorization, summarizes some of the difficulties: "To understand the concept 'visible minority' and to measure its incidence in the population requires consideration of both elements of the term – both the word 'visible' and the word 'minority' ... How is visibility to be measured? What is to be the focus of inspection? Race? Colour of skin? Height? Colour of eyes? Mode of dress? Other unspecified and non-quantifiable measures?" (Statistics Canada 1990: 3). The challenge facing Statistics Canada was to reduce the discrepancy between the numbers declaring themselves as members of a visible minority and those who might be so identified on the basis of ethnic background or "the numbers which may be revealed through visual inspection" (Boxhill, undated: 32). Boxhill did not consider the contribution that might be made by the provision of colour charts to assist census enumerators in closing the gap.

The definitions of bureaucrats did not necessarily correspond to those of other Canadians. In practice, the number of those classified as visible minorities is strongly influenced by the construction of the data-gathering instrument – a fact that raises substantive questions about both the reliability and comparability of data in this area. Ted Wannell, a Statistics Canada analyst, has noted the problems with the agency's own personnel data in this regard. These include the assumption that any employee who does not have an "x" for designated group status is not a designated group member: "it is impossible to distinguish between those who have never received an identification form, those who received one but did not return it and those who returned the form but are not in a designated group" (Wannell undated: 6).

The problems for the bureaucrats assigned to racial categorization are compounded by the failure of Canadians to fall neatly into the allotted categories: "Routine cross-tabulations disclosed that many persons with a place of birth in Haiti (and very likely non-white) had reported their ethnic origin as French." This caused real concern since "it would have been a serious aberration to accept the position that Haitians who reported themselves as French were European and therefore white" (Statistics Canada 1990: 32).

A further difficulty arose in the allocation of particular ethnic groups to larger generic clusters. In 1981 Pacific Islanders, "conceptualised as a group encompassing persons with origins in countries often visualised and portrayed as exotic islands in the Pacific," included not only Samoans Fijians and Polynesians but Indonesians and Filipinos (ibid.: 6). By 1986 Filipinos and Indonesians had lost whatever exotic charm they may have had. Indonesians were allocated to the Southeast Asian category and Filipinos received an independent count. Meanwhile bureaucrats fretted over appropriate generic terminology: "Some terms and aggregations were contentious. The title 'Indo-Pakistani' has sometimes been questioned. Should it have been 'East Indian'? Might it have been 'Persons with Origins in India,' or 'Indo-Canadians'?" (ibid.: 7). The generic term was subsequently changed to South Asian. Unfortunately this failed to solve Statistics Canada's problems: further testing of questions for the 1991 census indicated that "many respondents were confused by the term South Asian" (White 1988: 16).

There was not even agreement on who the census should count. In 1991 the net was extended to capture refugee claimants and temporary residents. Less than 1 per cent of non-visible minority respondents fell into this category compared to some 7 per cent of visible minorities. Equity targets would in future be measured against this larger figure, notwithstanding the fact that it now included a number of people with no right to seek permanent employment. It is indicative of the continuing search for evidence of discrimination that no mention is ever made of the inclusion of this group in the population that sets equity benchmarks.

Intermarriage and resulting miscegenation pose an additional challenge to any bureaucracy charged with racial measurement. What to do with those who report both a visible ethnic origin and a not-visible ethnic origin? What to do with those who report more than one visible minority status? Again these were questions which would have been familiar to those who laboured in the Afrikaans bureaucracy, where the issue could have particular sensitivity since many of the Afrikaans elite "visibly" had some African heritage. In South Africa this was not by itself enough to result in reclassification. Canada, in contrast, determined that any mention of a "visible" ethnic origin would result in allocation to the visible group. For example, "individuals who reported Filipino and British ethnic origins were included in the Filipino group." To avoid double counting, those who reported more than one visible origin "were assigned to the multiple visible minority group" (Statistics Canada 1989: 4).

The decision to consign those who reported any visible ethnic origin to the visible category was consistent with the history of the census. Back in 1901 the issue of racial purity was openly addressed: "The races of men will be designated by the use of 'w' for white, 'r' for red, 'b' for black and 'y' for yellow ... only pure whites will be classed as whites; the children begotten of marriages between whites and any one of the other races will be classed as red, black or yellow, as the case may be, irrespective of the degree of colour" (Boxhill undated, appendix A).

The present-day allocation of any respondent mentioning a visible ethnic group to that category increased the overall numbers, but may, together with the confusion of those who think they are just regular Canadians, help to explain the under-reporting that is a common feature of employment equity self-identification surveys. Boxhill, reviewing these problems, raises other problems that may arise if, as an alternative, supervisors are used to collect data: "While some persons who are undoubtedly in a visible minority in Canada, may be identified as such by a supervisory identification, *the phenomenon of passing*, suggests that this approach is not one which is removed from the possibility of major errors" (Boxhill undated: 28, emphasis added).

Boxhill's turn of phrase is a curiously revealing one, rooted in the experience of racially polarized societies in which to "pass" was to gain access to opportunities otherwise denied. The suggestion that this has any salience in contemporary Canada is remarkable. An alternative perspective was provided by a participant in one of the focus groups established to help Statistics Canada find ways of addressing widespread opposition to census questions on race. The focus group in Halifax included only blacks, and one member suggested that their ethnic background should appropriately be described as African. Others disagreed. The exchange is instructive:

"I guess if you want to think about our true origins, all Blacks came from Africa but I think of myself as a Canadian. My great grandparents came to Canada a century ago and I think that qualifies me to be considered a Canadian. I don't identify with Africa at all."

"But you should. We would be better off if we could gain this identity. One of the problems facing blacks is that they don't see themselves as a homogeneous group. We will never have any sense of identity until we band together."

"I'm not interested in doing that. I just want to be thought of as a Canadian, nothing else."

"But you can't because your skin is black."

"I don't see why this makes me any different than other Canadians. In fact, I dislike being described as a Black. Actually I have a white grandmother and lots of white relatives."

The dialogue is described by the consultants as "not untypical of what we have found in various focus groups with various visible minorities who have assimilated into the mainstream" (Breedon 1988: 36–7). For its part, Statistics Canada has no hesitation in assigning a racial label. In the 1996 census the focus group participant would have found that being Canadian is not enough.

Boxhill raises a number of questions about the reasons for pursuing the data. Noting that employment equity legislation does not encompass immigrants who are white, whatever adjustment difficulties language may cause, he asks, "Is the over-riding issue one of employment, both hiring and promotional opportunities for those *who are systematically excluded because of visible differences from the majority population?*" (Boxhill undated: 35, emphasis added). There is no evidence that *any* ethnic group in Canada faces systematic exclusion. If this is indeed the real reason, the racial questions on the census are unnecessary.

The success of Japanese Canadians cautions against the assumption that the key influence on outcomes is racial discrimination. One of the interesting aspects of Japanese success is that it was achieved not through a focus on community insularity but through the evolution of high degree of cultural assimilation. At least half of third-generation Japanese Canadians are estimated to have intermarried with white Canadians (Lampkin 1985: 668). It can be argued that this strategy was in part a defensive response to the brutal treatment meted out in wartime; nonetheless, it suggests a level of contemporary tolerance that contrasts with claims of pervasive discrimination. It also raises questions about the likely success of policies that explicitly cater to the proliferation of hyphenated-Canadians. Canadians of Japanese origin, like Canadians of Jewish origin, sought not separate provision and measures to secure group preferment but acceptance into the mainstream.

Contemporary policies insist on the primacy of genealogy over nationality. The policies lead to results that are profoundly offensive to those who would assert the prior claims of a common humanity and a common nationality.

The direct adverse effects are not always confined to white males. In 1995 the University of Alberta, which has a singular reputation for politically correct excesses (see chapter 11), became embroiled in a grievance arising from the failure to renew the contract of its director of Native Student Services. The former director, June Kaida, who came to Canada from Tanzania, should have benefited from the university's enthusiastic promotion of preferential hiring but failed to have her contract renewed when aboriginal students complained she could not understand their problems because she was not an aboriginal. The reason for these communication difficulties is not immediately apparent. Kaida had worked in the area of aboriginal education for more than a decade. The university's director of Native Studies, James Dempsey, a blood Indian, responded that if native students believed that "communications are better with a native and when a non-native is appointed, there is an automatic barrier" (*Alberta Report*, 14 October 1996) – an argument that might equally apply to the concerns of professed anti-Semites for ethnically compatible service provision. Dempsey had succeeded Richard Price to the director's position in 1992, when the latter was "purged," in part because he was non-Indian (ibid.).

In subsequent negotiations with the Academic Staff Association the university agreed that "judging an employee on the basis of group membership when that had not been a criterion in hiring was unfair." Both sides agreed that in other circumstances membership in a particular "historically disadvantaged group" could be a prerequisite for employment. The incident illustrates both the way in which preferential policies reinforce ethnic separation and the collapse of any commitment to merit or an insistence on the right of individuals to be judged on that basis.

ABELLA'S LEGACY: ENTRENCHING RACIAL DIVISION

The logic of funding service provision through ethnic-specific organizations or through organizations that seek to differentiate their potential clientele on the basis of skin colour is to deter assimilation. Equally, the benefits that may be claimed through preferential hiring measures encourage individuals to continue to adhere to a racial identity. The existence of such measures appears, simultaneously, to confirm the view that such an identity carries with it the need for legislated protection against the prejudices of fellow citizens.

The Abella report and subsequent legislation resulted in significant growth in the preferential hiring industry. The government required bureaucrats to collect the data necessary for implementing and monitoring policy. Companies seeking to comply with the legislation depended on a growing number of human resources equity personnel and on specialist outside consultants. As in the United States, those who found careers in the industry sought ways to expand business opportunities. It is the nature of such programs that the problems they address turn out, on examination, to be far worse than anyone suspected, the available resources too few, the remedies too limited. Pressure immediately began to build for more resources and stronger, more extensive legislation.

Further expansion could also be pursued by giving attention to new jurisdictions, provincial and municipal. Perceived weaknesses in federal legislation might be used to shape ever more draconian provincial legislation – a development that was to reach its nadir with the Rae government in Ontario. At the municipal level, most notably in Toronto, local politicians were quick to see electoral advantages in promising to support preferential hiring for key ethnic constituencies and in channelling tax dollars to groups claiming to represent ethnic constituencies or other identity groups.

8

Lies, Damn Lies, and
Federal Employment Equity Data

> Long and painful experience has taught me one great principle
> in managing business or other people, viz., if you want to
> inspire confidence, give plenty of statistics. It does not matter
> that they should be accurate, or even intelligible, so long as
> there is [sic] enough of them.
>
> Lewis Carroll, in Coren, 1995

THE FEDERAL VIEW

A review of the federal government's contribution to the debate over
employment equity reveals a consistent pattern: statistical data are mis-
represented; evidence challenging the assumptions on which preferential
hiring is based is ignored; exaggeration is endemic. The federal government, politicians and civil servants alike, have systematically distorted
evidence in pursuit of the claim that gross discrimination is the norm and
ever-increasing intervention the answer. In doing so the government has
promoted a profoundly inaccurate view of the Canadian labour market.

The official federal view is given unequivocal expression in a guide
on employment equity provided to employers who are expected to
comply with federal legislation. Under the heading, "Why Employment
Equity Is Needed," employers are advised:

There is ample evidence in all sectors of society that equal access to employment has been denied to members of certain groups because of their sex, racial
or ethnic characteristics, or disability ... Women, aboriginal peoples, visible
minorities and persons with disabilities face significant but different disadvantages in employment. Some of these include high unemployment, occupational
segregation, pay inequities and limited opportunities for career progress
(Employment and Immigration 1991: 8).

What is notable is the sweeping nature of the claims. The problem exists in "all sectors," discrimination is active as employment is "denied," the groups face "high unemployment." In contrast, the data portray a much more complex picture. In federally regulated industries the government's own figures indicate that 8.24 per cent of the work-force covered by the Employment Equity Act were visible minority members, compared to 9.1 per cent of the total Canadian labour force in the 1991 census. Visible minority men and women working full time both earned 96.5 per cent of what all men and women in the federally regulated work-force earned (HRD 1995: 31). That this group includes a very large number of recent immigrants with a shorter history in the Canadian labour market might suggest considerable success in a tight labour market. The proportion of visible minority employees had in fact increased by more than 50 per cent from 5 per cent in 1987 to 8.24 per cent in 1994 (ibid.: Table 6).

The 1995 HRD Employment Equity Annual Report, covering federally regulated industries, contained a statement directly contradicting the government's claim that in *all sectors* racial and ethnic groups are being denied employment: "Over the years, the share of hirings of members of visible minorities has systematically been higher than the group's representation in the workforce, and their share of terminations has been lower than the group's representation" (ibid.: 30). As well, visible minorities comprised 8.24 per cent of all employees but 11.12 per cent of promotions (ibid.: Table 10).

Visible minorities, as a group, experience higher levels of unemployment. But the conclusion that this is a function of discrimination is tendentious, as again the age and length of experience in the labour market need to be considered, in addition to such central factors as qualification and skill levels. If race is the decisive factor, it might be expected to effect all visible minority groups. Census data for 1991 (excluding Atlantic Canada) indicate that the unemployment rate stood at 9.0 per cent. Visible minorities as a whole experienced an unemployment rate of 12.1 per cent but the level for the constituent groups varied. The unemployment rate for those of Chinese ethnic origin, at 8.2 per cent, was lower than the Canadian average. In contrast, the West Asian/Arab group had a rate of 16.1 per cent (Canadian Heritage 1994b: 3). If visibility is a key issue, this is a surprising outcome, for the group West Asian/Arab fall in the generic category "caucasian" and include many who in common-sense terms have no great "visibility" relative to other Canadians of Mediterranean ancestry. Other ethnic groups that had large numbers of new immigrants had higher than average levels of unemployment: 10.5 per cent for Greek Canadians, 10.4 per cent for Portuguese Canadians. Length of residence in Canada and area of settlement could both be expected to influence unemployment patterns. "The low participation rates and high unemployment rates for Latin Americans and South East Asians may relate to their recent arrival in Canada," suggests Kelly: "over half of their populations arrived during the 1980s. In addition, many Latin Americans and South East Asians as well as West Asians and Arabs, lived in the Montreal CMA in 1991, where unemployment was higher than in Canada's other two largest CMAS. In the week before the 1991 Census, 11 per cent of the non-visible minority population living in Montreal were unemployed, compared with 9 per cent of those in Vancouver and 7 per cent of those in Toronto" (Kelly 1995: 7).

Unemployment levels are strongly influenced by language capacity. Analysis of 1991 census data found that among female immigrants who arrived between 1986 and 1991, unemployment levels were 25.8 per cent, while among those who spoke English the level was 16.4 per cent. Overall, more recent immigrants exhibited significantly higher unemployment levels than longer established immigrants (*Ottawa Citizen*, 11 January 1997).

Occupational segregation might seem to suggest parallels with apartheid; certainly in the mantra of the employment equity industry it appears that disproportionate concentrations, whether characterized by race or gender, are prima facie evidence of discrimination. In contrast, as we have noted, data on the occupational distribution of ethnic groups suggests that disproportionate representation in certain sectors is the norm not the exception, and is not readily attributable to discrimination. Italians and Portuguese workers are heavily represented in the construction sector, Greeks in the service sector, blacks in the medicine and health sector, Chinese in natural sciences, engineering, and mathematics. The diversity of the experience of visible minorities is clear from any review of the data (Policy Coordination and Strategic Planning 1994). What is most striking is that the federal government should distribute such a demonstrably inaccurate document to employers. The document is illustrative of a pervasive willingness to make inflammatory claims regarding labour market discrimination, even where the government's own research indicates that such claims are demonstrably false.

SEARCHING FOR GENDER DISADVANTAGE
IN THE FEDERAL PUBLIC SERVICE:
BENEATH THE VENEER

Treasury Board President Pat Carney established the Task Force on Barriers to Women in the Public Service in September 1988. The task force, set up four years after the Abella report, is indicative of the ability of feminist activists to maintain a continuing focus on the alleged discrimination faced by women. Yet the need for further federal measures to secure women's equality in the public service was not immediately obvious. A study reported in the annual collection *How Ottawa Spends* reviewed departmental assessments of women's representation in twenty-one federal departments including issues such as competition for promotion and performance appraisals and found the "staffing process in government departments has generally not discriminated against women in the recent past." In regard to promotion the federal government was "a model employer" (Swimmer and Gollesch 1986: 246–7).

Carney's task force produced a four-volume report *Beneath the Veneer*, which purported to document the continuing barriers faced by women in the public service. The task force based its approach on the assumption that any statistical evidence indicating under-representation of women in particular occupational categories, over-representation in other categories, and concentration in the lower levels constituted proof that equity had yet to be achieved. The task force defined its objective as a "balance of gender" at every level. It faced some difficulties in making its case since, while women were disproportionately concentrated in certain occupational groups and in the lower grades, the evidence of widespread discriminatory practices was hard to find. A range of other factors may account for such differences, including seniority or length of time in the work force, occupational aspirations, and level of formal qualification.

The task force set the scene with an eclectic mishmash of statistics intended to demonstrate the national scale of discrimination. In fact they were more convincing as evidence that task force members were happy with any figures, so long as they pointed to the right conclusion. The demonstration of discrimination depends on the comparison of groups whose relevant labour market characteristics are similar. If group members share such important factors as age, level of qualification, length of service, hours worked per week, and occupational aspirations, then some conclusion might be drawn from statistics documenting unequal labour market earnings or status. The task force instead preferred to orient its audience to the debate by use of statistics which, while at first glance striking, fail to stand up.

Readers are informed that earnings of women clerical workers, employed full time in 1988, were only 73 per cent of the average salaries of men employed full time as clerical workers. Could such a discrepancy be explained by the lower average hours of work of the female clerical workers, their shorter length of time in the work force or differences in relative qualifications? These factors are not considered.

Other studies have shown that in general women who work "full time" work shorter hours than men. The rapid growth in female employment suggests that female workers will not only be disproportionately younger than male workers but will also have less labour force experience – both factors that have a major effect on earning levels.

The task force displays an equally cavalier attitude in its comparison of the earnings of male and female graduates: "A woman with a university degree, working full-time for a full year, earned an average (in 1988) of 72.3 per cent of the average earnings of a man with the same education and a full-time job" (Edmonds *et al.* 1990a: 11). Readers who were still insufficiently shocked were also informed that a woman with a post-secondary certificate or diploma, working full-time for a year in 1988, earned less than a man working full-time with only Grade 8 education or less.[1] This is a truly striking contrast, which appears to confirm the claims of pervasive discrimination. Closer examination suggests that in fact the comparison is useful only in providing an aura of legitimacy to the task force's wider polemic. The comparison of a group containing disproportionate numbers of older male workers with a group containing a disproportionate number of younger female workers tells us more about the differentials attributable to age than to gender. Certainly the contrast illustrates a disregard for meaningful statistical analysis. Government task forces with multimillion dollar budgets might reasonably be expected to use such basic statistical techniques as age standardization to ensure that like is indeed being compared with like.

The task force does not compare similar groups of workers in which the only significant difference is gender but groups in which the primary difference may lie in the time of entry into the labour market. The last twenty years has seen a profound change in the experience of labour market entrants at all levels. The prospects of those who entered the work-force with grade 8 in the 1950s, in a period of relatively full employment and sustained growth in real wages, were markedly different than those faced by their counterparts today. Women's labour force participation has risen rapidly, a point noted by the task force. In 1975 44 per cent of Canadian women worked outside their homes, compared to 58 per cent in 1989 (Edmonds *et al.* 1990a: 8). This rise has occurred at a time when the incomes of new labour market entrants have declined. The average employment earnings of a high school-educated man fell 27 per cent from 1979–1993, a result of growing unemployment and declining real wages. For women in the same group the number employed increased but average employment earnings fell 12 per cent (Statistics Canada, *The Daily*, 5 September 1995: 5).

The impact of age is readily illustrated. Males in full-time full-year employment in the 15–24 age group earned an average of $22,783 in 1993 compared to $45,241 for the 45–54 age group (Statistics Canada, Cat. 13-217). What is driving the disparity is the much less favourable labour market faced by younger entrants and the overwhelming power of seniority in enhancing incomes and protecting the jobs of older workers: "In the mid-1970s, families headed by a person under 25 had a median income of about 80 per cent of that enjoyed by all families. Since that time, their situation has deteriorated almost without respite, until by 1992 they had a median income of only 54 per cent of the median income of all families" (Child Poverty Action Group *et al.* 1994: 8).

If labour market discrimination against women is pervasive, it should affect single women, not simply married women, yet Statistics Canada data demonstrate no difference between the earnings of single female graduates and single male graduates. Recent data reflect little difference between the earnings of contemporary male and female graduates. Analysis of three PHD cohorts found no difference in male and female earnings. What of the fabled advantage of males with Grade 8 education? If the narrower comparison is made between women with university degrees in full time employment, and males with Grade 8 or less in 1993, the women made $40,669 compared to $29,127 for the male group (Wannell and Caron 1994b, Statistics Canada, Cat. 13-217). Age standardization would substantially increase the difference.

The task force's misrepresentation of the labour market experience of male high school dropouts and female graduates is not surprising. This egregious example is a favourite. In a 1993 article, Maureen O'Neil, former general secretary of the Canadian Human Rights Commission, cites the same figure in a lament for women's continuing subjugation (O'Neil 1993: 317). Again the figure is offered as though it is nothing less than a clear measure of "income inequalities."

Examination of labour market data indicates that marital status, not gender, is the more important predictor of earning disparities. Income differentials for unattached women are much smaller than for women with spouses. Overall, single women between the ages of 15 and 64 earned 85.6 per cent of male earnings. In the 25–44 age group the differential (97 per cent) is much narrower (Statistics Canada 1995a: 84). This stands in contrast to the 72 per cent female to male earnings ratio for all workers in 1993. As we have noted, comparison of the earnings of single women with single men show only small differences.

The task force approach to statistical analysis of the situation of women in the federal public service was equally facile. The task force encountered considerable difficulty in finding the empirical data to support its agenda. The absence of convincing evidence of gender discrimination in the contemporary practices of the civil service forced the task force to use global labour market statistics, in which claims of discrimination ultimately depended on the assertion that equity demanded women be represented equally at every level. The fact that historically, when fewer women were in the labour force, men had predominated ensured that the use of global figures appeared to confirm the continuing marginalization of women. The task force accepted that some change had taken place; current practices were increasing the representation of women, but the pace was too slow.

The creation of an "equity index" sought to invest the task force's findings with an aura of mathematical precision. The index measured the representation of women at each level in an occupational hierarchy. A mathematical formula was devised which weighted representation at particular levels and permitted the creation of a scale in which equitable representation was reflected in a score of 100. A score below 100 was said to indicate that women were "compressed" in the lower levels. The index may measure representation, but the problem arises in the inference that this is relevant to the discussion of "barriers." If women are overwhelmingly represented in recruitment into positions demanding lower qualifications or are disproportionately concentrated among recent recruits, the score will inevitably be less than 100. Males in the federal civil service are disproportionately represented in the groups with higher qualifications. The Statistics Canada survey of the federal work force, commissioned by the task force, cast some light on these questions. Men constituted 67 per cent of those who had graduated with a Bachelor's degree, 73 per cent of those with a Master's degree and 86 per cent of those with a doctorate (Edmonds et al. 1990b: 87).

A more effective measure of discrimination depends on the study of the progress of similar cohorts of men and women over time. Statistics Canada commissioned a range of cohort studies for the task force. In the face of objections from the task force, the consultants who undertook the studies insisted that age and experience be taken into account in measuring outcomes.[2] The studies demonstrated no general pattern of gender discrimination. In the lower paid cohorts men gained slightly higher pay increases over the ten year period 1978–87 than women, 26 per cent compared to 20 per cent; but no similar trend was observed in the intermediate cohorts. An examination of management cohorts found that female managers had experienced more rapid promotion and a slightly higher growth in salaries than male managers.

Among the factors that characterized women who were "rapid advancers" was the fact that they were more likely to belong to a visible minority (Edmonds et al. 1990a: 51). This would appear to contradict the claim that visible minority women are doubly disadvantaged – a claim that continues to inform Treasury Board employment equity policy (Treasury Board 1995: 22). In common with other findings which run counter to the wisdom of orthodoxy, this had no effect on subsequent considerations of employment equity. The Consultation Group on Employment Equity for women, set up in the wake of the task force report, announced that it was actively considering the situation of "doubly disadvantaged" women, including visible minorities (Consultation Group 1992: 17).

In addition to analysing existing employment patterns the task force commissioned Statistics Canada to survey 10 per cent of public servants to investigate perceived "barriers" to progress. This survey, like the cohort studies, raises substantive doubts about the discriminatory assumptions that underpin the task force's approach. Respondents were asked why they thought they might have missed out on a promotion in the last three years; if discrimination against female personnel is widespread, this question might have been expected to identify this barrier. The most common "first most important factor" identified concerned the views of respondents' managers: 7,876 for example, reported that their manager or supervisor did not want to replace them. Gender discrimination ("I am a woman") was reported by 801 women as the most important factor. This compares to 1,517 men who identified this as the major barrier to their promotion ("I am a man"). A further 241 women were categorized as responding that they "wanted a job for which they would not normally hire a woman," and thirteen men responded that they "wanted a job for which they would not normally hire a man." When the first, second, and third most important factors are combined, and the categories that refer explicitly to the respondent's gender (I am a man) are combined with the responses that identified the gender associated with the position sought (would not normally hire a woman), 6,932 female respondents and 6,288 men identified gender as one of the reasons they missed out on promotion. In total, 7 9 per cent of all female respondents and 5.4 per cent of male respondents identified gender as one barrier to promotion.

These figures are not notably high. Indeed, given the repeated focus on the alleged disadvantage faced by women in the labour market, the results are surprising. The barriers women perceived as being attributable to gender were lower than those attributed to membership of a particular linguistic group. The survey explicitly informed respondents that it was part of a study of barriers to women. Many of the possible responses focused on gender issues, yet a higher number of women (8.4 per cent) mentioned their membership of a language group as a barrier to promotion ("I am an anglophone," "I am a francophone") than mentioned gender (7.9 per cent).

Respondents were also asked if they had sought a developmental opportunity in the past three years and to offer reasons why they were refused. Again more men than women, 648 compared to 414, identified gender as "the first most important factor." Overall 3,328 women and 3,191 men identified gender as *one* of the reasons for refusal.

Pervasive discrimination might be expected to lead to demands for more rigorous employment equity legislation. Yet when respondents were asked what they thought would help them "most" in overcoming possible barriers to their career advancement, only 310 women identified "reinforcement of the employment equity program." In contrast 3,107 men identified abolition of the employment equity program as the factor that would help them most. These findings might have given pause to any thoughtful researcher, for if they indicate that discrimination exists, they also cast doubt on the proposition that this is the defining experience of *women* in the public service.

The survey asked respondents a number of attitudinal questions. The conclusions drawn by the task force are worth noting: "a surprising degree of support for sexist attitudes showed up ... On stereotyping, 65 per cent of men and 52 per cent of women agreed that "some jobs are more suited to the skills men have, while some jobs are more suited to women." Most people disagreed with the statement that "men make better managers than women do" but 20 per cent of men and 11 per cent of women supported it. The suggestion in an official government report that those who believe women and men may have differing labour market skills are sexist is an example of how far politically correct thinking has penetrated the Ottawa bureaucracy. The degree of arrogance that allows a group of civil servants to define a majority of their colleagues (including 52 per cent of women) as sexist is astonishing. Is it sexist to speculate that men may continue to dominate occupations such as mining and that, given free choice, many women will be quite happy to allow them the privilege? Are all differences between the genders to dissolve once equity has been engineered?

The task force compensated for the weakness of its empirical evidence regarding gender based discrimination with a lengthy treatment of anecdotal evidence. Some one-third of the final report was devoted to such evidence. Much of this consisted of statements by women regarding the difficulties of receiving equal treatment:

I still meet men who are astonished by the level of my capabilities on the job. Some have made it clear that their astonishment is because I am a woman.

You have to make sure that you behave in an acceptable manner by a man's standards. We are still in a male-dominated era.

These accounts proved an important selling point, particularly among senior managers, many of whom may have given little attention to the statistical data but were justifiably concerned by some of the attitudes that were portrayed. Undoubtedly, in the public service as elsewhere, there are some who hold prejudicial attitudes. The impact of those attitudes cannot be measured by anecdotal evidence, no matter how detailed. The task force in effect sought to bury its weak empirical data in a mass of carefully selected material portraying women as continually confronted with a work environment dominated by hostile male values and attitudes. But other data sources confirm that women do not face significant contemporary barriers in the public service. Data for 1991 and 1992, compiled by the Public Service Commission, indicate that the proportion of women recruited into various occupational categories generally exceeded that of their "labour market availability," as measured by the numbers in relevant occupations in the Canadian labour market.[3]

The commission failed to standardize for age or length of service (factors that would significantly favour males in promotion). However, women's promotion share was only slightly lower than their "internal availability." In the scientific and professional category, for example, their internal availability was 32.4 per cent and their promotion share 31.8 per cent in 1991 and 33 per cent in 1992 (Public Service Commission 1993: 37). In 1993–94 54.5 per cent of those who were promoted were women, though they constituted only 47 per cent of the staff (Treasury Board 1995: 24).

Faced with evidence from cohort studies of promotions and recruitment that fail to support the proposition that women face contemporary discrimination, federal employment equity activists simply fell back on global statistics. The Consultation Group on Employment Equity for Women, established by Treasury Board in the wake of the task force report, gave up further attempts to measure the relative progress of contemporary employees in favour of the regurgitation of statistics showing the "over-representation" of men in the upper echelons of the public service (Consultation Group 1992). The preponderance of males in the senior positions is ensured, as we have noted, by the fact that they predominated in earlier recruitment cohorts.

THE REWARDS OF "DISADVANTAGE"

To outsiders employment equity initiatives in the public sector often seem indistinguishable from other measures taken by public sector workers to enhance their pay and benefits. In the name of equity, salaries are increased, pay scales rewritten, more generous leaves provided, and fully funded scholarships offered to those deemed disadvantaged enough to secure such advantages. The Canada Mortgage and Housing Corporation was identified by the Consultation Group on Employment Equity for Women as one of a number of "best practice" case studies. Among the innovations highlighted was the provision of five days of paid annual leave for family related responsibilities. Transport Canada, another "best practice" agency, provides fully paid educational leave, a network of employee assistance counsellors, and no less than the equivalent of nineteen full-time positions to the employment equity function (Consultation Group 1993).

VISIBLE MINORITIES
IN THE FEDERAL PUBLIC SERVICE

The Visible Minority Consultation Group on Employment Equity was established by Treasury Board in 1991 to advise on a range of issues regarding recruitment and promotion of visible minorities. The work of the group is primarily of interest in revealing the shaky foundations on which policy is based. The group was made up of eleven senior civil servants, all of them members of a visible minority. They quickly embraced the politics of identity, heralding the VMCG success in bringing together public service representatives of diverse cultures and races to give "reality to the McLuhan vision of a 'global village'" (VMCG 1992: 2). The group was less enthusiastic about those Canadian members of the global village who were not members of a visible minority. The first report noted Canada's history of racism and what it saw as the contemporary legacy: "In researching the mandated items, the Group encountered many beliefs, attitudes and behaviours that are inimical to employment equity. It became clear that these patterns of thought are deeply imbedded in our culture. We believe these patterns of thought are among the most serious impediments to the equitable treatment of visible minorities within the Public Service of Canada" (ibid.).

This is a disturbing and sweeping indictment, suggesting a federal civil service in which racist attitudes are deeply entrenched. Unfortunately the reader has to take this on faith, as the report offers no further insight into the specifics of the patterns of thought that have been detected. Readers who are dubious about the group's research are not likely to be reassured by the claim about the future of public service recruitment. Highlighted on the next page, it would cause some surprise to demographers: "By the year 2000, 50 per cent of all applicants will come from visible minority groups" (ibid.: 3).

The group considered the problems of data collection through self-identification but curiously make no reference to the survey of 10 per cent of the public service conducted for the Task Force on Barriers to Women. This survey found that the self-identification process had understated visible minority representation in the public service by 50 per cent (Treasury Board 1994b: 10). The finding was not surprising: a number of sources point to a tendency for employer generated statistics to under-represent designated group membership, with the exception of women. Collection of figures on gender is normally straightforward whether from personnel data or self report surveys; many respondents will be less willing to provide information on disability or ethnicity. Such data collection is also affected by the wording of the questionnaire and by return levels. Employers who secure inadequate responses must make a judgment on whether the returned questionnaires represent the distribution in the company as a whole.

One expert, writing in the industry publication *Managing Diversity*, suggested that the problems of under-reporting in a system of voluntary self-identification were "insoluble." Many visible minorities, it was suggested, rejected the idea of being hyphenated-Canadians; national pride in being Canadian made under-reporting a common occurrence (Juriansz 1993). Treasury Board has acknowledged the difficulty this poses: "there is general agreement within the public service that some members of designated groups choose not to self-identify. Yet self-identification remains essential for the Treasury Board to judge progress in terms of numbers" (Treasury Board 1994a: 2).

Statistics Canada analyst Ted Wannell noted the seven-fold difference in the representation of people with disabilities in the agency's employment, depending on whether the data were collected from the information on personnel files or from the Statistics Canada Employee Opinion Survey (Wannell undated). The survey undertaken for the Barriers task force study found there were two and a half times as many civil servants with disabilities as the number who had self-identified (Treasury Board 1994b: 10). (The wording of any question on ethnicity will also have a strong influence on responses; questions which offer a respondent the option of multiple responses will result in different figures than a question which offers only one option, since many Canadians have a mixed ethnic background (Wannell undated).)

The VMCG placed considerable emphasis on the fact that visible minority representation in the federal public service at 3.6 per cent, in 1991, was lower than in the country as a whole; but the group failed to ask a number of important questions. If the survey undertaken for the Barriers task force is accurate, the actual representation is around 5.4 per cent. This compares to 1986 census data which showed that 6.3 per cent of the work-force belonged to visible minority groups. The number of visible minorities in Canada had increased by 1991, but it is unrealistic to assume that the composition of federal employment will immediately mirror major demographic changes. Turnover in the federal government is relatively low, and in the absence of significant increases in the number of employees it is reasonable to anticipate a significant time-lag between federal employment figures and Canada's changing ethnic composition. The lag will be increased where large numbers of new immigrants are fluent in neither French or English, and there is a contraction in government employment.[4]

The group failed to consider these issues but apparently attributes the disparity in representation to discrimination. The group also noted the low representation of visible minorities at the management level suggesting that this resulted from a "visibility ceiling" (VMCG 1992: 10). Again what is remarkable, in a document endorsed by eleven senior civil servants, is the absence of any critical review of the data. Central to the current management structure of the federal public service is the historic composition of the recruitment intake. In order to ascertain whether there is any prima facie evidence of discrimination, a minimum requirement would be to look at the length of service of visible minority employees relative to the public service population as a whole. The report fails to ask or answer the question of whether visible minorities are promoted more slowly than similarly qualified whites with similar lengths of service. The Barriers report, it will be recalled, actually identified visible minority women as more likely to be promoted.

A second report issued by the group the next year started with the astonishing claim that the previous report had offered "evidence of systemic discrimination against visible minorities within the employment practises of the Public Service of Canada" (VMCG 1993: v). The conclusion to be drawn from this must be that either the group has failed to understand the meaning of systemic discrimination or it had failed to acquaint itself with the basic research principles necessary to establish whether or not it might exist. Leaving no doubt as to the magnitude of the challenge that the group addressed, the foreword advised readers: "We submit our findings during an upsurge of racial and ethnic violence throughout the world. People everywhere seem to be retreating into ever smaller orbits of tribe, race, culture and geography ... There is disquieting evidence within the Public Service of Canada of those very biases that underlie so much disharmony in the global village" (VMCG 1993: v).

The group broke new ground with the suggestion that some women faced "triple jeopardy: visibility, gender and unassertive behaviour." This was said to be a particular problem for Asian women (ibid.: 4). The search for new victim attributes is consistent with the thrust of employment equity activists, but the allocation of a common characteristic to women from a wide range of cultural, linguistic, religious, and geographic backgrounds is notable. In any other context such racial stereotyping might invite serious strictures. Elsewhere, observing the fact that visible minority members (notwithstanding the claimed systemic discrimination) are disproportionately located among those who earn $45,000 a year or over, the group attributes this to the large number who are in the scientific and professional group. What accounts for this? The group offers another stereotype, "the often recognized pursuit of academic excellence and qualifications among visible minorities" (ibid.: 12).

Apparently unaware of the contradiction with its views on the pursuit of excellence, the group gave voice to a theme more prominently found in deliberations on employment equity in the Ontario Public Service: "credentialism." Yet the requirement for a particular qualification does not appear to be inherently discriminatory; indeed, it might be thought that such requirements increased the probability that appointment would be made on merit.

The attraction of the attack on credentialism is two-fold. Firstly it increases the latitude for appointment on the basis of a desirable group characteristic such as race or gender. Secondly, for current employees possessing such group characteristics, it removes potential barriers to promotion. In order to fit within the contemporary mantra it must be expressed in terms that (illogically) suggest a discriminatory consequence from the application of universal qualification requirements. The VMCG captured this well: "Visible minority women feel they were also unfairly winnowed out of some competitions because of the excessive 'credentialism' required to fill the respective positions" (ibid.: 4). Why this should affect visible minority women but not others is not explained.

The weakness of the VMCG's analysis does not deter sweeping conclusions. What are required are not only measures to increase the representation of visible minorities in management training but cross-cultural training for the whole public service: "for managers, for staff within the employment equity function, for the colleagues of visible minority individuals and for the visible minority individuals themselves" (ibid.: 18).

The VMCG reports may have lacked empirical detail, sociological insight and common sense, but they were not without influence.

Appearing before a Canadian Human Rights Commission tribunal considering allegations of discrimination at Health Canada, Nan Weiner, testifying as an "expert witness," relied on three reports in her identification of supposed "barriers" faced by visible minorities. One was American, the other two were those of the VMCG, which appear to have been accepted by the tribunal as though they actually had some scholarly basis (CHRC 1997a).

The Canadian Human Rights Commission has been a particularly energetic protagonist in claiming pervasive discrimination in the public service and offering an enthusiastic embrace to those who attribute their thwarted career ambitions to discrimination. We return to the commission's habitually meretricious statistical legerdemain below; here we will confine our concern to its report, *Visible Minorities and the Public Service of Canada*, prepared by Carleton University sociologist John Samuel. News coverage, notably on CBC Radio, suggested that the study had provided evidence of extensive "barriers" to the recruitment and promotion of racial minorities in the public service. CBC listeners were also provided with news clips featuring visible minority public servants who were confident that only their group membership stood in the way of the promotions they knew they merited (7 February 1997).

Samuel's study was a curious affair. The claim that the Canadian government pursues discriminatory employment policies is explosive, reflecting on the motives and practices of public servants and offering apparent endorsement to the views of those who claim Canada is a society in which racism is rampant. The publication of such claims could be expected to result from exhaustive investigation that demonstrated, beyond any reasonable doubt, that similarly qualified racial minorities experienced consistently lower levels of success in job applications compared to other candidates. Equally, public servants who are members of a visible minority must experience lower promotion rates than others with similar qualifications and lengths of service. Anyone looking for such evidence in the CHRC report will be disappointed.

Cohort studies, comparing groups with similar characteristics differentiated by race or gender, represent a widely recognized research technique for measuring discrimination. It was used, for example, as we noted, in the 1984 Task Force on Barriers to Women in the Public Service. In contrast Samuel preferred to rest his case on questionnaires probing qualitative issues, which encouraged respondents to record perceived grievances. In a context in which visible minorities in the public service had been repeatedly encouraged to perceive themselves as victims of discrimination, Samuel in essence asked his visible minority respondents whether they thought their visibility had hindered the achievement of their career aspirations and whether they would like to see stronger preferential hiring, training, and promotion programs. In the circumstances what is surprising is not that many replied in the affirmative but that some did not.

The study's authors did not design the research to ensure a representative sample. Among many methodological problems, the authors report, it was "not possible to calculate a response rate." Participating departments distributed the questionnaires through a variety of differing mechanisms, while individuals also contacted the study's authors directly, requesting copies. It is in the nature of such exercises that those responding to and requesting copies are likely to have a disproportionate interest in the issues under consideration. Measuring crime victimization, for example, by such an approach would produce a grossly inflated figure, since victims would be predisposed to respond.

The problem is evident in the study's treatment of promotions; visible minority respondents, it reports, received fewer promotions than those in what the study authors designate as a "control group." It is unclear how this group was constructed or why it is less than one third the size of that of the visible minority; nonetheless, readers are left in no doubt that promotion shares was the subject "uppermost in the minds of almost all visible minority participants in the group discussions." In the context of federal downsizing, this is not surprising, but do visible minorities in fact receive a disproportionately low share? Not mentioned in the text but buried in the tables at the back is a global figure for promotion shares in the public service. In 1995, when those who had designated themselves members of a visible minority comprised 4.1 per cent of the public service, they received 4.1 per cent of all promotions, even though, as a group, they had shorter lengths of service.

Was 1995 an exceptional year? Surely the chief commissioner of the CHRC, Michelle Falardeau-Ramsay, would not endorse a report claiming pervasive disadvantage for visible minorities in promotions in the public service without some reasonably convincing evidence? Certainly, it would be reasonable to assume, the Human Rights Commission would not simply rely on an egregious exercise, in which visible minorities were encouraged to attribute their frustrated mobility plans to race? In 1991, when self-identified visible minorities constituted 3.6 per cent of the public service, they received 3.9 per cent of the promotions; in 1993 with 3.8 per cent of positions, they received 4.0 per cent. (No figures are available for 1992, or for other earlier years.) In 1994, again with 3.8 per cent of positions, they received 3.9 per cent of promotions (CHRC 1997a: 93, Table 1 and Table 2).

The absence of empirical evidence has not deterred visible minority public servants from attributing frustrated career goals to discrimination – a more attractive explanation than limited competence. And, whereas downsizing or wider failures to reward merit afford no easy remedy, attributing such frustrations of ambition to discrimination legitimates the implementation of policies affording opportunities to those blessed with the requisite designated group status, at the expense of their less "disadvantaged" colleagues.

To buttress its less than convincing data, the Samuel study, like the Barriers to Women report, makes great use of the anecdotal accounts of those who claim to find the federal government an uncomfortable place. The study's statistics fail to support the case. A section headed "Comfort in the Environment of the Workplace" (ibid.: 46–7) offers the unambiguous conclusion that visible minority employees were less comfortable and proceeds at some length to detail the alleged discomforts. The questionnaire data indicate that 17.5 per cent of visible minorities replied in the negative to a question on comfort levels, compared to 15.8 per cent of the control group. Given the way in which respondents were recruited and the continual focus on racial grievance, these data provide no support for the study conclusion.

Other questions afford equally little backing to claims that the experience of racial minorities is distinctive, though they raise concerns about public service morale. Asked if working conditions were conducive to higher levels of achievement, 63.4 per cent of visible minorities replied in the negative, compared to 67.6 per cent of the control group. Asked if the "best qualified" receive promotions, 76.6 per cent of visible minority respondents replied in the negative, as did 74.3 per cent of the control group.

Not surprisingly, visible minority respondents were overwhelmingly in favour of measures that would provide them with a competitive edge in an increasingly tight labour market. Of the self-selected visible minority respondents, 67 per cent favoured such "special measures," as did a notable 26 per cent of the control group.

Samuel claimed, "evidence also indicates that the Canadian-born visible minority employees fare no better than their foreign-born counterparts" (CHRC 1997a: 67). It is difficult to know what "evidence" Samuel is referring to, as a review of some of the dubious reasons offered for the alleged disadvantage of visible minorities suggests that no case can be made in regard to those who are Canadian-born. At Canadian Heritage, for example, among the obstacles identified by visible minorities was "proficiency in the French language" (ibid.: 17). Focus group participants also raised bilingualism and "problems in terms of cultural differences" (ibid.: 27). Managers referred to the fact that "visible minority candidates do not respond in the same manner in interviews (with respect to eye contact, for example) and interpretation of answers is different" (ibid.: 52).

There may no doubt be specific issues for candidates and public servants who were raised outside Canada, but these are properly attributed to immigrant status, not visibility. Visible minorities in Canada are disproportionately concentrated in CMAs with above-average access to French immersion education programs. The suggestion that those who have graduated through the Canadian education system retain "cultural variations" that affect interview success is highly dubious. Samuel's claim that the Canadian-born "fare no better" is important in making the case that the public service is guilty of race-based discrimination which must be addressed through a variety of preferential recruitment, training, mentoring, and promotional programs. When Samuel, who immigrated to Canada from India thirty-six years ago, was interviewed by the *Globe and Mail* (which afforded entirely uncritical coverage to the study claims), he professed surprise "to learn from the study" that Canadian-born minorities do not fare any better than their foreign-born counterparts. "That really bothers me," he said, "because my children, born here, should have the same opportunities as everyone else" (8 February 1997). Samuel's study did not provide the evidence to support his conclusion, but his children could no doubt benefit from the preferential policies proposed.

The study, as is customary in the preferential hiring industry, made extensive reference to other reports that endorsed its perspective, notably those of the VMCG. Samuel's readers might assume that the VMCG reports bore evidence of some research: "The VMCG noted the "double Jeopardy" faced by visible minority women … The VMCG found that 'employment practices are believed by most visible minority employees interviewed to be unfair, to lack integrity, and to be racially biased'" (CHRC 1997a: 14–15). In fact, as we have seen, the reports are primarily of interest as evidence of the shoddy thinking that has characterized discussions of the issue at the federal level.

Samuel notes the existence of some problems with self-identification – remarkably, even in Canadian Heritage, a department obsessively preoccupied with the politics of identity; a 1996 survey found only 85 per cent of visible minorities had self-identified (ibid.: 16). Strikingly Samuel fails to draw any conclusion about what this may mean for actual representation in the public service, leaving readers to assume that the 4.1 per cent figure he cites reflects an accurate measure of current representation.

In a particularly egregious exercise he compares the record of the public service with the private sector, choosing as his example the Canadian banks which have been assiduous in recruiting visible minorities. Among the many unacknowledged differences in the two workforces is the higher turnover in the banking sector, the large number

of positions located in the CMAs where visible minorities are disproportionately resident, and the different qualification requirements.

Any reading of the study raises numerous questions about both the
methodology and the relationship of the findings to the conclusions
drawn by the CHRC. The most obvious one may be that the CHRC –
an organization that has spent many million dollars of taxpayers'
money and forced the federal government to spend many millions more
in a series of drawn-out tribunals alleging a variety of discriminatory
behaviour – has no understanding of the research required to evidence
discrimination. The CHRC has little concern as to how it dispenses
taxpayers' money and an apparently limitless propensity to issue
inflammatory charges of racial bias, without regard to the adequacy
of the evidence on which it bases its case.

Analysis of the situation of visible minorities within the federal
public service may owe more to fashionable polemics than scholarly
inquiry, but it has not been without effect. Many departments, including Canadian Heritage, provide official support to "visible minority
support groups," premised, it would appear, on the assumption that
such is the precarious condition of well-paid visible minorities in the
Canadian public service that they require the kind of therapeutic milieu
and continuing affirmation normally thought appropriate for those
such as battered women or recovering alcoholics. At CIDA the ten-
year-old Visible Minority Committee, with some seventy members, acts
as a lobby for the interests of visible minorities in the department. The
committee includes some whose blond hair and blue eyes might pose
a challenge to the most discerning bigot, but by reason of ethnic origin
and consequent designated group status, they have every right to
membership.

Many departments offer privileged access to training and promotion
opportunities to address the "historic disadvantage" faced by visible
minority public servants. This disadvantage has not yet been demonstrated, notwithstanding the considerable efforts expended on behalf
of Canadian taxpayers. Meanwhile, in the public sector, diversity
training, with its endorsement of grievance politics and its linked
portrayal of Canada as a society in which all but able-bodied, heterosexual white males face constant bigotry, is deeply entrenched.

FUN WITH NUMBERS:
CANADA'S HUMAN RIGHTS COMMISSION

Aside from the fact that the term "reverse discrimination"
implicitly admits a pattern of past discrimination, one must
question how far the pattern is really being reversed. Recent

figures suggest not far. In 1993, able-bodied white males, who represent forty-five per cent of the general labour force, received fifty-five per cent of hires into permanent full-time positions with employers coming under the Employment Equity Act. Far from falling behind, able-bodied white males appear to be getting a more than proportionate share of hiring.

Canadian Human Rights Commission, 1995

The Chief Commissioner of the Canadian Human Rights Commission (also) presented statistics indicating that in 1993 white able-bodied males received nearly 55 per cent of the hirings into full-time positions in this country. This number significantly exceeded their proportion in the labour market at that time, which was just under 45 per cent. The Chief Commissioner pointed out that when a group of people represent 45 of every 100 people available for work, but 55 are actually hired, it is difficult to see them as victims of reverse discrimination.

House of Commons, 1995

I continue to believe that Canadians are entitled to a fair and honest discussion of the merits and shortcomings of employment equity.

Max Yalden, chief commissioner,
Canadian Human Rights Commission,
"Letters," Globe and Mail, 14 March 1995

The statistics presented by the Canadian Human Rights Commission in support of Bill C64, which extended and strengthened federal employment equity legislation, appear at first glance to provide striking evidence of the advantage of able-bodied white males in the contemporary labour force. In the hands of the House of Commons committee reviewing the proposed legislation, it became evidence not of the experience of the 491,000 full-time workers covered by the Federal Employment Equity Act but a finding applied to the Canadian labour force as a whole. Selective evidence that misrepresents contemporary practices is adduced to strengthen the case for stronger legislative action and more resources for the commission. In the light of the commission's $18 million annual budget, high public profile, and penchant for pontificating on the perceived failings of those Canadians who pay its bills, a review of the statistics is instructive.

The Canadian labour force is made up of full-time *and* part-time workers. The Human Rights Commission conflates the two pools into one, then compares this with the full-time hires, a move that creates the appearance of gender imbalance since men outnumber women in the full-time pool.

The data from which the commission's figures were derived indicates that in industries covered by the act, designated group representation in full-time hirings, as compared to their representation in the total labour force, was: women 39.20 per cent (45.9 per cent), aboriginals 1.91 per cent (3.00 per cent), persons with disabilities 1.64 per cent (6.5 per cent) and visible minorities 8.15 per cent (9.1 per cent) (HRD 1994a: A-2, B-8). The most striking disparity is between the number of disabled hired and the proportion in the labour force. Since this is a group for which self-identification surveys fail to provide consistent and reliable data, no great credence can be given to this finding. The data on visible minorities may also under-report actual numbers. In 1988, the first year in which data were collected, 373 employers submitted reports, including 139 who included a textual commentary, and no less than 103 of these made reference to problems with self-identification surveys (Saveland 1993: 40).

Women and men are unequally divided between full-time and part-time employment. In 1994 80.7 per cent of employed men and 66.7 per cent of employed women were in full-time employment (Statistics Canada Labour Force Annual Averages 1994). Women made up no less than 69.4 per cent of all part-time workers; however, men working part-time were slightly more likely (37.4 per cent) than women (34.3 per cent) to give the failure to find a full-time job as the reason for part-time employment (Statistics Canada 1995a: 74). Overall male unemployment rates (10.8 per cent) were higher than female (9.9 per cent) (ibid.: 68).

Industries covered by the Employment Equity Act are not representative of Canadian industry as a whole. The industries include those in which women are heavily represented – notably banking and communications, and those in which they are not – federally regulated transportation and mining. This will have a significant impact on the gender balance in recruitment, as will changes in the relative recruitment in the different sectors. Women are over-represented in part-time work in industries regulated by the act. Overall women constituted 41.5 per cent of those holding full-time positions and 70 per cent of those holding part-time positions.

That the industries covered by the act are unrepresentative in their gender characteristics and cannot therefore be reasonably cited in support of the commission's claim of white male advantage is well known. A 1993 federal study on the labour market activity of designated groups noted: "Male employees outnumber female employees by 2–1 in the covered sector compared with a 55/45 split in the economy as a whole." (IDWGEED 1993: 42). The commission's statement is, in fact, simply an ideological polemic in support of further more invasive preferential hiring legislation and, of course, more resources for the CHRC.

Another measure of equity is the relative rate of promotions within the sector. The data on full-time recruitment were used by the then chief commissioner of the CHRC, Max Yalden, to support the view that progress towards equity was minimal. If discriminatory practices are prevalent they can be expected to impact on promotions to the detriment of the designated group members in employment. A comparison of the proportion of full-time promotions going to designated group members in 1993 in industries covered by the act, with their representation in the full-time work-force, provides no such evidence: women 54.08 per cent (full-time work-force representation 41.5 per cent), aboriginals 1.08 per cent (1.04 per cent), persons with disabilities 2.55 per cent (2.56 per cent), visible minorities 10.79 per cent (8.09 per cent) (HRD 1994a: B-9). Similar results were reported in other years. On this measure no designated group is disadvantaged, while women appear to enjoy a significant advantage. In contrast able-bodied white males were proportionately under-represented in promotions, holding 52 per cent of the full-time positions but receiving only 39 per cent of the promotions. It is notable that the Human Rights Commission report makes no comment on the significance of these findings.

Instead, the commission's statistical massage deflects attention away from the dire labour market situation faced by young males, precisely those who might be most likely to be seeking a "new hire." In 1994 no less than 18.5 per cent of males aged 15–24 were unemployed, compared to 14.3 per cent of women (Statistics Canada 1995a: 68). To the one in five young males who cannot find employment, notions of male privilege will have little salience.

The chair of the House of Commons Human Rights Committee, Dr Rey Pagtakhan, a former university professor of medicine, who, in 1996, became parliamentary secretary to the prime minister, not only misread CHRC commissioner Yalden's evidence, reporting that white able-bodied males received nearly 55 per cent of the hirings into *all* full-time positions in Canada – he also failed to understand other statistical evidence on discrimination. A Statistics Canada study of the labour market experience of visible minority, aboriginal, and disabled community college and university graduates found that visible minority graduates experienced somewhat higher unemployment levels, as did aboriginal college graduates but not aboriginal university graduates. However, "earnings of designated groups are very similar to the earnings of their classmates" (Wannell and Caron 1994a: i). The report caused some consternation among employment equity advocates in the public service since it failed to demonstrate pervasive discrimination. If discrimination is widespread, it should impact on earnings as well as employment levels and (in the case of aboriginals) on university as well as college graduates. Yet in the hands of the chair of the House of Commons Committee on Human Rights there is no ambivalence in the report's findings: "Obviously for the target groups indicated here, employment rates have remained lower. There is high unemployment. At the same time, the group earnings in fact are lower" (Minutes, 30 January 1995).

Pagtakhan made his comments while the committee was taking evidence from Human Resources and Development personnel. These included Syed Naseem, introduced to the committee as "a specialist in the area of statistics on designated groups in the labour market." Naseem failed to correct the inaccurate interpretation of the findings regarding earnings. Naseem first devalued the significance of the Wannell and Caron study, which now became "a very small sample of people graduating out of Canadian colleges." He then proceeded to confirm the inaccurate description of the report offered by Pagtakhan: "You are correct in saying designated group members have experienced employment disadvantage given the same level of education." The sample was not in fact "very small": rather, as Statistics Canada made clear in the report, it was "representative" of the 1990 graduates of Canadian universities and colleges university. There are a variety of possible explanations for the findings on employment levels, including the concentration of visible minority graduates in science studies, the restricted job market facing aboriginal community college graduates who live in remote communities, as well as the existence of discriminatory hiring practices. In contrast to the evidence offered by Syed Naseem on behalf of Human Resources and Development, the Statistics Canada study noted: "Given the equality of earnings, it is difficult to cite the unemployment disparity as unambiguous evidence of hiring discrimination" (Wannell and Caron 1994a: ii).

Commissioner Yalden categorically assured the House of Commons committee that "employment equity is not about quotas. A quota is an arbitrary number of positions in the workforce that must be filled regardless of whether qualified candidates exist for the job ... Targets make it clear what employers should be aiming for. They are not requirements for numbers of positions in the workforce that have to be met by hook or by crook" (Minutes, House of Commons Committee on Human Rights and the Status of Disabled Persons, 25:4, 31 January 1995). Curiously, when the CHRC tribunal delivered its verdict in a contentious case alleging discrimination at Health Canada, quotas were indeed imposed. The commission found that visible minorities experienced systemic discrimination which hindered their opportunities for promotion. The tribunal ordered that 18 per cent of all promotions in the next five years go to visible minorities.[5]

This might appear to be a quota. It certainly seemed that Health Canada was instructed to achieve it "by hook or by crook." The tribunal instructed Health Canada that, in any competition where a visible minority was a candidate, if the visible minority were not selected the hiring manager or selection board must write to the deputy minister or assistant deputy minister to explain why the visible minority candidates were not "found to be qualified." Twenty-five per cent of the positions in the ministry's Learning for Leadership programs were to be set aside for visible minorities. The tribunal set a similar quota for other training courses. What then of Yalden's concerns that quotas ignore the numbers of qualified candidates? The CHRC tribunal acknowledged that only 9 per cent of those who met promotion criteria were visible minorities (CHRC 1997b).

The Human Rights Commission has repeatedly assured Canadians that there can be no question of "reverse discrimination," the substitution of "one form of discrimination for another" (CHRC 1997c: 63). Yet the inevitable outcome of the tribunal ruling on Health Canada is overt discrimination against white employees in access to training and promotion opportunities.

The imposition of de facto quotas is also evident in CHRC-negotiated settlements. In a case alleging that the Department of Justice's hiring policies and practices created barriers to the employment of visible minority lawyers, the commission secured a commitment from the department to recruit at least 5 per cent visible minorities. In a settlement with Treasury Board Secretariat, which served as a model for fifteen other departments, the commission accepted a commitment that 3 per cent of all new hires be aboriginals (ibid.: 80–1).

The Human Rights Commission has shown a willingness to move far beyond the investigation of individual cases to intervention in wider debates. In its 1994 annual report it chided those who expressed concerns about immigration levels. In the commission's view, Canada includes "more than a sprinkling of racial, sexual and other biases." It cited in support of its claim "a persistent undertow of opposition to allegedly uncontrolled immigration from countries with 'different traditions,' a code phrase one suspects, for different racial make-up" (CHRC 1995: 14). The labelling as closet racists of those who had raised questions about the scale of immigration did not sit well with the Reform party. Reform critic Charles Strahl attacked the unctuous tone of the commission's interventions: "Instead of understanding that there are a variety of views that can be called legitimate, the Commission has taken an uncompromising stand on issues of extreme controversy in Canada, and thus just declares itself ideologically superior and directly opposed to the judgement of millions of Canadians who profoundly disagree" (Minutes, House of Commons Standing Committee on Human Rights and the Status of Disabled Persons, 45:12, 28 March, 1995).

The commission's report also served as a platform to air the commissioner's views on the debate over multiculturalism triggered by Neil Bissoondath's scathing attack on the promotion of hyphenated-Canadians. The commissioner disagreed.

Yalden used the opportunity provided by the release of the 1995 Annual Report to lecture the government on its failure to amend the Human Rights Act to add sexual orientation as a prohibited ground for discrimination (CHRC Communiqué 19 March 1996). When the Liberals responded by promising legislation, Yalden had no hesitation in telling Parliament how it should deal with the matter: "I don't think a free vote is appropriate" (*Globe and Mail* April 29, 1996). In the 1996 Annual Report the commission offered some insights into deficit reduction: "Rightly or wrongly, there is sometimes a perception that the 'hard' goals of fiscal probity and a vigorous economy may be less than fully compatible with the 'softer' goals of a fair, compassionate and harmonious society ... there was a suspicion that a continuing emphasis on deficit reduction and decentralization had once again proved the impossibility of serving both God and Mammon" (CHRC 1997c: 13). It is unclear what part of the commission's mandate might legitimate its involvement in such debates.

The CHRC has not confined itself to Canada[6]; 1995 found Yalden, a frequent traveller, in China where reporters were surprised to find Canada's human rights advocate curiously silent on the gross abuses which characterize China's ruling gerontocracy. Yalden had nothing to say on summary executions but praised China's progress on women's rights – this reflected the commission's curious ideological myopia, which results in a division between wider human rights such as free speech, and so-called "equality rights" that apparently exist in a discrete universe. It is also illustrative of the power of "relativism" – the assumption that all cultures are equally acceptable and that, in consequence, we cannot simply apply western standards to countries like China.

In a letter to the *Globe and Mail* defending his visit against those who argued that his presence had given legitimacy to a brutal dictatorship, Yalden offered his modest agenda. Canadians should let China know when we are "troubled" by actions that set aside individual liberties and should "exchange views on common problems relating, for example, to women's rights, children's rights and child labour, the rights of the elderly, of the disabled and of ethnic and religious minorities, and to a host of questions which we, like they, are trying to come to grips with" (9 September 1995). The suggestion that totalitarian societies and liberal democracies share "common problems" in these areas bears reflection. Is Ottawa's response to Canada's increasingly multiracial make-up to be understood as the counterpart to Beijing's attempt to "come to grips" with ethnic Tibetans?

How a discussion of equality rights and their realization could take place without freedom of debate is a mystery. As host of the United Nations women's conference, China displayed an authoritarian contempt for those who sought to question its policies. China's wider record on women's rights scarcely invites Canadian approval. The high birth rates of some countries are a legitimate matter for concern in the context of global resource demands, but the use of abortion as a tool of state policy replaces freedom of choice – the demand of Canada's human rights advocates – with state compulsion. Compulsory abortions are only one of the unsavoury consequences of China's birth control policies. Families faced with a female birth may commit infanticide since they fear a daughter will bring significant costs but not incur any parallel obligations to support aging parents. Some parents use ultrasound monitoring to establish the sex of the foetus. The ratio of infant boys to infant girls has risen from 103.8 to 100 in 1964 to 118.5 to 100 in 1995 (*Globe and Mail*, 10 January 1996).

Human Rights Watch/Asia issued a report on China's orphanages soon after Yalden's return, documenting the death by starvation of children and claiming that the high mortality rates in the orphanages were a result of a deliberate policy to reduce the number of abandoned children (ibid.). Amnesty International, in a report entitled *No One Is Safe*, reported human rights violations "on a massive scale" and cited a former family-planning official who claimed that authorities enforcing the one-child policy threatened violence to get pregnant women to agree to abortions (*Globe and Mail*, 13 March 1995).[7]

In Canada the commission promotes a concept of equality rights that lacks subtlety and coherence. The assertion that such rights demand equal gender distribution, for example, in every area, at every level is reflective only of knee-jerk feminism. Societies in which gender roles remain to some degree differentiated may offer equal or better opportunities for self-fulfilment. To believe otherwise is to embrace the proposition that interests and abilities are not simply distributed across genders but occur in equal proportions and that given free choice men and women will distribute their activities identically. Totalitarian societies may be better equipped to accomplish the conformity envisaged in this view of equality rights. Women or other designated groups can simply be legislated into conformity with the planned outcome in the same forceful way in which countries like China tackle other complex issues.

In other areas it is difficult to see the commission's foreign ventures as anything more than a desire to appease its political paymasters and afford commission staff the opportunity for foreign travel. The Canadian Human Rights Commission, for example, has played a key role in coordinating Canadian assistance to the Indonesian Human Rights Commission, with which it has signed a bilateral agreement (CHRCb 1997: 14). The commission, set up by Indonesia's genocidal military regime, is accountable to the Suharto government, which has continued to imprison trade unionists and bar opponents of the regime from running in elections while maintaining its sanguinary hold on East Timor and Irian Jaya. The Indonesian Human Rights Commission serves, on the other hand, to deflect international criticism and foster the illusion that the Indonesian dictatorship is open to reform. In Canada, support for the Indonesian Commission is used to suggest that Canada's courtship of the Suharto regime is not entirely mercenary and has (astonishingly) even been claimed as evidence of CIDA's progressive aid policies (Fried 1996).

STRENGTHENING THE FEDERAL EMPLOYMENT EQUITY PROGRAM

If you look at the federal statistics, employment equity has had very little impact on changing the composition of the workplace. In fact equity doesn't exist in most places.

Judy Rebick, Rebick and Roach, 1996

Since the 1960s, the white overclass has sought to co-opt potential black leaders of dissent (and, to a lesser extent, Hispanic leaders) by means of a racial preference machinery that has grown more elaborate with each passing decade.

Michael Lind, 1995

There are lots of jobs in racism. If all the people who are employed with the ostensible purpose of fighting racism were actually to achieve some success in their struggle, many of them would be out of work. This does not seem likely to happen.

Robert Martin

The repeal of the Rae government's employment equity legislation in Ontario may have reflected the growing unpopularity of government intervention in the labour market to favour some groups over others, but this had little impact on the federal Liberals. At the same time, Lloyd Axworthy was pushing new legislation through Parliament, enthusiastically backed by the Canadian Human Rights Commission and others hopeful of improved career opportunities. While the Ontario legislation was the subject of continuing controversy and played a significant role in the NDP rout and Harris government's election, there was little media or public interest in federal proposals that brought the federal public service within the scope of the legislation and gave the CHRC the right to audit public and private sector employers.

Justifying the new legislation provided speakers from the government benches with an opportunity to make a further contribution to the welter of misinformation which supports preferential hiring policies. Ethel Blondin-Andrew, secretary of state for Training and Youth at Human Resources, informed the House of Commons that the 1994 Employment Equity Act Annual Report "painted a depressing picture for people with disabilities, members of visible minorities, women and aboriginal people" (Hansard 16 October 1995). This is a surprising interpretation, as the report noted, *inter alia*, "Despite the reduction of the workforce under the Act between 1992 and 1993, the representation of members of the four designated groups in the workforce actually increased" (HRD 1994a: 5).

The minister's confusion may have stemmed from her inability to distinguish between federally regulated industry figures and broader economic measures (a problem, as we have noted, she shared with Rey Pagtakhan, chair of the House of Commons Human Rights Committee). Drawing the attention of the House to the plight of aboriginals, Blondin-Andrew advised, "It is a source of national shame that our first peoples account for only 1.04 per cent of the workforce, occupy the lowest paying jobs and are on the losing end of the wage gap when compared with other Canadians." In fact the 1.04 per cent figure refers only to the small and unrepresentative group of industries subject to federal regulation. More astonishing was the minister's claim that university-educated young aboriginals faced unemployment levels twice as high as their white male counterparts – a consequence, the House was asked to believe, of discrimination.

The claim of dramatically higher unemployment levels for aboriginal graduates prompted me to contact the minister's office to track down the source of the statistic. After repeated phone calls, Paula Jardine, one of the minister's numerous assistants, finally advised me that the figure came from an unpublished analysis of census data provided by Statistics Canada (telephone, 29 November 1995). Published analysis of the 1992 National Graduates Survey by Statistics Canada indicates that male aboriginal graduates have higher labour force participation rates and slightly higher unemployment rates than other Canadians. Male aboriginal participation rates for 1990 graduates were 97.6 per cent, in 1992, compared to 92.7 per cent for all others. The unemployment rate was 13.6 per cent compared to 10.6 per cent. In contrast, female aboriginal graduates had a slightly lower rate of unemployment – 10.4 per cent compared to 10.8 per cent. There is no evidence of any national pattern that might be suggestive of discrimination. In Ontario, Quebec, Manitoba, Alberta, and British Columbia (including the Territories) aboriginal unemployment rates were the same or lower than rates for other graduates. Nationally, aboriginal graduates (many of whom enjoy tax-exempt earnings) gained slightly higher average salaries than other graduates (Wannell and Caron 1994a).

Statistics Canada was unable to assist me in providing a source for the minister's figure, but they did advise me that according to 1991 census data the unemployment rate for aboriginal male university graduates was 6 per cent, the rate for their non-aboriginal counterparts 4.9 per cent (personal communication 18 December 1995). The concentration of aboriginals in more remote parts of the country, often in areas of high unemployment, makes it difficult to draw any conclusion from a 1.1 per cent difference, except that it is far smaller than the figure provided by Blondin-Andrew to the House of Commons.

Blondin-Andrew was not the only member of the government benches to seek support in dubious statistics. Maurizio Bevilacqua, parliamentary secretary to the Human Resources minister, drew the House's attention to what he believed to be the concentration of women in low paid jobs: "many women continue to be ghettoized in low paying and part-time work. In spite of that fact, in 1990 women obtained 55 per cent of university bachelor degrees" (*Hansard* 17 October 1995). This was a curious juxtaposition, suggesting that female graduates were failing to achieve equal treatment, a fact disputed by Statistics Canada data. Full-time male graduates worked an average of three to four hours a week more than full-time women; when women's earnings are expressed as an hourly rate, they are actually higher than men's. There was no ambiguity in the Statistics Canada review of the data at a number of points conclusions were expressed in bold: "**This means that controlling for differences in characteristics, female graduates earned more than men**" (Wannell and Caron 1994b: 16, emphasis in original).

Bevilacqua (or his speech writer) was equally unsuccessful in interpreting data on employers' views on the need for legislation: "Roughly two thirds of Ontario businesses responding to a poll just after the recent election reported they are in fact in favour of reforming or keeping that province's employment equity law as it is. The business position is reform it but do not repeal it" (*Hansard* 16 October 1995). This would suggest that enthusiasm for government regulation was much higher among businesses than among the general population, as opposition to the legislation had been a major issue in the Conservatives' election. What "poll" could Bevilacqua be referring to? His office provided the source: a survey by Omnibus Consulting, a company that gains significant business from companies obliged to comply with equity legislation. Omnibus surveyed two thousand companies, receiving responses from 221 – 11 per cent of those who received the survey responded, a rate so low as to make any results meaningless. It is a well-established principle of survey research that low response rates raise substantive questions of respondent bias; with so many failing to mail back the questionnaire, the self-selected respondents are unlikely to represent the views of the other 89 per cent.

But the claims of Blondin-Andrew and Bevilacqua were modest in comparison to those of the parliamentary secretary to the minister of Citizenship and Immigration, Mary Clancy. Remarkably, Clancy has a reputation for being a "walking encyclopedia" when it comes to data recall. Perhaps, like one of my former professors, this stems from her endless willingness to offer a number. Clancy advised the House that "white males get 50 per cent of federal government jobs. They get 60 per cent of the jobs nationally in both private and public sector combined. Even more overwhelming, white males get 90 per cent of the promotions" (*Hansard* 6 October 1995).

Compare these figure with the Public Service Commission 1993–94 Annual Report indicating that women received 59 per cent of new appointments to the public service and 55 per cent of promotions within the service. The government's 1995 report on employment equity in federally regulated industries indicated that white males were consistently under-represented in promotion shares, while visible minority hirings were consistently higher than their proportion in the labour force, their terminations disproportionately low, and their promotion rate disproportionately high (HRD 1995). There are no national figures on promotion shares, but in federally regulated industries where data does exist, white males obtain a disproportionately small share. No separate calculation is made for the non-designated groups (white males), but women who comprised 44 per cent of all employees received 55 per cent of promotions. Visible minorities held just over 8 per cent of the positions and received just over 11 per cent of promotions (HRD 1995: A-8, A-10). Clancy's suggestion that white males receive 90 per cent of all national promotions is indicative only of the excesses to which politicians are prone in justifying preferential hiring policies.[8]

9

Immigrants and Refugees

Policies in Search of a Rationale

Canada now leads the world in the number of immigrants admitted relative to its population size. Immigration is no longer driven by economic logic: in 1985 Canada admitted 85,000 immigrants; by 1992 in the midst of a deep recession Canada admitted 254,000. Entering a labour market which was shedding workers, immigrants all too often found their prospects far different than the rosy picture painted by the immigration officials, lawyers, and consultants who had smoothed their path into Canada. Support for preferential hiring policies has been driven by claims that many visible minorities do not experience equivalent labour market success compared to other Canadians. For many recent immigrants this is undoubtedly true.

The speed of transformation of Canada's major cities was dramatic. In the Toronto CMA the 1996 census reported that 42 per cent were immigrant. One in five of Toronto's residents are immigrants who arrived after 1981. Where once European countries dominated the source countries, newer immigrants came from Asia, Africa, the Middle East, Central and South America, and the Caribbean. The debate over immigration quickly became structured by the change in the immigration flows. Those who adopted the traditional position of the left and urged restrictions in the context of rising unemployment were dismissed as racists. For its part, the government worked with the immigration industry to ensure that a positive spin was placed on policies that afforded a comfortable living to lawyers and immigration consultants and brought significant benefits to developers and low wage employers, and major social and economic costs to other Canadians.

Yet even immigration boosters were sometimes compelled to acknowledge that many workers had experienced negative effects. Don
DeVoretz, co-director of one of the so-called centres for research
excellence, funded by the Immigration department to foster research
sympathetic to its agenda, admitted in a recent article: "In short
workers in 47 major industries are losing jobs or suffering wage
compression from immigration" (DeVoretz 1996).

The provision of a privileged and well-funded platform to those who
view Canada as a profoundly racist society has served to deter those
who might otherwise have raised questions about Canada's immigration and refugee policy. The debate, in consequence, is dominated by
the sizable constituency who make a living in the immigration and
refugee industry and by those who benefit from high levels of immigration. The government has intervened directly to afford financial
support to advocacy organizations and to academics and researchers
who support high levels of immigration.

In essence, in the post-war period, immigration policy reflected a
"tap-on, tap-off" approach, varying immigrant flows in accordance
with labour market conditions (Veuglers and Klassen 1994: 364).
Historically, organized labour campaigned against any policy that
threatened to result in downward pressure on wages, as labour supply
increased more rapidly than the capacity of the economy to create new
jobs. The Mulroney government unhooked the linkage between labour
supply and labour market demand; as immigration rose, the emphasis
on labour market skills declined. By 1994 less than one in five immigrants were selected for their skill levels (*Globe and Mail*, 25 October
1994). The Liberals, conscious of the electoral popularity of this
approach in some ethnic constituencies, committed, in the Red Book,
to increase immigration to more than 300,000 per annum. Immigration
levels were even more striking when Quebec was factored out. Quebec
has the right to select its own immigrants; in 1996 and 1997, for
example, it was expected to receive some 11 per cent of Canada's
immigrants, far less than its population share would suggest (Citizenship and Immigration 1996).

The Mulroney government faced continuing criticism from the
Canadian Labour Congress and its allies on the left over a variety of
policies including free trade and the government's frequently proclaimed intention to address Canada's mounting national debt. The
issue of immigration, in contrast, remained out of bounds even when
it became clear that as the economy moved into steep recession the
government intended to maintain record immigration levels. This
silence reflected a sensitivity to charges that, in the changed immigration
environment, organized labour's traditional opposition to high levels

of immigration in a stagnant labour market would be portrayed as racist.[1] Those on the right of centre who raised questions, notably the Reform party, invited the epithet.[2]

The Liberal government maintained high immigration levels even though 1.4 million Canadians were out of work and 800,000 were involuntary part-time workers. Such figures actually understate the magnitude of unemployment, since they do not capture so-called "discouraged workers" who have left the labour force. Economist Arthur Donner suggested the unemployment rate would be closer to 13 per cent if these drop-outs were included (*Globe and Mail*, 20 April 1996). The recovery that began in 1994 saw little improvement in the employment situation. In 1990 Canada and the United States had the same employment rate, 625 jobs per thousand adults. The Canadian rate fell more rapidly than the United States and failed to show any comparable recovery. By 1996 the American rate had returned to its 1990 level; in contrast, Canada had only some 587 jobs per thousand adults (Fortin 1996).

Particularly impacted by rising unemployment were young people, a group which might be assumed to be competing for some of the same entry level jobs sought by many new immigrants. Some responded by simply dropping out of the labour market: participation rates for people under 25 declined from 71 per cent to 61 per cent between 1989 and 1996, but unemployment levels by the end of 1996 for those aged 15 to 24 were above 16 per cent (*Globe and Mail's Report on Business*, 11 January 1997).

Immigrant recruitment is driven by a level of official boosterism that might surprise Canadians familiar with the country's parlous labour market. A computer disk provided to would-be applicants features a cover note proclaiming Canada "The Number One Country in the World." Immigration officers attend recruitment fairs, often sponsored by the immigration industry, to promote Canada's attractions. Potential immigrants are greeted by an array of stalls advertising the services of companies who will assist potential entrants to secure a favourable outcome, move their goods, or provide a range of other services.

Canada's immigration program has undergone significant transformation, as the increase in the numbers admitted was parallelled by a sharp decline in the importance of labour market skills in shaping the immigrant flow. Changes to sponsorship regulations in 1978 allowed citizens and landed immigrants to sponsor parents under the age of sixty. Daniel Stoffman summarizes the consequences: "These working-age parents are the opening through which large extended families are able to move to Canada. Because they can sponsor their children once landed, it is through them that the siblings of the original immigrants can enter Canada without passing through the points system. These siblings can then sponsor *their* children, who can sponsor *their* fiancees, who can sponsor *their* parents and so on" (Stoffman 1993: 13, emphasis in original). Stoffman cites one case in which an immigrant from India reported that no less than sixty to seventy of his relatives followed in his wake.

The decreasing skill levels of the immigrant population were captured in a Statistics Canada study comparing international literacy levels. This found a disproportionate concentration of immigrants in the lowest literacy group; 31.1 per cent of immigrants compared to 14.8 per cent of native born Canadians (*Globe and Mail*, 7 December 1995). Where immigrants are admitted on the basis of relevant labour market skills, the process is less than rigorous, affording little assurance that those admitted possess skills in contemporary demand. The judgment of occupational demand depends on points allocated on the basis of a list which is often outdated. In early 1997 the operative list originated in 1993 and included occupations that might have surprised many young graduates and others seeking employment. A long list of various chefs and cooks (head chef, caterer, cook institution, etc.) all received the maximum ten points.

The case of a potential immigrant from the U.K. who is a qualified social worker is illustrative of the dubious utility of the classification. In 1997 a wide range of social workers and social service workers received five points for occupational demand. An applicant normally requires a minimum of seventy points to secure admission as a skilled worker. Someone with a Master's degree in social work, with four years experience, under the age of forty-four, with some knowledge of French, would score eighty-three points. In addition to occupational demand the candidate would receive eighteen points for specific occupational preparation and sixteen points for formal education.[3] Canada emphasizes that immigrants need to be flexible, but the transferable skills of social workers apply to a relatively narrow range of occupations. Those entering as social workers are unlikely to seek work in high-tech industries or the financial services sector. The reality is that there are few jobs available for those with social work skills and a large number of qualified job seekers already in Canada. Nonetheless, the putative U.K. applicant would normally be certain of success.

Sponsors undertake to ensure that sponsored dependents will not be a charge on social assistance payrolls. A study based on 1994 tax filers found that in Metro Toronto one in five sponsored parents and grandparents were claiming social assistance three years after their arrival (Thomas 1996: 42). By 1996 there were some thirty thousand sponsored immigrants on welfare in Ontario (*Globe and Mail*, 30 March

1996). Nonetheless, where parents and grandparents arrived in Canada as visitors and then applied for admission through sponsorship, the route usually recommended by lawyers and immigration consultants, in 1996 86 per cent were successful (Trempe 1997: 49).

A significant number of immigrants first arrive in Canada to work as nannies, gaining in return the right to apply for landed immigrant status after two years of live-in work. The beneficiaries of this program are upper income Canadians who gain access to workers at rates well below those which otherwise would prevail in the Canadian market. Employers or "sponsors" are obliged to show that they have first tried to find a Canadian to do the job, but since wage rates for live-in foreign nannies are around $300 per week, this is scarcely an insurmountable barrier. Without access to foreign workers prepared to work long hours at low rates of pay, upper income households would be forced to pay higher wages, with benefits for unemployed Canadian workers.

The child-care problems of Zoe Baird, Clinton's nominee for attorney general, became a *cause celébre* in 1993 when it was reported that she had hired an illegal immigrant nanny. Feminists erupted in predictable outrage when Baird's nomination was challenged, arguing that it reflected a lack of understanding of women's child-care problems. Baird, who was reported to earn more than U.S. $500,000 a year as a corporate lawyer, paid her live-in nanny U.S. $250 per month.

The incentive for many foreign workers lies in the facts that wages are higher than at home and those who undertake to remain in domestic service for two years are eligible for landed immigrant status and then able to sponsor relatives to come to Canada. Historically this was a favoured route for Caribbean immigrants, particularly in Toronto and Montreal (Calliste 1989). The largest contemporary group are from the Philippines, currently an estimated 90,000 (*Globe and Mail*, 20 January 1996). The family disruption which this policy causes and the long-term problems that may surface when husbands and children are reunited with the absent mother lead to significant costs to Canada's social and educational services – costs borne by all taxpayers, to assure a cheap labour supply to a few.

Immigration has not only excceded the capacity of the labour market to provide additional employment and placed growing pressure on educational and social services but also entails continuing ecological changes. Conservative estimates suggest the population of greater Toronto will increase by an additional 2.5 million to 6.7 million by 2021. This will inevitably place additional stress on an area already experiencing transportation problems. In British Columbia the population increased by 13.5 per cent between 1991 and 1996; most of the new immigrants moved into the Lower Mainland. Combined with the movement of Canadians from other parts of the country, the effect of new immigration was not only sky-rocketing real estate prices but mounting concerns that such rapid growth would severely damage the quality of life in the area (*Globe and Mail*, 16 April 1997). Pressures on Vancouver's school system are evidenced by the fact that 57 per cent of children speak a language other than English at home, and close to 50 per cent of students are in ESL classes. The high costs resulted in increasing funds for ESL while the board of education announced cuts to other educational funding (Dwyer 1997).

The flow of the overwhelming majority of immigrants into a small number of urban centres is driven by the desire to live close to relatives and other members of the same ethnic group rather than economic demand. The Toronto urban area, which remains the destination of 42 per cent of immigrants (Trempe 1997: 29), has experienced a devastating recession with a significant loss of manufacturing jobs. A 1997 study prepared for the Ontario government's Task Force on the Greater Toronto Area found that the city was lagging behind virtually every major American city in economic growth and had one of the worst records of job creation. The flow of immigrants was paralleled by marked increase in the number of area residents between twenty and sixty who reported that they had effectively withdrawn from the Greater Toronto labour market. In 1990, 150,000 people reported they were no longer seeking work, a figure that rose to some 340,000 by 1995, reflecting the economic downturn. The economic recovery elsewhere in Canada was accompanied by some job growth, but this was not the case in the Greater Toronto area (*Globe and Mail*, 15 January 1996). Employment growth there climbed sharply in 1997 but scarcely enough to compensate for the 441,035 immigrants the 1996 census reported settled in the Toronto CMA between 1991–96 (*Globe and Mail*, 5 November 1997).

Immigrants taking advantage of Canada's generous admission policies may hold quite unrealistic expectations about their economic prospects. The expanding economy, relatively low unemployment levels, and the absence of massive public sector debt afforded earlier generations of immigrants opportunities that are not open to many contemporary arrivals. Mahler's study of Central and South American immigrants into suburban Long Island, predominantly arriving to work in low-tech industries and the service sector, found few opportunities for economic mobility even in the more dynamic American market (Mahler 1995). In Canada the dominant attribution of failure to discrimination rather than the weak labour market and low skill levels of many immigrants may have explosive social consequences. The claim that the labour market is profoundly discriminatory is endorsed by a range of governments and government-funded organizations. It would be surprising if many of those who had entered Canada with high hopes of social and economic mobility, only to find few well paying jobs and limited prospects, did not conclude that their failure was due to skin colour.

IMMIGRATION AND PREFERENTIAL HIRING

The interface between employment equity programs and immigration policy reflects a certain perverse logic. As the flow of skilled independent-class immigrants decreased and the number of those admitted without regard to their ability to compete in the labour market grew, the consequence, particularly in an unfavourable economic climate, could only be increasing failure. Employment equity programs, with their emphasis on numerical targets, de facto quotas, and special recruitment and training programs, offered opportunities to some immigrants which they were unlikely to access on merit. Immigrants have been given access to specific vocational training not readily available to Canadians. In March 1997, for example, Immigration Minister Lucienne Robillard announced a further $63 million in funding for adult education and employment retraining for immigrants. Others, selected as skilled immigrants only to find that this bore little relationship to any demand for their skills in the Canadian labour market, could also seek benefit from preferential hiring policies.

Such policies often give new immigrants opportunities to access employment vacancies not open to long-term Canadian residents. Large numbers of Canadians with teaching qualifications have been unable to obtain work in their profession, but in Ontario some recent immigrants with teaching qualifications gained overseas are able to gain more favourable access to opportunities by enrolling in a York University program, partly funded by the Ontario Ministry of Education. The program, which not only provides provincial certification but also experience as teachers' aides, "aims to kill two birds with one stone – school staffing demands for diversity and ministry regulations for certification," as the *Globe and Mail*'s education reporter enthused (Lewington 1996). The logic of admitting immigrants intending to seek employment as teachers and paying significant sums for their further training, in a situation in which large numbers of teachers are on recall lists following lay-offs, and less than one in four contemporary graduates from Ontario education faculties find public school teaching positions on graduation, is not readily apparent. However, there is no doubt that in some boards membership in the right designated group has replaced merit in selection.

The Peel board, under the leadership of its black director, Harold Braithwaite, announced that in 1995 it intended to set aside "at least" 34 per cent of new teaching positions for aboriginals, racial minorities, and people with disabilities. The announcement gave particular emphasis to recruiting racial minority teachers, noting "Peel Board statistics indicate that 34 percent of students identify themselves as being part of a racial minority" (press release, 18 December 1994). This statement reflected what by then had become the common-sense view that the racial composition of students and teachers should be matched, though not long ago such a suggestion would have been dismissed as racist. The board provided the customary assurances that they continued to uphold "the principle of hiring the best qualified people for the job" (ibid.) but failed to explain how this was consistent with offering at least 34 per cent of the positions to groups comprising a mere 9 per cent of contemporary graduates from Canadian education faculties (Wannell and Caron 1994a). Given the shortfall in candidates possessing both the requisite qualifications and the required group membership for such discriminatory recruitment campaigns, the York course has no doubt identified a market niche.

Training programs not only afford immigrants opportunities not available to other Canadians but also provide further patronage opportunities to government. The campaign of Ginny Hasselfield for the leadership of the Manitoba Liberals was subject to some unwelcome attention when it was revealed that her company, Cross Cultural Communications International, had received a $3 million untendered contract to provide job training to immigrants from Human Resources Development. The contract was issued at the time when Winnipeg South Centre MP Lloyd Axworthy was the responsible minister. Hasselfield acknowledged the lobbying assistance of another Winnipeg MP, Reg Alcock, whose election campaign she had chaired (*Globe and Mail*, 16 October 1996).

THE REFUGEE OPTION

> Canada spends more most years on legal aid fees to refugee lawyers and on IRB salaries than it does actually helping refugees.
>
> Daniel Stoffman, 1997

Immigration is further increased by the unprecedented generosity of Canada's refugee admissions program, which affords generous assistance to those who make a refugee claim on reaching Canada, no matter how improbable. Sweden, a country with an international reputation for assisting refugees, admits 5 per cent of applicants, Denmark 10 per cent. Germany, which admitted a mere 4.3 per cent of 438,000 asylum seekers in 1992, many from the former Eastern Bloc, then removed its constitutional guarantees of asylum and substantially tightened admission. The number of asylum seekers fell to 120,000 and the admission rate rose to 10 per cent. In Canada, in 1996, some 58 per cent of refugee claims were successful, and history suggests that many of those refused will stay in Canada under one or other humanitarian exemption.[4] The high level of Canadian admissions owes much to the changes introduced in 1989 when the Immigration and Refugee Board was set up.

The board, whose members are political appointees, quickly demonstrated a willingness to accommodate the demands of the legal-aid funded lawyers appearing before it. Unqualified board members were no doubt encouraged in their favourable rulings by the fact that whereas a refusal required a written decision, an acceptance necessitated no such laborious effort (Stoffman 1993: 10). Before the recent introduction of one-panelist hearings, whereas one member of a board could admit a refugee, two had to agree to reject an application. In the board's first year of operation some 90 per cent of those applying secured admission (Cox and Glenn 1994: 298).

The problems around excluding transparently dubious claims rest in significant measure on the 1985 Singh decision of then Supreme Court member Bertha Wilson, a decision for which Canada has paid a considerable price. Jeffrey Simpson sums up the effect: "The so-called Singh decision ... gummed up a reasonably effective [refugee determination] system by extending protection under the Charter of Rights and Freedoms to 'everyone' who put a foot on Canadian soil and by insisting that 'everyone' was entitled to a full oral hearing" (*Globe and Mail*, 13 February 1997).

A number of groups have found the refugee route a useful way of by-passing ordinary immigration requirements. Among the many dubious claims of persecution recognized by the boards are those of Russians who, claiming to be Jewish, emigrated to Israel under that country's Law of Return. This entitled them to have their travel costs paid and to receive generous resettlement allowances. Some thousands of these "Jewish refugees," having decided that Israel was not to their liking, then successfully obtained refugee status in Canada on the grounds that they were not in fact Jewish and in consequence allegedly faced persecution in Israel (Abella 1996a).

In 1996 the board received claims from a number of countries not widely recognized as posing grave dangers to political activists, including the small Caribbean democracy of St Vincent, from which 59 people fled persecution. The Ukraine contributed 277 refugees, Hungary 64, India 1,367, Jamaica 132, Chile 2,824, Venezuela 379, Czech Republic 144, Israel 1,270, and Costa Rica 95. Even the European Union made a contribution with 9 fleeing from persecution in Italy, 1 from Denmark, 12 from France, 3 from Germany, 3 from Greece and 12 from Portugal (IRB 1997). What is striking is not simply the incidence of widespread persecution in the most unlikely places but the fact that those facing such persecution have been driven to escape not to a neighbouring country but to the other side of the world.

The generosity of the Canadian system is well known, affording rich opportunities for enterprising lawyers. In 1997 a sudden upsurge of Czech refugees followed a television program that claimed that Romanies, protesting discriminatory treatment at home, would receive a sympathetic hearing on making refugee claims in Canada. The Czech airline CSA reported that all economy-class seats were booked for the next three months. One town council offered departing Romanies assistance with air tickets in return for vacating their apartments. The TV program featured an interview with Toronto lawyer George Kubes, who provided information on how Romanies might seek refugee status. One of Kubes's Czech clients was filmed eating dinner in the CN Tower restaurant to demonstrate how well she had done in Canada. Kubes told the *Globe and Mail* that he already represented some forty Czech Romany families seeking refugee status, some of whom had already been successful; more had sought his assistance following the program (13 August 1997). In the week following more than one hundred additional refugees arrived, and Kubes was reported to represent more than fifty families (*Globe and Mail*, 20 August 1997).

Reports that in Europe Gypsies were disproportionately involved in criminal activity caused some concern. Canada's vice-consul in Rome reported frequent complaints from tourists who had been robbed of their money or passports by Gypsies; RCMP Inspector Soave, who had formerly served as liaison officer in Rome, expressed concern over the implications of an influx of Gypsy refugees for the force's goal of "safe homes, safe communities" (ibid.). Canada's refugee advocacy groups had no such concerns. Sharry Aiken, president of the Canadian Council of Refugees, opposed the reintroduction of visa requirements for Czech nationals, calling the influx "a drop in the bucket." Aiken's law office was reported to be representing some twenty Gypsy families (ibid., 23 August 1997).

Those making refugee claims in Canada can stay in the country until their case is heard. In 1997 it took more than a year for a case to be referred for a hearing and another fourteen months before it was heard. The influx of Czech Gypsies forced Toronto hostels to set aside beds previously intended for battered women. Some 20 per cent of the reported two thousand hostel residents were said to be Gypsies, awaiting the necessary documentation to enable them to claim social assistance and medical benefits and send their children to school, while awaiting a hearing at which they may be represented by counsel paid for by legal aid (ibid., 22 August 1997).

The board has proved itself willing to adopt an ever more expansive definition of "refugee." In early 1997, for example, the Toronto board afforded refugee status to a British family, in which a twelve-year-old boy had experienced sexual abuse at the hands of his biological father. British social services and police authorities, it was alleged, had failed to take action (ibid., 17 April 1997). It is unclear how the board could test the accuracy of such claims, and there is no evidence that British authorities are any less assiduous than Canadian authorities in pursuing such matters.[5] Nonetheless, the board concluded that the child was a member of "a particular social group" with a well-founded fear of persecution, though the board had heard the abusive father might be dead.

The seriousness with which the Chrétien government treated the board's obligations was indicated by the appointment to the posts (which pay between $83,900 and $86,400) of a number of youthful, inexperienced members to serve on the Montreal Board. The new members had not only their youth in common; they also had parents who were prominent Quebec Liberals. Another appointee, Inderjit Singh Bal, a former chairman of the Liberal Party's multicultural committee, admitted to a Commons committee that he had entered Canada illegally in 1976 by jumping ship and had subsequently entered into a brief marriage of convenience (ibid., 5 November 1994).

Board chair Nurjehan Mawani has sought to deflect criticism of the board's patronage-driven appointment's system: "Important changes have been made to our appointment's process. Vacancies to the Board are publicly advertised" (Mawani 1997). The contemporaneous announcement that Deborah Coyne, former constitutional adviser to Liberal Newfoundland premier Clyde Wells, was among the latest appointees to the positions, suggested that such changes remained cosmetic. Among those joining Coyne in Chrétien's year-end patronage list was David R. Cooke, a former Ontario Liberal MLA (*Globe and Mail*, 4 January 1997). Immigration Minister Robillard had earlier reappointed her ex-husband, Jacques Lasalle, to a further four-year term. Yasmin Yar Khan, a former television journalist, also joined the board; coincidentally, Khan is married to Haroon Siddiqui, editorial page editor of the fervently Liberal *Toronto Star*.

Prominent among board members are those who have made their careers in ethnic organizations in immigrant and refugee advocacy organizations, or as immigration and refugee lawyers. Diane Smith, first appointed in 1997, is a past member of the executive of the Citizenship and Immigration Law Section of the Canadian Bar Association; Gladys Macpherson, reappointed in 1997, is a former information officer with Amnesty International; Dale Noseworthy, reappointed in 1997, is an immigration lawyer; Ian Clague, another lawyer, reappointed in 1997, is a former vice-chair of the Vancouver Refugee Council; Judith Ramirez, reappointed in 1997, is the founder of Intercede, an immigrant advocacy group; Milagros Eustaquio, reappointed in 1997, is a former executive director of the Peel Multicultural Council; Felix Mora, reappointed in 1997, is former national president of the Canadian Hispanic Congress; Joel Moss, first appointed in 1997, is a former executive director of the Jewish Immigrant Aid Services; Edith Nee, reappointed in 1996, is a past vice-president of the Asian Canadian Association; Queenie Hum, reappointed at the same time, is a former board member of the Chinese Canadian National Council; Errol Townshend, reappointed in 1995, is a former vice-president of the Jamaican-Canadian Association. Others like Lucie Blais, a prominent Liberal from northern Quebec, first appointed in 1997, reflect the continuing importance of links to the government of the day.[6]

The cost of Canada's refugee program, including such items as legal costs, health, and welfare, amounts to some $1 billion a year. In Ontario, for example, in 1992 legal aid costs for refugee applicants were estimated at $31 million and welfare costs $155 million (Cox and Glenn 1994: 299–303). Many of these costs are incurred not on behalf of genuine refugees but of those who have correctly recognized that a claim for refugee status can be a viable alternative to a conventional immigration application.

In 1994 it was reported that one in six of those making application for refugee status in the first half of the year had been charged with or convicted of a crime since their arrival in Canada.[7] A tally undertaken by the RCMP found that of 8,377 refugee claimants checked in the first half of 1994, 1,299 had been charged with or convicted of a criminal code offence; 419 had been "investigated for or found to have" a criminal record elsewhere; and 217 had broken immigration regulations by filing more than one application (*Globe and Mail*, 5 November 1994).

An investigation by *Maclean's* (5 August 1996) reported that some 10,000 Tamils who had entered Canada, largely through the refugee process, had received guerilla training and taken an active part in the civil strife in Sri Lanka. Many were former members of the Liberation Tigers of Tamil Elan, classified as a terrorist organization by the Canadian government and alleged by the European Union to have links to the Mafia and international drug trafficking. *Maclean's* claimed that some thirty important Tamil leaders were now in Canada. Many of those who had sought "refuge" status remained active partisans, raising an estimated $7 million a year in funds to support the conflict in Sri Lanka. Fund-raising was assisted by extortion: targeted Tamils were expected to pay 6 per cent of their gross income. Many "refugees" arrived only after payments were agreed: "If a Tamil wants to leave an LTTE-controlled area and travel to Canada to make a refugee claim – dozens do so each week – the Tigers will not grant them passage until a relative in Canada begins making the payments" (ibid.).

The result of Canada's failure to distinguish genuine refugees from protagonists has been the transfer to Canada of many of the problems arising from Sri Lanka's ethnic strife. In the words of *Maclean's*, the "climate of fear reaches deep into Canada's Tamil community" (ibid.). Earlier in the year the *Globe and Mail* had reported on the "disturbing escalation of crime" in the Tamil community in Toronto and the apparent increase in intimidation to silence critics of the LTTE, including vendors of *Muncharie*, a Toronto-based Tamil newspaper. The report noted police concerns "that the violent subculture that has been nurtured in the decade-long Sri Lankan civil war is now spilling over into Canadian life" (19 January 1996). In Scarborough in Toronto's east end police report a growing problem with heavily armed Tamil gangs involved in a range of criminal activity (*Globe and Mail*, 10 May 1997).

In 1996 the Board received 2,946 new claims from Sri Lanka. In the same year it granted a positive decision in 82 per cent of all the Sri Lankan cases it decided (IRB 1997).

The danger that violent political conflicts originating overseas might, through immigration and refugee decisions, be imported to Canada is evident elsewhere. Canada's Sikh community has provided fertile ground for extremists. In 1988, for example, the moderate publisher and editor of the *Indo-Canadian Times*, Tara Singh Hayer, was shot by Harkirat Singh Bagga and paralysed from the waist down. The trial judge concluded that Bagga was acting on behalf of Sikh militants opposed to Hayer's politics (*Globe and Mail*, 14 August 1996). Sikh militants are also suspected in the still-unsolved bombing of an Air India plane which exploded over the Atlantic in 1985.

Political and religious conflict in the Sikh community in British Columbia's Lower Mainland erupted into a bloody melee at a Sikh temple, where moderates had displaced traditionalists in the temple leadership. More than a thousand were involved as militants drew swords and attacked chair-wielding moderates. The rioting followed an earlier incident in which shots were fired at the home of the temple president. Moderates, claiming the police had sided with fundamentalists by allowing them into the temple area, hurled missiles at police vehicles as they removed people from the temple. Among the reasons offered for the dispute was the allegation that substantial sums had been channelled from the temple to militants in India fighting for Khalistan, the proposed Sikh homeland (*Globe and Mail*, 13 January 1997).

Immigration officials appear to have been equally ineffective in preventing the admission into Canada of a number of Serbs suspected of serious war crimes in the ethnic cleansing that took place during the breakup of Yugoslavia. Canada has made no response to the efforts of the Bosnian government to extradite those involved (CBC, *The National*, 14 April 1997).

Palestinian Gazi Ibrahim Abu Mezer, charged in 1997 in an alleged plot to bomb the New York subway system, arrived in Canada in 1993 and made a claim for refugee status. Like others, Abu Mezer found Canada's extraordinarily lax border controls provided an easy access route to the United States. Mezer was returned to Canada twice after being apprehended making an illegal entry; on the third occasion Canada refused him re-admission. Abu Mezer then made a refugee claim in the United States, but dropped the request promising to leave voluntarily before being arrested in connection with the alleged bombing plot (*Globe and Mail*, 8 August 1997).

The record of the RCMP in dealing with an earlier generation of undesirable immigrants does not encourage complacency about their capabilities to subsequently identify and deport those with records of terrorism or human rights offences. In the post-war period considerable resources have been devoted to identifying those who were guilty of war crimes, including mass murder, in the Second World War. To date only one (Jacob Litjens) has been deported, though an independent American investigator, Steve Rambam, had no difficulty identifying 157 alleged war criminals resident in Canada and interviewing sixty of them while posing as a professor from a fictitious university. Even when Canadian authorities were provided by the American government's Office of Special Investigations with detailed evidence against an individual alleged to be involved in horrific mass murder in Lithuania, the only RCMP response was to interview the individual. Ten years later, as the RCMP and the courts come under growing pressure to take action, the individual is absent from the current list of those targeted for investigation (Sher 1997).

The Immigration Department has identified some two hundred people admitted to Canada who are suspected of other war crimes or crimes against humanity, from countries such as Rwanda, Somalia, and Honduras. The department has succeeded in deporting a mere fifteen (*Globe and Mail*, 11 February 1997).

Konrad Kalejs, alleged to have been a member of a pro-Nazi Latvian killing squad, Arajs Kommando, and a former high-ranking officer at a slave labour camp, was deported from the United States in 1994. Kalejs came to Canada as a tourist. After Canada initiated deportation proceedings, Kalejs left for Australia and then returned to Canada where he was re-admitted. Kalejs, who had no status in Canada except as a tourist, was finally removed in August 1997, three years after his first arrival (*Globe and Mail*, 20 August 1997). Simon Wiesenthal Center files indicate that at least four members of the Arajs Kommando, responsible for the massacre of twenty thousand Jews, remain in Canada (Sol Littman, Letters, *Globe and Mail*, 23 August 1997).

The lack of careful investigation characterizing many refugee board decisions was highlighted by the admission of an Iranian "refugee" Mirsalah-Aldin Kompani. Kompani had been sentenced to a fifteen-year penitentiary term for robbery and assault in Lexington, Kentucky, in 1987. Kompani was deemed mentally ill and his sentence reduced to three years probation. Soon after, he returned to Iran. In 1991 Kompani arrived in Canada and applied for refugee status, claiming imprisonment and torture in Iran, a claim accepted by a Toronto refugee board. He told officials he had graduated from a Lexington university, but no background checks were done. Kompani's case came to light because he was one of three homeless men whose freezing deaths were the subject of a 1996 coroner's inquest; a *Toronto Star* investigation revealed the background (3 July 1996). In August 1996, a Vancouver adjudicator received some unwelcome attention when he released a Colorado "refugee claimant" pending a hearing. The would-be refugee had escaped from an American prison, where he was serving a twenty-year "dangerous offender" sentence for a serious assault and robbery. In this case no background check was necessary: the adjudicator was aware that he was dealing with an escaped felon.

Refugees who fail to secure admission may, nonetheless, remain in Canada. In 1996–97 38 per cent of those considered ready for removal in the Quebec region failed to report when required. Nationally since 1993, 31,200 refugee claimants had abandoned their claims or had them denied, but only 4,300 had a confirmed departure. In 1996 the Immigration department removed only 2,465 failed refugee claimants, a sharp decline from 4,672 removed in 1992 (Auditor General 1997: 25:29–25:32).

The refugee admission process is influenced by active lobbying by MPs, legal-aid funded lawyers, and a range of social service groups.

The Canadian Council for Refugees is a persistent advocate of more generous admission policies. The council, in common with many of its affiliates, receives financial support from the federal Ministry of Citizenship and Immigration. Reports that Canadian immigration officers had successfully thwarted an attempt by ninety-six Indian nationals, many from the Punjab, to undertake a hazardous boat journey from Gambia to Canada led to protests from council president Sharry Aiken, an immigration lawyer. The decision to hand the would-be migrants over to the Indian authorities for return to India suggested, claimed Aiken, that Canada had forgotten the lesson to be drawn from the return of Jews aboard the St Louis to Nazi Germany in 1939, where most died in the concentration camps. There had, in fact, been no suggestion that those returned to India encountered any persecution, let alone faced organized genocide.

The council president presented no evidence that the group were anything other than economic migrants but claimed that they should "at the very least" have had the opportunity to explain whether they were fleeing human rights abuses (Aiken 1996) – an invitation, in short, to claim refugee status and presumably be brought to Canada to begin the lengthy and costly process of refugee determination. Since, as Aiken notes, 60 per cent of refugee claimants from the Punjab are admitted, they could have anticipated some success. What remains unclear is why, if they were indeed desperately fleeing persecution, they should have travelled all the way to Gambia without making any attempt to secure asylum.

Aiken linked the Indian migrants to the case of the Romanian stowaways allegedly thrown overboard off the Maersk Dubai: "That makes a total of 99 people who might now have been in Canada claiming refugee status. Why aren't they here?" It may indeed have been the intention of the Romanians to claim refugee status, but again no evidence is offered that they actually faced political persecution or, if they did, what prevented them making a claim for asylum in Europe. The most interesting aspect of Aiken's intervention was the insight it provided into assumptions underpinning Canada's immigration and refugee lobby. Those heading to Canada by illicit means must be given every opportunity to avail themselves of Canada's generous provisions for those who wish to portray themselves as refugees. This includes legal-aid funded access to the many lawyers who support the work of the Canadian Council for Refugees.

IMMIGRATION AND CRIME

There is remarkably little public discussion about the relationship between immigration and crime. Apparently racial sensitivities preclude serious debate or, in the case of Canada's national public broadcaster, much of the relevant information. Vietnamese gangs in Edmonton have engaged in a series of bloody encounters, frequently in such public places as shopping malls. The ferocity of the attacks, which have resulted in serious injuries and fatalities, has ensured that some have made the national news, but those who depend on the CBC for information will remain ignorant of the ethnic origins of those involved. CBC policy generally precludes such information being aired.

The issue of immigration and crime is nonetheless of growing importance. Canada appears to afford a particularly attractive venue for those who might expect to experience considerable difficulty in gaining entrance to other countries. Immigrants and refugees who commit serious crimes subsequent to their arrival can also depend on a high degree of leniency, most notably from the appeals division of the Immigration and Refugee Board.[8] Those who have failed to secure access, whether as visitors or immigrants, through the normal screening process may request a special-entry permit from the minister. Special permits appear to be easily obtained: in 1995 Immigration Minister Sergio Marchi granted 5,483 special-entry permits, including 394 to individuals convicted of offences carrying a maximum sentence of ten years or more and 1,155 to individuals convicted of offences carrying less than a ten-year term (*Globe and Mail*, 10 June 1996).

A number of those admitted to Canada through the normal operation of the immigration process appear to have sources of wealth that might surprise law-abiding Canadians. In Toronto's exclusive Bridle Path area, where homes sell from $3 to $6 million (though more expensive properties are also available), properties are increasingly snapped up by buyers from the former Soviet Union and mainland China – countries, as the *Globe and Mail* notes, with "endemic corruption and alluringly primitive income tax systems" (18 June 1996). Questionable sources of wealth appear to be no barrier to immigration into Canada, though one Russian purchaser, Dmitri Iakoubovski, a neighbour of Conrad Black's, was forced to put his house up for sale when he was arrested and put on trial in St Petersburg, charged with stealing $130 million in rare manuscripts from the Russian National Library (ibid.).

Citizens of the former Soviet Union who have entered Canada as entrepreneurs in the last few years have included a significant number with illicit incomes. This has been on a large enough scale to attract comment in the annual report on organized crime, produced by Canada's Criminal Intelligence Service: "Links are continually surfacing between FSU [Former Soviet Union] organized crime and entrepreneur class criminals from the FSU. This category of criminals tends to consist of conspicuously wealthy businessmen, who are associated with large international trading companies ... the majority of these entrepreneur class criminals are now linked to organized crime" (CISC 1996: 11).

Canada's refugee admissions program provides an avenue of entry to many who fail to fit any conventional definition of those fleeing political persecution. Vitali Papsouev came to public attention in 1997 when the collapse of the European Union Bank of Antigua caused the loss of millions of dollars of deposits. Papsouev claimed to be a simple depositor, but Antigua's solicitor-general said Papsouev was being sought as one of the directors. Papsouev, a martial arts expert, had arrived in Canada in 1992 with Dimitri Iakoubouvski but denied being Iakoubouvski's bodyguard (*Globe and Mail*, 9 August 1997). Papsouev originally held a temporary permit as a business immigrant, but when that was not renewed he claimed refugee status on the grounds that his wife was Jewish and would face persecution in Russia. Papsouev awaited the outcome of his claim in comfort, purchasing a mansion in Richmond Hill, where in addition to two leased cars he also garages his $50,000 1998 Mercedes. Five years after his first arrival in Canada his application is still undecided.

Asian organized crime is now well established in every metropolitan area. Asian criminal organizations, with links to Southeast Asia, control an estimated 80 per cent of the heroin entering Canada. Hong Kong police sources claim that Toronto is now the central transmission point for heroin distribution throughout North America, with organized criminal gangs an increasing force in the city with links across North America and into Hong Kong and mainland China.[9]

The most celebrated recent beneficiary of Canada's immigration policies is Lee Chau-Ping, the so-called Ice Queen. Chau-Ping entered Canada from Hong Kong as a business immigrant, with the improbable promise that she and her family intended to move to La Ronge, a remote, predominantly aboriginal community in northern Saskatchewan, and invest in a fast-food chicken franchise. Chau-Ping's business interests were rather more exotic. The family never moved to La Ronge or invested in any chicken franchise but did garner national headlines when Chau-Ping fled Canada as an RCMP investigation closed in. It was reported that she was also wanted by police in China, Hong Kong, and Thailand: Chau-Ping's business acumen, it transpired, was directed not to fast food but a highly addictive crystallized methamphetamine known as ice (*Globe and Mail*, 19 June 1996).

Many of the victims of Canada's failure to distinguish between meritorious and criminal immigration and refugee claims are Asian: "Much of the increase in violent criminal activity can be attributed to street gangs that exploit victims in the Asian community. Canadian law enforcement agencies are concerned with the mobility and propensity for violence of these gangs, which are often armed with semi- and fully automatic weapons. Extortion, loan sharking, witness intimidation, illegal gambling, prostitution, drive-by shootings, 'home invasion' and commercial robberies are typical gang signature crimes" (CISC 1996: 9).

In Vietnamese and Chinese communities, violent gangs appear to operate with virtual impunity. Even in sedate Ottawa most restaurants in the capital's Chinatown are reported to pay protection. Refusal to pay results in violent disruptions engineered by young gang members; patrons flee. If the police intervene it is a simple case of juvenile delinquency, rarely inviting any serious legal sanction. In this as in other areas, racial sensitivity precludes the collection of data, intelligent discussion, or the call that those who devised and implemented the immigration and refugee policies that created these problems be made accountable.

Where the Immigration Department do take measures to curtail entry or remove those deemed undesirable, they may be over-ruled by the courts. A deportation order against a Hong Kong billionaire convicted of bribery in his own country was overturned by the Federal Court of Appeal, reportedly on the grounds that he would not necessarily have been convicted if he had been tried in Canada (*Globe and Mail*, 22 August 1996). Hong Kong at the time was a British crown colony.

An immigration department ruling to declare a convicted Jordanian criminal a danger to the public and order him deported under the new powers granted to the minister in July 1995 was set aside by Madam Justice Barbara Reed, who determined that there had been insufficient opportunity for the defendant to challenge the decision. Nedal Mohammed Ibrahim had been charged with trafficking in hashish and convicted of two gas station robberies and driving dangerously while trying to evade police (ibid., 30 November 1996). Reed's judgment will make it substantially more difficult for the department to expedite the removal of those convicted of serious crimes.[10]

David Matas, the lawyer who acted for Ibrahim, is co-chair of the Canadian Helsinki Watch Group, in which capacity he has argued to the United Nations Human Rights Commission that the removal of those determined a public danger without a proper hearing (at which no doubt legal-aid funded counsel will be required) is a violation of Article 5 of the Universal Declaration of Human Rights, which prohibits cruel, inhuman, or degrading treatment. Such removals will of course have been precipitated by criminal convictions which might be thought to have established guilt. Matas has also claimed that the removal to their country of origin of (non-citizen) adults, who came to Canada in their youth and have been subsequently convicted of criminal offences, is a further violation (ibid., 3 April 1997). Matas further claimed that the absence of an appeal process for unsuccessful refugee claimants and the lack of counsel at ports of entry when refugee claimants are interviewed by immigration officials also constituted violations.

Matas travelled to Geneva to present his claims to the commission, with financial support from the Canadian International Human Rights Network, which administers funds provided by the tax-funded International Centre for Human Rights and Democratic Development. Canadian taxpayers financed the denunciation of their government in Geneva and provided funding for a campaign which would make it significantly more difficult to remove criminals from Canada, while providing yet more tax-financed work for immigration and refugee lawyers.

The appeal division of the Immigration and Refugee Board reviews deportation orders. In the wake of the fatal shooting in the Just Desserts Café in Toronto, it was revealed that one of the suspects, Oneil Rohan Grant, had been given a five year "conditional" stay of deportation by board member Irene Chu, in spite of a lengthy record of assault and drug related offences (*Globe and Mail*, 19 May 1994). In 1993 the board had authorized 145 conditional stays for individuals with criminal records, some worse than that of Grant. The nationalities of seventy-nine were specified, of whom twenty-five were from Jamaica (ibid.).[11] Clinton Gayle, the killer of Toronto police officer Todd Bayliss, had also been released from jail where he awaited deportation, at the order of adjudicator Ivan Rashid.

Canada's generous legal aid system, backed by Supreme Court decisions giving foreigners extensive opportunities to access Canadian lawyers at taxpayers' expense, makes Canada a destination of choice for fugitives from foreign justice. Toronto is believed to be a particular favourite with those fleeing American authorities. Explaining the attraction of Canada, a member of the Toronto squad charged with hunting down foreign fugitives contrasted the harsh penal regime in some American states with Canada: "Here, prison life is nice, they have cable, ping pong, video games. And they'll hold up the entire extradition process, fighting forever at public cost," said detective Larry Dee (*Ottawa Citizen*, 6 January 1996).

Lax immigration and customs controls facilitate entry into Canada of many who might otherwise be excluded. *Globe and Mail* reporter Jan Wong followed her own experience of being detained at Pearson International Airport with an article highlighting the heavy dependence on part-time students with little training to provide front-line customs and immigration services. Students averaged 80 per cent of such workers at Pearson. The manager of immigration operations at Terminal 2 acknowledged that a large number of undesirables were getting through: "Obviously we have a lot" (14 October 1996). Canada appears to be unique in entrusting such responsibilities to students. The growing dependence on students appeared to be accompanied by reduced detection: while passenger volume had increased substantially, the number of drug seizures fell.

Immigration procedures also fail to afford protection against the admission of those who may pose significant health threats. Immigrants are tested for tuberculosis but not for the HIV virus, though the former is still a far more treatable condition. The failure to test for HIV appeases vocal lobby groups but at considerable risk to Canadians. Immigrants from countries with epidemic levels of HIV infection, where predatory male sexual behaviour is widely condoned, pose a potentially lethal risk to their partners. The case of Ugandan immigrant Charles Ssenyonga who knowingly infected numerous Canadian women with the fatal virus has been well documented (Callwood 1995). Ssenyonga arrived in Canada before there was sufficient knowledge to raise the question of screening, but workers in the AIDS field are familiar with a number of other equally harrowing cases. These could have been prevented by the introduction of effective screening of would-be immigrants as the nature and scale of the AIDS epidemic became clear.

ILLEGAL IMMIGRATION

A substantial number of illegal immigrants arrive in Canada each year, although there appear to be no estimates of the numbers involved. Included in the flow of illegals will be a disproportionate number whose lifestyle makes conventional entry difficult. In the United States the issue has assumed considerable electoral significance. An investigation by officials of the State Department, Justice Department, Immigration and Naturalization Service, CIA, Coast Guard, and FBI reported to President Clinton in November 1995, describing an international trade in human cargo running into billions of dollars and involving hundreds of thousands flowing through highly profitable human pipelines. Up to fifty thousand a year were reported to be smuggled into the United States from China alone (*Guardian Weekly*, 7 January 1996).

In Canada the introduction in 1995 of legislation allowing officials to open mail and seize false papers resulted in the seizure in Vancouver of 306 illegal documents in seventy-two parcels. The following year the RCMP reported that they had cracked a counterfeit passport ring centred in Montreal believed to have produced thousands of illegal passports. A Sri Lankan national was charged, and the ring was said to have dealt extensively, though not exclusively, with Sri Lankans (*Globe and Mail*, 5 September 1996).

The break-up of a major smuggling ring in the Netherlands highlighted the ease of access into Canada and the less than rigorous response of politicians and law enforcement agencies. The Dutch investigation was said to be one of the largest criminal investigations in recent years; the exposure of the smuggling ring, said to have sent some five thousand Iranians and Iraqis into Canada, resulted in numerous arrests in the Netherlands and a political uproar. In Canada police arrested and charged two Iranians, both of whom had made successful refugee claims and been granted landed immigrant status a year earlier. The RCMP reported that they had traced twenty-five individuals who had made refugee claims (*Globe and Mail*, 6 December 1996 and RCMP Milton, personal communication, 9 December 1996) and were immune from further police action until these had been processed. There was little political response though Solicitor General Herb Gray did suggest the Dutch should make their passports more difficult to forge (*Globe and Mail*, 7 December 1996).

The smuggling of mainland Chinese into North America is inextricably linked with the growth of Asian crime, which law enforcement agencies now consider a threat second only to that posed by the Mafia. The same individuals are frequently involved in the heroin trade, the export of stolen luxury cars, and the importing of illegal immigrants. Those who refuse to pay the loans required to finance their trip are at risk of substantial retribution including death. The absence of papers, in turn, drives many illegals into the underground economy and compels them to work for employers who ignore minimum wage and benefit regulations (CBC *Newsworld*, "Rough Cuts," 9 December 1996).

The relative ease of illegal access to Canada is suggested by the growing numbers who use the country as a stepping-stone into the United States. In 1996 the United States apprehended some twelve thousand "illegals" attempting an illicit entry across the Canadian border (CBC *Radio News*, 7 February 1997). In Ontario significant smuggling occurs across the St Lawrence, using Mohawk territory near Cornwall. The death of a woman in 1996 when an overloaded boat sank attracted some publicity. One of those apprehended told a Canadian immigration detention hearing that he had paid some $5,700 in New Delhi to be brought to Canada and smuggled into the United

States (*Globe and Mail*, 26 October 1996). All of those detained claimed refugee status in Canada. Nancy Worsfold, the executive director of the Canadian Council for Refugees, suggested that those "forced into the hands of sleazy smugglers" were often refugees: "That people have recourse to exorbitant and dangerous methods is testimony to their desperation" (ibid.). It was unclear what persecution might have been involved in this case or why those fleeing persecution would not have immediately sought refuge in Canada rather than being smuggled into the United States, a country with a far less generous refugee admission program.

The arrest of a number of people in Vancouver, Toronto, and Cornwall was linked to the operation of a major smuggling ring bringing Chinese immigrants through Canada into the United States at $45,000 each. Those arrested and charged with conspiracy to smuggle aliens included immigrants, refugee claimants, and Canadian citizens. Those being smuggled through Canada were reportedly advised to make a claim for refugee status on entering Canada (ibid., 6 November 1996).

The failure to afford effective deterrence to the organized smuggling of would-be immigrants results not only in significant costs to Canadian taxpayers and the erosion of confidence in the efficacy of Canada's admission's procedures; it also poses serious dangers to those tempted to use such routes to secure entry. Illegal immigrants may be subject to continuing threats from those who assisted their entry. Chinese smuggling organizations have a particular reputation for the brutal recovery of money from those who default on the frequently usurious arrangements made to secure passage. Would-be immigrants are often attracted to smuggling rings by quite unrealistic expectations of the prospects that await them in the country of destination. Those able to afford the $5,000–$10,000 advance payments which are often demanded are recruited not from the very poor but from more affluent groups, who combine inflated expectations with little knowledge of the risks. In a particularly gruesome case, a smuggling ring bringing Sri Lankans, Indians, and Pakistanis into Italy, from where many intended to secure onward passage to other countries including Canada, some 280 migrants were forced at gunpoint from a ship off the coast of Sicily into a small vessel which quickly began to sink. The vessel was then either intentionally or accidentally rammed by the mother ship, and all on board were lost. The remaining migrants were put ashore in Greece, again at gunpoint. Greek authorities issued arrest warrants for mass murder for the three Greeks involved (Ferguson 1997).

Historically, Canada has responded to illegal immigration by declaring periodic amnesties.

SOME INTERNATIONAL COMPARISONS

Although the United States has a much lower unemployment rate than Canada, concerns over the pace of demographic changes and the pressures on preferred immigrant destinations have led to moves in Congress and the Senate to reduce current immigration levels – which are already on a per capita basis much lower than Canada's. Conscious of the effect that illegal immigrants have on wages at the lower end of the labour market, the black Democratic caucus have played an active role in seeking stronger enforcement measures. The economic plight of many black Americans has ensured that in the United States concern over high immigration levels is also found on the left of the political spectrum, where the use of immigration by some large American corporations to secure access to cheap labour has been highlighted (Beck 1996).

In 1996, Australia announced a reduction in its immigration intake of 10.8 per cent. The number admitted under the family reunification scheme would fall sharply, with greater emphasis on English language competence and labour market skills. The changes were linked to high unemployment levels among some immigrant groups with poor English language skills (*Guardian Weekly*, 14 July 1996). Prior to the changes Australia, with a population of 18 million and an unemployment rate significantly lower than Canada's, admitted some 83,000 immigrants annually.

SHAPING THE IMMIGRATION DEBATE

The linkage of immigration with race in Canada ensures that there is little debate over immigration levels. This linkage appears to find favour with the Ministry of Citizenship and Immigration, which provides funding to the pro-immigration Ontario Council of Agencies Serving Immigrants to study racist and anti-immigration references and to encourage and assist the media to portray immigration in a positive light. The project organizers left no doubt that those who opposed immigration were racist. As *Globe and Mail* columnist Michael Valpy noted, "what we have here is the federal government funding academic and social agency research ... to defend an immigration policy (and to help the press support an immigration policy) that a segment of the population legitimately doesn't like" (26 March 1996).

OCASI's government-funded project produced a number of so-called "fact sheets" for circulation to the media and elsewhere. This allowed the project to parade a series of contentious claims under a veneer of scholarship, ostensibly supported by an array of evidence. Fact sheet number 2, for example, offered the statement: "unemployment is a serious problem in Canada, but it is caused by fiscal policy not immigration." The carefully footnoted sources for this facile view of the relationship between immigration, unemployment, and fiscal policy are the Canadian Council for Refugees and a 1987 statement by the National Executive of the Canadian Autoworkers. In contrast, in the introduction to a collection of academic studies generally sympathetic to high levels of immigration, the editor offers an unambiguous comment: "expanding immigration in the early 1990s as central Canada's unemployment rose no doubt exacerbated the unemployment in central Canada" (DeVoretz 1995: 25).

The marked decline in independent-class immigrants is a matter of record. OCASI maintains instead that "Immigration selection criteria puts increasingly great emphasis on education and qualifications." Warming to its theme, OCASI notes that 17 per cent of immigrants had degrees between 1981 and 1991, compared to only 9 per cent before 1961 (OCASI 1996) – a figure that points to the project organizers' willingness to cherry-pick any statistic so long as it points to the right conclusion. Any meaningful comparison would need to take into account the whole range of immigrant educational attainment and the rapid growth, over the comparative periods, of post-secondary education.

Why does Canada admit so many immigrants? The OCASI project offers a clear answer: "Canada brings in immigrants because it needs to stimulate the economy through population growth" (ibid.). This apparently ignores the miracles that might be achieved by fiscal policy and raises some question as to why Metro Toronto's burgeoning population has failed to provide the promised stimulus. The council is in no doubt that "studies show there is no economic growth without population growth," a finding that might surprise those European Union countries whose economic growth is accompanied by static population levels. The council is equally confident that current immigration levels are too low: "At the present rate of 200,000 immigrants per year, not enough immigrants are admitted to meet these needs" (ibid.). The council is of course in the immigration business – higher immigration levels will ensure higher levels of funding. But the tax-funded "facts" offered here stand in sharp contrast to the views of demographers: "There was no demographic basis for the high immigration levels of the early 1990s ... Canada's population would have been increasing even without any immigration ... A federal investigation of Canada's demographic future, the Demographic Review, proved that no demographic case exists for high immigration levels" (Foot and Stoffman 1996: 203–4).

British Columbia has experienced a disproportionately high level of immigration, both internally and externally. During the early 1990s it seemed that the province had avoided the economic downturn affecting the rest of Canada, though welfare rolls grew by some 100,000 and unemployment remained at the 10 per cent level. In an expert collection of papers assembled by the C.D. Howe Institute and the Laurier Institution, the diminishing returns from immigration were noted, but B.C. was singled out as "one province where immigration and inward capital flows continue to result in significant benefits" (Keirans and Kunin 1995: vi).

Subsequent data on the economic impact of immigration from B.C. Stats suggested that in fact much of the growth in provincial GDP was simply a reflection of population increases. In contrast to the claim that immigration provides net economic benefits, the province's rapid population growth had been accompanied by little real growth in GDP per capita. This had risen only $600 since 1981 (a period that saw significant increases in the female labour force participation rate). In 1981 British Columbia had a per capita GDP 8.4 per cent above the national average; by 1996 it had a per capita GDP 4.4 per cent below (*Globe and Mail*, 20 November 1996). The argument made by those who advocate high immigration levels depends not on the assertion that some growth will result but rather that there will be general economic benefits of which per capita GDP is a good measure.[12] The relationship between immigration policy, economic growth, and a range of social issues is complex. What OCASI offers is not a contribution to the debate but government-funded propaganda.

The efforts of the Department of Citizenship and Immigration to promote its agenda are not always characterized by such obvious attempts at the manipulation of public opinion. The department provides extensive funding to scholars and others researching its programs. It is in the nature of such relationships that those who are funded share many of the perspectives of those providing the funding. The rewards for participants are considerable, extending beyond access to scarce research funding for travel to foreign conferences. A joint venture between the Canadian Department of Citizenship and Immigration and the Australian Bureau of Immigration and Population Research brought Australian and Canadian academics together at seminars in Melbourne and Toronto to examine the issues of immigration and refugee policy from a comparative perspective. The resulting two-volume publication, not surprisingly, provides a less than critical account. A discussion of immigration and crime, for example, seems intended more to provide reassurance than to probe the issues that underlie public concerns and raise questions about the efficacy of mechanisms intended to protect Canada from immigration by those involved in crime. Figures are offered to show that the foreign-born are less likely to be involved in crime: "The most likely explanation is that the foreign-born are simply less disposed to crime. This should not be too surprising given that immigrants are screened for criminality before being admitted to Canada" (Borowski and Thomas 1994: 645).

The authors acknowledge the over-representation in crime of those born in the West Indies and Central America, but there is no suggestion that this may reflect any failure in the immigration recruitment process. What is offered instead is a picture of social victimization: "Immigrants from the Caribbean, Central and South America may experience problems in the integration process generally ... criminal means have taken the place of legitimate means due to the existence of barriers" (ibid.: 646). There are many problems with this account, not least the question of why immigrants from different Caribbean islands are not equally affected and why other immigrant groups such as South Asians and Africans are not driven to "criminal means" in similar numbers.

More recently Citizenship and Immigration together with the Social Science and Humanities Research Council launched a more ambitious international venture with cooperation and seminars planned between researchers in Canada, the U.K., Germany, France, Italy, Sweden, the Netherlands, Finland, Israel, Croatia, and the United States. Four Canadian research centres were promised $8 million over six years (SSHRC-CIC 1996). The program placed the interests of immigrant advocacy groups in a central position. The "research partners" of the centre established by York University, Ryerson Polytechnic, and the University of Toronto included OCASI, which appeared to have already provided answers to most of the relevant questions. The Alberta-based centre of excellence boasted the racially exclusive "Women of Colour Collective" among its partners.

THE IMMIGRATION INDUSTRY

Many of those offering to assist would-be immigrants advertise their former connections with the immigration service. A full page in *Canada News*, a British monthly directed to would-be immigrants, offers the services of Hall and Associates Professional Immigration Consultants. The ad contains extensive information on partner David Hall, a former "national Director General" in the immigration department "who has more than twenty five years making decisions in Canada's immigration department" (July 1996).

An article in the same issue of *Canada News* recounts the experience of Prashant Ajmera, who employed the services of Montreal immigration lawyers Brownstein and Brownstein to assist his application. Ajmera was advised that "his chances of immigrating under Quebec's immigration policy were bright, providing he learnt some French." Brownstein arranged an attorney for hearings that resulted in Prashant's acceptance. Simultaneously Prashant organized seminars for other would-be immigrants to meet with Brownstein and Brownstein in Delhi and Ahmedabad. This was the beginning of a mutually beneficial relationship: "Ever since Prashant has not looked back. He has provided consultations for hundreds of clients in India and has conducted seminars in India on Canadian immigration" (ibid.). Prashant is now employed in Montreal with Brownstein and Brownstein, whose advertisement appeared adjacent to the "news" story.

The provisions for more favourable immigration access to those prepared to invest a minimum of $350,000 in Canada (outside Ontario, Nova Scotia, Quebec, and British Columbia the sum is $250,000) have been repeatedly criticized. The scheme has been subject to extensive abuse as Canadians have taken advantage of the scheme to establish investment schemes that have proved less than advantageous to immigrant investors. The program provides a significant advantage to immigrants from wealthier areas and to more affluent applicants. Why wealth should be thought to constitute such an important qualification is unclear: many of those admitted under the program have no obvious entrepreneurial skills but have merely benefited from the soaring property prices and booming stock exchanges in Hong Kong and Taiwan. The sale of an apartment for $1 million may create sufficient wealth to apply under the immigrant investor program and allow for the purchase of a comfortable Canadian property, but it has no relevance to the likelihood of an immigrant finding worthwhile employment in Canada – as many immigrants have found to their cost. In British Columbia the so-called "astronauts," as those commuting frequently between Vancouver and Hong Kong have been dubbed, include many who failed to find employment in Canada. Not all such commuters are rich; they include many who can only return to visit their families infrequently, as they pursue work in Hong Kong. There is little glamour in such lifestyles, as the *Globe and Mail*'s correspondent Miro Cernetig writes: "they will often find they have grown estranged from their families who have gone on with different lives in Canada, which astronauts call 'passport land'" (8 May 1997). One consequence of this peripatetic lifestyle is that Canadian taxpayers pick up the costs of families whose own taxable income is earned abroad.

The investor program is open to easy manipulation by immigration consultants. Imperial Consultants, for example, with offices in Taiwan,

Vancouver, Hong Kong, Montreal, and Moncton, have assisted thousands of Taiwanese to move to Canada since 1987. The company's activities received some unfavourable publicity in 1996, when it was reported that Imperial's owners, Gordon and Robert Fu, faced charges of attempted bribery. The brothers were alleged to have offered immigration officials $50,000 to change rules that had suspended several of their investment funds (*Globe and Mail*, 24 June 1996).

A Quebec investment firm developed an apparently legal scheme which provided further support to the charge that the program was simply an invitation to wealthy immigrants to purchase their entry into Canada and, in doing so, enrich those Canadians who had seized the opportunities afforded. The scheme, developed by Lévesque Beaubien Geoffrion, a major player in the management of immigrant investor funds, required would-be investor immigrants to put up not $350,000 but $97,000; the dealer would arrange a five year loan for the remaining $253,000 (ibid., 10 February 1997). The reduction in capital requirements came at a price – those investing in the scheme would receive no refund or return on their "investment," which would be used to finance the loan and, no doubt, provide a worthwhile return to those who had dreamed up this ingenious plan. In a context in which most Taiwanese immigrant investors have lost money in a variety of schemes, it would perhaps be reassuring to know the cost from the outset. Tai Yao, past president of the Taiwan Entrepreneurs and Investors Association of Canada, noted that the majority of investors who moved to Canada lost money. Those who only lost $100,000 were "very happy" (ibid.).

Many Canadians might be surprised to learn that the immigrant investor program, justified on the grounds that it will bring investment and business talent into Canada, could be subject to such interpretation; but Lucienne Robillard, a former Quebec cabinet minister, had no such concerns. Specifically defending the Lévesque Beaubien Geoffrion scheme, Robillard said she had heard of no abuse or fraud in the province, which receives some 50 per cent of all money invested under the investor program (*Globe and Mail*, 11 February 1997).

Those seeking to enter Canada from mainland China as business immigrants make extensive use of immigration consultants. A *Globe and Mail* report suggested that a Chinese government crackdown on corruption, which threatened those whose wealth had been gained by syphoning profits out of state enterprises, had resulted in a sharp increase in applications. The wealth of some other would-be immigrants was believed to stem from involvement in organized crime, the "Triads." Careful scrutiny of immigrants at the Beijing Embassy resulted in increasing applications at other Canadian embassies, assisted by immigration consultants. Canada allows application at any embassy and as one immigration department official commented, "They go shopping. I know that if I were an immigration consultant I would certainly not have my Chinese client apply in Beijing" (15 November 1996).

Lai Tong Sang, identified by the Macau police and the Immigration Department as a Triad gang leader, was granted immigration status at Canada's Los Angeles consulate. Lai had previously applied in Hong Kong but withdrew his application. Applying in Los Angeles in May 1996, Lai was admitted to Canada in September – a speed no doubt reflecting the intervention of legal counsel. He moved to Vancouver where his home was the target of a drive-by shooting. Local press interest compelled the minister to admit that no check had been made with the Hong Kong consulate before Lai was accepted (*Globe and Mail*, 23 August 1997).

The allegiance of many wealthy immigrant investors to their new country is questionable. Some appear to view a Canadian passport as little more than a protection against political uncertainty in Hong Kong and Taiwan. Citizenship claims, on which access to Canadian passports depends, are intended to follow the establishment of a continuous period of permanent residence in Canada. Many of those who have "moved" to Canada continue to live in their countries of origin and to conduct the bulk of their business there.[13] Recent proposals to compel Canadians to reveal their overseas assets were greeted with outrage by wealthy Chinese Canadians in Vancouver, who claimed it would result in many of those affected leaving Canada. The protest was sufficient to ensure a meeting with Finance Minister Paul Martin, who reported that "they don't want to be discriminated against" (*Globe and Mail's Report on Business*, 18 October 1996). This commendable sensitivity begged the question as to why the issue of discrimination was relevant to a proposed tax law with universal application.[14]

The pursuit of high levels of immigration appeals, as Daniel Stoffman notes, to influential constituencies. Immigration lawyers get more work, bureaucrats more resources. Ethnic groups see their numbers swell, and politicians hope for votes from those admitted. Landlords in the major immigrant centres raise rents in response to growing demand, land developers get richer, employers are offered an apparently limitless supply of low wage workers. In contrast, opposition is diffuse, particularly where those who urge more modest admission goals risk being accused of racism. Proposals by Immigration Minister Sergio Marchi in late 1995 to focus recruitment more closely on skilled workers fluent in one of Canada's official languages were quickly placed on hold following intense lobbying by immigration lawyers who claimed such changes would leave too much discretion in the hands of immigration officials (thus reducing the opportunities for immigration lawyers and consultants) (*Globe and Mail*, 9 January 1996). The proposals were scarcely draconian, providing applicants with an opportunity to "self-assess" such matters as language skill.

A ruling by the British Columbia Supreme Court barring Jaswant Singh Mangat from continuing in business as an immigration consultant, since the Immigration Act did not allow non-lawyers to do the work for a fee, highlighted the lucrative nature of the industry. Mangat, who had been in business for twenty-seven years, was said to handle more cases than anyone else in western Canada. Before the Law Society of British Columbia sought an injunction against Mangat, he was reported to have around one thousand clients, at a fee of some $1,500 a case (ibid., 20 August 1997). Don DeVoretz, director of the Centre of Immigration Studies at Simon Fraser University, which is supported by the Immigration Department, assured the *Globe*, "I don't see a scandal out there involving immigration consultants" (ibid.).

The announcement by the new Immigration minister, Lucienne Robillard, that immigration targets for 1997 were set at between 195,000 and 220,000, with an increase in the proportion of independent class immigrants, provided an insight into the way the industry structures the debate. Robillard acknowledged that the Liberals had failed to meet the Red Book target of 1 per cent of the Canadian population, blaming Canadians who accepted the "myth" that immigrants take jobs from Canadian residents: "I have to recognize the myth is there. To have more immigration in Canada we need the support of the population" (ibid., 30 October 1996). The headlines succinctly summarized the minister's spin: "Minister holds the line on immigration: 'Public Opinion' forces Robillard to keep 1996 levels" (*Ottawa Citizen*, 30 October 1996), "Immigration levels reflect backlash" (*Globe and Mail*, 30 October 1996).

The minister's approach no doubt explains the department's financial support for those who share her view that the only barrier to increased immigration is the ignorance and bigotry of other Canadians. The resulting public debate was, inevitably, dominated by those who work in the industry or have a direct stake in increased immigration. David Matas, head of the immigration law section of the Canadian Bar Association, condemned the government's obeisance to erroneous public opinion, calling on the government to take "some leadership in shaping that opinion." Alan Li, speaking for the Canadian-Heritage funded Chinese-Canadian National Council, added to the public's alleged misconceptions the belief that immigrant investors and skilled professionals are more economically valuable than dependents, claiming the increased emphasis on economic class immigrants "perpetuates the myth that the family class is a burden on society" (ibid.).

The intervention of Nancy Worsfold, executive director of the Canadian Council for Refugees, confirmed the council's view that Canada's immigration policy should minimize any barriers to entry. Worsfold expressed concern that a drop in the number of children, spouses, parents, and grandparents might result from the imposition of immigration processing fees intended to defray the costs of the immigration program, as part of Liberal deficit reduction measures. The council appeared to see no difference between these policies and the very different philosophy that underpinned earlier, racially specific immigrant control measures: "If there's been a steep drop in applications, I'm worried the head tax [sic] is too high," Worsfold said. The tax-funded Ontario Council of Agencies Serving Immigrants charged the Liberals with being "driven by re-election objectives" (ibid.). Certainly the Liberals' immigration and multicultural policies are driven by the party's overt cultivation of ethnic constituencies, but not in the way OCASI suggests.

Entirely absent from the public discussion of the new immigration targets were those who might raise such heretical questions as whether potential immigrants would be advised about levels of unemployment in Canada and the large numbers of recent immigrants who, unable to find work, had been compelled to seek social assistance. Equally lacking was any discussion of the way in which, contrary to the minister's anodyne assurances, the government's own preferential hiring policies ensured it was certainly not a "myth" that immigrants might take jobs from Canadians.

The way in which the government presented the immigration target led to the inevitable conclusion that an enlightened immigration policy would have offered a much higher target had not ill-informed and prejudiced Canadians prevented further increases. Yet again government policy offered explicit endorsement to the claim that large numbers of Canadians are racial bigots. The consequences of regular repetition of this allegation include the encouragement of those who are the putative victims of this bigotry to interpret their life experiences accordingly. As for those Canadians who legitimately question immigration policies that seem driven more by political expedience and the interventions of well-paid lawyers and "consultants" than economic logic, there will no doubt be some who respond that if this is bigotry, then bigots they will be.

10

Alabama North

Race, Gender, and the Politics
of the Rae Government

Cultural and demographic changes made us push very hard
on issues like pay equity and employment equity. This made
some people, powerful people – who tend to be white middle-
and upper-class men – very uncomfortable.

Bob Rae, 1996

Far from being an assault on the white power structure, racial
preference is a means by which the black and Hispanic affirmative action elites are turned into dependent clients of the
white overclass.

Michael Lind, 1995

The Rae government's employment equity legislation played a prominent role in the electoral campaign that saw the NDP reduced to third
party status. But contrary to Rae's retrospective above, those who were
made uncomfortable were not predominantly middle- and upper-class
white men. Corporate Canada is quite comfortable with legislated
employment equity and the related diversity industry, though the particulars of the Ontario legislation may have caused concern. The upper-
class men Rae conjures up as his opposition may serve to provide the
NDP with the cachet of crusader against the elite, but there was scant
evidence of upper-class opposition to the Chrétien government's moves
to strengthen federal employment equity legislation. The courts,
scarcely the preserve of the working classes, have also proved enthusiastic supporters of legislated preferential hiring. Michael Lind has
described a similar American phenomenon: "to be opposed to affirmative action is thought to be an admission of the prejudices of a
lower class white ... an insistence that even white Americans should

be protected from legal discrimination is considered not so much immoral as simply *vulgar*" (Lind 1995: 150, emphasis in original).

More important to the NDP's defeat was the neglect of the concerns of its traditional constituents, who sought not group advantage but greater social equality. Responding to a question about the "shift to the right," Rae acknowledged the real pressures faced by ordinary Canadians and drew attention to the link between his government's failure to address these and its preoccupation with the political demands of various identity groups. Rae rooted the shift to the right in "the fact that living standards have not really improved over the last twenty years and we have not focused enough attention on that. The NDP was perceived by the public as preoccupied with other issues and I think we got punished for that. People care about their taxes and jobs and living standards. They want the government to focus on these issues more than on equity issues" (Dahlin 1996). With no evident logic Rae then proceeded to identify the main opposition to such measures in the white male middle- and upper-classes. A more convincing but, for the NDP, unsettling argument, might suggest that it was primarily working-class Canadians who turned against the NDP's growing preoccupation with the politics of grievance. They, after all, were historically far more likely to vote for the party.

The Rae government's enthusiasm for preferential policies responded to the agenda of upwardly mobile women and visible minorities, who saw in such policies the opportunity for accelerated advancement at the expense of white male competitors. The agenda pursued by Rae, even where it targeted women and visible minorities, was not an agenda directed to the concerns of the genuinely disadvantaged, who lacked opportunities for upward mobility. The American experience had already demonstrated the irrelevance of affirmative action to the life chances of poor blacks. William Julius Wilson, a black social democrat and a University of Chicago professor, summarized the con-clusions to be drawn from the American experience: "programs of preferential treatment applied merely according to racial or ethnic group membership tend to benefit the relatively advantaged segments of the designated groups. The truly deprived members may not be helped by such programs" (Wilson 1987: 115). What Rae offered, at the expense of able-bodied white males, was to provide further advan-tages to those who were already relatively well placed.

Rae came to office as the recession and the effects of the North American Free Trade Association took a devastating toll on Ontario's manufacturing industries. To many of those facing lay-off or increasing job insecurity, the NDP's preoccupation with legislating preferential hiring and other facets of grievance politics appeared at best an irrelevance, at worst a move to create additional insecurity.[1] The high level of immigration which persisted even as employment declined might have prompted a government more influenced by the concerns of ordinary Ontarians to call for restraint until the economy improved. In the rarefied circles that informed the NDP's policies, such a call would have been denounced as "blaming the immigrants."

The legacy of the new government included not only its own political rhetoric, which frequently portrayed women and racial minorities as victims of the grossest discrimination, but also programs and policies already put in place by the Peterson Liberals. Preferential hiring in the Ontario Public Service had already seen some ministries, notably Housing and Citizenship, place increasing emphasis on skin colour in recruitment. The Race Relations Directorate in the Ministry of Citizenship, and the Ontario Women's Directorate, were both active protagonists in advocating race and gender driven policies. The Peterson government had developed a Multiculturalism Strategy and Race Relations Policy involving many of the same groups that depended on federal patronage. A meeting in 1988 with the minister responsible for women's issues included the National Organization of Immigrant and Visible Minority Women, the Congress of Black Women, the Canadian Ethnocultural Council Women's Committee, the Chinese Canadian National Council Women's Issues Committee, and the Coalition of Visible Minority Women (Gabriel 1996: 188). The organizational names are indicative of the confusion that must have arisen over who could lay claim to represent which constituencies. According to one account, "women of colour" were concerned to "redefine the ways in which they were included and excluded from decision-making processes; in doing so they raised the issue of institutional sexism and racism, and their particular position of multiple marginality [sic]" (Gabriel 1996: 190).

THE VIEW FROM ROSEDALE

The major beneficiaries of racial preference, it can be argued, are overclass whites, who by this policy of ethnic division and co-opting buy social peace. They also, incidentally, undermine any mass based populism in the country.

Michael Lind, 1995[2]

I have to tell you there is great concern about the progress of the government's intended employment equity legislation ... there may be no other explicit legislative initiative which will mean so much to establishing a positive climate of race

> relations in the minds of every single minority grouping ... If
> one accepts the argument ... that the Ontario Public Service
> (OPS) must set the example for everyone else, then we have
> a problem on our hands.
>
> Stephen Lewis, 1992

The perception of pervasive racism and discrimination in the province was given widespread credence in the 1992 "report" of former NDP leader and UN ambassador Stephen Lewis on the Yonge Street mini-riots. The disturbances, triggered by protests against the beating of Rodney King, testify as eloquently to the Americanization of Canadian discussion of racial questions as the actual Lewis report. To read the report is to find not an examination of what may well be the most successful multi-ethnic society in the world but a catalogue of racism and discrimination more commonly attributed to our southern neighbours.

Lewis's recommendations had a seminal influence on the political direction of the Rae government. Every ministry was expected to play a part in implementation, with the Ministry of Citizenship taking the coordinating role. Lewis held no formal position with the Ontario government. Nonetheless, in May 1994, two cabinet ministers (the attorney general and the minister of Citizenship) submitted to him a seventeen-page letter, described as an "informal status report on our response to the spirit and the letter of your recommendations" (Ziemba and Boyd, Letter to Lewis, 3 May 1994). Lewis's own "letter" might stand as a textbook case for those interested in the workings of orthodoxy. He eschewed facts and figures or scholarly reference in favour of sweeping observations. Where facts, figures, and other research evidence exists, Lewis was usually wrong.

Lewis was asked by Rae to become his adviser on race relations, but it remains unclear how Lewis defines racism. The emphasis in the report is on the central importance of race in program provision and employment entitlement, not the fostering of colour blind practices.[3] Lewis reported the views expressed by those he talked to as though they were representative of some broad consensus on the "facts." This allowed him to reach decisive conclusions that might puzzle those aware of either the diversity of view found in all ethnic communities or the empirical data examined by serious researchers. Lewis learned, for example, of the great concern to see the government's employment equity legislation passed. No other legislation, Lewis assured the premier, would mean so much "in the minds of every single minority grouping it matters not, public and private sector alike" (Lewis 1992). Curiously, a contemporary *Toronto Star* poll reported that among

South Asians "only 16 per cent consider prejudice and discrimination to be one of the most pressing issues facing their community" (*Toronto Star*, 28 June 1992).

Lewis denounced the failure of the Ontario Public Service to make progress on employment equity. An accelerated program had been in place since 1987, but the results were "truly disappointing," the gains "marginal at best." Giving voice to the enormous scepticism he claimed to have encountered among visible minorities in the public service, Lewis talked of a real "crisis of faith." He also detected the same problem in the political staff in the different ministries. Clearly something was amiss in the public service. Or was it? Entirely lacking from the Lewis report was any empirical data.

Yet relevant research is easily accessible. Before the Rae government's equity legislation, Bill 79, was introduced, there was already a veritable army of employment equity officers at Queen's Park. The staffing, recruitment, and promotion practices of every government office were exhaustively monitored. If the charge of intentional and systemic discrimination made by Lewis and repeated in the preamble to the soon-to-be-legislated Employment Equity Bill were well based, we would expect there to be very few racial minorities in the Ontario Public Service. In addition to possible discrimination there were good reasons to expect visible minorities to have a disproportionately small number of positions in the Ontario Public Service: many members of this group arrived in Canada relatively recently; 1991 census data indicate that only 17 per cent of visible minorities were born in Canada (Canadian Heritage 1994: 1). Fifty per cent of recent immigrants to Toronto do not speak either of Canada's official languages.

According to the 105-page *Employment Equity Annual Report, June 1991 to May 1992* (Management Board 1993), visible minorities represented about 8.6 per cent of the Ontario working-age population at the time of the 1986 census; by 1991–92 they made up 12.7 per cent of the Ontario Public Service. In the Ministry of Citizenship 36 per cent of employees were visible minorities, 76 per cent of all employees women; in Housing 34 per cent were visible minorities, 56 per cent women. This might be thought reassuring to those worried about discrimination. It might also have suggested scope for cutbacks in employment equity staff. Given the characteristics of visible minorities in the province, including the recent origin of many and the large number fluent in neither English or French, some of the figures might be thought to reflect such a degree of preferential hiring as to raise concerns about the application of the merit principle.

This was not the conclusion of the Ontario government. The fact that racial minorities were over-represented must be set in context:

Management Board, who masterminded this exercise in social engineering, determined that the objective was not to achieve a reflection of the contemporary population – the intent was that the workforce should "mirror the diversity of the population in the year 2001," when there would be a significantly larger visible minority population. For most positions the target was to mirror not the representation of visible minorities in the province but the much larger proportion in the Metro Toronto area.

Given the rapid changes in Ontario's demographic characteristics, it is reasonable to hypothesize that visible minority members will be disproportionately represented among more recent public service recruits. The importance of seniority in securing higher earnings and accessing promotion opportunities would suggest that on average the visible minority group would be lower paid. Instead the report notes that visible minority men earned, on average, the same as white males – evidence, perhaps, that they do not face discrimination? No such conclusion is drawn. Rather, it is suggested that the explanation lies in the fact that they are under-represented in lower paying blue-collar jobs. Visible minority women were reported to earn less than white males and marginally less than white females – evidence, we are to believe, of systemic discrimination. Yet the statistics presented might well result from visible minority women having a lower average length of service or lesser qualifications. However, Management Board employment equity staff have confirmed that they have not sought to analyse the earnings of visible minority women taking these factors into account to determine if there is prima facie evidence of discrimination. The reason no such analysis has been undertaken, they advised me, is that the focus was on program implementation not program justification. Again fashionable belief takes precedence over serious analysis.

It should be emphasized that the statistics cited above are not a consequence of the effects of the Rae government's employment equity legislation. Rather, this was the situation in the Ontario Public Service when the Ontario government stated in the preamble to Bill 79 that visible minorities faced intentional and systemic discrimination in the public service. These were the circumstances which gave rise to Lewis's "crisis of faith."

Were visible minorities, as Lewis claimed, excluded from political staff and from the influence such staff exercise? The demographic composition of the Ontario Public Service is a historical construct. Many current employees were hired and promoted when the ethnic and gender characteristics of the provincial labour force were very different than they are today. In contrast, the staffing of ministers' offices is a result of very recent decisions. Such staffing should reflect a snapshot of the contemporary provincial labour force, with candidates recruited from a disparate geographic area.

Management Board's response to a Freedom of Information request (27 September 1994) indicated that no less than one in five of the 350 staff in ministers' offices were members of visible minorities. Women made up 40 per cent of the full-time labour force in Canada but 66 per cent of the ministers' staff (Statistics Canada Labour Force Averages 1994). The group most clearly disadvantaged in employment was white males. In the Ministry of Citizenship, for example, the ministry responsible for employment equity, the discrimination against able-bodied white males evident in the ministry's wider employment statistics was also apparent. In the minister's office, only one of the thirteen staff fell into that category (Response to FOI request, Citizenship, July 24, 1994).[4]

It is possible, notwithstanding the broader statistics, that discrimination in particular ministries or particular occupational groups might exist. When the Rae government left office, having added some $50 billion to the provincial debt, there was an extensive panoply of employment equity staff, in addition to the rapidly growing Office of the Employment Equity Commissioner. Individual ministries each had staff with an employment equity function. Management Board, with oversight of the OPS, had 130 staff with such a function. In September 1994, under Freedom of Information legislation, I asked the following question: "What evidence from Ontario government research (or other research reports) has been considered by Management Board (or other relevant Ontario Government bodies) regarding the practise of discrimination in recruitment or promotion of currently designated employment equity groups?"

The reply, three months later, was: "There are no records which involve a quantitative analysis of whether or not discrimination against designated groups based on comparisons between designated and non-designated groups in various occupations has taken place in the OPS" (Letter, J.R. Thomas, Management Board, 7 December 1994).

FROM EQUALITY OF OPPORTUNITY TO EQUALITY OF OUTCOME

The ill-founded assumptions of the equity industry are nowhere more clearly articulated than in the proposition that any under-representation of any target group in any field is *prima facie* evidence of contemporary discrimination. Equality demands not equality of opportunity or treatment but equality of outcome. To ensure equality of outcome, it is argued, it may be necessary to treat people unequally.

The Rae government engaged in considerable intervention in the educational curriculum, driven by the conviction that the schools could and should deliver equality of outcome. More thoughtful critics would have pointed to the powerful influence of external factors of class, income, culture, and family status. A 1974 Statistics Canada study, for example, found students from affluent families five times as likely to attend university as students from poor families (Coyne 1996). Contemporary research indicates that it is the educational status of parents, not race or gender, that is the most important predictor of access to higher education: children in households where one or more parents has a degree are some five times more likely to attend university than children in other households.

Ontario's Royal Commission on Learning articulated the equality-of-results argument: "We can expect that, in a truly equitable system, roughly the same proportion of each [racial or ethnic] community will excel, do satisfactorily or do poorly, as in the total student population. If, as is currently true, they do not, the system needs to be fixed" (in Valpy 1995).

This reflects a degree of faith in the potential of social engineering that might surprise those familiar with the extremely modest achievements of previous educational reforms. It denies the impact of social class on educational outcomes, for how else could one expect ethnic groups that are significantly less affluent to do as well as those that are significantly more affluent? The commission would seem to justify the claims of those who attribute educational failure to the school; more disturbingly, it legitimates groups who explain their own failure by blaming such abstractions as systemic racism. This in turn deflects attention away from individual and group behaviours that maximize the chance of success and failure. Those who lose are viewed as victims of a system that needs to be fixed, not held responsible for their failure to maximize opportunities as they were presented.

The Rae government, backed by an array of tax-funded advocacy groups, introduced a number of reforms to the school curriculum.[5] Educational restructuring resulted in de-streaming the school system, which it was claimed was currently failing many low-income children and those from racial minority backgrounds. The intent was not to secure equality of opportunity but to legislate equality of outcome. The educational reforms were an essential part of a wider political mission that placed the issue of identity at the forefront of the government's agenda: "The drive to end streaming is, at bottom, part of the drive to convert Canada from a country based on the equality of opportunity for the meritocratic inequality of result into a racialist and sexist state where the government distributes entitlements, jobs, and status so as to exactly replicate at all times the distribution of the two genders and visible minorities in the population at large" (Emberley and Newell 1994: 18–19).

The demand for proportionate outcomes requires that racial or ethnic groups which currently do poorly in the school system become fully represented among the high achievers. It also, logically, requires the appropriate representation of groups which are now disproportionately successful, among the low achievers. Black and Portuguese students must do substantially better; Jewish and Chinese students significantly worse – at least in relative terms.

There are considerable differences in outcomes between ethnic groups, mediated by such factors as culture, geographic residence, and relative economic status. Not surprisingly, children born to more affluent parents have a greater chance of success. A test of student math achievement by the North York Board of Education, a board with a large number of visible minority and immigrant students, found socio-economic variables the most significant in predicting achievement. For students from high socio-economic environments, for example, there was "very little" difference in Grade 8 math benchmark achievements, regardless of length of time in Canada (North York Board 1995: 6).

Other factors, including family stability, also play an important role in influencing educational outcomes. Children in single parent families are at significantly greater risk of educational failure. A study of 334 black student dropouts by the Canadian Alliance of Black Educators found that three-quarters were from single parent families. Many of the dropouts seemed destined themselves to become single parents: more than half of the girls had unplanned pregnancies (*Globe and Mail*, editorial, 12 December 1995). In Toronto the proportion of black lone parents is three times as high as for the wider population. Nationally, 1986 census data showed some one in three black children were raised in single parent families, compared to some one in eight of other Canadians (Kralt and Allen 1992).

Statistics Canada's National Longitudinal Survey of Children and Youth reported the increased incidence of a range of problems for the children of single parents, including a growing number of students who had to repeat a grade at school (*Globe and Mail*, 18 October 1996). It is unclear what responsibility the Royal Commission's "system" should bear for such issues. What is clear is that a myopic focus on "race" may detract attention from action in areas far more likely to improve performance. The suggestion that failure should be attributed to such abstractions as "systemic racism" not only directs attention to the wrong area but may also serve to legitimize educational failure.

Lewis's discussion of the education system is illustrative of a wider willingness to embrace any claims of grievance he encountered, without the tiresome business of considering research evidence that might raise questions about his endorsement of whatever fashionable remedies lay to hand.

Lewis reported a disturbing failure in the education system to assist racial minority students. To read Lewis is to conclude that there is a dramatic and widespread failure to afford equitable treatment to visible minority students: "The lack of real progress is shocking." The views he reports are apparently unanimous, the pernicious effects of contemporary policies pervasive:

Everywhere, the refrain of Toronto students, however starkly amended by different schools and different locations, was essentially the refrain of all students. Where are the courses in Black history? Where are the visible minority teachers? Why are there so few role models? Why do our white guidance counsellors know so little of different cultural backgrounds? Why are racist incidents and epithets tolerated? Why are there double standards of discipline? Why are minority students streamed? Why do they discourage us from University? Where are we going to find jobs? What's the use of having an education if there's no employment? How long does it take to change the curriculum so that we're a part of it? (Lewis 1992: 20–1).

Lewis does not deal at any length with the substance of this litany of complaints. The history taught in Ontario schools is extremely limited, a result of educational innovations that have eroded many traditional parts of the curriculum (Davis 1995).[6] The argument for offering ethnically differentiated curricula appears to depend on a number of questionable assumptions. The claims of black history rely largely on the popularity of this approach in the United States and the lobbying of Afrocentrists. Canadian blacks constitute some 3 per cent of the population; the majority are first-generation Canadians. Are schools to similarly offer courses in aboriginal history, South Asian history, and East Asian history? What of the claims of Italian, Ukrainian, or Portuguese history?

The primary role of history in the curriculum might be thought to be to provide a common sense of place and a common understanding of the key events in the creation of a young nation, or at least the differing perspectives on those events. Canada is more than a haphazard collection of ethnic migrants, and the central mission of a Canadian history curriculum must be to address the ongoing process of nation-building, to assist in the creation of that informed citizenry essential to effective democracy. Under the aegis of the Lewis report, however, Canadians who happen to be black are to be taught not the history of their country but some diasporic, largely American-driven account of those who share some perceived racial heritage and (implicitly) a consequent grievance.

The suggestion that counsellors should be familiar with different cultural backgrounds is, at first sight, a reasonable one, but in a situation where students come from more than one hundred different countries, there are some limitations on what can be achieved.

In essence Lewis reiterates and thereby endorses a number of fashionable charges. A careful assessment would suggest they are largely misconceived. There is no evidence that "visibility" is a predictor of educational outcomes, though there are measurable differences between different clusters of ethnic groups. A 1991 "census" by the Toronto Board of Education found significant differences in achievement by gender. Thirty-two per cent of female students were in the group "high in English and math," 21 per cent of male students. Asian students were above average, black students below. Forty-three per cent of female Asian students but only 28 per cent of Asian male students were "high in English and math," and more white female students (31 per cent) were in the group than Asian males. Twenty-one per cent of white males were in the group, compared to 15 per cent of black females and 10 per cent of black males (Yau *et al.* 1993: 23). The gap between white males and Asian females is notably larger than the gap between white and black males. Overall, the statistics provide no support to Lewis's claim that the schools are failing minority students.

A review of Toronto Board data by the *Toronto Star* drew attention to the relative lack of success of other ethnic groups. In the white group those who were "high in English and math" ranged from 42 per cent for those of Jewish origin to 16 per cent for both Italian and Portuguese origin students. Sixteen per cent of "Canadian" blacks were in that group but only 9 per cent of Caribbean blacks. The drop-out rate for black students who entered high school in 1987 and should have completed in 1992 was 42 per cent; for Portuguese students it was 41 per cent (11 February 1995).

The composition of the schools' teaching staff is determined by historic recruitment. Implicit in the regularly repeated observation on the colour of the staff is the suggestion that discrimination is the cause of the low representation of racial minorities. Toronto has undergone a rapid ethnic transformation, and many recent arrivals have been fluent in neither English or French; relatively few have had relevant teaching qualifications. Should the school boards fire current staff to adjust the ethnic/racial mix to reflect Toronto's shifting demographics? Should they refuse to recruit any new white staff, no matter how qualified? Why, in the absence of evidence of discrimination, should the colour of staff be an issue? These are among the many questions left unanswered as Lewis rushed to endorse grievance politics.

Great play is made of role models, but women have become a significant majority of contemporary undergraduates without benefit of large numbers of role models on university teaching staff. The proportion of females among those graduating in dentistry, for example, rose from 22.6 per cent in 1982 to 40.3 per cent in 1990, with few apparent role models (Wannell and Caron 1994b: 4). Students of Chinese ethnic origin have better than average outcomes in the school system with few obvious "role models." There is, in any case, something intrinsically offensive about a society that claims a common citizenship continually labelling individuals on the basis of their colour. The relevant issue is the capacity of teachers to motivate and educate all their students.

Lewis is little concerned with empirical data, though he does cite an unnamed director of education who told him that hiring night at the faculties was "not much different" from the 1960s and 1970s. Lewis unequivocally lays the blame for low visible minority enrolment on the faculties of education: "Why are there still faculties of education out there that rely on marks alone, that won't provide educational upgrading, or transitional help, prior learning assessment or simple employment equity in order to make our schools a reflection of society?" (Lewis 1992: 23). Again there is little evidence that Lewis has considered the implications of these well-meaning sentiments. There is no evidence that admission on the basis of marks discriminates against racial minorities. What he proposes, however, is that some students be admitted on the basis of skin colour in ways not open to others. Like other preferential measures this is unlikely to foster good race relations, improve the selection process, or address the problems of quality that beset the Ontario education system.

Lewis endorses the demand for a quota to guarantee the right of racial minorities to 9 per cent of places in faculties of education on "a right-of-first-refusal basis." Racial minority candidates would, additionally, be eligible for all other places.

The report, notwithstanding its lack of research or any evidence of careful consideration in the proposals that flowed from Lewis's brief deliberations, resulted in a flurry of demands from the Ministry of Education, including affording preferential treatment in admissions to education faculties and teaching recruitment. In July 1993 eight initiatives at a cost of $1.4 million, were announced, intended to increase the representation in teaching of racial minorities, aboriginals, and members of "ethnocultural communities." In a world of finite opportunities, measures that privilege one group of applicants adversely affect others. An assistant deputy minister for Anti-Racism, Access and Equity was appointed. School boards were required to develop and implement policies on "anti-racism and ethnocultural equity" and submit them for approval by 31 March 1995. Bill 21, passed in July 1992, included a provision giving the education minister the power to require school boards to implement employment equity (Letter to Lewis, 3 May 1994).

The ministry called for the establishment of speech codes in universities and colleges to ensure that no student experienced a "negative environment." The government announced that it had adopted a policy of "zero tolerance" of harassment and discrimination at the province's universities. Universities, notwithstanding their formal independence, were required to submit annual reports on their response to complaints received under the policy. The government's initiative was welcomed by the Ontario Confederation of University Faculty Associations and the Canadian Association of University Teachers, even as its members warned of the threat to academic freedom and professors at Trent University and elsewhere insisted on the right to be "offensive" as a fundamental tenet of academic freedom. The zero tolerance policy flowed directly from the government's response to the Lewis "report," which had called on the province to adopt anti-harrassment policies.

The anti-harrassment co-ordinator at the Ontario Institute of Educational Studies (OISE) captured the essence of politically correct approaches to the need for thought purification: "I don't think zero tolerance is about intolerance ... It's about changing societal mores. We have never tolerated murder, does that mean we are intolerant?" (Klein 1994). Murder is, generally, a relatively easy crime to identify. In contrast, as UBC learned to its cost, a negative environment may be claimed on the basis of nothing more than an enthusiastic search for grievance.

The ministry, under the direction of Education Minister Dave Cooke, issued guidelines on *Antiracism and Ethnocultural Equity in School Boards*. These gave explicit endorsement to the ill-founded charges of the cultural relativists who complained of the disadvantages of minority students faced with a Eurocentric curriculum:

Much of the traditional curriculum focuses on the values, experiences, achievements, and perspectives of white-European members of Canadian society and *excludes or distorts those of other groups in Canada and throughout the world* ... This affects students' values, attitudes, and behaviours and, whether intentionally or not may have a discriminatory effect.

Antiracist curriculum ... consciously examines and *challenges* the Eurocentric nature of curriculum *and of* the society in which young people are growing up (Ministry of Education and Training 1993: 13, emphasis added).

Curiously, Asian students, a group that includes many who by reason of history, language, and religion are furthest removed from the "Eurocentric" focus, are nonetheless the most academically successful.[7] Cooke's ill-informed meddling did, however, legitimate a wide range of equally ill-informed local responses. The enthusiasm of some school boards for book banning, in the name of racial sensitivity, was evident in Ottawa where the Board of Education, under pressure from some Jewish groups, removed Shakespeare's *Merchant of Venice* from the curriculum (Greenfield 1994).

Within the Ministry of Education the zealotry evident in the Lewis report gave renewed strength to bureaucrats who were charged with approving material suitable for the province's students. The Circular 14 Advisory Committee lists the books approved for use in Ontario schools. Following the Lewis report, "new criteria" were developed: "Select textbooks, currently in Circular 14, are being re-evaluated in terms of bias" (Letter to Lewis, 3 May 1994). The 1994 version of the circular insisted that all texts "be free from racial, national or ethnic, religious, cultural, or sexual bias or bias against the aged, disabled persons, persons in certain occupations, or individuals belonging to a specific group" (Ross 1995).

Circular 14 operates without much public scrutiny or discussion, but in 1995 Tom Flanagan, a University of Calgary political scientist, described his experiences when a textbook of which he was co-author was dropped from the circular on grounds that the book was guilty of "racial, religious and sex bias." Evidence for the sex bias lay in the fact that far more men were named than women. Bias against Jews was alleged: "Israel is not included in the index; the PLO and Palestinians are included. This appears to be a calculated omission." The Society for Academic Freedom and Scholarship wrote to Cooke, who promised a review, but none apparently took place. Flanagan's efforts to gain clarification from the ministry's book banner, "the implausibly named John Smith, co-ordinator of English-Language Learning Media in the Curriculum Policy Department Branch," were unsuccessful, but "someone in the ministry called Nelson Canada to tell me to back off, or the Government of Ontario would not buy any more of its books" (Flanagan 1995).[8]

As we have noted, contrary to Lewis, racial minority students were not disproportionately failing in the school system or being streamed away from universities. In 1990, when racial minorities made up some 9 per cent of the Canadian population, they represented 10 per cent of all those graduating with a Bachelor's degree and a remarkable 19.3 per cent of those graduating with a doctorate. It is true that racial minority students are under-represented in faculties of education. Should this lead to the conclusion that this is a consequence of systemic discrimination? This requires the belief that education faculties, where only 4.1 per cent of 1990 graduates were from racial minorities, are guilty of discriminatory practices which are absent from engineering, maths, and the physical sciences where racial minorities constitute more than 20 per cent of 1990 graduates (Wannell and Caron 1994a: 4).

Among the many initiatives launched in Lewis's wake were a number that sought to provide access to services not on the basis of a common citizenship but skin colour. The Rae government funded the establishment of an African Canadian Legal Clinic which, like some of the increasingly racialized women's shelters, quickly became enmeshed in conflict between blacks of different ethnic backgrounds.[9] Funding was provided to the Canadian Caribbean African Credit Union. A Black Business Resource Centre was established to provide services to black business people (Letter to Lewis 1994). Even the response to the threat posed by AIDS took racial form, led by the burgeoning Black Coalition for AIDS Prevention with no less than nine staff members ("Employment," *Globe and Mail*, 2 July 1994). The government saw combatting racism as a central priority, but the continual emphasis on race as a basis for entitlement appeared designed to entrench racial separation rather than to diminish any racial divisions.

ORTHODOXY CONFIRMED: THE JUDICIAL LEGACY OF LEWIS

The absence of any credible research supporting the issues addressed in Lewis's report was of no concern to Justice Doherty who, in a 1993 Ontario Court of Appeal ruling, cited Lewis's "conclusions" in support of his finding that "a significant segment of our community holds overtly racist views. A much larger segment subconsciously operates on the basis of negative racial stereotypes" (R. v. Parks in 84 C.C.C. (3d): 369).[10] This was held by Doherty to justify challenging jurors for racial bias in an appeal case involving a Jamaican drug dealer charged with murder and convicted of manslaughter in the death of a drug addict.[11]

Doherty's ruling was subsequently confirmed by the Ontario Court of Appeal, in a case where the black accused was appealing conviction for possession of narcotics for the purpose of trafficking, possession of the proceeds of crime, and possession of a prohibited weapon. The Court of Appeal ruled that the "challenge for cause" should not be restricted to Toronto. The judge who heard the original case in Whitby had rejected a defence application for challenge, claiming that in fourteen years of experience on the bench, "I have never yet seen a jury that came back with a verdict, in my view, that was influenced at all by prejudice, in this jurisdiction." The Ontario Court of Appeal, under Chief Justice McMurtry, preferred, in contrast, to rely on the "studies" to which Doherty had referred (Court of Appeal for Ontario 1996, R. v. Wilson: C 20964).

Jurors in Ontario may now be routinely challenged for racial bias, a development that will increase legal aid costs and aid the defence counsel in securing a sympathetic jury. The rulings provide judicial sanction to the claim of orthodoxy. In Doherty's judgment, "Racism and in particular anti-black racism, is part of our community's psyche." The impact of the ruling, widely favoured by knee-jerk liberals, may create some unpalatable results. The O.J. Simpson case provided insight into the way in which defence counsel can use jury selection to secure a jury whose racial composition appears favourable.

A study undertaken by the Washington-based Centre for Equal Opportunity examined relative black and white acquittal rates. The researchers found that generally blacks experienced higher acquittal rates. This might in part be attributed to discriminatory policing and prosecution policies, which result in more blacks being charged on questionable evidence. Some differences are nonetheless striking. Fifty-one per cent of blacks charged with rape had their charges dismissed or were acquitted, compared to less than a quarter of whites. Where the charge was heard before a jury, no less than 83 per cent of blacks charged with rape were acquitted, compared to only 24 per cent of whites (Chavez and Lerner 1997).

LEGISLATING EQUITY?

> There is no evidence to suggest that members of non-designated groups will be disadvantaged by employment equity.
> Office of the Employment Equity Commissioner, 1992

Bill 79 required employers to proportionately reflect the gender and racial composition of the wider community in their workforce and imposed penalties up to $50,000 on those who failed to comply. The bill was introduced following a series of provincial consultations, led by the recently appointed employment equity commissioner Juanita Westmoreland Traoré. The agenda was set well in advance of the consultations and was based on the conviction that in Ontario discrimination on the grounds of race and gender is systemic and pervasive. This conviction was so strong that the Office of the Commissioner found it unnecessary to conduct any original research to measure contemporary labour market discrimination or to review any research evidence. As leader of the opposition in 1990, Rae had introduced Bill 172, an even more draconian piece of legislation. Indeed critics of Bill 79 condemned the government for failing to go as far as Rae's private member's bill (Legislative Assembly of Ontario, Standing Committee on the Administration of Justice, 2 September 1993: J-634).

Rae appears to have given little thought to the philosophical implications of the legislation. In his autobiography, *From Protest to Power*, he acknowledges the "political reaction, which we would feel full bore in the election campaign" but other than asserting the need to "steadily reduce systemic discrimination" offers little evidence that he had thought through the complex array of factors affecting labour market outcomes. There is a striking absence of any recognition of the onerous burden his legislation would place on those unable to seek the advantages of "designated group" status (Rae 1996: 249–50 and *passim*).

The government introduced its employment equity legislation at a time when demographers were predicting that visible minorities would form a majority of the population of the province's largest city soon after the year 2000. More thoughtful politicians might have paused to re-evaluate how far such concepts as "minority" continued to have salience. But the Rae government's approach exemplified orthodoxy: social investigation took second place to embracing demands raised on behalf of supposed victims, whose status was assumed to flow from their group membership. This avoided difficult questions, such as why the (white) son of an unemployed construction worker should be assumed to have greater advantages than the daughter of a Chinese Canadian surgeon.[12]

Traoré found it unnecessary to commission research or even consider any existing research on labour market discrimination. Following the example of Judge Abella, she simply assumed that her fellow Canadians were bigots.[13] Instead the Ontario government preferred to disburse money to a range of self-appointed advocacy groups to lobby for the new legislation.[14] In this scenario evidence of discrimination depends not on hard data but the relentless repetition of the same egregious claims. Groups whose continued receipt of tax dollars depends on their claims that racism and discrimination are pervasive are unlikely to find the problems have been exaggerated or to report that they have now been successfully addressed.

The Employment Equity Commissioner eschewed research in favour of consultations with those who shared her agenda. Typical is the reproduction of a claim by NAC, printed in bold type in one of the promotional pamphlets: "For women as a group, progress is glacial" (Office of the Employment Equity Commission 1992a: 24). The then

NAC president, Judy Rebick, served on the Consultation Advisory Committee, which no doubt goes some way to explain the similarity between the claims and policies of the Office of the Commissioner and those of NAC.

Bill 79's publicity material reports that "in 1986, 59% of all women aged 15 and over were in the labour force, compared to 79% of all men" (Office of the Employment Equity Commission 1992b). This, we are to conclude, is evidence of historic discrimination. Low-paid women wrestling with child-care problems, domestic labour, and a full-time job are hardly likely to see those who have the financial ability to leave the labour market for a few years as victims of discrimination. The legislation, however, undertook to remedy this situation. Women were in future to be represented in employment not in proportion to their numbers in the labour force but in the community. The legislation promised each "designated group" proportionate representation in every area of the labour market at every level. The representation was not limited by the numbers in the labour force or even the number in the qualified pool: "Over time, every employer's workforce at each level and in each job category, should reflect the representation of designated groups *in the community*" (Ministry of Citizenship 1994: 3, emphasis added).

Rebick suggested that the issue of appointment on merit raised by critics of the bill was a diversion to deflect attention from pervasive current discrimination: "If employers hired strictly on the basis of merit, and didn't discriminate either systematically or intentionally, we would have 50% women, we believe today, in almost every position of authority" (Legislative Assembly of Ontario, Standing Committee on Administration of Justice, 30 August 1993: J-509). The most cursory examination of those in positions of authority suggests that a disproportionate number are in their fifties and sixties, having entered the labour market in the 1950s or early '60s. If this is a major pool of recruitment, it is reasonable to ask how many women were in the labour force in that period, and do they now constitute 50 per cent of the pool? Female participation rates have risen dramatically in the last twenty years. In 1951 a mere 11 per cent of married women were working. Participation levels rose slowly, but as late as 1961 only slightly over 30 per cent of all women were in the labour force (Conway 1990: 14–15).

Rebick was, however, reflective of the ideology that underpinned Ontario's legislation. Any under-representation was to be deemed prima facie evidence of systemic discrimination. It is impossible to find in the commission's statements any acknowledgment of the influence of such issues as age, language capacity, length of labour market service, qualifications, length of time in Canada, or desire for full-time employment. The commission quoted with approval the "six measures of equality" identified by Metropolitan Toronto: "representation of designated groups in the workforce; their range of occupational choice in the workplace; the authority and decision making ability of designated groups; their job security and tenure; employment conditions; and finally pay and benefits for designated groups" (Office of the Employment Equity Commission 1992a: 11). Groups whose representation in the labour force has increased rapidly and which include those with limited fluency in English or French will be concentrated in less favourable positions. The commission endorsed the claim that this resulted from discrimination.

Bill 79 legislated an entitlement to favourable treatment. Women, for example, may have had less seniority and be a minority of the full-time labour force, but employers were required to provide proportionate demographic representation at every level. This could only be achieved if designated groups were treated more favourably than able-bodied white males who had similar qualifications. Indeed, since the legislation did not specify that employers should be guided by the availability of qualified workers in the different groups, they would be encouraged to waive normal requirements in order to meet equity targets. While necessarily resulting in real discrimination against able-bodied white males, the employment equity legislation's passage simultaneously endorsed the claim that outcomes were previously driven by overt discrimination. The explosive consequences of such official sanction for claims that the under-representation of racial minorities resulted not from the ordinary, colour-blind operation of the labour market but prejudice scarcely need spelling out. Any member of a racial minority who had failed to realize his or her ambitions was encouraged to view this as the inevitable result of a grossly discriminatory labour market.

The under-representation of racial minorities in the upper echelons of the Ontario Public Service, for example, can be readily explained by the very small number entering the OPS in the 1960s and early 1970s. The Rae government, in contrast, attributed this to "systemic discrimination." It is difficult to find any other government which engaged in such inflammatory racial rhetoric while proclaiming a concern to improve race relations. Those entrusted with the development of the legislation showed no concern to examine empirically the relationship between gender and racially neutral factors such as age and length of service, and labour force representation.

The commission's use of statistics was grossly misleading, designed to paint a picture of profound discrimination. In one of its many so-called "Fact Sheets," in a section that purported to address "historic discrimination and sexism in the workplace," the commission claimed, "Women and men who have the same level of education are not paid the same. White women with a university degree earned 66 percent of the income ($31,647) that white men with a university degree earned ($48,037). Racial minority women with a degree earned 56 percent of the income that white men earned" (Office of the Employment Equity Commission 1992b).

Readers could be in no doubt that what they were seeing was irrefutable evidence of the most grievous discrimination. In fact what was offered by the commission, under the authority of the Rae government, was propaganda. There is, as we have noted, no evidence, when contemporary groups of university graduates are compared, that women, white or racial minority experience *any* earnings penalty (Wannell and Caron 1994a, 1994b). The commission simply chose to exclude the influence of age and length of service and compare groups that were dissimilar in order to garner support for its legislation. A group that included a large number of older white males was compared with a group that included large numbers of more recent graduates and others with discontinuous labour market service. A group with large numbers of recent immigrants, including many with overseas qualifications, was then compared with the same white male group.

Osgoode Hall law professor Judy Fudge, an active participant in these debates, notes the marginality of employment equity to workers in non-standard employment or in the small businesses excluded from Ontario's legislation. In the larger companies, where better paid jobs predominate, "the assumption is that, as older workers leave standard jobs in large firms, they will be replaced by workers from the equity target groups" (Fudge 1996: 82). Fudge does not dwell on the consequences of this for those young white males who would have historically sought such positions.

The unions had ensured that the legislation excluded seniority rights in lay-offs and recall from the equity agenda. There was no coherent philosophical argument behind the exclusion – indeed, if systemic discrimination really had some historical force, it was precisely the more senior able-bodied white males who had gained the greatest advantage. Certainly the historic construction of the labour force ensures that the group that dominated the labour market in earlier years will have the most seniority. Conversely, women and racial minorities will be disproportionately represented among new recruits and therefore less likely to benefit from seniority. The seniority exclusion was simply the price paid to keep union support. Certainly many preferential hiring advocates wanted to tackle seniority; Traoré report-edly wanted to "jump all over seniority in hob-nailed boots" (Walkom 1994: 216). The protection of seniority rights ensured that the burden of accommodating groups whose labour force participation was increasing rapidly would fall on young white males. Unions were quite ready to pose as champions of what passes for progressive thinking so long as their members paid no price. The eloquent support union leaders offered to the bill was delivered secure in the knowledge that the members who paid their generous salaries would not be calling them to account for any sacrifices offered on their behalf.

It was impossible under the new legislation to employ too many designated group members. One ministry, for example, may count 70 per cent females on its staff, but another ministry must still bring its representation up from 40 per cent to 52 per cent. Racial minorities may be over-represented in the total staff but further targets will be established in any specific area in which they are under-represented. Ministries could continue the existing practice of setting equity bench-marks not on the basis of the contemporary demographics but on the basis of projections five or ten years down the road.

In a tight labour market, for those blessed with the requisite "dis-advantages," the prizes at stake in securing uninhibited access to public sector employment are considerable. The average pay in the Ontario Public Service, excluding the senior management group, is $45,000, 50 per cent higher than the average for earnings in the province. Benefits are worth another $6,000. The average pay for the two thousand employees at the senior management level is an impressive $79,000. Historically these have been secure jobs with obligations that are not necessarily burdensome. Increasingly they could be accessed with no formal educational qualification, in a context where gender and ethnicity are critical factors in appointment decisions. Provincial employment is funded by taxes levied across the province and should be equally accessible to all residents. In practice, equity targets for most OPS employment were based on the demographics of Metro Toronto, offering a marked advantage for racial minorities. The non-designated group members who would be adversely affected by such practices had no legal recourse.

The Office of the Employment Equity Commissioner, backed by the government, gave explicit endorsement to the concept of group enti-tlement in employment allocation. Members of designated groups had a "right" to a proportionate share of employment in every area at every level, irrespective of qualification, length of service, labour-force participation levels, English or French language fluency, or any other factors that might reasonably be expected to influence outcomes in a merit based system. Indeed, as we will see, the logic of Ontario's policies required a diminishing emphasis on qualification in order to meet the requirements of preferential recruitment and promotion.

The rights of designated groups were not circumscribed by the countervailing rights of the non-designated group, able-bodied white males. It was quite legal to staff an entire organization with designated group members; proportionate representation was simply the minimum goal. The staffing in the minister's office in Citizenship might be seen as illustrative of what could happen once the focus on group membership became pre-eminent. In March 1994 36.4 per cent of the staff were racial minorities, 64.3 per cent female, 9.1 per cent non-designated males (FOI Request 940040 MC).

The onus placed on male dominated industries, which would be obliged to take urgent steps to increase female hiring, had no counterbalance. No parallel obligation was imposed on female dominated industries. Those who charged that the government had declared open season on able-bodied white males were roundly denounced. Indeed, the typical progressive response was exemplified by *Globe and Mail* columnist Rick Salutin, who described the legislation as "toothless" (16 June 1995). The legislation's critics were, nonetheless, right.

DUMBING DOWN FOR EQUITY

> Supporters stress that affirmative action programs never entail hiring or promoting the unqualified. In fact, hiring the unqualified would be counterproductive if that produced a high degree of failure among those chosen.[15]
>
> Library of Parliament, 1989

The claim that any under-representation of any designated group at any level in the work-force evidenced discrimination resulted in increasing pressure to remove any "barriers" to recruitment and promotion. Such "barriers" could include many traditional requirements for formal qualification as well as the revision or abolition of specific testing. The Canadian experience paralleled the American, where under pressure from an array of enforcement agencies employers were required to demonstrate that any test did not discriminate against minority groups. The U.S. federal Civil Service Commission, for example, under relentless pressure from the Civil Rights Commission, engaged in significant revision of its merit based testing program, largely eliminating mathematical components. The Civil Rights Commission questioned the relationship between test outcomes and job performance and disputed the claim that the system was merit driven, querying whether any "merit system" could indeed be operational (Glazer 1987: 55).

The response of American employers, who faced the loss of federal contracts and punitive legal penalties for failure to comply with the directives of federal enforcement agencies, was to move increasingly to a de facto quota system in which group membership took precedence over merit (ibid.: 45 and *passim*).

Canadian preferential hiring advocates have assiduously denied that their proposed policies will lead to the end of merit-based hiring. Traoré was pressed on this point, in a question from the legislative committee reviewing her appointment. A committee member gave voice to business concerns that there would be pressure to hire unqualified workers and that there might be insufficient eligible potential employees in the target group. Traoré dismissed these concerns:

The whole phobia around forcing employers to hire unqualified people – if we look, for instance, at one group, people of different racial and ethnic origin in one setting, we will find that on average within that group we have persons who have more qualifications. We have 27 per cent of the group with university education as compared to 17 per cent of the general population in Ontario. These are Ontario figures. So when we look at the bottlenecks that have been created for this particular target group, we will say that it is not related to qualification in terms of education and experience, that in fact there is a pool of people that is being underemployed and underpaid (Standing Committee on Government Agencies, 20 March 1991: A-347).

If racial minorities are over-represented in the qualified pool, presumably all that is required is a recruitment process that does not discriminate on the basis of race. Certainly there can be no justification for recruiting racial minority candidates who lack normal qualification requirements while rejecting other candidates who have them. Or can there?[16]

Preferential hiring advocates have argued that discriminatory employment practices result in less qualified applicants from privileged groups securing preferment over more qualified disadvantaged applicants. One way of ensuring recruitment by merit is the clear specification of relevant qualifications. Yet the Office of the Commissioner's approach, in contrast, was to remove any formal requirement such as a degree or professional qualification, even for posts such as senior policy adviser, on a salary scale in excess of $66,000. For this post the ability to word process was not a requirement, though it was recognized as a "useful asset." In the absence of stated formal qualification requirements it is difficult to demonstrate that appointment is based on competitive merit.

The Office of the Commissioner funded a considerable number of research projects (although, as we have noted, none sought to examine the evidence of discrimination apparently necessitating the new legislation). Again there was a marked absence of any concern for an open competitive process; not a single research undertaking was competitively tendered.

The abolition of formal qualification requirements was also evident in the recruitment of adjudicators who would be "cross appointed" to hear cases before the Employment Equity Tribunal, Boards of Inquiry under the Human Rights Code, and the Pay Equity Hearings Tribunal. This might be thought to suggest the need at least for a university degree, perhaps accompanied by some formal legal training. The notice of recruitment made no mention of such criteria but did indicate that applications from designated group members were "particularly welcome." Again, as in recruitment to the commission and, as we will see, in the evolution of staffing policies at the Ontario Human Rights Commission, what was sought was unfettered opportunity to recruit and promote those who possessed appropriate group membership and the correct ideological disposition – expressed, in this case, as "a commitment to fairness, social justice, equity and access issues" (advertisement, *Globe and Mail*, 21 January 1994). Those appointed to adjudicate the new legislation were to share the same myopic ideology as those who drafted it. What they may have lacked in competence they would make up in zealotry.

The focus on creating a "representative" work force and the reinforcement of group claims to proportionate shares, reflected in preferential policies, quickly leads to demands that barriers posed by qualification criteria be reviewed. This trend is not unique to Canada. Thomas Sowell, surveying the international experience, notes: "The sense of entitlement – independent of skills or performance – has long been an accompaniment of preferential policies" (1990: 123). He argues that such policies discourage the pursuit of excellence by target group members, since they are assured of consideration by virtue of group characteristics. Those who are members of any group adversely affected by preferential hiring also may respond by reducing their efforts, since their chances of success are no longer determined in merit-driven competition.

Employment equity proponents argue that systemic discrimination may not be intentional; it may, for example, simply result from failure to widely advertise available employment positions, reliance on word-of-mouth communication, or nepotism. And how did the Office of the Employment Equity Commissioner proceed in recruiting staff?

The commissioner was appointed by the premier's office. The second executive director was appointed without external advertising. Names of potential candidates were canvassed from deputy ministers and managers of employment equity in different ministries. A short-list was constructed – a process that might be thought a quintessential example of word-of-mouth recruitment. Only once did the Office of the Commissioner advertise a position in a provincial newspaper, preferring to rely on what it called "outreach." Unsurprisingly, no able-bodied white males were hired.

ABLE-BODIED WHITE MALES NEED NOT APPLY

> Changes in the nature of work have laid waste the traditional sources of unskilled male employment ... As their jobs have declined so have their prospects of marriage ... For women, work and family are often competing spheres; for men they are linked. When the link is broken, some men, in some places, become loose molecules: uneducated, unskilled, unmarried and unemployed.
>
> *The Economist*, 28 September 1996

Prior to the passage of Bill 79 the Ontario government was already engaged in an accelerated employment equity program in recruitment and promotion. The explicit discrimination which this entailed became public with the report that the government was using "limited eligibility" competitions, which restricted applications to designated group members. This became widely publicized when Management Board posted a limited eligibility contest for the well-paid position of Director, Information Technology. The government, as it scrambled to deal with the political fallout, directed staff to undertake a detailed and, no doubt, costly review: "Between Nov. 9 and Nov. 24, 70 separate [news] items were tracked ... 32 items appeared in print media for a total of 258 inches of copy" (Media Analysis, undated).[17] Management Board bureaucrats noted "a very negative knee-jerk reaction since all the facts and information wasn't [sic] out there" (ibid.).

The controversy resulted in the announcement that limited eligibility competitions would not be used in the future, but the Orwellian arguments of Management Board chair Brian Charlton were scarcely reassuring: "Employment equity is about making the most of our workforce ... taking advantage of the skills and capabilities of *all* our people rather than overlooking the talents of some." The sentiment is difficult to reconcile with the explicit exclusion promised by limited eligibility. Charlton announced that he was withdrawing the measure, not apparently because he had been persuaded that there was anything intrinsically offensive about such crass discrimination but because of concern that the measure might damage its supposed beneficiaries: "Until I am satisfied that this measure will not have an effect opposite to its intention; until I am satisfied that this measure will not discourage members of designated groups from putting themselves forward; until I am satisfied that this measure will not jeopardize the goals of employment equity, limited eligibility will not be used (Statement to the Legislature, 15 November 1993).

Management Board refused (under Freedom of Information requests) to release documentation regarding their intended future policies, but documents that were released indicate that a range of options were under review, which would continue to privilege designated group members without attracting the same public opprobrium. The policies being canvassed included allowing non-designated group members to apply but making it unlikely that they would be appointed: "designated group member *must* be selected if designated and non-designated candidates are found to be relatively equal" (Evaluation of Staffing Positive Measures, undated). Other options included allowing able-bodied white males to apply but giving preferential treatment to designated group members in selection for interview.

ACADEMIC SCHOLARSHIP VS. RACIAL IDENTITY: CARLETON UNIVERSITY AND THE OHRC

> Opponents of affirmative action have effectively conveyed the erroneous impression that affirmative action is about *lowering standards* in order to hire women, racialized [sic] people, people with disabilities, and so on.
>
> Council of Ontario Universities Committee
> on the Status of Women in Caplan, 1993; emphasis in original

The claim that preferential hiring policies do not mean hiring unqualified candidates is, at least in Ontario, demonstrably false. In the view of the Ontario Human Rights Commission, it is perfectly legal to waive normal qualification requirements for designated group members and to recruit such candidates in preference to able-bodied white males who hold the qualifications normally required for the position. There need be no evidence that the designated group who benefit from discriminatory hiring programs have experienced any previous disadvantage in recruitment.

In December 1990 the School of Social Work at Ottawa's Carleton University advertised four full-time positions and one half-time position. This was an unusually large number of openings. Three full-time positions were advertised at the assistant professor level, one at the instructor level. The school's advertisement declared, "we are anxious to increase our understanding of the way in which race and ethnicity affect the lives of people in Canada. We want to develop a culturally sensitive program and an active anti-racist practice."

It is unclear what caused the school's faculty suddenly to notice the fact that Canada included people with different cultural backgrounds. The fact that a culturally sensitive approach still required developing might be thought to reflect a degree of myopic lassitude raising questions as to what competence previous graduates acquired. More baffling was the concept of an active anti-racist practice. Is this supposed to exist in contrast to the racist practice being carried out by other social workers? Certainly the advertisement's wording suggested careful attention to the politically correct buzz words.

"Normally appointment to professor positions requires a doctoral degree, but under affirmative hiring practises, visible minority and aboriginal candidates without a doctorate will be considered," the advertisement noted. The school was as good as its word. Seven candidates were short-listed for the three assistant professor positions. Four were racial minority candidates who lacked a PHD. Two of the three appointed were racial minority candidates who lacked a PHD. No qualified able-bodied white male made the short-list. A racial minority candidate was also appointed to a position at the instructor level.

The intervention of my constituency MPP was necessary to secure a response to a complaint sent to the OHRC.[18] It took the OHRC four years to "investigate" the matter. The investigating officer's conclusion was that Carleton's actions were consistent with Section 14 of the Ontario Human Rights Code. This includes the provision: "A right under Part I (of the Code) is not infringed by the implementation of a special program designed to relieve hardship or economic disadvantage or to assist disadvantaged persons or groups to achieve or attempt to achieve equal opportunity."

In essence, the OHRC investigating officer Lisa Taylor constructed a "special program" defence for Carleton. Taylor reported that in the late 1980s the Carleton University School of Social Work "instituted a wide-scale review of its programmes in order to develop an employment equity policy." Following what the investigating officer describes as "Multicultural Brainstorming Sessions," the school decided to increase "affirmative action student admissions" and "hiring of new faculty in order to reflect more closely the multicultural, multiracial society ... As a formal step to enhancing this process, the School announced in September 1989 that the administration had approved the hiring of three new professors for the BSW programme. Of these positions, one was designated as an employment equity position for which a PH.D. would not be required" (Taylor 1994).[19] In fact not one but three positions were to be filled by racial minority candidates without a PHD. The university's unequivocal linking of employment equity with the removal of customary qualification requirements is noteworthy.

Did the university have evidence that racial minorities were under-represented on academic staff? In 1988 a survey found that racial minority groups constituted 9.6 per cent of Carleton's work-force. Fifty-seven per cent of the group earned $40,000 or more. Carleton claimed that representation was comparable to the national work-force. In fact, as we will see, as the investigation moved to the Ombudsman's office new figures emerged indicating a substantial over-representation of visible minorities in academic appointments.

In the Ottawa Carleton area the 1986 census indicated that 7.6 per cent identified themselves as members of racial minorities. It was suggested to the investigating officer that if proportionate representation were the goal of equity, some relevant geographic benchmark was required and that one such might be the surrounding region. Taylor preferred a more ambitious mandate: "For purposes of employment equity, it would not have been reasonable for the university to use statistical information from the limited geographical area proposed by Dr Loney ... a more reasonable comparator would have been the area of search used by the university, which might have included all of Canada and the United States" (Taylor 1994).

That the goal of Canadian employment equity measures should be to reflect the proportion of racial minorities south of the border is a novel idea, but illustrative of the rapidly moving goalposts set up by the beneficiaries of the burgeoning employment equity industry. In this case it would necessitate a change to immigration policy that requires universities to direct their advertisements to Canadian citizens and permanent residents.

Subsequent correspondence, following a complaint to the Ontario Ombudsman, produced entirely new figures: "People from visible minorities had been more highly represented with 10.3% of faculty members at Carleton as compared to 9% in the external work force in 1986" (Jamieson 1997: 5). The 10.3 per cent figure (for faculty as distinct from total employment) had never appeared in the OHRC report, perhaps because it suggested little need for a special program.

It is unclear where the (egregious) figure of 9 per cent was conjured up. The correct figure for 1986, used by Treasury Board, based on work-force availability, was 5.9 per cent (Treasury Board 1995: 35). In short Carleton launched a discriminatory hiring program to benefit visible minorities in academic appointment when the group was *over-represented* in academic employment by some 175 per cent. Given the well-established under-reporting that occurs in data collection on racial minority employment, the number in post at Carleton may well have been much larger.

It is a testament to the investigative skills of the Ontario Ombudsman and the OHRC that after seven years the fact that the beneficiary group were already over-represented remained unacknowledged. That the Ombudsman's office should happily recycle a figure for labour force representation, a critical benchmark for any claim of "disadvantage" or "systemic discrimination," 50 per cent higher than the accurate one suggests a striking indifference to assessing evidence.

Taylor's report had necessarily to address the issue of the recruitment of unqualified candidates. The challenge was made more difficult by the unequivocal view of experts, summarized by Keene and noted by Taylor: "Nowhere in the literature of affirmative action has there ever been a serious recommendation that opportunities for employment or higher education be extended to unqualified persons, nor has there ever been an affirmative action program ordered by a court that suggested that unqualified persons be hired."

The solution to this dilemma lay in the investigating officer's pronouncement that Carleton's actions were "consistent with the standard employment equity practices described in Human Rights in Ontario (Keene 1992), *if one accepts the premise that an individual can have "equivalent qualifications"* without being able to lay claim to a PHD." (Taylor 1994, emphasis added). The question of "equivalent qualifications" might therefore be thought a central question for the investigating officer to define. What would constitute such qualifications? What evidence exists that those appointed to the positions at Carleton possess equivalent qualifications? These are not matters covered in the report or in the subsequent "investigation" by the Ontario Ombudsman.

For Taylor the real contribution of those appointed lay not so much in formal qualification but who they were:

One of the successful candidates was a woman of South Asian origin, while the other was a black woman from Nova Scotia. Many employment equity programmes, in addition to seeking proportional representation of members of disadvantaged [sic] groups, seek as a general principle diversity of the employee population. This concern would be of particular relevance in a post-secondary academic setting, which has traditionally sought to provide a diversity of academic and political opinion ... A diversity of racial and gender perspectives promoted by the School's employment and educational equity programmes would presumably enhance the broad spectrum of opinion that is ideally reflected in a university setting.

Taylor's enthusiasm for racial perspectives would not be out of place in the theorizing of racial thinkers for whom race does indeed imbue the individual with a distinct vision and unique characteristics, usually in some perceived hierarchy.

The Ontario Human Rights Commission reportedly had research on the "disadvantages" faced by racial minority women in seeking university appointments. The investigating officer's report noted that the commission's Policy Unit had advised that there is statistical evidence to suggest "a trend for *qualified* racial minority women to be under represented as members of faculty at universities in Ontario" (Taylor 1994, emphasis added). Why such evidence should support the recruitment of *unqualified* candidates is unclear; nonetheless the evidence from the Policy Unit would appear to give at least some substance to the claim that racial minorities experience substantive disadvantage in seeking university appointment.

I pursued this issue through Ontario's Freedom of Information provisions. I requested:

• All records held by the commission's Policy Unit regarding the under-representation of qualified racial minority women in Ontario Universities, and;
• All records regrading the perceived under-representation of other designated groups in Ontario universities.

I was advised, in reply: "there are no records responsive to your request." This absence caused no subsequent comment by the Ontario Ombudsman.

Taylor's report went to the commissioners in February 1995, four years after the matter was first raised. The commissioners determined that no board of inquiry need investigate the matter, as the complainant had not been discriminated against: Carleton had a legitimate program "designed to assist First Nations and racial minority persons to achieve equality of opportunity for employment as social work faculty" (Ontario Human Rights Commission 1995).[20]

I appealed this decision, which was subsequently endorsed in a ruling signed by the then chief commissioner, Rosemary Brown. The Ontario Ombudsman found little fault with the OHRC; its investigation largely consisted of a reiteration of the OHRC position. The Ombudsman did

undertake to bring to the attention of the OHRC the need to acknowledge letters but appeared less concerned that letters to the executive
director and another senior officer were not only unacknowledged but
had simply disappeared: "I agree that your letters should have been
acknowledged ... There is no record of other letters received by the
Commission in June, July and October, and, *accordingly*, I will not
pursue this issue further" (Jamieson 1997: 10, emphasis added). The
letters were sent by fax and their arrival is in no doubt.

THE POLITICS OF DIVISION: THE ONTARIO HUMAN RIGHTS COMMISSION

> Half of all black managers and professionals in the United
> States, according to one estimate, work for government at
> some level ... There is a striking contradiction between the
> radical talk of many members of the black overclass and their
> dependence on the white oligarchy that promotes and subsi-
> dizes them for reasons of its own.
>
> Michael Lind, 1995

The Ontario Human Rights Commission has been the focus of a
number of allegations of racism. These became prominent in the late
1980s when the Liberals' newly appointed head of the Human Rights
Commission, thirty-two-year-old lawyer Raj Anand, came under attack
for what were called "lily white" hiring practices. The attack, led by
the *Toronto Star*, focused on the absence of racial minorities in hiring
for seven senior positions. Charles Roach, a prominent black lawyer,
entered the fray to call for the abolition of the commission. A subsequent inquiry found no evidence of discrimination – not surprisingly,
since Anand had an established reputation as an active campaigner
against racism – but by then Anand had been forced to resign (Ehring
and Roberts 1993: 228–9).

The commission, ostensibly committed to equality of opportunity
and the enforcement of sanctions against discriminatory behaviour,
might be thought the concern of all Ontarians, not an opportunity
for preferential employment for those endowed with the right group
characteristics. Its inept response to the "lily white" hiring allegations
encouraged others to play the race card in an attempt to secure
advancement.

The strength of allegations of racism might seem surprising, given
the high proportion of racial minorities at the commission. At the time
the allegations were made against Anand, some 25 per cent of the
commission's staff were estimated to be members of a racial minority.

The commission's own figures, obtained under Freedom of Information requests, indicate that in 1992, when the commission's benchmark for proportion of racial minorities in the Ontario population was 8.6 per cent, they comprised no less than 38.8 per cent of commission staff. In contrast, able-bodied white males, who made up 40 per cent of the population, accounted for 9.2 per cent of commission staff (OHRC Workforce Profile 1992). Some employees claimed that racial minority members had insufficient senior posts and that clerical workers, who lacked post-secondary qualifications, could not gain promotion. The charge that discrimination was evidenced by the disproportionate concentration of racial minorities at lower levels illustrates the muddled reasoning that underpins many claims of "systemic" discrimination. It also provides an insight into the use that can be made of such claims by those who seek advancement.

What was demanded by activists at the commission was numerically proportionate representation of every designated group at every level in the commission. If racial minorities were over-represented at the lower levels and lacked the qualifications for promotion, then criteria must be changed. The demand was not that the commission reflect the provincial population but rather that racial minorities, having captured a disproportionate share of positions, now could assert a proportionate right to all senior positions. This view was never challenged in the commission's lengthy deliberations.

The story of the commission's efforts to address the alleged racism provides a classic study of what has been called "producer capture." Publicly funded agencies, established to meet service demands, are increasingly subverted to meet the needs not of clientele but staff. In response to the allegations the commission sought and obtained funding for the hiring of staff to join an anti-racism project team. Two consultants' reports purported to examine the charges (Minors 1992, Young 1992). Hundreds of hours of staff time and hundreds of thousands of taxpayer dollars were devoted to the production of a plan of action for "anti-racism organizational change." Consultant Arnold Minors was hired to recommend ways of eliminating "racism" from the OHRC. His report suggested that racism was indeed endemic to the commission. Most interviewees, claimed Minors, "often feel victimized" by racism at the commission. For some it was reportedly so bad "that a significant minority experience physical symptoms: 'It's killing us'" (Minors 1992: 4).

Minors's report is interesting in the insight it provides into the orthodox mantra on race relations, in which a series of contentious claims are paraded as though they are no more than self-evident. Their acceptance creates an apparent context of societal racism from which minorities must be protected and "dominant" whites made aware of their culpability. Minors identifies racism as a peculiarly white vice: "people of colour and Aboriginal people may discriminate in employment for example, against other Aboriginal persons or persons of colour. In doing so, however, they are using the referred power of members of the dominant (i.e. white) culture" (Minors 1992: 5). Since racism was everywhere, its identification was difficult: "Racism, by virtue of its very pervasiveness, is largely invisible in its effect and must, therefore, be actively attended to in order to eliminate it. It is kept going in organizations by a complex web of normative ideas, institutional practices and individual behaviours each feeding on the other by the interconnected strands of the web" (ibid.). With a definition at once illusive and expansive the employment prospects for those charged with eradicating this problem look rosy indeed.

Minors repeated a number of the favourite chestnuts of the race industry. Under "normative ideas" the commission was informed: "If I am a person of colour or an Aboriginal person then *I won't normally see people of my race represented on the front page of newspapers or on television or in magazines.* When I do see them, they are much more likely to be presented in a negative light." (ibid., emphasis added) This industry cliché originates in the United States and dates back at least to the 1950s. Anyone familiar with the media in Metropolitan Toronto will recognize this as ludicrously inaccurate; it is of interest only because it speaks volumes to the lack of careful, empirical analysis that epitomizes the race industry.

Moving on to "institutional practices," Minors assured the commission that (presumably in contrast to visible minorities) "If I am white, I can be reasonably sure that the rules for promotion won't change when I apply for one" (ibid.: 6). The reality of preferential hiring policies, in contrast, meant that for many – particularly able-bodied white males – the rules had changed quite markedly, in ways that made the unchangeable attribute of group membership of increasing importance in accessing promotion.

To demonstrate the pervasive nature of racism at the commission Minors relied not on such tedious measures as cohort studies, which might, for example, have investigated whether similarly qualified whites and visible minorities with similar lengths of service experienced differential promotion. Minors preferred to offer an eclectic list of comments from his interviews, many of which had no apparent relevance to the charge of racism, except in the sense that it provided a useful label under which to group a range of discontents.[21]

Not surprisingly, in the burgeoning culture of grievance and entitlement that characterizes the OHRC, Minors found no shortage of those

willing to embrace the charge of racism. It is doubtful that the cultivation of racial grievance would have been diminished by the adoption
of his numerous recommendations, which, inevitably, included man-
datory anti-racism education, the dismissal of any manager who failed
to respond to complaints about racism, and the demand that the OHRC
Anti-Racism Committee monitor all appointments and promotions
(34–8). The latter recommendation would have placed considerable
power in the hands of the commission's racial advocates.

   One outcome of the lengthy and costly deliberations was the introduction of appointment and promotion criteria that depended not on
universal measurable standards such as the possession of a degree but
on criteria that would privilege certain groups and afford recognition
to desirable ideological characteristics. The requirement that investigating officers hold a university degree was removed and new criteria
were introduced such as "a demonstrated commitment to challenging
racism"; qualifications "such as community development, work on
human rights ... were to be seen as a valuable asset, and in some cases,
as a requirement for specific jobs." Languages other than English or
French might equally be a specific requirement (OHRC 1993: 21–2).
This agenda was directed at the concerns of commission staff who
lacked formal qualifications but desired promotion opportunities. In
future they would be able to claim eligibility based on the display of
the right attitudes, membership in the right groups, and the accident
of having been born in a country or raised in a household where the
dominant language was neither English or French.

   The commission's employment equity plan in 1989 had established
as a "goal" the creation of "a representative workforce across all jobs
and all levels" (OHRC "Employment Equity," undated). A review of
the plan's three-year targets indicated an unusual view of representation.
The goal for human rights officers was that aboriginals be 12.1 per
cent, persons with disabilities be 15.2 per cent, and that the "proportional representation" of racial minorities be maintained at 37.5 per
cent and women at 57.5 per cent. What is immediately apparent is
that these levels bear no relationship to the representation of these
groups in the provincial labour force. Oddly, in documents that display
an obsessive concern with identity, I was unable to find any reference
to the dramatic under-representation of able-bodied white males. The
introduction of revised criteria for promotion would result in the
further marginalization of white males in commission employment,
since they would be unlikely to be thought to exhibit the kind of
characteristics now prioritized for recruitment and promotion.

   In retrospect it is hard not to conclude that what underlay the
charges of racism at the commission was the politics of entitlement.

Racial minorities may have been disproportionately represented in employment, but for those eager to secure career progression, barred by existing qualification requirements, the temptation to play the race card was overwhelming. Once an emphasis on race or some other group characteristic has become accepted as a central organizing principle, with a focus on the entitlements and grievances that are believed to flow from membership of a particular racial group, the probability of further race-based conflict is increased. The Human Rights Commission remains an arena of racially charged conflict, increasingly staffed by those whose qualifications may make competent job performance challenging.

In 1996 one disgruntled former employee launched a $5.5 million lawsuit against the commission. Glen Morrison, a black ex-Toronto police officer, claimed he was fired after complaining about the poor investigative skills in the agency's racially troubled Mississauga office, where racial conflict between different visible minority groups dated back to the late 1980s. The commission had earlier investigated complaints from a Filipino employee of racial discrimination by Morrison. The OHRC had reportedly claimed mismanagement and discrimination against non-blacks in dismissing Morrison, while a government investigation reported that a "poisoned environment based on race" pervaded the Mississauga office (*Ottawa Sun*, 25 August 1996).

The incestuous preoccupation with race and the development of more flexible appointment and promotion criteria has done little to help the commission's abysmal investigative record. The commission experiences considerable difficulty in getting its investigating officers to process complaints speedily. Even simple cases frequently take up to five years.

The Ontario Human Rights Commission is not unique in providing a tax-funded venue for racial skirmishing. The perspective of some protagonists is exemplified by the black Citizenship bureaucrat who advised a white colleague that if she were really a committed anti-racist she would resign her job and give it to a woman of colour (Walkom 1994: 223).

In the U.K. the pursuit of similar racially driven policies by a number of Labour councils and the widespread use of anti-racism training, which served to confirm the inevitable culpability of whites, created growing conflict. In a situation where any racial minority facing a management instruction that he or she objected to could cry "racism," even the most basic controls could quickly break down. *The Observer*, a liberal newspaper, reported on "the spectre of political correctness haunting the new model Labour Party" (28 May 1995). The story was triggered by the results of an inquiry into allegations that lax management and ill-conceived employment policies had left children in the care of London's Islington Council vulnerable to pimps, drug dealers, and pedophiles. The report described the council as "paralysed by equal opportunity and race issues." Applicants for appointment, for example, could not be asked for a reference from a previous employer or about disciplinary or absence records, since, it was suggested, minority applicants may have had poor past records which should not be a barrier to recruitment. In the words of the paper's well-respected correspondent, Melanie Phillips: "Not only were grossly unsuitable child care staff recruited as a result of equal opportunity policies, but managers were then too terrified to deal with them for fear of being labelled homophobic or racist."

The problems faced by Islington existed, in less dramatic forms, in other councils. In the London Borough of Hackney, the white head of the housing department and the black head of the race unit were both accused of racism and sacked after uncovering what they claimed was fraud and corruption among a group of council employees of African origin. Herman Ousely, the black head of Britain's Commission for Racial Equality and a former chief executive in the London Borough of Lambeth, noted that many council equality units had been "hijacked by zealots." Ousely warned: "Racism awareness training whipped people into a frenzy of guilt which built up resentment and fear. Managers became too frightened to challenge anyone black who was inadequate."

Phillips notes the problem created by the reigning orthodoxy in social work education: "Social work itself was caught up by zealotry during the 1980s. Social workers were taught that society was endemically oppressive, and students were marked down on their course if they did not conform to the correct line on racism." This pedagogic approach has not been confined to the U.K. When Dalhousie University's Maritime School of Social Work recently advertised for a new director (*University Affairs*, January 1996), the announcement left no doubt as to the necessary ideological perspective: "The School is interested in advancing the development of theory/practise that accounts for systemic inequities based on social factors such as gender, sexual orientation, race, class, disability, is rooted in knowledge of political economy, and is useful in community development and social action."

Academics who think scholarship is more than a shopping list of putative victims and should not be confused with advocacy are unlikely to find this encouraging. Subsequent recruitment notices for additional faculty afforded similar instruction as to the requisite political perspective. Potential applicants were advised that the school "seeks to further curriculum development and scholarly work in the areas of diversity and anti oppressive [sic] social work" (*University Affairs*, March 1997). Academic freedom at Dalhousie apparently does not require intellectual diversity.

SHOW BOAT: POLICING CULTURE

> To be charged with racial or ethnic bias, or with sexism, was like being accused of child molesting: you were guilty until you could prove yourself innocent. A new "treason of the clerks," a betrayal of culture by the intellectuals was in progress. And where the left actually held power (as in the case of Bob Rae's government in Ontario) a new class of *apparatchiki* emerged and began to apply their social quotas to the creative process.
>
> Thomas Henigan, 1996

> The Ontario Anti-Racism Secretariat views the conflict around Showboat [sic] as an example of systemic racism.
>
> Secretariat paper, 1993

> It goes without saying that we share your urgent desire to reach out to members of racial minorities who are the victims of racism and are looking to the government for leadership.
>
> Elaine Ziemba and Marion Boyd,
> Letter to Stephen Lewis, 3 May 1994

The Rae government's involvement in and financial support for the Coalition to Stop Show Boat might stand as an epitaph to the government's inability to resist the lure of grievance politics. Rae subsequently denied any involvement of his government in the campaign, but the record demonstrates otherwise.[22] It may be that the government's support for the coalition proceeded without the premier's direct approval, but the context had been established by the Lewis report:[23] the subsequent increased role for the Anti-Racism Secretariat in the Ministry of Citizenship and the conviction that Ontario was a profoundly racist society.

The focus on Show Boat is also indicative of the enthusiastic search for symbolic injustices that characterized the politics of those who claimed to speak for the "black community." The fact that so much of the resources of black activists and Ontario bureaucrats could be directed to the issue suggests either that there were few substantive racial concerns or that those charged with identifying them were unequal to the task.

Show Boat, while undoubtedly replete with racial stereotypes in its original form, was not an immediately obvious cause for offence. Those with any knowledge of the musical's history might have been given pause by the fact that this was the platform which made the black American communist Paul Robeson internationally famous. Equally notable is the response that the same production received in the United States, whose southern history provides the backdrop. No American government saw fit to deploy its bureaucracy to deal with the question of Live Entertainment's right to produce the musical. The black press in the United States were, in contrast to Canadian black critics, lavish in their praise.[24]

The Toronto protests were triggered by the announcement that Garth Drabinsky's Live Entertainment, which managed the new North York Municipal Arts Centre, planned to open the theatre with a production of Show Boat. This resulted in a swift reaction from various black activists who condemned the musical as racist and insensitive. The position of the protesters is aptly summarized in the account of York University professor Frances Henry in her academic text *The Colour of Democracy: Racism in Canadian Society* (1995: 218–22). Henry quotes with approval the view of the chair of the Coalition to Stop Show Boat, fellow York University professor Jeff Henry: "Show Boat has resonated in the Black community ... It is the symbol of systemic and cultural racism. It symbolizes what we suffer in our daily lives, no matter what we have achieved in this society, no matter who we are" (Henry 1995: 220).

Jeff Henry is married to Frances Henry, although readers are not advised of this or of the fact that he had received a $60,000 grant, with the Jamaican Canadian Association, from the Anti-Racism Secretariat, to help young people "understand racism in the performing arts" (Walkom 1994: 223).

In common with other debates of this nature, those who might reject the protesters' views simply gave further evidence of the pervasive nature of racism: "The continued racism and oppression that were an everyday reality for Black Canadians were considered irrelevant by the decision-makers of Live Entertainment Productions as well as the mayor of North York and other politicians" (Henry *et al.* 1995: 220).

The involvement of the Ontario Anti-Racism Secretariat (OARS) in the campaign resulted in a $20.5-million lawsuit by Live Entertainment. In response a ministry spokeswoman told reporters: "The ministry is on record as having denied providing funding to stop Show Boat" (*Globe and Mail*, 21 December 1994). The ministry made some effort to conceal the scale of its involvement, refusing to release many documents under Freedom of Information requests until ordered to do so by the Information and Privacy Commissioner.[25] The material released remained incomplete but included extensive documentation of the ministry's involvement. The "Record of Approval" for a contract with the Center for Dispute Settlement in New York for example, included in the "background" section: "The Secretariat would like to assist the community in its efforts to address the ShowBoat [sic] issue." The "rationale," in the "Record of Approval," appeared to directly embrace the views of the protesters, who claimed Show Boat was an example of widespread racism: "The persistence of systemic racism, and the rise in racial incidents indicate the need for proactive strategies and new directions for working with the Community."

The funding for the New York centre was approved by Anne-Marie Stewart, assistant deputy minister and head of the Ontario Anti-Racism Secretariat (22 March 1993). Stewart played a central role in the Rae government's race relations policies, chairing the committee established by cabinet to coordinate a government-wide response to the Lewis report. The Anti-Racism Secretariat in turn was held in high regard by the Rae government. Reporting on their good works to Stephen Lewis, Citizenship Minister Elaine Ziemba and Attorney General Marion Boyd observed "in the Anti-Racism Secretariat the Ontario government has developed a unique little gem that is working ... the Secretariat has risen to your challenge to serve as a kind of central agency to monitor, inspire and facilitate anti-racism work throughout the government and the broader public sector" (Letter to Lewis, 3 May 1994).

The OARS had already made clear its interest in the Show Boat production. Stewart had written to Garth Drabinsky, repeating the secretariat's demand for a copy of the script and proposing a meeting to discuss the matter. Lest Drabinsky should hesitate to meet with a government bureaucrat to discuss a cultural production, Stewart's letter left no doubt as to her expectations for compliance: "My secretary will be calling to set up an appointment" (18 February 1993).

A meeting at the North York Board of Education on 24 February 1994, attended by OARS staff, gave a substantial boost to the campaign when trustee Stephanie Payne compared the play to hate propaganda and called on the Stephen Lewis report for support. Payne's subsequent claim on CTV that "always a Jewish person is doing plays that denigrate us" caused some adverse comment (Valpy 1993).

By March OARS were actively involved; a "staff team" had been assigned to deal with the Show Boat issue and was mandated to "assist the community (behind the scenes) to organize itself to effectively address the issue." Among the team's tasks: "identify key individuals who may be able to support the community." Stewart had met with the Black Action Defence Committee, which in January had received a $35,000 grant from OARS. In 1993 the secretariat provided some $1 million in funding to a bevy of groups claiming to be fighting racism (Briefing Note, 27 September 1993). The Black Action Defence Committee called on the government to stop the production (Issue Note, 9 March 1993). Other groups that had received OARS funding were also involved in the campaign.

By April OARS had still not seen the script. An informational update noted: "The Secretariat expects that Black activists, community groups and civil rights organizations which are prepared to take action against hate propaganda [sic] will demonstrate against this production" (Information Note, 19 April 1993). The secretariat did not openly state its position regarding cancellation of the production: "Secretariat staff will ensure the community takes the lead on any actions." But its internal position was clear, as was its advice to school boards who might think of sending students – an important source of revenue, its loss one of the subjects of Livent's lawsuit:

It is the Secretariat's position that stereotyping is harmful to communities and especially to the self-worth of youth in particular. Show Boat is also harmful to youth in general because it exposes them to stereotypes which inhibit the formation of socially useful relationships with their Black peers ... the production will have a negative impact on young people's understanding and respect for racial difference and therefore school boards should discuss openly the potential effects of the production on the youth in their systems (Issue Note, 21 April 1993).

The secretariat remained involved, sending one of its paid "consultants" to attend the demonstration on 5 October 1993, the production's opening night. The staff presence was no doubt welcome. In spite of the efforts of OARS, which saw Show Boat as one of its main priorities, only 135 demonstrators attended.[26] Apparently the "communities" OARS claimed to be assisting, and on whose behalf they were acting, had few members.

In Toronto Show Boat remained tarred by the controversy. It was more successful when it moved to Vancouver and more still when, in 1994, it opened in New York. In that liberal and ethnically diverse city, with a black population of far larger size and deeper historical roots than Toronto, the musical became the most successful of the 1994–95 season, both in terms of revenue and awards. It was nominated for seven Drama Desk Awards by New York critics, won four Outer Critics Circle awards offered by journalists covering Broadway from outside New York, and won five Tonys, including "Best Musical Revival."

The campaign against Show Boat was illustrative of larger attempts to censor or condemn works that failed to meet standards imposed by those who claim to speak for the sensitivities of millions. When Disney's *Pocahontas* hit the screens, CBC Radio's *Commentary* provided air time to Winona Stevenson at the University of Regina to express at length her concern that the portrayal of the wispy Indian girl "will traumatize our daughter's self-image" (23 June 1995). I asked my (then) ten-year-old daughter, who had seen the movie, whether she had any thoughts on this erudition. Her reply was a welcome breath of common sense: "It's a cartoon, Dad."

EPITAPH

> We want you to be in no doubt that any action to revoke the equity law, without introducing satisfactory alternative legislation, will be regarded as an act of racism and sexism.
>
> Beverley Gardner, president of
> the Federation of Women's Teachers Association,
> in a letter to Citizenship Minister Marilyn Mushinski

The campaign against Show Boat, in common with other race and gender based issues, relied heavily on groups whose influence rested more on their ability to secure public subsidy than to attract widespread support. The cacophony of demands for ever more draconian preferential hiring legislation, and the parade of witnesses constantly at hand to assure politicians that the situation of those they claimed to speak for was immeasurably worse than anyone had previously suspected, were kept lubricated by generous patronage.

The election of the Conservatives, whose victory owed much to the electorate's distaste for a politics driven by the divisive demands of special interests, might have been expected to pose problems for those who were reliant on regular transfusions of tax dollars. In fact many simply sought new sources of subsidy. Citizenship bureaucrats may no longer have been signing cheques, but at the Trillium Foundation there was still a welcome mat. The foundation does not undertake direct fund-raising, receiving its money from the Ontario lottery at the government's discretion. In 1995–96 its thirteen staff dispensed $13 million in grants (requiring, apparently, one staff member for each million dollars of grant funding).

The Alliance for Employment Equity may have decisively lost the battle for public backing for quota-based hiring policies, but it secured a three-year $105,000 Trillium grant to support its work "to eliminate discrimination in employment against women, people with disabilities,

aboriginal people and people from ethno-racial [sic] communities."
The Urban Alliance on Race Relations, which had secured a modest
$50,000 from Citizenship in fiscal 1992–93 and again in 1993–94,
was even more successful, obtaining $280,000 over four years "to
build a volunteer leadership model to conduct public education and
training in the area of race relations" (Trillium Foundation 1996).[27]
Race based groups are also well represented. The black Tropicana
Community Services Organization, for example, received $26,250
from the Ministry of Citizenship anti-racism program in 1993–94. It
secured a $120,000 grant from Trillium.

The foundation's explicit endorsement of the fractious politics of
identity was perhaps most clearly exemplified in the award of $6,000
to the Trent student newspaper, *The Arthur*, "to publish four special
issues produced by four different communities [sic]: First Nations, gay
and lesbian people, people of colour and women." Again Trillium's
largesse appears not to extend to "communities" that fail to fall into
these fashionable confines.

The language with which Trillium describes its beneficiaries speaks
as eloquently as its granting pattern to the perspective of those charged
with distributing lottery proceeds. Most Canadians reject the fostering
of "identity" constituencies, which claim sponsorship on the grounds
that they "represent" particular communities. They equally reject the
provision of service to those differentiated by race, ethnicity, gender,
and sexual preference rather than to those who share a generic need
or interest. The existence of "communities" bounded by gender, ethnicity, and sexual preference is a radical feminist construction, but the
use of the concept in the allocation of public funds serves both to
legitimize it and to give it life. Increasingly access to resources rests
not on the assertion of a common citizenship but on the particulars
of group membership.

The foundation appears to attribute considerable credence to the
Lewis report. Pressed on its enthusiasm for funding advocacy groups
and on the belief that visible minorities experience substantive race-
based discrimination justifying preferential funding provision, the
foundation's executive director Julie White referred me to Lewis's letter
to the premier (persona communication, 4 March 1997).

The League for Human Rights of B'Nai Brith Canada secured a
substantial $180,000 "toward the prevention of hate crimes through
the development of educational materials and community based training," a worthy, if perhaps illusive, goal. A host of other advocacy
groups have found Trillium an equally supportive funder. Many of the
grant recipients are pursuing avowedly feminist agendas, with a plethora of grants explicitly targeting women. The largest, a $750,000 grant

to the Canadian Women's Foundation Consortium, appears to be no more than a contribution to another gender based fund "involved with women's economic development." It is unclear why women should merit such generous treatment. One third of Canadian firms are owned by women and the number of women-led firms is growing at twice the national average (Statement by the minister for International Trade, Art Eggleton, 3 May 1997). It is no doubt coincidental that the executive director, chair, and eleven of the foundation's thirteen staff are women.

The foundation undertakes a gender and "ethnic" analysis of its grants, and its gender analysis indicates that 27 per cent of grant expenditure was distributed to programs specifically directed to women. The foundation's support for programs specifically directed to men stands at o per cent (Trillium Foundation, Grants Allocation Breakdown, March 1996). While the foundation provides support for a number of programs designed to improve the position of low income women, low income men attract no similar concern.[28] The foundation's grant summary contains a number of comments; under the gender breakdown it notes: "this is acceptable."

Preferential hiring policies may have been decisively rejected by provincial voters, but within hospitals, school boards, universities, and municipalities in the province, zealotry remains largely unchecked. The Toronto Board of Education precipitated some controversy when it was revealed that its planned recruitment of one hundred new teachers in the fall of 1997 would be driven by overt preferential ranking, which awarded an additional ten points to any candidate who fell into a target category: aboriginals, the disabled, visible minorities, or women teaching in "non-traditional" areas such as woodworking. Thus an able-bodied white male or a white female teaching in traditional subjects could score a maximum of 38 points, while a target group candidate could score a maximum of 48. The board has established a target of 29 per cent visible minority teachers by the year 2000, a figure far exceeding labour force availability (*Toronto Sun*, 21 March 1997).

The Toronto board continued the concern with policing culture exhibited by the OARS bureaucrats. A play, *Bedtimes and Bullies*, staged by the award-winning Young People's Theatre resulted in a board warning that the production, which cast a black actor as (toy) gun-toting bully, was reinforcing negative stereotypes. The same role had been played in a 1987 production by a white actor without any problem. The board's Equity Studies Centre instructed teachers accompanying students to the show to contact the centre to "arrange for adequate resource support addressing the issues raised by analysis of the play." Teachers were required to preview the show and present their principals with a written lesson plan approved by the centre before their students would be allowed to attend. Not surprisingly some schools cancelled bookings (*Globe and Mail*, 1 February 1996).

The announcement by the new OHRC chief commissioner, Keith Norton, that the commission would seek faster resolution of cases through mediation provided some assurance to those worried that, under the new regime, the grievance industry had fallen on hard times. In the hands of the commission's highly partisan staff, mediation could afford a useful means of securing compliance without the time-consuming requirements of a full investigation. The commission's staff were to receive training to assist them in this role from the University of Windsor Law School, where Juanita Westmoreland Traoré had recently been appointed dean.

Mediation would provide little help to any white males who were subject to discrimination, however gross. Employers would be free to continue to claim a "special program" defence, over which, in the view of the new Conservative-appointed chief commissioner, the OHRC had "little jurisdiction" (K. Norton, personal communication, 27 May and 20 June 1997).

11

Spare Me the Facts

Orthodoxy and the Flight
from Scholarly Inquiry

> Post-modernism? I don't know what that means but I suspect
> it's a scam thought up by intellectuals to keep themselves
> employed.
>
> Noam Chomsky, *New Internationalist*, December 1996

Much of the intellectual support for preferential hiring and the wider
politics of grievance originates in the universities. Those who speak in
the name of the new orthodoxy do not confine themselves to the
assertion of the prior claims of group membership over merit in
academic appointments – their assault strikes at the heart of academic
freedom and traditional norms of scholarly inquiry. The academic crisis
facing Canada's universities is the subject of growing comment (Fekete
1994, Emberley 1996, Bercuson *et al.* 1997).

Universities are expensive institutions. Those who teach in them
acquire considerable social prestige: salaries for full professors, some
of whom owe their position more to longevity than scholarly brilliance,
are commonly in the $80,000 to $110,000 range, and opportunities
to pursue lucrative second careers are widespread. The power the
professoriate holds in educating the young can be used to ensure
conformity or to encourage students to develop the critical skills
required to draw their own conclusions. A disturbing amount of
evidence exists that in many courses what students learn is not intellectual analysis but the ideologically loaded beliefs of the politically
correct. Recruitment to faculty positions in the humanities and social
sciences depends increasingly not only on the display of the requisite
biological characteristics but on an embrace of a particular political
agenda which challenges the alleged influence of patriarchy and the
dominance of a Eurocentric curriculum.

Within the universities the humanities and social sciences are characterized by many conflicting interpretations, yet much of the writing and teaching of those who detect a pandemic of racism and sexism is based on assertion rather than objective inquiry. There is a reasonable apprehension that many students are required to accept the caricatured view of Canada offered by their professors in order to meet course requirements. More disturbing is the vilification of those who challenge the new orthodoxy. Critics of feminist excesses, and those who reject the vision of Canada offered by the champions of grievance politics, risk not intellectual rebuttal but a punitive campaign to secure retribution, public apology, and academic marginalization.

The influence of the grievance-based politics of radical feminism is no longer marginal. Such politics now play a central role in academic life. University feminists are highly organized, and those who oppose them may do so at considerable personal and professional cost. The pusillanimous response of university presidents and senior administrators to even the most scurrilous assaults on academic freedom speaks both to their egregious embrace of the politically correct perspective on matters of race and gender and the careerist opportunism of many who have sought senior academic positions.

In 1993 the University of Toronto Press published a report on the plight of women academics, commissioned by the Council of Ontario Universities, which draws its income from taxpayers and student fees. *Lifting a Ton of Feathers: A Woman's Guide for Surviving in the Academic World* purported to destroy "academic myths about women's career chances in the university" (Caplan 1993). The meretricious use of statistics which characterizes preferential hiring debates was evident in the opening description of the text: "Women account for more than half of all undergraduate students in the United States and Canada, yet they make up only 10 per cent of faculty members at the level of full professor. What keeps women out of the highest levels of academia?"

The writer, Paula Caplan, a psychology professor at the Ontario Institute for Studies in Education, provides an exhaustive list of feminist grievances, portraying the university as a bastion of able-bodied white heterosexual male hegemony. A plethora of anecdotal evidence leaves no doubt as to the hardship faced by female academics and the courage required to pursue an academic career.

Feminist orthodoxy with its emphasis on the centrality of group membership to social understanding is eagerly endorsed: "Just as men often have a great deal to learn from reading the words of women, so white or heterosexual or able-bodied or young women have a great deal to learn from reading the words of racialized, lesbian, bisexual, and old women and women with disabilities" (Caplan 1993: xv).

The book, "proudly" introduced by the Council of Ontario Universities Status of Women Committee in a prologue signed by York University President Susan Mann, and University College of Cape Breton President-designate Jacquelyn Thayer Scott, is replete with advice, including the following to graduate students: "At any point in your graduate work, consider organizing a group of students to request that seminars be held for professors about the effects of the chilly climate on the learning and achievement of women and on members of racialized groups, students who are not able-bodied, older students, and lesbian and gay students" (ibid.: 117).

The "chilly climate" controversy in the University of British Columbia's political science department received national prominence and gave a first-hand insight into the unwillingness of university administrators to defend traditional concepts of academic freedom from the claims of those who would cleanse the universities of incorrect thought (Marchak 1996, S. Martin 1996). The controversy originated in 1992, when a small group of graduate students produced an unsigned report alleging racism and sexism in the department. Emboldened by the university administration's cringing response to their first attacks, apparently vindicated by the $246,000 report produced by feminist labour lawyer Joan McKewen (the most expensive cataloguing of unsubstantiated allegations in legal history[1]), the dissident graduate students unveiled their agenda, demanding a full apology from the targeted professors (*Globe and Mail*, 6 September 1995). Offending faculty were to be "re-educated"; those who demurred were to be retired. In language redolent of China's cultural revolution, professors were to publicly apologize for their thought crimes – "racism, sexism and harassment" in the contemporary vernacular – and to undergo a twelve-week "recovery program." Professors would have to recant their previous errors prior to being allowed back in the classroom. Those willing to follow this ignominious path to renewed acceptability would find their powers closely circumscribed by students who were to have access to unlimited letters of reference and considerable power in defining their own grades.

UBC did not ultimately concede the demands of the student rump, but that they could be seriously posed in a contemporary Canadian university is illustrative of the current offensive being waged against critics of orthodoxy. Equally disturbing was the failure of UBC's most senior academics to learn anything from this debacle. When President Strangway finally lifted the suspension of the political science department's graduate program, he did it, as SAFS president John Furedy observed, conditional on the department's "continuing to progress towards equity objectives" (Furedy 1996: 9). Whatever this Orwellian mumbo-jumbo might be supposed to mean, there could be no doubt that it constituted an apparent endorsement, if not of the specifics at least of the broad thrust of the unfounded, politically motivated, *ad hominem* charges that had set the whole sorry affair in motion.

UBC is by no means an isolated case. The political science department at the University of Victoria was also the subject of prolonged investigation, following feminist charges of a "chilly climate" (Fekete 1994: 286–318). Included in allegations by a committee headed by Somer Brodribb, a radical feminist appointed to the department two years earlier, was the critical attitude some faculty members had displayed towards aspects of feminist thinking. In addition to the general opprobrium heaped on the male political science faculty, a particular target was Warren Magnusson, a left-of-centre professor who had displayed an active interest in "women's issues," though apparently without displaying the requisite zealotry. A specific student complaint included a harassment charge triggered by an article he had written on the controversy. His ordeal included a range of investigatory commissions, the attentions of the university's equity officer, and a reference to the British Columbia Council of Human Rights on the grounds that his article, addressing feminist perspectives, violated the student's human rights.

UBC rejected the demand that its political science faculty be "re-educated," but Carleton president Richard Van Loon had no hesitation in endorsing a demand that Red Cross workers be subject to such a regime. Gay, lesbian, and bisexual students demonstrated at campus clinics in protest against the offence claimed to arise from questions posed to would-be blood donors in an attempt to exclude high-risk groups. Carleton's response was to bar the Red Cross from holding further clinics until it provided "sensitivity training" to its workers. The demand for such training provided an explicit endorsement to the tendentious claims of the demonstrators. Red Cross workers were to be re-educated to display only approved attitudes and opinions and would no doubt be encouraged to recognize their earlier "thought crimes." When the Red Cross failed to fulfil its agreement to deliver such training, it was barred from campus. Defending the ban, Carleton's president wrote "they will be welcome back when they have done so" ("Letters," *Globe and Mail*, 29 March 1997).

Preferential hiring policies and the battery of equity officers, women's officers, anti-harassment officers, and race relations advisers which seem *de rigueur* at any self-respecting Canadian university do not come cheap. The University of British Columbia has a staff of seven equity officers, headed by an associate vice president. The President's Advisory Committee on Equity has sixteen members, the Advisory

Committee on Discrimination and Harassment, seventeen members (UBC 1997). The University of Toronto's forty-one-person Presidential Advisory Committee on Race Relations, established in 1991, had a budget of $100,000. On the assumption that committee members might otherwise have been engaged in productive activity, the real costs of the committee would have been considerably higher. The committee was to determine whether anything in the university's curriculum might be offensive to a minority or member of a disadvantaged group (Furedy 1994: 20). Many academics warned that such policies were anathema to higher education, which inevitably required students to confront ideas and facts that some would find uncomfortable.[2]

The University of Toronto currently provides some $1.5 million for eight Equity Officers Advisory Groups, enough resources to run a small academic department (Furedy 1995).[3] Costs far exceed the stated budget, not least since the meddlesome actions of those appointed to these policing functions necessarily involve an extensive diversion of energy to those targeted for investigation. Attempts to persuade the university to devote attention to the issue of academic freedom proved less successful. A proposal by John Furedy, president of the Society for Academic Freedom and Scholarship, that the University appoint a *part-time* academic freedom officer was defeated by the university's Academic Board. University president Robert Prichard opposed the motion on the grounds that it was unnecessary and premature (*The Newspaper*, University of Toronto, 31 March 1993). This would have surprised anthropologist Jeanne Cannizzo, driven from her post at the university after controversy erupted over her ROM exhibit on attitudes of white missionaries in Africa. The university's administrators failed to protect Cannizzo, apparently mesmerized by the speed of events and careful, no doubt, to avoid offence to the zealots who hounded her.

Activities of equity and anti-harassment bureaucrats can cause significant disruption. At York University (whose faculty association endorsed the Rae government's speech codes) sexual harassment officers sought in 1989 to tape-record the lectures of psychology professor Irwin Silverman. The officers wanted to evaluate whether his views on biology and sex differences might constitute sexual harassment. Silverman refused to teach, the officers refused to leave, and the matter was only resolved when, at Silverman's request, the associate dean placed security guards on the lecture room door to keep the officers out (Fekete 1994: 238). Taxpayers had the privilege of financing both the sexual harassment officers and the security guards required to protect Silverman from their attentions.

Silverman has expressed some doubt that he would be so fortunate today. Certainly a similar 1994 case cited by the Society for Academic

Freedom and Scholarship gives cause for concern. At the University College of the Cariboo, Professor A. MacKinnon was suspended for "sexual harassment" after discussing average or group differences in cognitive abilities between the sexes. It was recommended that when MacKinnon was allowed to return to teaching his lectures be "monitored" (Furedy 1995).

At UBC, at the height of the "chilly climate" battles, nearly 40 per cent of the complaints of harassment and discrimination were categorized under the heading "insults/slurs/unacceptable jokes." The figure fell to just over 20 per cent in 1996. The Equity Office offers the following as illustrative of the 1996 complaints, investigated at great cost:

- A student complained about a student newsletter which contained an offensive joke at the expense of men with disabilities.
- A mature student experienced the class-room as a poisoned environment [sic] when the professor made demeaning remarks about age and aging students.
- A staff member sought ways to intervene with a male employee who was making offensive remarks about female staff.
- A staff member complained anonymously that a department manager was overlooking ethnic and homophobic jokes in the workplace.
- A faculty member sought information on UBC's policy on Discrimination and Harassment after a colleague accused him of making harassing comments (UBC 1996: 15).

At Simon Fraser University the dismissal and subsequent reinstatement of swim coach Liam Donnelly, following contentious allegations of sexual harassment by a student (who secured a $12,000 compensation settlement and credit for an incomplete course) failed to resolve the increasingly complex bevy of charges and counter-charges as Donnelly claimed that he had in fact been the victim of sexual stalking. The resulting farrago did highlight the endemic problems in the university's attempts to police its members. In the ensuing furore SFU president John Stubbs requested medical leave to recover from depression (*Globe and Mail*, 30 July 1997).[4] Stubbs subsequently resigned, following a $315,00 payment.

Ann Brown, the sexual harassment advisor at Brock University, has offered some insight into the assumptions of those who occupy these powerful offices. Responding to the suggestion that there appeared to be a regrettable presumption of guilt when allegations were made, Brown gave voice to the industry's epistemology: "Impact, not intent, is the relevant criterion in determining whether one has been harassed, many respondents are not aware that their behaviour is offensive and harassing to others ("Letters," *University Affairs*, February 1997).

Some students might in these sensitive times feel harassed by professors or fellow students who fail to embrace the latest feminist pieties. This is, as we have seen, a rapidly moving field in which there is more than enough case history to cause concern. Brown's comment that "It is not necessary to find someone 'guilty' in order to start the process of re-education [sic]" is not reassuring.

In the fervour generated by those who believe they have uncovered feminist "truths," traditional notions of academic freedom and scholarly inquiry are quickly jettisoned; indeed, for some they apparently provide no more than another legitimation of white male power. Jackie Stalker, a former professor of higher education at the University of Manitoba and one of the more strident champions of feminist academic grievances, makes the point succinctly: "I just love the way the question is being posed now ... the smoke screen, we're talking about academic freedom. That's a beautiful tactic. It's one that encourages and protects the bigots, encourages sexist and racist speech, promotes backlash politics. It's just wonderful because it protects the deeply entrenched institutional network of sexist practises and attitudes" (CBC Radio, *Cross Country Check-Up*, 22 October 1995).

THE DEMISE OF THE MERIT PRINCIPLE

University recruitment policies increasingly target those whose primary qualification is group membership. In 1995 the School of Journalism at Ryerson Polytechnic, always at the forefront of political fashion, advertised a new Chair of Editorial Diversity, concerned with the hiring and depiction of minorities in the media. It was the first such chair (but surely not the last) in Canada. The requirements on the incumbent, who was obliged to teach only one course in journalism, were not onerous. The successful candidate would also consult with faculty on how to address so-called "diversity issues" in other courses. It was open to the appointee to continue to work part time in journalism. In essence, Ryerson offered a tax-funded sinecure to whoever was deemed sufficiently exotic to adorn the school's masthead.

It is unclear what diversity issues the school had in mind or how it had previously been possible to be a successful journalist in Toronto while being ignorant of the city's diversity. Some insight into the thinking behind the appointment might be found in a contemporary *Globe and Mail* column by Ryerson journalism professor Rick Salutin. Salutin reports a study which purports to reveal that "only" 2.6 per cent of journalists at Canadian newspapers are non-white, evidence of "a historic injustice" (17 March 1995). Apart from such obvious questions as whether the ethnic press were included in the survey[5] and how many journalists actually responded, the figure tells us nothing about whether contemporary recruitment practices are discriminatory or even whether historic practices resulted in discrimination. The figure is, however, sufficient for Salutin to conclude that those who have "benefitted" from this discrimination should make the sacrifice: "So why not start by replacing Lloyd Robertson and Peter Mansbridge? They've had the gain, now let them feel some pain. Hand their jobs to younger native women – or older black men." Curiously, but in common with other aging, fully employed white males who wear their equity credentials on their sleeves, Salutin neglected the contribution he might make to rectifying this historic injustice by falling on his own pen.

Some universities now routinely require candidates to provide employment equity data prior to applications being considered. St Thomas University, for example, informs applicants: "The Employment Equity provision of the St. Thomas University Collective Agreement requires the Department Chairperson to request that each applicant for a full-time faculty position complete a self-identification questionnaire." Dalhousie sends applicants a long questionnaire which, *inter alia*, seeks information on designated group status.

Preferential hiring is extended not simply to those who can claim victim status but to those who share the political agenda of entrenched academic factions. At the University of Alberta the appointment of Patricia Clements as dean of arts in 1989 was reported to have significantly boosted the power of feminists in the university (Verburg 1996). In the same year the university's English department offered all five new positions to women, claiming with no apparent sense of contradiction that this was consistent with the requirements of the Federal Contractors Program that the university address the position of "disadvantaged groups," and that the appointments were made on the basis of merit (Wallace 1996: 148). The reference to federal legislation to justify the university's foray into preferential hiring is of some interest. The scheduling of a review of the university under the program in the academic year 1991–92 provided leverage to preferential hiring activists and enabled them to claim that the discriminatory hiring policies were simply a consequence of complying with the 1986 federal Employment Equity Act.

The 1989 hirings produced intense controversy, but they did not curtail the power of radical feminists in the university. This was reflected in the 1996 appointment of Janine Brodie, a high profile radical feminist, as chair of political science. Brodie was recruited from York, though the majority of the Alberta political science department favoured an internal male candidate. The most unusual feature of the hiring process was the simultaneous offer of a job in women's studies to another York political scientist: "To lure Prof. Brodie, Dean Clements agreed to hire her close friend Lise Gotell" (Verburg 1996). Feminists make great play of the alleged existence of an old boys' network which serves to exclude women from fair competition. In the Gotell appointment, contrary to university policy, no position was ever advertised.

The University of Alberta arts faculty appears to be less than tolerant of those who fail to conform to the new orthodoxy. Bob Solomon, a twenty-eight year veteran in the English department, and a self-described liberal, took early retirement, publicly regretting his earlier support for Clements: "it has become a very unwelcome place for non-feminists." Internationally recognized scholar Greg Kelly, an expert on British women writers, resigned after being excluded from a group bidding for a federal grant to study women's literature (ibid.).

In common with other universities, Alberta has seen significant curriculum revision. Postmodern theorists, for whom all knowledge frequently seems little more than a mask for race and gender privilege, have sought to reduce the attention given to classical texts and writers, remove core curriculum requirements, and introduce new areas of study, typified by the English department course "*Post Modernism and Queer Praxis*" (ibid.).

Group membership may be a requirement not only for appointment but for the exercise of "scholarly" judgment. Paula Caplan reports the problem of an "openly lesbian" faculty member who was asked to "recommend other lesbian or lesbian-positive [sic] faculty for a doctoral dissertation committee" (Caplan 1993: 16). The issue that preoccupies Caplan is the lack of faculty who have made a public issue of their sexual preferences and might thus be known to be eligible; others might wonder what such preferences have to do with the composition of a committee empowered to recommend the award of a PHD.

Academic preferential hiring policies purportedly rest on the same claims to "historic disadvantage" as underpin other such programs. In the case of those whose high salaries depend on their assumed scholarly abilities, it seems reasonable to demand a high standard of proof. In contrast what is offered are sweeping assertions. The Canadian Association of University Teachers, which has an indifferent record when it comes to defending broader aspects of academic freedom, has shown little commitment to appointment on merit. Many of the faculty associations affiliated to the CAUT have, as at York University, used collective bargaining to insert preferential hiring practices into appointment procedures.

Spurred on by its Status of Women Committee, the CAUT has been eager to publicize the alleged plight of women but reluctant to allow equal time to those who would interrupt such laments with empirical evidence. Grant Brown of the University of Lethbridge, who has been one of the more courageous and rigorous crusaders against the tyranny of feminist orthodoxy on university hiring, wrote a critique of the thirty-two page Status of Women Committee "Special Report" published in 1991. The CAUT refused to publish it. Brown wrote a letter to the CAUT *Bulletin* alerting members to the fact that they could obtain the critique direct from him. The *Bulletin* refused to publish the letter (Brown 1992: 60).[6] In 1996 the Status of Women Committee again offered misleading claims regarding systemic discrimination. Again Brown wrote, and again the *Bulletin* failed to print his letter. The letter did appear in the newsletter of the Society for Academic Freedom and Scholarship (December 1996), an organization which, unlike the CAUT, has campaigned since its formation in 1992 for the defence of scholarly standards through appointment on merit and for academic freedom. We return to the issue of the empirical data on university hiring below.

The usual requirements of scholarly debate are irrelevant not simply to the CAUT but to many other preferential hiring advocates in Canadian universities. The controversy generated by UBC's search for a new president, a search that was accompanied by the statement that employment equity designated groups were "especially" welcome to apply, illustrated the power of orthodoxy. Political science professor Philip Resnick's attack on preferential hiring met with the inevitable outrage (Resnick 1996). Such measures, it was claimed, were necessary to create a level playing field. In the Orwellian reasoning of preferential hiring advocates, only by introducing such measures could appointment on merit be assured. Sunera Thobani, speaking from her new position as the Ruth Wynn Woodward Chair of Women's Studies at Simon Fraser, illustrated the approach: white men have benefited for decades from preferential hiring, ensuring that "merit is not the principle [sic] basis for hiring in the labour market." Only by taking affirmative action can "this historic preference can be countered, and a level playing field created whereby merit can indeed become the principle [sic] criterion in hiring" ("Letters," *Globe and Mail*, 23 September 1996). Those who oppose policies that appear to afford "especially" favourable consideration to some groups are simply attempting "to preserve the privileges enjoyed by a certain sector of society, and to maintain existing discriminations and barriers which work against the designated groups." Thus, in feminist newspeak, to be in favour of treating every group in the same manner is to be in favour of discrimination, while to favour being "especially" welcoming to some groups is consistent with ensuring that merit is the principal criterion in hiring.

The University of British Columbia's associate dean of science, Judith Myers, joined the debate to claim that some Canadian university departments had operated zero quotas for female recruitment in the 1960s (ibid., 1 October 1996). I requested further information, including where evidence of the existence of such quotas might be found and of which quotas Myers had direct knowledge but received no reply. Myers reported that UBC sets science hiring targets based on the numbers in the qualified pool, and that this resulted in the recruitment of women for 25 per cent of the 1995 positions (ibid.). Myers failed to respond to a request for clarification as to how this figure was obtained, but statistical data suggest the estimate was generous: women doctoral candidates are disproportionately concentrated in education, social sciences, and the humanities (HRD 1994b: 19).

UBC political scientist Kathryn Harrison captured the prevailing conventional wisdom, eschewing the messy business of sifting evidence or even offering any. Responding to Resnick in the *Globe and Mail*, Harrison boldly asserted what she knew to be obvious: "white males in the university still enjoy a considerable advantage" (Harrison 1996). University professors writing articles in national newspapers might be assumed to have at least a passing acquaintance with relevant studies, yet a number of detailed analyses have failed to find any support for the claim that qualified female candidates experience any contemporary discrimination. In fact an examination of recruitment, relative to the numbers in the qualified pool, indicates that women experience some considerable advantage (Brown 1992, 1994, Groarke 1996, Irvine 1996). Grant Brown, reviewing a range of statistical evidence, argues that the data "suggests that qualified women are twice as likely as qualified men to be hired for university positions" (Brown 1994b: 99).[7]

Harrison prefers simply to assert the existence of discrimination against women: "merit-based hiring has been more myth than reality." Where she did essay to offer facts, they appeared to rest on little more than casual observation. Women, for example, were present in undergraduate programs in "roughly equal numbers to men." In 1993–94 women comprised 58 per cent of those graduating with an undergraduate degree (HRD 1995a: 33) – this is not what feminists might describe as "roughly equal" were it women rather than men who comprised only 42 per cent.

Harrison assured *Globe and Mail* readers that "it is explicitly not UBC's policy, when hiring, to give preference to designated groups;

merit remains the prime criterion" (Harrison 1996). This begs the question of what other criterion apart from merit might influence the selection process. It also contradicts the contemporaneous advertisement for the UBC law faculty, which invited applications from all qualified candidates but affirmed that appointments "at a more senior rank" would only be considered for those who were members of a designated group (*Globe and Mail*, 24 August 1996). Harrison was, however, accurately reflecting the public representation of UBC's preferential hiring policies, which as with other such policies, are consistently represented as merit driven. This is categorically stated by Sharon E. Kahn, associate vice president, Equity: "UBC's 1991 Employment Equity Plan seek[s] to diversify the workforce without jeopardizing the merit principle ... The Equity Office continues to advance merit as *the foundation and guiding principle for all hiring activities*" (UBC 1997: 2, emphasis added).

Kahn is economical with the truth. Confronted with a complaint that the law faculty's advertisement violated Section 6 of the Human Rights Code of British Columbia which prohibits employers from expressing preferences or limitations on the basis of race and gender, UBC's lawyers offered a very different view: "It is in the nature of an effective employment equity plan that its provisions will benefit certain identified groups over others ... The University does not deny that the Plan, of which the disputed advertisement is a manifestation, may result in preference being given to one of the four designated groups over white males."[8] UBC's lawyers simply claimed that discrimination was legal since it was intended to ameliorate the conditions of disadvantaged individuals – to wit, the women who sought a comfortable position in the law faculty.

Turning her attention to the case for preferential hiring, Kathryn Harrison finds an absence of data on hiring decisions in Canadian political science and turns to the American data on political science hirings. The relevance of such data to the Canadian debate is not self-evident, but Harrison reports that among PHD graduates women were slightly more likely (72 per cent) to obtain academic jobs than men (70 per cent), and men slightly more likely to obtain contract as opposed to permanent jobs (35 per cent compared to 31 per cent). These figures, which indicate success rates for graduates far in excess of contemporary Canadian experience, are provided to counter Resnick's claim that universities have declared "open hunting season on one group, that is, white males."

The American data are inadequate to the task; they relate only to one academic discipline area and appear to assume male and female PHD graduates were equally likely to apply for positions. More relevant are generic Canadian data, and these indicate no under-representation in recruitment relative to the number of women in the qualified pool; rather, they suggest a clear gender advantage. In 1992–93, for example, in one sample surveyed, women are reported to have obtained twenty-five of the fifty jobs given to new PHDs (Renner 1996a: 1; see also Brown 1992 and Irvine 1996). Assuming that male and female graduates were equally likely to apply for an academic position, the two-thirds of PHDs who were male secured only half the available positions. Qualified women were twice as likely as qualified men to secure an appointment – a ratio that, had it been reversed, would have undoubtedly have been seen as powerful evidence of systemic discrimination.

Harrison extends her claims of discrimination from women to minorities, who, we are advised, also face "conscious and systemic practices" that discourage them from pursuing graduate studies and academic careers. This claim reflects feminist orthodoxy,[9] which insists on the deep-rooted sexism and racism of Canadian institutions but does not explain why visible minorities comprise some one in five of contemporary Canadian PHD graduates, twice their proportion in the wider student population, or why women comprise close to half of all Master's degree graduates (Wannell and Caron 1994a, 1994b). Women may comprise only 34 per cent of PHD graduates (HRD 1994a: 33), but the claim that this reflects "conscious and systemic practices" would be more convincing were it accompanied by evidence. Why do such practices only come into play at this and not the undergraduate or Master's degree levels? A more convincing argument suggests that the very rapid expansion in female participation levels in the universities in the last thirty years reflects the absence of systemic barriers. Universities have responded with little apparent difficulty to rapid changes in social values, female labour force participation levels, and demand by women for post-secondary education.

The existence of de facto hiring quotas, contrary to the claims of preferential hiring advocates, is widespread. Two professors at the University of Victoria note that "covertly if not overtly" 50 per cent of new and replacement appointments at that institution are reserved for women: "The official position is that the 50 per cent is only a goal – but a goal actively pursued and enforced by the vice-president academic, with the support of the president and the board of governors, is a quota in all but name" (Cutt and Hodgkinson 1992: 8).

Misao Dean, a supporter of preferential hiring at the university, notes: "The best equity hiring records on campuses usually amount to no more than achieving numerical parity between men and women in the most recent hirings" (Dean 1995:15). One University of Victoria department that refused to "follow the university equity policy and actively seek to hire women," she reports, was not allowed to recruit (ibid.). Transparently the university's policies discriminate against male candidates, but Dean remains unsatisfied: "departments can always make a case that offering a job to *this* male candidate justifies winking at equity hiring goals *just* this one time" (ibid., emphasis in original). Dean, a former chair of the faculty association's Status of Women Committee, appears to endorse what would be a de facto female-only policy.

The University of Moncton openly pursues preferential policies that place able-bodied white males in a residual category: "Where there are several excellent qualified candidates with one or more belonging to underrepresented groups, the person responsible must recommend a person from this underrepresented group" (*Telegraph Journal*, 31 March 1997). Prior to the formulation of the policy the university was already under attack for hiring unqualified staff in order to meet equity targets. White males with PHDs were reportedly passed over in favour of less qualified candidates who then received time off from the university to complete PHDs.

York University president Susan Mann defends her institution's hiring and promotion criteria, which she reports without any sense of contradiction, "require a rigorous external and internal assessment of candidates." Mann goes on to boast that, in the last ten years, 56 per cent of all full-time faculty appointments have gone to women ("Letters," *Globe and Mail*, 26 April 1997). This contrasts with their representation in the qualified pool (including recent and earlier generations of PHDs) at less than 25 per cent. This may, by some statistical quirk, be entirely consistent with the application of the merit principle, but would President Mann be equally eager to endorse the rigour of York's approach if more than 75 per cent of the candidate pool were women, but women secured only 44 per cent of the positions?

York's actions have in any case proved insufficient to appease union militants. Linda Briskin, one of York's many women's studies professors, has charged that the university has "systematically underpaid" female faculty. In support of this claim Briskin cites an $11,049 difference between average male and female salaries and demands the implementation of pay equity ("Letters," *Globe and Mail*, 1 May 1997). Briskin's figure is of no statistical merit, since it fails to note the large age and length of service discrepancies in the male and female pools – factors central to salary determination – or the possibility that at York, as elsewhere, a disproportionate number of women have accessed jobs without being required to hold a PHD.

ENTER THE PHILOSOPHERS

There is nothing so absurd but some philosopher has said it.

Cicero

Wayne Sumner, who headed Canada's pre-eminent philosophy department at the University of Toronto, has become known as one of the discipline's more aggressive proponents of preferential hiring. The University of Toronto has an explicit policy of awarding two-thirds of all new appointments to women who, Sumner claims, amount to 25–30 per cent of the candidate pool (Sumner 1996: 381). Since women constitute only 13 per cent of all those holding academic posts in philosophy and many of those teaching at less prestigious or well-paid institutions might wish to seek employment at Toronto, Sumner's figure would appear to exaggerate the proportion of women in the qualified pool.

Strikingly, neither Sumner or the other well-remunerated male professors who embrace the department's discriminatory hiring policy have been moved to offer any sacrifice on their own behalf. They have, however, found no difficulty articulating a myriad of ethical arguments in favour of the sacrifices that might be made by male students currently graduating with philosophy PHDs or those males teaching elsewhere who might wish to be considered for appointment at University of Toronto on the basis of merit. It may be thought, of course, that women in philosophy had experienced some particularly pernicious discrimination which only overt preferential policies could redress, but a study undertaken for the Canadian Philosophical Association suggested that 93 per cent of female PHDs had been awarded university posts. Indeed, critics suggested Toronto's preferential hiring simply made it more difficult for less prestigious departments to recruit qualified women philosophers (Groarke 1996b: 389).

The University of Toronto's decision to adopt a two-to-one preferential hiring policy parallels moves within the Canadian Philosophical Association to endorse such hiring, an argument justified in part, as at the University of Alberta, by reference to the 1986 federal legislation (Brown 1992: 59). There is inevitably among those who find themselves on the cutting edge of progressive thinking a desire to go one step further. The Philosophical Association was content to recommend only a modest 50 per cent hiring rate for the minority of candidates who are women, not the four out of five-and-a-half appointments proudly achieved by Toronto.[10]

Sumner is aware of the statistical evidence which demonstrates the contemporary advantage of qualified women candidates but prefers to seek justification elsewhere. Anecdotal evidence, as any bar-room politician knows, is always available to render the most well-evidenced argument suspect, and Sumner offers the example of Melissa Franklin who, if Sumner's account is correct, experienced overt gender discrimination in her application for a post in the University of Toronto physics department (Sumner 1996: 376–7)[11] According to Sumner, the physics department engaged in blatantly illegal discrimination, since while it is perfectly legal to discriminate against white males, as Sumner's department does, it is not legal to discriminate against those who can claim group disadvantage; if a visible minority male applied to Sumner's department and faced the discrimination standardly afforded male applicants, Sumner might find himself faced with a legal rather than philosophical quandary.

Sumner's response is not to call for the dismissal of those physicists responsible or to suggest any remedy to the alleged problem but to maintain that this example provides reason not to rely "solely on hiring statistics." It was open to Sumner as a senior academic to seek a university inquiry into the physics department and to press for appropriate disciplinary action, though this might have required confrontation with similarly powerful tenured academics. Instead the story is proffered in support of policies that overtly discriminate against relatively powerless men applying for philosophy positions in Sumner's own department.

There are other problems with Sumner's resort to anecdote – not least that far more men will have accounts of occasions in which they were denied appointment or promotion because of their gender, including applicants to Sumner's department. Sumner's defence of his department's discriminatory policies rests on such improbable observations as the fact that women who have received explicit preference in hiring have, nonetheless, "easily been the equal of their male colleagues" (ibid.: 380). It would, no doubt, take a full professor of philosophy to explain how the deliberate recruitment of some 80 per cent of new appointees from a pool containing (at best) 25 per cent of qualified applicants could result in such an outcome.

Sumner's other defences for his department's refusal to recruit on merit include a fashionably postmodern bow to the possibility that knowledge is, if not biologically determined, then certainly biologically informed: "The small number of women in the department was also a problem for female students ... Many of them had perfectly legitimate reasons for wanting to work with female faculty, especially in one-on-one situations or when they were undertaking feminist projects. With so few women on staff, they experienced difficulty in finding available supervisors. Some also reported feeling marginalized or trivialized in classes taught by men when they tried to articulate points of view at variance with the reigning ideology of the classroom" (ibid.: 378). There are a number of possible implications in this account, including that some faculty in Canada's pre-eminent philosophy department are so lacking in pedagogic and social skills that they are unable to communicate effectively with members of the opposite sex or to distinguish between the task of an educator and that of an ideologue. Such problems will not be addressed by any preferential hiring program.

Toronto's pioneering efforts inevitably encouraged other philosophy departments to emulate their approach. In 1996 the University of Winnipeg advertised a tenure-track philosophy position for which the gender requirements were unambiguous. The successful candidate required not only familiarity with feminist research and theory but was also required to "have experience with community based women's organizations." In case there was any remaining doubt that the position called for a proselytizing approach, candidates were also required to be able "to present non-academic public talks on women's issues" (*University Affairs* January 1996: 40).

HAREMS AND OTHER DIVERSIONS

> After completing their graduate study, women are less likely
> than men to be hired by academic institutions.
>
> Paula Caplan, 1993

The claims of white male domination in the university are buttressed by the undisputed evidence that white males are "overrepresented" in faculty positions. This can be expressed in a variety of ways. Carleton psychology professor Edward Renner, surveying a large sample of academics, compares the number of women appointed to the proportion of women in the undergraduate population, noting that in 1971, at the peak of the academic hiring period, women secured only 12.5 per cent of the appointments but made up 38 per cent of the students: "By 1992–93, women got twenty-five out of the fifty jobs given to new PHDs, close to the 54% proportion of women students" (Renner 1996a: 1). The purpose of the comparison, other than polemical, is unclear. The real test of systemic discrimination lies in the relative success of qualified candidates: since Renner notes that only 67 per cent of female faculty have a PHD compared to 83 per cent of males it might appear that selection procedures have been less demanding for women (ibid.: 2).

The most striking charge, widely used by feminist polemicists, is that the proportion of female faculty is unchanged since the 1930s. Jackie Stalker has compared the position of women in universities to harems, with men "exerting their will over women who are students, staff and even a small number of colleagues" (Stalker 1995). Stalker's grasp of the realities of life in a harem may be limited, but she offers an interesting illustration of the apparently limitless capacity of those who have led lives of consummate privilege to claim victim status.

Stalker points to the fact that in 1931 women accounted for 19 per cent of full-time university faculty, compared to 21 per cent in 1994. The reason is apparently simple: "Had qualified women been appointed over the years, we wouldn't have this problem now. Budget is obviously not the underlying reason" (ibid.). If universities claim an absence of qualified female candidates, the reason again is discrimination: "If they can't find any women who are qualified, the question we should ask is, why aren't they producing them? Why are they still excluding them?" (ibid.).

For a former professor of higher education Stalker seems to have a surprising faith in the power of universities to mould student preferences: women may constitute a significant majority of undergraduates, in spite of the "chilly climate" she claims they face, but they steadfastly refuse to distribute themselves equally between disciplines. In 1990 95 per cent of nursing graduates were women, as were some 76 per cent of those graduating in psychology, sociology, anthropology, and demography. This compares to a mere 13 per cent of those graduating in meteorology or physics – but should we conclude that the climate in these subjects was really that much chillier than in chemistry, geology, and metallurgy, where no less than 59 per cent were female (Wannell and Carron 1994b: 4)? If physics departments "exclude" women, by what mechanisms do they do so? Certainly the challenge of recruiting equal numbers of qualified female professors in some disciplines is immense. In 1991, only 17 per cent of those granted doctorates in mathematics and the physical sciences were women, compared to 53 per cent in education and 46 per cent in the humanities (HRD 1994b: 19).

These differences may be rooted in significant differences in values and goals. A study commissioned by Industry Canada on discipline choices and retention patterns concluded: "There are gender differences in basic attitudes, values, motivations, social support and perceptions of self and science that affect recruitment or discipline choice, experiences, achievement, retention or program behaviour and career directions" (Gilbert and Pomfret 1995: 49).

Stalker's selection of comparative years (1931/1994) serves a polemical purpose but casts no light on contemporary practice. Self-evidently those currently teaching in universities were employed in a much later period, starting in the late 1950s. In 1961 women constituted 11 per cent of the faculty at Canadian universities, rising to 22 per cent by 1992 (Renner 1996a: 1). Female recruitment has risen rapidly; with the increase in the number of women in the qualified pool, the explanation for the slow rate of change lies not in systemic barriers but the low attrition rate among academics. Many of those currently teaching in universities were recruited in the late 1960s and early 1970s when relatively few women were in the qualified pool. The changing demographic composition of university faculty is illustrated by the much larger proportion of women among younger faculty. Fifteen per cent of the faculty over the age of fifty are women, compared to 35 per cent of those under the age of thirty-five (Renner 1996a: 2). This share exceeds female availability in the contemporary qualified pool. The share, however, must be set in context: less than 6 per cent of university faculty are under thirty-five (Renner 1996b: 1).

Irvine has estimated that in the 1960s women constituted some 8.6 per cent of the qualified pool and secured 7.6 per cent of the appointments (Irvine 1996: 259). Irvine is prepared to concede that discrimination may account for this small discrepancy, but an equally convincing case could be made for the claim that in a period when women were less likely to pursue full-time careers, some may have exercised other preferences. This is the only period in which there is any evidence that women may have faced discrimination. In the 1972–74 period, for example, women comprised an estimated 11 per cent of the qualified pool but 19.6 per cent of the appointments. Irvine concludes: "the data are consistent with there being significant discrimination in favour of women and against men" (Irvine 1996: 260).

These statistical debates are of little importance to feminists. Anne Dagg, who is identified as the academic advisor to the independent studies program at the University of Waterloo, opts for conjecture and anecdote to account for women's historically low hiring rates: "I believe the reason is that … universities were now offering comparatively good wages that attracted more than uncommonly dedicated academics; men were so often available for openings that there was little need to hire women" (Dagg 1993: 14).

Feminist victimology supports Dagg's argument that women and racial minorities bear the brunt of discriminatory hiring practices: men, she says, may be "hired and tenured for non-academic reasons – because they are not women, because they are white, because they have families to support, because they have friends in the right places. *Such discrimination is documented in thousands of articles and books"* (ibid.: 15, emphasis added). Dagg offers a further spin in claiming that even where women are hired in academic positions, "feminist" women experience additional barriers to recruitment and promotion. Again she turns to anecdotal evidence, but in the absence of hard data, those who have observed the rapid growth of women's studies (with extensive funding support), the penetration of feminist orthodoxy into large areas of the humanities and social sciences, and the documented evidence of women's advantage in hiring may not be easily convinced.[12]

Jackie Stalker, in a discussion prompted by the events at UBC and elsewhere, has suggested that the problems of women in academia extend far beyond discrimination in hiring. If Stalker is to be believed, the minority of white males on campus exercise truly extraordinary power:

There has always been a chill ... Women who were once the minority because they were even excluded from universities are now the majority of students and they cannot speak out freely. All graduate students, in fact, cannot speak out freely, nor can the minority of faculty who are women. They have never been able to: women in post-secondary institutions are always relegated to a lower status, and that's whether we're talking about – rank, research, publications, ideas, recognition of their scholarship, or even salaries.

Women are all in the Triple-A category: assistant, associate, or acting positions.

The consequences are quite vicious: if you're a student speaking out, well, you have to worry about graduating. If you're a faculty member, you have to worry about getting promotion or never getting tenure or possibly losing your term position (CBC Radio, *Cross Country Check-Up*, 22 October 1995).

When host Rex Murphy (unusually, for those who customarily serve as CBC Radio gatekeepers) suggested this scenario was improbable, Stalker responded, "Oh, Rex, stop that. You're saying that from your perspective, and you're one more white male. You don't see the world the way the majority of people do."

In contrast to Stalker's allegations, the striking fact is that those who face being silenced or find it necessary to express their views with increasing circumspection are those who fail to share the views of radical feminists. There are no university officials whose mandate is to protect their rights. In a catalogue of abuses against academic freedom, it is not the voice of feminism that faces suppression (Fekete 1994: 199–318).

Stalker is of course not alone in presenting a view of female academics as prisoners of male power. Paula Caplan suggests that women
are victims of a pervasive social tyranny: "Most women consciously
or unconsciously know that the band of behaviour that is acceptable
for females is extremely narrow: many of us constantly monitor our
behaviour, realizing that with every step we take, we are in danger of
being labelled either as cold, rejecting, castrating, and bitchy or as
smotheringly warm, overly emotional, hysterical and intrusive"
(Caplan 1993: 3).

The claims that women face a "chilly climate" in university employment often appear to rely on nothing more than the capacity of well-
paid female academics to resituate their privilege and claim victim
status. Misao Dean laments that "the job of [the] university professor
... is still designed for men who have stay-at-home wives who cook,
take care of the kids, do the laundry and pack for them when they go
to conferences ... Female faculty, especially those with families, don't
have the luxury of shutting out the merely personal in order to work
16 hours a day on their teaching and research" (Dean 1995: 15).[13]
Among the outrages Dean reports are late afternoon meetings, when
day-cares want parents to pick up children by 5:15: "That means
leaving campus by 4:30" (ibid.). It is a striking example of the sense
of entitlement of middle-class feminists that they should suppose that
highly paid, prestigious occupations providing unusually generous benefits and extensive vacations should also provide incumbents with the
right to routinely leave their posts at 4:30 p.m. Many low-paid Canadians have no such expectations.

Research into the experience of male and female university administrators casts substantial doubt on the chilly climate claims. A survey
of male and female university administrators found, in contrast to
previous surveys that had surveyed only women, that many of the
alleged indicators of chilly climate, such as the claim that others took
credit for a respondent's ideas, were affected by the respondent's
hierarchical status as department head, dean, vice-president or president: "the significance of most of the chilly climate indicators was no
longer attributed to gender but turned out to be related to positional
power" (Berkowitz, 1996). As a report on the study noted, "For
example, one chilly climate indicator is a positive response to the
statement: 'Others take credit for the ideas which I openly express.' In
this survey, both male and female department heads reported that
deans take credit for their ideas" (Berkowitz 1996). The research was
conducted by Sheryl Bond, a professor in the Centre for Higher
Education Research at the University of Manitoba, where Stalker
formerly professed.

BROADENING THE NET

The earlier focus on the perceived plight of women is now giving way to an emphasis on the claims of another group that has sought the benefits afforded by "historic disadvantage." It is noteworthy that no evidence has been produced to suggest that racial minorities ever experienced discrimination in hiring to academic appointments in Canadian universities in any period relevant to current staffing. This is not to deny the possibility that the occasional bigot may have influenced a hiring decision, a factor that may influence appointments affecting a wide range of people. "Systemic discrimination" is nonetheless commonly claimed. Bill Graham, president of the University of Toronto's powerful faculty association, and a member of the philosophy faculty, has no hesitation in assuring *Globe and Mail* readers that "many men" experience such discrimination: "vastly more men (*but not men from targeted groups*) are in Canadian universities than are women" ("Letters," 14 May 1994, emphasis added). This is the voice of orthodoxy. Graham offers no statistics: he simply knows that this is the way Canada is, his fellow citizens (and academics) unremitting bigots.

The position of the orthodox is also put forward by York University professor Frances Henry, in a book intended as a college and university text. In a chapter bluntly entitled "Racism in Universities," Henry states that one of the "manifestations of racism" is a lack of academic representation. It is worth examining Henry's argument in some detail, since it is indicative of what contemporary students are being taught in pursuit of the argument that Canada is a deeply racist society.

University and college social science courses should introduce students to the existence of competing perspectives to familiarize them with the nature of contemporary debates and to equip them with investigative tools to examine relevant empirical and theoretical issues. Henry's approach, in contrast, appears to rely on telling students "truths" about Canada. There is rarely any suggestion that there may be other interpretations of the data or profound disagreements about its meaning. Henry advises her readers that a review of staffing at the University of Toronto reveals a "pattern of inequity" (Henry *et al.* 1995: 197). Visible-minority student enrolment at the University of Toronto was almost 40 per cent, "yet less than 10 percent of its faculty were members of racial minority groups" (ibid.). Readers will by now be familiar with this approach: find two superficially connected figures, put them together and shout foul.

Recruitment of faculty to Canadian universities is national (Canadian immigration regulations give preference to permanent residents and Canadian citizens). If a comparator is required for the number of racial minority faculty, it is not the local student body but the proportion of racial minorities in the Canadian population. This might be further refined by looking at the size of the qualified pool (those holding PHDs) and the numbers at historic junctures when existing faculty incumbents were recruited. In fact the number of visible minorities on faculty at the University of Toronto in 1993, according to Henry, stood at 9.5 per cent. This was slightly higher than the proportion of visible minorities found in the 1991 census and a percentage considerably higher than would be suggested by reviewing the proportion of visible minorities in Canada in the late 1960s and early '70s when many faculty were recruited. The figure may well under-estimate the actual number of visible minorities on faculty since, as we noted earlier, there is a consistent pattern of under-reporting in self-identification procedures. Even if the figure accurately captures the representation of visible minorities, the conclusion which is suggested is that the figure affords no evidence of discrimination in hiring.

The figures on the number of visible minority students might be thought to merit comment even taking account of the large numbers in the metropolitan Toronto area. In 1994 a university survey in fact reported that 41.3 per cent of students were members of a visible minority, 58 per cent of whom were members of that doubly disadvantaged group, "women of colour."[14] The figure suggests a truly remarkable level of access to one of Canada's top universities.[15] This might appear inconsistent with claims of widespread discrimination in the education system, yet the tone of the previous chapter, "Racism in Canadian Education," is illustrated in the selection of an opening quote from Esmeralda Thornhill, who currently occupies the racially exclusive James Robinson Johnstone Chair in black Canadian studies in Dalhousie's law faculty: "Visible-minority students are exposed to discriminatory educational practices which, like a multitude of timeless voices, tells them loudly or softly that they are intellectually, emotionally, physically and morally inferior." This message apparently failed to reach the very large visible minority population at the University of Toronto.

Henry proceeds from a comparison of the proportion of visible minorities who are students and faculty to advise students: "Even more revealing is the fact that this 10 percent were heavily concentrated in a few fields, such as engineering and computer sciences. Disciplines such as the social sciences had very few minority faculty, and the sociology department did not have a Black faculty member" (ibid.: 197). "Revealing" of what is unclear: are students to assume discrimination in the social sciences, an area generally associated with a plethora of progressive attitudes, is greater than in engineering? The shift from a discussion of minority faculty to black faculty is equally notable. Should every department have one or more black faculty members?

Census data for 1986 indicate that visible minorities comprised 6.3 per cent of the Canadian labour force. In establishing employment equity benchmarks, it is common to use a figure derived from the last census. Treasury Board, for example, reporting on the representation of designated groups in the public service, as of 31 March 1993, offered a work-force availability for visible minorities of 5.9 per cent based on 1986 census data and an estimation of those in the group "with skills similar to those in the public service" (Treasury Board 1994: 11 and Table 1).

Henry offers no benchmark other than the "almost 40" per cent of University of Toronto students she reports as members of a visible minority. Turning her attention to York University, she reports "even fewer" visible minority faculty, 6.4 per cent. A tabular representation offers further data: UBC 9.3 per cent, Simon Fraser 7.0 per cent, Dalhousie 7.8 per cent, Manitoba 7.2 per cent, Calgary 11 per cent. The data are either from 1990 or 1991. Based on any conventional labour force benchmark, the conclusion that should be drawn is that racial minorities are highly successful in securing appointment. Henry's unequivocal conclusion, in support of her claim that this is a "manifestation of racism," is: "Universities clearly face a problem of non-representativeness at the academic and senior management levels" (Henry 1995: 198).

The alleged racism is also evident, according to Henry, in promotion and tenure decisions, where, for example, traditional standards of excellence may discriminate against women and minorities. This is illustrated by the fact that women's studies was only recently added to the curriculum and is "not as highly regarded as other areas of specialization" (ibid.: 199). If true, this may well reflect the highly ideological nature of much that passes for pedagogy and research in that field. Henry offers no evidence that those espousing women's studies face any problem in securing appointment or promotion. Any review of the last twenty-five years suggests the reverse.

Henry suggests that minority faculty may also publish in "smaller community oriented or advocacy publications" which are not as credible in tenure decisions and attend less prestigious locally organized conferences. It is not clear where the evidence for this stereotype might be found, particularly since Henry has previously advised her readers that minority faculty are concentrated in fields such as engineering and computer science – areas not known for the prevalence of community oriented or advocacy publications. Henry illustrates her claim by reference to the fact that she must present more detail in support of applications for financial support to attend the meetings of the Caribbean Studies Association than is required to attend meetings of the American Anthropological Association. It is unclear why minority faculty should be particularly affected by this requirement which is of a generic nature having nothing to do with the ethnicity of the applicant (Henry is white).

Minority faculty are also said to be disadvantaged in the added burden they face in student counselling, advising, and graduate supervision because there are too few to meet student demands. Why students in subjects such as mathematics and engineering should think the ethnicity of a supervisor relevant is unclear. Students normally seek a supervisor whose area of academic specialization most closely corresponds to their own. In the humanities and social sciences expertise in such areas as women's literature or African politics is a function of scholarship, not gender or ethnicity.

Although Henry fails to offer any convincing evidence for the disadvantage of racial minorities in promotion and tenure decisions, students are left in no doubt that this exists. Just as affirmative action is required to address the imagined under-representation of racial minorities on faculty, so promotion and tenure committees are urged to become "sensitive" to "the extra demands made on minority faculty" (ibid.: 199) and presumably afford them more generous consideration than faculty not burdened by such "disadvantages."

Turning her attention to students Henry draws attention to the problems posed by the "Eurocentric" curriculum. Curiously, she fails to note that in spite of these pervasive problems, visible minority students have been extraordinarily successful in completing PHDs, where nationally their representation, in 1990, was twice as large as in the undergraduate population (Wannell and Caron 1994a: 4).

Support for preferential hiring is not confined to those who explicitly champion the grievance-driven politics of race and gender. Carleton political science professor Peter Emberley in *Zero Tolerance: Hot Button Politics in Canada's Universities* offers an apocalyptic vision of universities "on the verge of financial, spiritual and political collapse" (1996: 257) and demands a return to the "scholarly culture." In Emberley's view universities are being torn apart by the competing demands of the "cultural left," dedicated to extirpating sexism and racism in the curriculum, and the "corporate right," demanding business relevance. Emberley, who heads the university's elite College of the Humanities, distances himself from some of the excesses of preferential hiring advocates but has no dispute with the underlying philosophy: "Hiring quotas (though never so-called) for aboriginal people, people with disabilities, members of racial minorities and women exist, in fact, at most of Canada's universities ... Some find these practices abhorrent ... But modest efforts to steer institutions in the light of approved public policy and constitutionally guaranteed principles are not unjustifiable" (Emberley 1996: 231).[16]

Dalhousie political scientist David Cameron affords equally fashionable accomodation. In a paper on academic freedom published by the Association of Universities and Colleges of Canada, he suggests that this concept is in competition with affirmative action programs: "At issue here is competition between two ideas: the commitment to the unremitting search for truth through scholarship, and a social responsibility to ensure that faculty of publicly-funded universities are broadly representative of the society they serve. It is not necessary to argue that these ideas are incompatible to conclude that they are in competition" (Cameron 1996: 9).

Cameron, remarkably, fails to offer any resolution or to explain at what stage universities assumed the responsibility to be "representative of society." Universities might resolve the issue by appointing on merit, but in the muddled world of preferential hiring it is no longer enough to condemn and prevent discrimination in selection. We have now moved to a situation in which we must seek to reconcile discrimination (against white males) with the principles of academic freedom and recruitment on the basis of excellence. Cameron is in no doubt that the task at hand is "to agree on what compromises of academic excellence may be acceptable in pursuit of employment equity" (ibid., 9–10).[17] It is a measure of the shift in the universities that even those who claim to defend the ideals of a classic liberal education have no difficulty endorsing policies which reject appointment on merit.

THE EPISTEMOLOGY OF THE ORTHODOX

> The lived experience of women in the academy is one in which we learn that to be successful, we must disassociate our rational selves from the rest of ourselves. The bifurcation of persons, particularly those in marginalized groups, in the academy is supported by the hegemony of objectivity over subjectivity. Thus, learning in the classroom and conducting research are activities in which women and minorities are profoundly vulnerable.
>
> Drakich, Taylor, and Bankier, 1996[18]

It is not only in the area of preferential hiring policies that unsupportable claims proliferate. We have already reviewed many of the allegations that underpin the academic cultivation of the politics of grievance. York University sociology professor Himani Bannerji assured her Vancouver audience in 1985 that the ideology of racism "combined with the neo-colonial nature of South Asian countries" ensured South Asian women "our place on the lowest level on the scale of exploitation in Canada" (Bannerji 1993a: 146). The casual claim of a university professor to inclusion in "our place" at the bottom of the scale is noteworthy, but of greater interest is the fact that Bannerji found it unnecessary to explain in quite what ways India, the world's largest democracy, was embraced by the neo-colonialism label or to offer any statistical evidence that South Asian women were on the "lowest level." Census data from 1986, as we have already noted, showed no evidence of discrimination against visible minority women born in Canada.

Bannerji claimed that researchers "have shown, for example, that South Asian women are generally found in factories which are farthest away from dense population centres, working in areas with almost no transportation, in the lowest or inner-most part of factories" (Bannerji 1993a: 146). No studies are cited, nor is it clear how South Asian women, who predominantly live in major urban centres, are able to access their jobs in far-away factories with "almost no transportation." The subordinate position of South Asian women is said to be maintained through stereotypes: "Passivity, docility, silence, illiteracy, uncleanliness, smell of curry, and fertility are some of the common-sense things the dominant culture 'knows' about us" (ibid.: 147). Again no evidence is offered in support of assertions that might surprise those familiar with the family-centred, entrepreneurial, and success-oriented culture of many South Asians. More than one-third of South Asians recorded in the 1991 census arrived between 1982 and 1991, but the proportion of South Asians in professional positions (13 per cent) is the same as for the population as a whole (Kelly 1995: 4–7). Indira Gandhi and Benazir Bhutto scarcely reinforce the docile stereotype, which is grounded in nothing more than Bannerji's search for evidence of grievance.

Elsewhere, in yet another tome funded by the Canada Council and the Ontario Arts Council, Bannerji observes in reference to the effects of NAFTA that in Canada in 1993, with a population of "approximately" 25 million, 150,000 or more are unemployed "in Ontario alone" (Bannerji 1993b: viii). The number of unemployed, excluding discouraged workers and the involuntary part-time workers in Ontario in 1993, stood at 604,000 (Statistics Canada Labour Force Annual Averages 1989–94). The York sociology professor "lost" more than four million Canadians, but more remarkable, for an academic whose discipline is ostensibly concerned with social questions, is the under-estimation of Ontario's unemployed. If Bannerji's figure was accurate it would represent an unemployment level of 2.6 per cent, a figure which would result in little involuntary part-time unemployment and very few discouraged workers. If the Canadian economy were able to realize such a level, it would be functioning more effectively, in employ-ment terms, than any contemporary western economy. In contrast, the real unemployment level, including discouraged workers and the invol-untary part-time exceeds 13 per cent. The last time the Canadian economy saw a figure approximating 2.6 per cent was in the early 1950s. Transparently for some practitioners of orthodoxy, facts have receded into virtual irrelevance.

Linda Carty, in a contribution to an anthology (again supported by the Canada Council and the Ontario Arts Council) that looks at the university "as a site of feminist struggles," makes explicit the prior claim exercised by life experience over empirical data. Carty offers a litany of anecdotal accounts intended to illustrate the claim that knowl-edge produced through universities is "Eurocentric, white and male and therefore inherently gender-biased and racist" (Carty 1991: 16). Illustrating the way "Black feminist scholarship" is "put down," Carty cites the example of a university professor who challenged the claim that blacks in the media were portrayed in stereotypical terms. The anonymous professor reportedly said that while this may have been true in the 1960s, it was no longer the case. The comments, Carty observes, "were without any basis in knowledge because those of us who are Black continue to see ourselves reflected in the media largely as criminals or idiots of one sort or another" (ibid.: 21).

Carty offers no evidence beyond what she claims to "see," but one task of scholarship is to seek ways of resolving such disputes through research. D'Souza cites just such research, a survey by Lichter and Rothman of six hundred programs aired in prime time, over three decades. The study found that blacks committed only three in one hundred TV murders, and were eighteen times less likely to commit homicide on TV as in real life (D'Souza 1995: 263). Notes D'Souza, "Today television series and films self-consciously depict blacks in counterstereotypical roles: as physicians, scientists, supervisors" (ibid.).

At the extreme, Carty appears to argue that black women have nothing to learn in the classroom, having acquired their own knowl-edge elsewhere: "So, as a black woman, I entered the classroom knowing that what I was about to undertake was not something new about the world or something that would help me deconstruct any complexities in my own world. Instead, it was merely to learn the process of how the dominant knowledge forms are validated and given legitimacy for what counts as knowledge" (Carty 1991: 23). Carty has now graduated from student to professor, a role that will enable her to insist on the acceptance of such epistemological approaches by those taking her courses.[19] It is unclear whether her non-dominant knowledge is of similar equivalence in areas such as physics, mathematics, or possibly brain surgery.

Three tenured women professors who served on the CAUT's powerful Status of Women Committee endorse a similar position in *Beyond Political Correctness*, insisting that "the concept of academic freedom is improved by including the subjectivity of women and minorities and acknowledging that the personal and experiential are of equal importance to intellectual words and ideas" (Drakich, Taylor, and Bankier 1996: 130). It is not clear why white males who have no claim to minority status (other than the obvious statistical one) should not have the right to have their "subjectivity" taken into account. More puzzling is what role highly paid academics might play when students insist on rival truths derived from experiential knowledge, or perhaps truths that are at odds with intellectual words and ideas. There must, for example, be many young people in Saskatchewan whose personal experience might lead them to believe the world is flat. However, since the book in which this epistemology is articulated was prepared with financial support from Carleton University and published by University of Toronto Press, such pedagogic approaches are obviously becoming mainstream.

Krista Soots reported on a University of Toronto conference organized as part of the university's "Equity Days," Rescuing Graduate Studies: Equity and How to Get It, in the Society for Academic Freedom and Scholarship newsletter (March 1997). She noted the pervasiveness of the claim that all opinions are of equal merit:

Epistemological equity means that all "knowledges" are equal (except of course the views that disagree with this). As to the "epistemological equity" between, for example, a supervisor and a graduate student, it was maintained that equity must be viewed as complete, because the professor has merely a different experience from the student, and not a superior understanding ... there was a seamless conceptual unity in the voices of all the speakers – everyone spoke in the same highly abstract, ponderous and often profoundly incoherent idiom of "deconstruction." No dissenting viewpoints were considered.

THE PULPIT IN THE CLASSROOM

Racist beliefs and practices continue to pervade Canadian society.

Frances Henry, 1995

> The most useful contribution male pedagogues can make to the feminist cause is to mobilize the support of their male students.
>
> Stephen Richer, 1995

Carleton university sociology professor Stephen Richer openly proclaims his intention in teaching a course, misleadingly entitled Introductory Sociology, to act as a recruiting sergeant for feminism: "I slowly realized that as male I had a unique opportunity to reach the men, to make feminist thinking an appropriate male pursuit" (Richer 1995: 195). Necessarily, Richer's goal, which might appear messianic rather than scholarly, includes familiarizing students with just how profoundly women are oppressed. He notes the dominance of men among the founders of sociology: "I asked whether much had changed, citing the national average of eighteen percent women among the professoriate" (ibid.: 202). Richer's statistic is wrong but illuminating. What if he were to compare the proportion of female undergraduates today with forty years earlier? This could prove subversive to the whole venture.

Richer offers further evidence of women's oppression, comparing the annual incomes of males and females in full-time employment in various sectors of the labour market. There are many striking aspects to these statistics, though not the ones Richer would have the students note. The figures are drawn from a 1981 study by York University's Institute for Behavioral Research; they are obviously dated, but by how much it is impossible to know, as this would require information about York's original sources. But they are at least fifteen years out of date, and why fee-paying students should not be provided with contemporary information is unclear. The apparent failure, in an introductory sociology course, to provide students with any critical understanding of how to use statistics is notable. Richer, former chair of Carleton's sociology department, compares the earnings of males in the "professionals, managers" category who are high-school dropouts with females in the same category with a university degree. A similar comparison is made in the "clerical, sales, service" categories and the "manual" category. This allows students to draw the obvious conclusion that "women university graduates possess less earning power than male high school dropouts" (ibid.: 214).

The comparisons in fact indicate little beyond the parlous state of sociology teaching at Carleton University. The groups being compared are not similar in a number of relevant ways, including age. The average male with "less than high school" in the professionals, managers category earned (in whatever distant year these statistics originated) $24,938; the average female with a university degree, in the same category, earned \$23,901. Could the pool of female graduates in this category be younger, with substantially less labour force experience than the pool of male high-school dropouts?

Richer could have resolved some of these difficulties by comparing like and like. A good comparator might be earnings of contemporary university graduates. Richer would have his students believe that female graduates face a dire level of discrimination and are fated to under-perform male high school dropouts. Yet, looking at the graduating class of 1990, a Statistics Canada report notes: "we found that female university graduates are rewarded slightly better than their male counterparts, after controlling for experience, job tenure, education and hours of work" (Wannell and Caron 1994b: i).

Frequently academics who would persuade students that Canadian society is pervasively sexist and racist rely on simple repetition, the charges so self-evident that evidence would be redundant. In a recent textbook, *Women and Canadian Public Policy*, edited by Janine Brodie, the newly appointed chair of the University of Alberta political science department, students are informed: "Racist practices dictated that the experience of many new immigrants from the south, *as well as people who had been in Canada for generations*, would be *fundamentally different* from European immigrants. The concerns of the former *revolved around systemic discrimination* not just on the basis of language, but also *in the areas of housing, employment and education*" (Gabriel 1996: 182, emphasis added).

The writer, Christina Gabriel, a PHD student in political science at York University, Brodie's former department, finds it unnecessary to offer a single piece of empirical evidence. No doubt at York such beliefs are so widespread that no social science graduate student questions them. This is the new orthodoxy. Lest students be in any doubt, they are informed that "systemic racism and sexism [is] endemic to Canadian society" (ibid.: 186). Editor Brodie suggests Gabriel's contribution is important in showing how "spaces created at the margins of the state apparatus provided a place for women of colour to contest their subordination and exclusion" (Brodie 1996: 19). This description might be thought to suggest the kind of relationship ethnic Tibetans enjoy with their Chinese colonizers, but according to the University of Alberta's top political scientist, it describes the life experience and political status of visible minority women in Canada.

In the same text Osgoode Hall Law professor Shelley Gavigan writes of the "social and legal marginalization of women of colour." Again this is offered as though it were no more than self-evident (Gavigan 1996: 255). Gavigan provides students with no indication of quite how such legal and social marginalization occurs, why it appears to afflict women but not "men of colour," or whether it embraces people like Windsor law dean Juanita Westmoreland Traoré. Students are offered little information that would enable them to judge whether the learned professor is giving voice to fashionable feminist sentiment or empirically informed social analysis, to the fruits of academic scholarship or the repetition of ideological truths.

The Colour of Democracy, a recent textbook by Professor Frances Henry and others, is illustrative of the fervour of those who would have students believe Canada is a pervasively racist society. Henry opens the book with a series of propositions designed to overcome any doubts students may have about the magnitude of the problem. The central concept of "democratic racism" is defined as a system that facilitates "the justification of the inherent conflict between the egalitarian values of justice and fairness and the racist ideologies reflected in the collective mass-belief system as well as the racist attitudes, perceptions, and assumptions of individuals" (Henry *et al.* 1995: 17). This concept is introduced by a summary of the views of "new racists" in the U.K. and "aversive racism" in the United States.

According to Henry, new racists "have defined a national British *culture* that is homogeneously White." Reflective of the new racism is the proposition that pathological cultural patterns contribute to criminal behaviour, "poverty, poor achievement and an assortment of other social problems" (ibid.: 17, emphasis in original). It is difficult to see how social scientists, investigating the disproportionate involvement of some groups in crime, can avoid questions such as the relationship of social pathology to crime, or if its incidence in particular groups. The relevance of the British experience to the Canadian one is, in any case, questionable. In the U.K. Third World immigration took place into a largely homogeneous white society, whose history and culture were deeply influenced by Britain's imperial past. Canada, in contrast, was not a colonial power but is a country of immigration. Immigration is the central force that has shaped Canada's twentieth century history. To suggest that the response to new immigrants in Canada shares close similarities with that in the U.K. is to defy common sense.

Aversive racism is loosely defined, apparently embracing those who "believe in fairness and equality for all" but unknowingly harbour aversion to blacks or other minorities (ibid.: 19). The concept appears to be primarily of use in labelling those who reject racism but fail to endorse whatever demands for action are made by those who claim to speak for "disadvantaged groups." This becomes clear when Henry turns to the Canadian experience. Students are advised that one aspect of democratic racism is "a lack of support for policies that might ameliorate the low status [sic] of people of colour" (ibid.: 21). The

implication of Henry's argument is clear: Canadians who oppose preferential hiring policies are racists. Since most Canadians do indeed
oppose such policies, this in turn provides support for the claim that
most Canadians are racists. Opposition to high levels of immigration
is also evidence of democratic racism.

It is, according to Henry, reflective of democratic racism to equate
earlier discrimination against white immigrants with that experienced
by visible minorities today since this "ignores the importance of the
history of colonization, subjugation, and *oppression* of people of
colour by Canadians of European origin" (ibid.: 22, emphasis in
original). It is not clear what history this refers to, although Canadian
aboriginals can reasonably claim to have experienced colonization,
many years ago, before the ancestors of most contemporary Canadians
arrived. Canada's larger role in the colonial mission was marginal, and
the culpability of most Canadians more marginal still. Accurate comparison of the experience of some earlier European immigrants with
those of contemporary racial minority immigrants indicates that while
the former included groups who experienced overt occupational exclusion or quotas and virulent prejudice which infected the whole of
society, contemporary racial minority immigrants encounter a range of
special programs and a society willing to seek accommodation for most
demands.[20] Yet Henry claims: "second-and third-generation Canadian
people of colour continue to *experience the same prejudiced attitudes
and discriminatory behaviour* as their parents and grandparents"
(ibid., emphasis added). Such a statement speaks volumes to Henry's
polemical mission but reveals a shaky grasp of history.

"New" or democratic racism is a concept now widely used in the
race industry, serving to extend the claims of racial activists by embracing an ever wider range of citizens who must be re-educated. This
sophistry allows the race industry to demand a degree of support
otherwise hard to justify: if racism is the prerogative of a small
minority of bigots, it scarcely becomes necessary to devote so many
resources to its eradication. By re-defining racism to capture all those
who oppose their agenda, racial activists legitimate an ever wider claim
on the political agenda and the public purse. Much that is presented
as anti-racism may be no more than the cultivation of ethnic grievance,
designed not to improve race relations but persuade racial minorities
that their every misfortune is a result of discrimination.

Li Zong, who teaches sociology at the University of Saskatchewan,
includes among the new racists those who oppose official multiculturalism (Zong 1997: 120–3). Behind opposition to multiculturalism,
claims Zong, is the demand that immigrants assimilate to Anglo-Saxon
culture. It is curiously static view of culture which also contrives to

entirely miss the point. The argument against official multiculturalism is not that we should all take afternoon tea in Victoria while reading Shakespeare, but that we should welcome the emergence of a universal, colour-blind Canadian culture demonstrably less and less confined by any Anglo-Saxon roots.

Henry portrays a society in which "skin colour" is the defining issue: "In a society that uses racial characteristics as a basis for discrimination, people of colour inherently provide a cue for discriminatory practices. Their skin colour, therefore, is not incidental, but is *the central factor in relations with White society*" (Henry 1995: 22, emphasis added).[21] This description of a society divided by racial boundaries is a travesty of contemporary urban Canada. Do the 41 per cent of the University of Toronto's students who are members of a visible minority find this to be the key factor in their relationship with the other 59 per cent? A survey at Henry's own university found that a majority of those Chinese Canadian students who spoke Chinese at home did not consider themselves to be members of a visible minority (*Globe and Mail*, 6 October 1994). How then can their skin colour be "the central factor in relations with White society"?

Henry offers students a series of "case studies" intended to familiarize them with the pervasive nature of Canadian racism. The studies provide an interesting illustration of the capacity of tenured professors to reconstruct events in ways that provide support to their ideological mission. The disproportionate involvement in crime of some black groups is a matter of record; the Commission on Systemic Racism in the Ontario criminal justice system found that black remand rates on drug trafficking/importing charges were twenty-seven times higher than white remand rates in 1992–93; the admission ratio for convicted persons was thirteen to one. Black remand rates on weapons charges were nine times higher and admission rates eight times higher (Commission on Systemic Racism 1995: 92).[22] In Professor Henry's "case study" the problem of the disproportionate involvement of some blacks in crime is nowhere to be found, unless in a discussion of "overpolicing" (Henry 1995: 111). The problem with which she regales students is that of media coverage: Henry singles out the *Globe and Mail*'s three-part series on Jamaican crime as "a particularly striking example of the media's role in fostering the racialization of crime" (ibid.: 237). She finds it unnecessary to actually confront the accuracy of the articles in focusing attention on the disturbingly high level of involvement by those of Jamaican origin in crime in Canada. Instead students are advised that what is occurring is a "pattern of the racialization of crime, developed primarily by the police but communicated and perpetuated by the Canadian media" (ibid.).

Another of Henry's "case studies" is the exhibition at the Royal Ontario Museum, *Into the Heart of Africa*, an important landmark in the debate over how a multi-ethnic society might address its history. The curator, Jean Cannizzo, intended to offer a critical view of the meeting of European missionaries with Africa. Although the portrait of the colonial enterprise was less than sympathetic, the exhibition became a focal point for black grievance politics. A small group of activists picketed the museum and charged the ROM with racism. The demands were, as usual, accompanied by claims for greater access to resources and control by those who claimed to represent the "black community."

Henry offers this episode as a further illustration of racism. There are many debates that might be pursued from the events surrounding this exhibition, but what is notable in Henry's case study is not only the according of a privileged position to those who leapt forward to criticise the exhibition, leading to the clear conclusion that this was "cultural racism," but the omission of some important facts. The protesters did not confine their attention to the ROM. Cannizzo's home was spray painted with graffiti, her classes at the University of Toronto were disrupted, she was threatened with physical violence, chased down the halls of the university, and finally driven from her post, subsequently leaving Canada and moving to Scotland. These events raised central questions about academic freedom, the failure of the University of Toronto to defend its faculty members, the intellectual quality of arguments that depended for effect on such tactics, and the complicity of those who had given such enthusiastic support to the protesters' exaggerated outrage. These issues will not concern readers of Henry's text: none of these occurrences are mentioned in the six-page case study (210–15).

Henry has had some influence on the evolution of Ontario's race policies. In the wake of the ROM protests, she headed a research consortium contracted by the Anti-Racism Secretariat of the Ministry of Citizenship to prepare a report on racial conflict/tension in the United States, United Kingdom, and Canada (Henry *et al.* 1991). The report's Canadian content was notably thin but served to set the context for the secretariat's subsequent, ill-conceived involvement in the Show Boat controversy; the report urged the Anti-Racism Secretariat to "bolster" the abilities of "minority communities" to intervene in such issues (ibid.: 296).

We have noted the bizarre antics of the Ontario government in regards to Show Boat and the curious contrast between the widespread praise the show received, notably in the United States, and the claims by some Toronto activists that it was "racist." In Henry's account, in a text for university undergraduates, there is neither ambiguity or ambivalence: "Show Boat is a clear example of how the cultural power and racist ideology of individuals and institutions converge to further marginalize, exclude and silence people of colour" (Henry 1995: 223).

THE CRISIS IN THE UNIVERSITIES

> There must be a willingness by administrations to get tough with those who simply fail to do the job they are paid for – and that includes those faculty who abuse the universities' facilities to set themselves up as consultants without even a shadow of oversight.
>
> Bercuson *et al.*, 1997

There is no obvious resolution to the crisis in Canadian higher education. Feminists and other advocates of orthodoxy are well organized and able to use their power to assist the appointment of those who share their agenda and to seek the marginalization of those who have the temerity to dissent. As in other areas of the economy, preferential hiring bureaucrats and the array of others hired to police the modern academy have been eager to extend their reach. At Queen's University, gays and lesbians have now been added to the list of those "encouraged" to apply. Where once progressive thinkers would be outraged that the sexual orientation of consenting adults would be thought a relevant criteria for employment, current fashion declares its centrality.

Queen's, one of Canada's most prestigious universities, illustrates the gathering strength of those who would assert group entitlement over merit in appointment and cleanse the curriculum. In the fall of 1997 Queen's created the new senior position of University Advisor on Equity. The lucky incumbent would be in one of three central agencies at Queen's devoted to the question of equity, including the Senate Committee on Equity and the Council on Employment Equity. The reach of Queen's flourishing equity bureaucracy is not confined to hiring, inevitably, but without regard to the question of academic freedom, it also embraces course content, more particularly the vexatious question of whether "academic choices may unintentionally restrict course content to the cultural and social values of one group and thus deny the influence of other cultural groups in that field" (Supplement to the *Queen's Gazette*, 7 April 1997). Thus, belatedly, Queen's has embarked on a project that has already done great damage to American education (Bernstein 1994, D'Souza 1995). Observers might be excused for thinking that the Queen's initiative arose in response to some overwhelming evidence of prior injustice. In contrast, as elsewhere, the prior claims of race and gender over merit are already well ensconced in the Queen's appointment's process, the agenda of biopolitics well covered.

Among those who have fallen victim to the expansive reach of the equity industry at Queen's is Professor Thomas Pearce, the 1996 recipient of the Career Achievement Award from the Geological Association of Canada. Pearce was the focus of investigation following complaints by two female graduate students that he behaved insensitively and inappropriately towards them on a field trip to Martinique in 1994. Three and a half years after the field trip, freelance journalist Donna Laframboise investigated Pearce's ordeal. Among the "emotional and mental hardships" alleged and subsequently investigated at public expense, the students claimed that they were forced, most days, to eat baguettes and Brie cheese, that Pearce's three-year-old son threw temper tantrums, and that they were briefly asked to look after the child. Pearce was also charged with suggesting to one of the students during a social occasion in Martinique that had he realized she was planning to get married he would not have accepted her. Pearce reported that the remark, in the context, was a jocular reference to his experience with another female graduate student who had quit in the middle of her project to arrange her wedding. In the McCarthyite climate that now encompasses such topics, no explanation was likely to prove adequate.

Pearce's case was reviewed by an ad hoc committee chaired by the acting dean of graduate studies, Suzanne Fortier, who had previously sat on a university committee addressing fashionable "chilly climate" concerns. Among that committee's insights, Queen's academic staff were encouraged to identify "bias against women, minorities, aboriginal peoples and persons with disabilities" in academic textbooks. The committee deemed the term "visible minorities" offensive because "categorizing all of those who do not have 'white' skin in one category could only occur in a racist society." The issue of categorization arises predominantly from the endless focus on such matters by the champions of identity politics; the problem identified might be thought central to such quintessentially PC language as "people of colour," which, unlike "visible minorities," acknowledges no plurality.

Pearce, who had been barred from accepting new graduate students while the investigation proceeded, reported that his career was "effectively over," his health seriously impaired (Laframboise 1997b). Given the vague but disparate nature of the complaints against him, the outcome was not surprisingly inconclusive. The complainants were awarded a term's worth of free tuition while yet another committee ruled that Pearce's grievance against the process to which he had been subject also had some merit. The incident stands as confirmation of the disastrous consequences that follow the creation and funding of a culture of complaint. None of the allegations merited the exhaustive attention they received. In other times, the students might simply have requested a change in supervisor.

The crisis in the universities will not be easily addressed, for institutional autonomy makes outside intervention unlikely. The most optimistic scenario would see a counter-offensive launched by academics whose disciplines have not been subject to the predations of those who confuse scholarship with proselytizing; but there are no signs that this is happening.

The triumph of grievance politics and the increasing emphasis on group membership in appointment complement other characteristics of the contemporary university. Tenure has allowed many professors to remain in post without making any continuing contribution to scholarship – "on permanent internal sabbatical" (Bercuson *et al.* 1997: 129). Many academics minimize their teaching and use their university positions as a base from which to pursue lucrative second careers. In these circumstances, the attraction of appointing colleagues whose own scholarly contribution is at best mediocre is obvious, and if the appointments can be presented as a progressive step necessary to redress some claimed historic injustice, so much the better. Those who get positions through their group membership and ideological zeal will, in turn, be ready to appoint others on a similar basis.

If there is a prospect for change, it may lie in the universities' increasing dependence on student fees and outside fund-raising. Those who are being called upon to pay the bill should ask some hard questions, including why, in many disciplines, a generation of male doctoral graduates have had their careers blighted by government-sanctioned discrimination.

12

The Pursuit of Division

Without the political division of the wage-earning white, black and Hispanic Americans along racial lines – a division exacerbated, though not caused by, racial preferences and multicultural ideology – it is doubtful that the white overclass in the United States, in the last generation, would have been able to carry out its agenda of destroying unions, reducing wages, cutting worker benefits, replacing full-time workers with temps, and shifting the burdens of taxation from the rich to the middle and working classes with so little effective popular opposition.

Michael Lind, 1995

The last two decades in Canada have been dominated by the politics of identity. Those who have urged the centrality of skin colour, gender, and sexual preference have had no doubt that they were on the cutting edge of progressive thinking. Among the progressive elite they have found scant resistance. Many in the unions and the NDP have been only too happy to embrace the latest identity politics fashion, though delegates to the 1997 conference of the Public Service Alliance of Canada did have the temerity to delete the word "male" from a motion condemning violence.

The agenda of the purveyors of identity politics has also proved popular with more conservative groups. Federally both Conservatives and Liberals have been generous in funding their radical opponents. The Conservatives in Ontario may have stopped much of the direct funding to grievance politics which characterized the Rae government but have been quite happy to see such funding provided by the Trillium Foundation.

The success of the champions of group grievance in dominating the progressive agenda should, if their analysis is correct, have resulted in a significant upsurge in radical politics. The constituencies on whose behalf they confidently speak amount to something close to 70 per cent of the population. In fact the growth of identity politics has been parallelled by a sharp decline in support for the political left, notwithstanding the enthusiastic embrace afforded to grievance politics provincially in Ontario by Rae and his colleagues, and nationally, first by Audrey McLaughlin and more recently by Alexa McDonough.

The politics of identity may have proved a rather slender reed on which to support a political movement, but no one could doubt that practitioners have secured considerable individual mobility. A growing number of women and a smaller but still significant group of visible minorities, of whom the most successful are lucky enough to combine the double disadvantage of race and gender, found in the new politics a rewarding route to upward mobility. Sunera Thobani claimed NAC office, after a scant four years in Canada, in the name of the most marginalized; she left early, to take a university chair.

Preferential hiring is now well established in the Canadian labour market, selection on merit a diminishing concern. The Canadian Labour Council's vice-president, Nancy Riche, appearing before the House of Commons Committee on Human Rights and the Status of Disabled Persons, dispensed with the usual mellifluous assurances that preferential hiring is compatible with the merit principle. Asked by the committee chair if employment equity was "about the principle of merit," Riche first prevaricated, "I don't believe it's about hiring unqualified people." Pushed on the question again, she responded "No, not necessarily" (Issue No. 28: 33, 8 February 1995). In the subsequent discussion it appeared that the CLC view was that if minimum qualification requirements were met then the designated group member should secure preference. In response to the suggestion by the committee chair that the position should go to "the best qualified for the job," Riche responded "Well, having the qualifications to do the job." In the public sector the adoption of such policies reduces efficiency and raises costs while implicitly confirming that public employment is a right rather than conditional on merit and performance. The adoption of such policies is no doubt more limited in the private sector, where employers who displayed so little interest in the relative merits of potential recruits would experience significant cost penalties.

The cacophony of grievance that has accompanied the upward surge of the professionally disadvantaged has had little impact on the lives of poorer Canadians. The enthusiasm of Canadian progressives for

high deficits and high taxes may make some kind of sense to those
whose comfortable incomes are drawn on the public purse, not infre-
quently by both partners in two-income households; but the reality for
poorer Canadians is a decline in real income, exacerbated by rising
taxes. The enthusiasm for public sector debt has led to inevitable
deterioration of the social safety net, but such enthusiasm must be seen
in the context of the alternative. This would have required some
attention to the inflated salaries and lax work requirements of many
beneficiaries of public sector employment. It is difficult to find large
groups of employees in the private sector who get "sick pay" for days
they are well and enjoy three-month vacations, but not hard to identify
such groups in the public sector.

The enthusiasm of many public-sector union leaders and their supporters for pay equity and preferential hiring fits well with a wider
culture of entitlement which, to the extent that the issue of who should
pay is actually addressed, depends on the assumption that if only "the
rich and the corporations" were appropriately taxed, there would be
limitless resources available. Even this rhetoric fails to find any reflection in political action. Union pension funds have proved singularly
unwilling to challenge such executive perks as share options, through
which corporate directors add large sums to their already generous
pay, at the expense of other shareholders. The pension funds of the
Ontario Secondary School Teachers Federation, members of whose
executive fly the province in a private plane, have been quite willing
to engage in the most predatory forms of vulture capitalism. The
victims, in consequent corporate restructuring and downsizing, are
frequently lower income Canadians. Indeed many unions do not
appear to have progressed far enough in their economic grasp to
understand that many of the policies of corporate taxation they
embrace would directly impact on the income of their own pension
funds.[1]

The focus on the politics of identity by Canadian progressives has
created the illusion of radical commitment without requiring any
sacrifices by those endorsing the prior claims of group membership.
Many envisage direct personal benefits from policies that afford an
"especial" welcome to people who look like them. Others calculate no
personal cost in embracing the rhetoric of preferential hiring and
discriminating against white male outsiders: rather, white males in
secure employment are able to garner support from powerful feminist
lobbies, curry favour with senior management which also endorses
such policies, and further their own promotion prospects even as they
damage those of the group to which they belong. In Canada, as in the
United States, successful blacks, with incomes that comfortably place

them in the top 5 per cent of earners, have had no hesitation in claiming to speak in the name of blacks as a whole, invoking the mantle of social justice. The preferential policies they embrace will do little for low income blacks but will secure further competitive advantage to the black elite.

A politics truly based on addressing social inequality, once it engaged with the real economy, would be compelled to recognize that notwithstanding the obscene salaries currently paid to some top corporate executives, any significant move to increase the disposable income of poorer Canadians would necessitate some belt-tightening by the army of teachers, university and college professors, and senior public servants whose idea of social justice never seems to involve a personal contribution. In the 1970s, under the Schreyer government in Manitoba, there was some discussion of the range of income differentials which social democrats could support; a ratio of two and a half or three to one was often mentioned as a reasonable goal. Few address such questions today, but it requires only a moment's reflection to recognize that between the income of those on minimum wage and the claims of physicians, university presidents, hospital executives, and others dependent on taxpayers for their pay cheques, the gap between their earnings and those of the minimum wage workers is far beyond these proportions and widening dramatically.

In the spring of 1997, York University faculty, who include a large number of tenured radicals, and a myriad deployed in York's women's studies program, had no hesitation in striking, at great cost to their students, for large pay increases and inflated buyouts for faculty reaching sixty-five – a group whose tax-funded retirement incomes would ordinarily be more than three times the income of a minimum wage earner, though the latter would not have a lifetime of savings to fall back on. In the face of the administration's refusal to comply with faculty demands, a delegation visited Lorna Marsden, York's president-designate, and advised her that if an acceptable settlement was not reached, the university would be "ungovernable and unmanageable" (*Globe and Mail*, 10 May 1997). The faculty also announced their intention of using their power in the university's senate to secure a more compliant administration. Among the issues in dispute was the faculty's demand to continue the practice of "selling" accumulated sabbaticals back to the university on retirement. Sabbaticals are, of course, supposedly justified by the research which is undertaken; but in the culture of entitlement which now predominates, they are simply another tax-funded perk. At York, "producer capture" is complete: the university's primary obligation is to meet the demands of its sinecured academics. The York strike might serve as a fitting epitaph to the politics of the progressive elite, a monumental comment on their irrelevance to low-income Canadians and the confusion of personal advancement with social progress.

The dividing line in Canada as in the United States, the country which Canada most approximates in its pattern of gross income inequality and growing polarization, is not between races or genders but social classes. Michael Lind offers a poignant vision for the American future: "The real threat is not the Balkanization but the Brazilianization of America, not fragmentation along racial lines but fissioning along class lines. Brazilianization is symbolized by the increasing withdrawal of the white American overclass into its own barricaded nation-within-a-nation" (1995: 14).

Canada has so far escaped the worst of America's inner city problems, but there are signs in Montreal, Toronto, Winnipeg, and Vancouver of a growing divide between affluent, well-policed areas and areas where poorer residents must accustom themselves to living under increasing risk of victimization. More worryingly, when the elite do address such matters, it is frequently to reprimand the police for overly aggressive intervention. The reality is that were affluent Canadians confronted with drug dealing, prostitution, and other crime in similar measure in their neighbourhoods, they would be marching on city hall to demand action.

The primary victims of ill-considered, poorly researched preferential hiring polices have been young, Canadian-born white males, who, in an increasingly tight labour market, have faced growing competition from those who exercise a prior claim based not on merit but group membership. Immigration policies, which have appeased powerful constituencies and promised electoral pay-offs, have failed to respond to Canada's changing labour market. In combination with preferential hiring policies, the result has been the marginalization of many native-born Canadians as jobs in education, the CBC, the RCMP, and other institutions are reserved for those with more fashionable group membership. In the name of inclusion, increasing emphasis is placed not on common citizenship but the qualifications and disqualifications which flow from a continuing emphasis on group membership.

As I was completing this book friends who were aware of my interests wondered whether identity politics were not, in fact, losing momentum. In contrast it seems to me that racial and gender thinking is now ubiquitous. The federal government is continually expanding programs that deliver services or confer benefits on specific identity groups. The most recent annual report on the operation of the Multiculturalism Act reflects the way in which multicultural policy is being transformed into a race-based policy, legitimating the provision of preferences to some Canadians at the expense of others (Canadian Heritage 1997). The report surveys a range of race-based initiatives sponsored by federal departments and a plethora of initiatives premised on the belief that race is central to the government's mission.

The National Research Council runs a Diversity Management Data Base, listing "ethnocultural minority organizations" that distribute NRC job openings and help locate applicants; a Research Associateships Program is targeted to "promising minority" candidates. The Orwellian wording is typical: what is clearly intended, but not said, is that Canadians of some colours are to be preferred over others. Native born Canadians who are white will be disadvantaged relative to others, including many recent immigrants who boast more fashionable melanin counts. CBC and the Société Radio-Canada (SRC) continue to afford explicit racial preferences. Some 60 per cent of projects approved under the HELP (Help Emergize Local Projects) Fund involved internships for visible minorities. In addition, the SRC runs a training program specifically for graduate students from visible minorities. Human Resources and Development runs a summer-employment program, the Native/ Black Internship program whose racially exclusive focus is explicit. CIDA boasted a retreat, exclusively open to visible minority and aboriginal employees, "designed to strengthen the group's identity" – a proposition based not on culture but on the racist assumption that those of a darker hue share some common identity. The Correctional Service of Canada sponsored four scholarships for post-secondary studies in corrections, exclusively open to visible minorities. The Canada Council took its myopic preoccupation with race some steps further with the release of a report on *Racial Equality in the Arts at the Canada Council*, recommending, *inter alia*, the creation of a Racial Equality Advisory Committee. The Canadian Human Rights Commission followed up its contentious report, which purported to document discrimination in appointment and promotion in the federal public service, with a further study which included a series of "focus groups" with employees and former senior managers who are members of visible minorities. This would provide a new platform for ethnic grievance, unconstrained by the need to offer any convincing empirical evidence of disadvantage.

Such government initiatives failed to appease those who claimed to detect a pandemic of racism. A public forum on racial discrimination in the federal public service was sponsored by PSAC, the Professional Institute of the Public Service of Canada, the Canadian Ethnocultural Council, the National Capital Alliance on Race Relations, and the Federation of Ontario Race Relations Organizations. The sessions featured, among other speakers, John Samuel, author of the CHRC report. The PSAC news release (6 February 1998) announced that current "policies and practices have in effect systematized racism in Canada."

The forum might serve as an appropriate epitaph to three decades of federal policies based on the centrality of race and the conviction that racism in Canada is a pervasive social ill. Such policies, if the forum organizers were to be believed, had transparently failed. Others might question whether the growing chorus of racial grievance did not, in some perverse way, testify to the government's success in nurturing an industry whose ever more expansive claims assure it a rosy future. The charges of gross discrimination received generous and uncritical coverage from the CBC, which introduced its report with the assurance that "those who have studied" the issue had reached these disturbing conclusions (CBC *Radio News* 9 February 1998).

For a government that has no clear agenda beyond the illusive pursuit of national unity, the politics of identity serves a number of purposes. It creates at low financial cost the appearance of progressive action, which no doubt appeals to many Liberals who find comfort in the belief that their party is a party of social reform; simultaneously, it appeals more directly to the real soul of the Liberal party, holding together a sufficient electoral coalition to assure political dominance. The ethnic and gender patronage which preferential policies entail are well suited to this purpose, particularly where dissident voices can be largely excluded from the debate. This has been most effectively achieved in discussion over the consequences of high levels of immigration, a policy playing directly into the Liberals' ethnic electoral strategy and appealing to powerful constituencies who make a living in the immigration industry and to economic interests which benefit from downward pressure on wages or upward pressure on housing costs.

The dominance of the issues of identity politics, like the social and economic pressures resulting from high immigration levels, has the effect of crowding other issues off the stage. Canada has failed to address child poverty and the attendant intergenerational marginalization of some Canadian families or the challenges of such extraordinarily deprived communities as Vancouver's downtown Eastside. Attention which might have been directed to these issues has been claimed elsewhere. The legacy is not, however, a society in which the fractious politics of identity have been assuaged: the result of the preoccupation with these issues is that biopolitical grievances are confirmed and enhanced. Canadians have financed an increasingly destructive agenda whose outcome is not unity, equality, or fairness but division.

Notes

1 The grant was administered by the University of Toronto which issued some ten cheques and pre-empted 5 per cent of the grant to cover its "costs." Donner's letter of 25 May 1995 announcing the grant to U of T specified "that there be no charge for administering the funds." In an exchange worthy of Lewis Carroll, I was told that the grant deduction was not for administrative costs but "indirect research costs." Society for Academic Freedom and Scholarship president John Furedy then made a further deduction to cover *his* "costs." When many tenured academics do little or no research and publishing (Bercuson *et al.* 1997), U of T's enthusiasm for taxing the grants of outsiders who do is notable.

2 Racial thinking informs the deliberations of the nation's highest court. In a statement extending the battered woman defence, Madam Justices Claire L'Heureux-Dubé and Beverley McLachlin warned against stereotyping: "Women who have demonstrated too much strength or initiative, women of colour, women who are professionals, or women who have fought back against their abusers … should not be penalized for failing to act in accordance with the stereotypical image of the archetypal battered woman" (*Globe and Mail*, 13 February 1988). The judges' own stereotyping endorses the radical feminist claim that "colour" is a defining characteristic.

CHAPTER ONE

1 Diversity training is based on the assumption that Canadian society, once characterized by the domination of a homogeneous group of heterosexual white males, must now be transformed to accommodate

ethnic, gender, and sexual diversity (Wilson 1996). This is history as caricature, frequently accompanied by astonishing levels of misinformation which presumably provide the diversity training script (Loney 1996). Trevor Wilson, the head of Omnibus Consulting, which houses the Canadian Diversity Network, offers a catalogue of erroneous statistics, including an underestimate of the percentage of visible minorities in the Canadian population by more than 50 per cent. Wilson informs his readers that racial minorities currently make up 6 per cent of the population, a number he believes will rise to 11 per cent in the next twenty years (Wilson 1996: 9). Projections based on 1991 census data and subsequent immigration suggest that the 1996 census will show that the 11 per cent figure has already been reached.

2 David Rose, reviewing Sivanandan's recent novel, *When Memory Dies*, set in the context of the civil strife which tore apart his native Sri Lanka, writes: "Two of the recurrent themes of his political writing find an echo in the novel. The first is a hatred for what he has termed 'skin politics,' the reductionist approach common to some black writers that blames everything wrong on imperialism, or white people in general; that emphasises separateness and ethnic difference; that is, in short, the mirror image of the old South African apartheid. The second flows from the first: a passionate belief in free will, in the ability of people and communities to change their destinies, irrespective of economic forces and historical legacies; to better their lot – or to ruin it" (*Guardian Weekly*, 19 January 1997).

3 Jewish Canadians experienced social and economic discrimination prior to the Second World War (Avery 1995, Levitt and Shaffir 1987). In 1991, 19 per cent of Jewish Canadians aged 15–64 reported earnings in excess of $60,000, compared to a Canadian average of 6 per cent (Canadian Heritage 1994: 7).

4 Gordon appears to have resolved this philosophical question with the answer that white reviewers are acceptable so long as they are favourable. Given a review of Cecil Foster's book commissioned from this writer by a replacement editor while Gordon was on leave, Gordon rejected it. When challenged, he offered the defence that I should never have been asked and that the review was "predictable," a reference perhaps to a number of articles I had published in the *Ottawa Citizen* criticizing the ill-researched demands of the advocates of biologically based grievance politics. I had held no preconceptions about Foster's book; much of interest could be written on the situation and challenges facing black Canadians, but Foster had chosen to write a poorly researched litany of complaints grounded in the certainty that government was somehow responsible for redressing the problems he claimed to have uncovered.

5 Half the students at Macnab High School in Hamilton absented themselves from a compulsory day-long conference on multiculturalism and
anti-racism, prompting the school principal to complain of a backlash
against "racial equity" (CP wire story, 24 May 1996).

6 Let us assume that in 1986 6 per cent (60) of the university's academic
employees are members of a racial minority, consistent with their representation in the wider population. In 1996, given the rapid growth in
Canada's racial minority population, the equivalent will be close to
12 per cent. If racial minorities simply receive a (growing) proportion of
the 200 new appointments reflecting their (growing) number in the population they will receive an additional 20 or so new positions (6 per
cent of those in 1987, 9 per cent of those in 1991, 12 per cent of those
in 1996, etc.). Assuming 6 per cent (15) of those who left will have
been racial minorities, the net increase will be five. The percentage of
the 950 current academic staff who will be members of a racial minority will now have increased to 7 per cent, not the 12 per cent target
established by legislation. To reach that target, 114 racial minorities
would have to be in post. This would necessitate offering sixty-nine
(34.5 per cent) of the two hundred new positions to members of racial
minorities, a greater share than would normally result from employment on merit. In fact, as we will see, universities have responded to
equity pressures by creating exclusive recruitment programs for racial
minority faculty or by giving implicit or explicit preference to such
candidates.

The same logic indicates that for groups who have been historically
under-represented in particular types of employment, the only way in
which equity targets can be met is through preferential hiring.

In some cases the problems caused by low turnover are compounded
by under-representation of target groups in the qualified pool. This can
be illustrated by the example of women in the universities. Historically,
women comprised a small part of the qualified academic pool, earning,
for example, only 11 per cent of the doctorates in Canada between
1955–76 (Brown 1992: 10). Women still comprised only 35.5 per cent
of PHD students in 1990, an 8 per cent increase since 1982 (Wannell
and Caron 1994: 4). If appointment is made on merit from the qualified pool, the achievement of equity targets will be very slow. Feminist
denunciations of male dominance in university teaching put pressure on
university administrators to go much further than simply ensuring that
women are recruited in proportion to their presence in the qualified
pool; not surprisingly, evidence indicates that a number of universities
hire significantly more women than their representation in the qualified
pool would suggest (Brown 1992).

In the United States pressures to meet academic equity targets has resulted in intense competition to recruit available black PHDs, with universities engaging in bidding wars and seeking to lure targeted faculty from rival institutions (D'Souza 1992: 169). In some highly specialized areas where there are few candidates, the introduction of hiring quotas, as the Canadian Society for Academic Freedom and Scholarship has observed, not only dilutes the merit principle but may discourage departments from offering courses where it is difficult to recruit competent faculty with the right race or gender characteristics (*SAFS Newsletter*, November 1992, Society for Academic Freedom and Scholarship).

7 Like the majority of NAC activists, Go is employed in the public sector, in this case in the racially exclusive Metro Toronto Chinese and Southeast Asian Legal Clinic. This is a creation of the Ontario government, which has sponsored the proliferation of apartheid-type racial provision rather than insisting on universal access to services defined by common citizenship.

CHAPTER TWO

1 The suggestion that some 65 per cent of the population of Canada are "marginalized" says much about the loss of common sense in feminist theorizing.

2 Cardozo and the Pearson-Shoyama Institute can also claim credit for one of the sillier pieces of research purporting to document employment inequities. Cardozo advised a House of Commons committee that the institute was making a list of the "top 500 most powerful and influential people in the country." Social scientists have laboured for many years to determine how power should be measured. The institute, within a year of its establishment, appeared not only to have answered that question but was able to advise the House of Commons that "at the most 4 per cent are from a visible minority" (Minutes, Standing Committee on Human Rights 1995: 37:28). If this figure could be believed, it would suggest a remarkable degree of mobility for a group whose members just surpassed the 6 per cent figure in the 1986 census.

3 Finlayson writes: "Studies show that women with families still work, on average, 15 hours more a week than their male counterparts." This is apparently so obvious that Finlayson finds it unnecessary to reference a single study.

4 Contemporary female university graduates earn more on an hourly basis than their male counterparts (Wannell and Caron 1994: 16). In contrast to such comparisons of like and like, equity advocates prefer to seek out figures that purport to document gross discrimination. Carleton university sociology professor Stephen Richer advises his students

that "women university graduates possess less earning power than male high-school drop-outs" (Richer 1995: 214) (see chapter 11).

5 Summarizing evidence to a conference at the Institute for Research on Public Policy presented by UBC economists Paul Beaudry and David Green, Institute president Jerome-Forget comments: "Their most notable finding concerned the 'gloomy' labor market experience of less-educated males, particularly those aged 25 to 34. This group lost out in both employment rates and job quality, expressed in access to full-year/full-time work. University-educated men experienced some declines in employment rates, but not to the same degree. Statistics for female workers across age and educational differences showed consistent improvement in employment outcomes, at least until the beginning of the 1990s" (Jerome-Forget 1997).

6 In Ottawa the report was the subject of an interview with CLC vice-president Nancy Riche on the local CBC noon-time program. The late-afternoon program carried an extensive extract from a speech by Riche declaiming against the increasing marginalization of women in employment. Again no alternative voice was heard.

 I raised my concerns regarding the news coverage with Jeffrey Dvorkin, managing editor and chief journalist of news and programming for CBC English Radio. Dvorkin agreed with my characterization of the report as "advocacy research." He concurred with the suggestion that the CBC failed "in this instance to take a journalistically sceptical approach" (Letter, 10 April 1997).

7 The questioner, who was identified as a PHD student in women's studies at York University, provided as an example the way in which rising fees prevent women from pursuing post-secondary education. The rising fees are a direct consequence of the growth of federal and provincial indebtedness and the resulting fiscal pressures, an issue on which radical feminists have had little to say beyond the suggestion that those who warned of the costs of continuing deficits were pursuing some "corporate agenda." In contrast to the questioner's claim, women constitute a majority of university undergraduates and those graduating from community colleges (Wannell and Carron 1994b).

8 NAC's contribution to the debate was to propose that the contributory CPP be extended to "homemakers." Cohen explains: "Women who worked in the home should be treated as workers, and that the people they work for (either the public, if they had children, or their husbands if they didn't have children) should contribute to the plans on their behalf" (Cohen 1993: 274). The suggestion that women who had no children and who stayed home enjoyed an employee relationship with their husband is as notable as the suggestion that raising children is an occupation undertaken for the public.

9 In 1992 the Kitchener Fire Department established a minimum cut-off of 85 per cent on the written test scores for white males and 70 per cent for other groups. A number of dissatisfied white male applicants made an unsuccessful complaint to the Ontario Human Rights Commission. Public pressure ultimately forced the fire department to cease such overt discrimination.

10 Hansard gives the figure of 426 for new recruits, but the correct figure was 642. In fact in 1995–96 the RCMP enrolled 630 cadets, including visible minorities (139), women (204), and aboriginal people (112). The RCMP took ten weeks to respond to a request for information on their actual recruitment and refused, in reply, to respond to a request for information on the relative test scores of successful candidates, insisting that such a request must be directed through Access to Information. There was no indication that such a request would be any more successful nor any evidence that such information could not be released at the RCMP's discretion, since it affects not individual records but mean or average scores. It would be surprising if the scores of successful white males were not higher than those of other successful candidates. The predictable outcome of the RCMP's approach is that lower-scoring designated group candidates take precedence over higher-scoring white males. The comment in the RCMP's reply is suggestive of the establishment of a qualification threshold for aboriginal and visible minority candidates, rather than the competitive recruitment process faced by others: "The hiring goals of visible minority and Aboriginal applicants have never been reduced. If goals have not been met, it is due to not having *sufficient numbers of qualified applicants* available at the time" (Letter, Sgt M.E. Anderson, Recruiting Section RCMP, 10 December 1996). The RCMP also refused to provide information on the distribution of the designated groups in the applicant pool. This would almost certainly have indicated far lower success rates for white males compared to other applicants.

11 "Numeric goals" had long been in operation in employment equity in the Ontario Public Service. The Ministry of Citizenship's 1990–91 Strategies for Renewal report, for example, prepared under the mandate of the Peterson government, "identified three year numeric goals for employment equity" (Ministry of Citizenship, undated).

12 The CBC's "sensitivity" to the prevailing orthodoxy is evidenced by the fact that the cash-strapped corporation maintains an "Office of Equitable Portrayal in Programming," with its own director.

13 UBC's advertisement stated that designated group members were "especially" welcome to apply for the position of university president (Resnick 1996).

14 The feminist influence on social policy is pervasive but little discussed, a further reflection of orthodoxy. Policies that are alleged to further women's independence may have unexpected consequences. In Quebec, where the intense conflict between separatists and federalists has given feminists a strong leverage, legislation is more "advanced." Legally only a woman's maiden name is recognized. The result, as Quebec columnist Lysiane Gagnon has argued: "The notion of family is stripped of public meaning" (Gagnon 1996). Many children carry both names but in the end must choose one or other parental name, or have their children encumbered with four surnames – a choice that, if made by every generation, might expose the full absurdity of the law.

A subsequent law, the Family Assets Act, stipulated that on separation a spouse was entitled to half of all family assets, whether or not acquired before or during the marriage. This provides a strong deterrent to marriage for older individuals and others who have acquired assets and for those who already have children from a previous marriage, who, on remarriage, must leave half of their assets to the new spouse irrespective of individual circumstance. Together, Gagnon argues, the two laws act as a deterrent to marriage and help explain the much lower rate of marriage in the province compared to elsewhere in Canada.

CHAPTER THREE

1 Henry's husband, also a York University academic, for example, received a $60,000 grant to help young people understand racism in the arts. Jeff Henry was also head of the Coalition to Stop Show Boat, which may give some indication of his concerns. Frances Henry, in addition to her full-time position at York University, has been employed by the federal and Ontario governments and by the Ontario Human Rights Commission to undertake a variety of projects.

2 The writer too has been given a blue card at Pearson, a result of approaching the desk marked "Canadian Citizens" with a U.K. passport but without a citizenship certificate. I hold Canadian citizenship and the passport presented was issued in Ottawa, but the officer made no attempt to establish the legitimacy of my status, asked for no other documentation, or asked any probing questions. The first time I realized there was a problem was when I was directed to a queue marked "Immigration." The officer, when I was interviewed, was quickly satisfied, but by then I had missed a connection and experienced a four-hour delay. I had travelled frequently on the same passport and, having never been asked for a citizenship certificate, had ceased carrying it. In contrast to

the profuse apologies obtained by Wong, a letter to my MP, Eugene Bellemarre, brought no response.

3 Nourbese Philip subsequently clarified the charge of under-representation, demanding that 50 per cent of the writers should have been Canadians of African, Asian, or native backgrounds. In response to PEN's suggestion that only 6 per cent of Canadians were members of a visible minority, a figure based on the 1986 census, Philip suggested these were simply the "survivors" – "genocide plus racism leaves a remainder of six per cent" Philip 1992: 157). Philip's somewhat tenuous grasp of numbers was given further illustration in 1995, when she offered the view that "only some six per cent" of Canada's population were visible minorities (Philip 1995: 8). The figure recorded in the 1991 census was 50 per cent higher and rose further in the intervening four years.

But the charge of under-representation should not be taken too literally; the claims of "women of colour" are not bound by normal concepts of proportionality. The demand that women might be entitled to preferential treatment on the basis of their colour had already received some official sanction. The Canadian delegation to the 1985 UN Nairobi conference, selected by the femocrats in Ottawa, for example, reportedly comprised some 40 per cent racial minorities (Pierson *et al.* 1993: 252), though they comprised only 6 per cent of the contemporary female population. Such generous accommodation does not appear to have assisted in forging unity in the delegation; at the orientation meeting in Toronto, "the women of colour came together separate from the white women" (ibid.).

4 Cannon's willingness to embrace collective guilt may be insufficient to ensure salvation. Her previous book, *China Tide: The Revealing Story of the Hong Kong Exodus to Canada*, was described by two academic critics as "anti-Chinese" and informed by a "racist slant" (Wong and Netting 1991: 115). Cannon's crimes included the suggestion that the Hong Kong Chinese would happily learn Swahili if this would secure business opportunities and the observation that the Chinese Triads rely on the same network of overseas Chinese as the Chinese business community, a comment no doubt intended to suggest a parallel, not identical, source of contacts. Once charges of racism become broadly fashionable, the word can have extremely broad meaning and, in consequence, none at all.

5 The hyperbole directed against those who fail to mouth uncritically the latest feminist truths is not unusual. In a scathing attack on Kate Fillion's *Lip Service*, *Globe and Mail* critic Bronwyn Drainie casually dismissed John Fekete's *Moral Panic: Biopolitics Rising*, a well-researched critique of the violence against women industry, as "a nasty piece of work" (*Globe and Mail*, 8 February 1996).

6 Kohli is not alone in adding Canadians of Jewish ethnic background to the list, an addition that may reflect the eagerness of some Jewish feminists to claim their own special place in the ever larger pantheon of grievance. Kari Dehli, a professor of sociology at OISE, suggests that white feminists have an obligation "to examine how non-Jewish whiteness works to position us in relations of power over other women, for example within the universities" (Dehli 1991: 63). Dehli provides no evidence in support of the claim that Jewish women occupy subordinate positions. The extensive representation of those of Jewish background in North American universities scarcely evokes images of marginalization; but in the search for new victims, empirical evidence is hardly central.

CHAPTER FOUR

1 Farrakhan's own meeting in Toronto was rather more successful, drawing an overflow crowd of more than 2,600 (*Globe and Mail*, 16 September 1996). Sol Littman, Canadian representative of the Simon Wiesenthal Centre, drew attention to Farrakhan's many racist comments over the years, including the claim that Hitler was a "great man," his reference to whites as "devils," and Judaism as a "gutter religion" ("Letters," *Globe and Mail*, 18 September 1996). No white supremacist has attracted any comparable contemporary audience in Canada.

2 Confronted with evidence of widespread slavery in the Sudan gathered by *100 Huntley Street* and Christian Solidarity International, Qasem Mahmud, the chair of the Islamic Schools Federation of Ontario, dismissed the charge (and the evidence), claiming it was simply an attempt to promote anti-Muslim sentiment: "I would not be surprised if the U.S. is not encouraging the evangelists and others to spread false information about Islam and Muslims to prepare public opinion for a future military invasion of Sudan" (*Ottawa Citizen*, 17 April 1997). According to Baroness Caroline Cox, deputy speaker of the British House of Lords, the Sudanese government has enslaved many Christians and animists as part of its campaign to force people in southern Sudan to convert to Islam. A former Sudanese cabinet minister, Bono Malwal, also claimed "overwhelming evidence" of enslavement (*Ottawa Citizen*, 24 April 1997).

3 Ordinarily *Border/Lines* is funded by taxpayers through the Canada Council, the Ontario Arts Council, and the Ontario government.

4 Canadian Heritage returned to the attack in the Brighton Research report, produced as part of the strategic review of multiculturalism programs. Bissoondath's views, readers were informed, are "refuted by the

available evidence," based on an "ahistorical misunderstanding of multi-culturalism." Bissoondath "fails to recognize how immature and fragile Canadian citizenship has been. His view of racism is equally naive" (Brighton Research 1996: 9–10).

5 Judy Rebick, who has done much to define the shape of contemporary "progressive" politics in Canada, writes: "Those to the left of the NDP argued up to about two years ago that the deficit was just an excuse being used by the corporate sector to justify slashing social programs ... But as we recognize now, the deficit *is* a problem. When a country spends thirty cents on the dollar to pay interest on the debt, there is a problem" (Rebick and Roach 1996: 18, emphasis in original). Why it should have taken more than twenty years for Rebick and her allies to recognize the blindingly obvious is unclear. Unfortunately insight may have arrived too late: social program cutbacks and the attenuated power of government are the inevitable result of the persistent deficit spending supported by many on the left. Contrary to the conspiracy theories that substitute for intelligent analysis on the Canadian left, it was not groups like the Business Council on National Issues that urged government to pursue the fiscal policies which made social program cutbacks inevitable but the CLC, NAC, and others who claimed to speak for poorer Canadians.

In 1992, for example, faced with yet another $35 billion Conservative deficit, a mere $7 billion higher than predicted, CLC President Bob White called for the GST to be cut to 5 per cent, creating a loss of $5 billion in government revenue. The deficit was to be further boosted by a major public investment program. As the deficit soared over the $40 billion threshold and headed into the stratosphere, White suggested cuts in interest rates and urged the government to let the dollar fall – an objective that could have been easily achieved, probably overnight.

6 Notwithstanding the many problems with Wilson's arguments (Loney 1996) his views have received glowing endorsement, introduced by a foreword from David Williams, president of National Grocers and Loblaws and endorsed by an array of luminaries including University of Toronto's Vice-President, Administration and Human Resources, Michael Finlayson.

7 Analysis of 1991 census data indicate that 69.5 per cent of black immigrants came from the Caribbean and Bermuda, 14.3 per cent from Africa, 10.1 per cent from Central and South America, 3.2 per cent from the U.K. and 1.9 per cent from the U.S.A. (Torczyner 57).

8 Slavery may not be too strong a term to use to describe the conditions of some domestic workers in Saudi Arabia, where rape, refusal to pay agreed wages, and casual brutality go unpunished while workers have little opportunity to escape ruthless employers (CBC-TV *Witness*, 5 November

1996). Canadian employers accused of the kind of activities routinely reported in Saudi Arabia would face criminal charges and, if convicted, imprisonment.

In France concern has been expressed over "quasi-slaves" working as domestics. The employers are diplomats or other foreigners who have brought compatriots from impoverished Third World countries, frequently without any legal status, to work as domestics in France (*Guardian Weekly*, 3 August 1997).

9 The organization was named after a black American who played a prominent role in assisting fugitive slaves and spent some years living in the St Catharines area in Ontario.

10 Considerable attention has been given to the relationship between blacks and the police force following a number of highly publicized police shootings. Discussion of this issue, as the Society for Academic Freedom and Scholarship pointed out in a letter to Stephen Lewis at the time of his "inquiry" into the Yonge Street disturbances, is handicapped by lack of relevant information: "Currently the Metro police are not allowed to indicate the race of arrested suspects, yet the figures on the race of the people shot by the police during arrests are given out. Both sorts of statistics (and additional ones) need to be collected before one can come to a sound interpretation of what is going on" (*SAFS Newsletter*, November 1992). The fatal shooting of Hugh George Dawson by members of the Toronto drug squad in March 1997, when Dawson allegedly tried to grab an officer's gun, resulted in the usual charges of racism and demands for action from a variety of black groups. Dawson, who was in Canada illegally, had previously been convicted of possession of crack cocaine and had been deported no less than four times since 1991 (*Toronto Star*, 3 April 1997).

11 Some of the news media contribute to an absence of intelligent discussion on these issues through self-censorship, apparently through a belief that their audience cannot be trusted to make the right use of any information. CBC Radio's current affairs program *As It Happens* provided extensive coverage to the violence that was threatening the future of high school basketball in Toronto in 1994 and early 1995. The coverage failed to mention that those involved were members of rival *black* gangs. Producer Karen Levine defended the coverage on the grounds that race was not an issue, since "the violence occurred within the same racial community" (letter, 10 February 1995). Since much of the conflict is between blacks of different ethnic background, CBC's self-imposed silence makes the story somewhat less than intelligible. More recently, the same program provided extensive coverage to the shootings that took place at an unauthorized party in an East York park (CBC Radio, 24 June 1996). Although 3,500 people attended, the police

reported little cooperation in their investigation into the shootings. Such parties, whether in parks or private dwellings, are a major problem in Metro Toronto, causing considerable distress in the neighbourhoods in which they occur. The police report great difficulty in controlling such events. Again CBC failed to inform its listeners of the salient details; no mention was made of the fact that those attending the "party" were overwhelmingly Caribbean Canadians. Since such parties are an innovation to Canada, with roots in West Indian culture, the story was again incomplete, leaving the listener to wonder just when and how public parks became sites for entrepreneurial, if unauthorized, all-night parties featuring a brisk trade in booze and drugs.

12 Surprisingly, the report notes that only 13 per cent of the respondents knew that slavery had once been legal in Canada – slightly more than half the number who knew that blacks had once been slaves. Whether this reflects on the structure of the questionnaire or the logical confusion of the students is unclear.

13 There is some question as to whether Henson and Peary actually discovered the North Pole.

CHAPTER FIVE

1 I requested a comment on the failure to age-standardize from Professor Torczyner, the principal author, but received no response.

2 These figures are not unique to Canada. In the U.S., 72 per cent of black children are born to single mothers (Stephney 1996).

3 Single parent status is strongly associated with poverty. The National Longitudinal Survey of Children and Youth, undertaken by Statistics Canada and Human Resources and Development, reported that while 17 per cent of children in two-parent families live in poverty, the figure for single-parent families is 68 per cent (HRD 1997: 3).

    The Economist, reviewing the relative success of Caribbean immigrants in the United States compared with native born black Americans, argued: "Black immigrant households bring in more money because they have more people working ... As a whole, two-thirds of Caribbean families are headed by a couple, and a quarter are headed by a woman alone. The figures for American-born blacks are almost half and half respectively" (11 May 1996).

    The Economist reports the claims of social scientists William Galston and Elaine Kamarck, who worked in the Clinton administration, that the relationship between crime and the presence of a father in the house "is so strong that [it] erases the relationship between race and crime and low income and crime" (28 September 1996).

4 A similar pattern is evident among blacks of Caribbean origin in the U.K., where no similar female deficit has been reported. A report by the

Office for National Statistics noted that only 34 per cent of children of black Caribbean descent were living with a married man and woman; 54 per cent were with a lone mother. By contrast, 90 per cent of children of Asian origin were living with a married couple (*Guardian Weekly*, 18 August 1996). The exclusion of such international comparisons by the research team at McGill is notable, permitting attribution of responsibility for what might be seen as dysfunctional parenting patterns to a source beyond those directly involved. If the reason is not readily reducible to Canadian immigration policies, the researchers appear to have offered a less than helpful agenda for addressing the issue.

5 The deterministic reasoning of the McGill group, consistent with the dictates of racial politics, appears to assume that the pool of partners is broadly fixed. In fact ethnic intermarriage is increasingly common, though it makes a mockery of the efforts of multicultural bureaucrats and their allies to preserve ethnic cocoons. In the U.K., for example, a country with a much less ethnically diverse but more racially polarized society, 1991 census data indicate that 40 per cent of Afro-Caribbean men, between 16 and 34, had a white partner, as had 21 per cent of Afro-Caribbean women. Among those in the age group who were married, 31 per cent of men and 21 per cent of women had a white partner (*The Economist*, 8 February 1997). A report by the Policy Studies Institute found that half of British-born Caribbean men and a third of Caribbean women have white partners (*Guardian Weekly*, 1 June 1997).

6 The academic practices of many foreign degree-granting institutions scarcely merit confidence. In Belarus the country's megalomaniac president, Alexander Lukashenko, personally sets the questions for university entrance exams (*Globe and Mail*, 5 August 1997). John Stackhouse has drawn attention to the problems of Indian universities: "casteism and corruption run riot in the land that gave birth to chess, algebra and astronomy ... In Uttar Pradesh, India's most populous state, with 150 million people, the vice-chancellors at six out of 18 universities have been suspended for corruption and misconduct" (Stackhouse 1997b). Arriving at Allahad University, Stackhouse found students beseiging their professors with the demand that exams be suspended, claiming they have had insufficient time to study. It is notable that in the voluminous, publicly funded analyses of the labour market characteristics of visible minorities in Canada, reference to the considerable disparity between Canadian degrees and those issued by many foreign universities is rarely to be found.

CHAPTER SIX

1 CBC guidelines appear to explicitly forbid such a confusing multiplicity of roles. Under the heading "Hosts and Interviewers," we learn: "Hosts

and interviewers must treat their guests fairly. They should not be critical or demanding of some, while conciliatory and sympathetic to others … It is also essential for the maintenance of their credibility *that they refrain from personal advocacy*, not only in their public statements but, as well, in their handling of discussions and their selection of questions" (CBC 1993: 73, emphasis added).

2 Foster received financial support from Canadian Heritage to write the book and additional financial support to promote it. Foster's appearance at a promotion meeting in Toronto was sponsored by the Alliance of Black Educators, and funded by Canadian Heritage (*Globe and Mail*, "Booksellers' Selection," 22 February 1997). It is difficult to identify any other country which provides such generous support to writers who, with no sense of contradiction, proclaim the enormity of the discrimination they face: "Racism with a smile on its face, as Canadian Blacks like to call the brand they live under. A racism that nonetheless still saps dreams and leads to despair about the future. Such is the current reality of being black in this country at the end of this millennium" (Foster 1996: 320).

Typical of Foster's case is the claim that "the sons and daughters of black doctors, lawyers and politicians are just as likely to drop out of school and to be harassed by the police as are the offspring of domestic servants" (ibid.: 112). Foster provides no reference in support of these startling claims. Research evidence, as we note elsewhere, indicates the continuing importance of social class, parental education, and family structure in educational outcomes. The suggestion that all blacks are equally likely to be "harassed" by police is improbable. The different black ethnic groups are not equally involved in criminal activity or equally present in areas where the police are particularly active.

The overwhelming fact driving the high involvement of (some) blacks in the criminal justice system lies in four particular charges: trafficking/importing drugs, possession of illegal drugs, obstructing justice, and weapons possession. The analysis of prison admission rates by different charges reveals that trafficking/importing reflects the greatest disparity, with a black-to-white admission rate of 22:1 (Commission on Systemic Racism 1995: 90). If the "harassment" hypothesis were accurate, it might be expected to be generalized, but in the admission rate for drinking and driving offences, for example, the black admission rate is half the white rate (ibid.). Even allowing for possible lower car ownership, this is scarcely suggestive of a general pattern of aggressive, racially motivated policing.

3 The notion of community mobilization was not confined to this event. Christina Gabriel, a former "economic analyst" at the Ontario Women's Directorate, captures the illusory sense of mass mobilization in the

accompanying mind-numbing prose: "Women of colour have mobilized around the policy and practice of multiculturalism in Ontario, demanding recognition of their particular intersectional status at the crossroads of gender and race" (Gabriel 1996: 185).

4 Economist Marjorie Cohen, who teaches in Women's Studies at Simon Fraser University, articulates the radical feminist belief in the apparently limitless power of the "state." It is the state that is "keeping the poor in a state of poverty"; it is the state that "makes people poor when it permits employers to pay some workers less than a living wage. The state makes people poor when it perpetuates an under-valuation of some forms of labour, particularly the labour involved in caring for and raising children" (Cohen 1993: 270). The state is not only able to determine the wages at which employers hire workers; it can also, apparently, ensure full employment: "The state makes people poor when it institutes policies that accept high levels of unemployment as inevitable" (ibid.). Economists may argue about the trade-offs to be made between minimum wage rates and employment levels or about government's capacity to secure full employment. When economics meets women's studies, such complexities disappear. There are victims and victimizers, the realization of utopia requiring no more than a shift in policy.

5 In 1995–96 the Status of Women–Office of the Co-ordinator provided $8.6 million in grants to women's organizations (1996–97 *Estimates*, part 2, *The Main Estimates*, 3–33). Other grant support was available from provincial and municipal governments and from sympathetic sources such as Ontario's Trillium Foundation, which, in dispensing money raised through the provincial lottery, has been singularly generous to feminist causes.

6 Hosek went on to become NAC president, serve in the Liberal government in Ontario, co-author the Liberals' imaginative Red Book and serve as director of Policy and Research in the Prime Minister's Office at the time when a successor, Sunera Thobani, claimed to have observed "a tremendous shift to the right."

7 In early 1996, during a trade mission to Indonesia, Chrétien announced a $300,000 contribution to the Indonesian Human Rights Commission, "as a reflection of the priority Canadians attach to human rights" (*Globe and Mail*, 18 January 1996). Before the official visit, a delegation of Canadian human rights professionals had visited Indonesia, under CIDA auspices, to assist the government-appointed Indonesian Human Rights Commission. The delegation included representatives of the Canadian Human Rights Commission, the Montreal-based Canadian Human Rights Foundation, the Ottawa University Centre for Human Rights, and the Quebec Human Rights Commission. What such

collaboration was expected to achieve, beyond giving credibility to the Indonesian dictatorship and deflecting criticism from Canada's Indonesian policy, is unclear. The head of the commission, Ali Said, is a military officer who previously served as attorney general and minister of Justice. Indonesia is a police state with one of the worst human rights records in the world. Following the publication of an Amnesty International report, *Power and Impunity*, journalist John Pilger wrote: "For the first time, Amnesty International has effectively declared a leading government criminal" (Pilger 1994).

CIDA also orchestrated extensive assistance by Canadian academics to the country's military dictators, much of it directed to assisting in programs designed to secure social peace through the implementation of the military's favoured ideology, Pancasila. The universities of Dalhousie, Guelph, and the University of British Columbia have been particularly assiduous in assisting CIDA in the expenditure of some $150 million on such programs.

It is a reflection of the incestuous relationships sustained by federal funding that organizations at the forefront of politically correct thought in Canada are to be found abroad engaged in the tawdriest collaboration with a corrupt and repressive regime – a collaboration driven by nothing more principled than Canada's perceived economic interests.

8 The federal government provided similar financing to some "ethnic" chairs. The result, as with women's studies, was some tension between traditional academic standards and a proselytizing mission. This came to a head at the University of British Columbia when fundamentalist Sikhs forced the resignation of Harjot Oberoi from the chair of Sikh studies, established in 1987 with $350,000 funding from Multiculturalism and a matching amount from the Sikh community. Fundamentalist Sikhs were outraged by Oberoi's research, which suggested that the Sikh religion had its origins in Islam and Hinduism. In contrast, Sikh religious leaders claim the religion is based on divine revelation with no connection to Hinduism (*Globe and Mail*, 18 July 1996).

9 Marsden was subsequently appointed to the Senate, later to the position of president of Wilfrid Laurier University, and recently to the presidency of York. She is the highest paid university president in Ontario.

10 Jaffer went on to become a federal Liberal candidate in the Burnaby-Douglas constituency, in a procedure that saw "party brass" ensure there would be no effective nomination contest. *Globe and Mail* guest columnist and former B.C. Liberal leader Gordon Gibson describes Jaffer as "the gender and visible minority combination the campaign makers love to put in the window" (7 January 1997).

11 According to the Washington-based Sentencing Project, one in three black males in the 20–29 age group is on probation, on parole, or in prison (*The Economist*, 8 June 1996).

12 In *Guardian Weekly*, 6 April 1997.

13 The Department of External Affairs, which allocates $4.6 million annually to assist artists to perform abroad, has also embraced the group entitlement approach to artistic support. *Globe and Mail* columnist Lysiane Gagnon wrote in reference to recent guidelines: "The new rules ... move right along into the soupy mix of political correctness and clientelism that has become the natural habitat of our cultural agencies" (22 February 1997). Among the obligations of grant beneficiaries, they will be required to represent Canada as "a bilingual country with various cultures." Artists will be selected on the basis of regional balance and cultural "diversity" (External Affairs 1997).

14 The CEC is understandably coy about its overwhelming dependence on government sponsorship. Appearing before the Ontario legislature's committee reviewing the Rae government's employment equity legislation, then vice-president Emmanuel Dick informed the committee that the CEC represented thirty-eight national ethnocultural organizations which in turn had over two thousand local and provincial affiliates. Dick advised the committee: "It is financed through membership dues, government funding, and fund-raising endeavours" (Standing Committee on the Administration of Justice, 2 September 1993 J: 644).

15 I phoned the department to obtain a copy of the report on the same day and was told it had not been released. Mr Cardozo had a copy of the report; MPs did not. The Reform critic Jim Abbot had been provided with some extracts by a journalist.

16 Whitaker is no stranger to such controversies. In 1994 he wrote an article published in the *Globe and Mail*, criticizing Ontario's proposed employment equity legislation. The university's advisor on the status of women, Selma Zimmerman, wrote to Whitaker suggesting that his opposition to affirmative action "may compromise your position as Chair of the Political Science department's hiring committee." Whitaker stood his ground and kept his position (Fekete 1994: 239–40).

17 Among the more bizarre defences of official multiculturalism is Cardozo's claim for the policy's successes: "Minority authors have successfully integrated into, and enriched the Canadian literature scene, such names as Joy Kogawa, Rohinton Mistry, M.G. Vassanji and Michael Ondaatje" ("Letters," *Globe and Mail*, 24 February 1997). It is unclear how the policy has contributed to this creative output or why such writers appear to secure similar success in countries not blessed with such policies.

18 Included in the examples of programs supporting the new direction for multicultural programs which followed the 1996 strategic review was: "A joint venture with the Conference Board of Canada and the Canadian Ethnocultural Council to find ways of creating stronger linkages between our cultural diversity and Canada's international economic advantage."

19 Repeated requests to Artur Wilczynski, Fry's media assistant, for a comment on the ministry's inability to monitor grant expenditure and for
the cost of the Brighton Research report (written by UBC professor
Charles Ungerleider) produced no response.

CHAPTER SEVEN

1 Readers who think this uncharitable should reflect on the 1993 Supreme
Court case involving lawyer Elizabeth Labour. Eberts appeared to argue,
unsuccessfully, that the charter provided protection to Labour as a
member of a disadvantaged group to deduct the costs of her nanny as a
business expense, since these were essential to her continuing employment. The claim that those with the resources to employ nannies are
disadvantaged suggests little need to parody radical feminists; this is
accomplished in house.

It would be wrong, however, to see Eberts as a radical extremist in
this debate. When Bertha Wilson retired, Eberts was actively promoted
by many, including influential Conservatives, to be appointed to the
Supreme Court (Simpson 1993: 102).

The Labour case is by no means the only example that might be used
to illustrate the egregious use of claims of gender disadvantage. In 1996
a group of female Alberta judges, led by Court of Appeal Chief Justice
Catherine Fraser, made a submission to Ottawa's triennial commission
on judges' salaries and benefits, calling for improved pensions. The
judges argued that since women were on average appointed at a
younger age than men, they paid more into the pension plan to receive
the same pension (Champion 1996). Preferential appointment policies
had indeed resulted in many relatively young women being appointed,
but the eight-year difference in the average age at appointment would
be largely compensated by women's greater longevity after retirement.
Again claims of gender disadvantage served to disguise what might
otherwise have appeared as simple greed.

2 Visible minority women are particularly favoured, consistent with the
fashionable but inaccurate claim that they are "doubly disadvantaged."
Thus, for example, when in 1990 Carleton University's School of Social
Work removed the requirement that racial minority applicants for professorial posts hold a PHD, no qualified able-bodied white males were
appointed to any of the three full-time professorial positions; but two
racial minority women, who lacked PHDs or any significant record of
publication, were appointed (this is discussed more fully in chapter 10).

3 This was evident in the evolution of policies on same sex benefits,
where the courts have played a key role in forcing the issue in the face
of the reluctance of legislators to act (Ross 1996). The resolution of

such issues by lawyers and judges rather than elected representatives is intrinsically elitist and removes the need for proponents of change to persuade other Canadians of the merits of their arguments. Social changes achieved by this route will necessarily be more precarious and increase the risk of a backlash from those who see this as a further example of the undemocratic power of special interest groups.

4 The chair of the California Civil Rights Initiative, the driving force behind Proposition 209, was black businessman Ward Connerly, who argued that racial preferences were unjust, provoked racial hostility, and entrenched the practice of identifying people on the basis of race (*Weekly Telegraph*, Issue No. 291, February 1997).

5 Characteristically CBC coverage highlighted the case of those who continued to demand preferential policies.

6 The bizarre consequences of racial classification were illustrated by the legal action brought against the United States government by Egyptian-born Mostafa Hefny, who claimed that although "black," with ancestry from the ancient kingdom of Nubia, he was not classified as such and thus was denied preferential access to scholarships, employment, and business opportunities (*Globe and Mail*, 5 June, 197). In Canada, black or white, Hefny, as Egyptian born, would be entitled to the benefits of preferential policies.

CHAPTER EIGHT

1 The use of Grade 8 as a cut-off point is interesting. Workers with Grade 8 or less will be represented largely among older workers, as few contemporary school drop-outs have an attainment level this low.

2 The potential significance of the age differences is illustrated by the fact that in 1993 27 per cent of women in the public service were forty-five years of age or older, compared to 41 per cent of men. Across the board women constitute a much higher proportion of younger workers. Women constitute 55.8 per cent of all employees aged 25–29 but only 33.7 per cent of those aged 55–59. Comparisons that fail to take age into account understate the contemporary changes. Thus while women make up 41.7 per cent of the executive group aged 30–34 and 39.2 per cent of those aged 35–39, the proportion falls to 5.5 per cent for those aged 55–59 (Treasury Board 1994: 19 and passim).

3 Wider analysis of public sector employment by the *Globe and Mail*'s Bruce Little suggests that women have been successful in securing a higher proportion of new public service jobs while experiencing a much smaller proportion of public sector lay-offs. In the last twenty years the number of male public sector employees has fallen almost continuously; while men lost close to 200,000 jobs, women gained more than

300,000. In teaching, women gained 60,000 of the 84,000 jobs created between 1990 and 1994 but experienced only two thousand of the fifteen thousand jobs lost in the subsequent period. Little concludes: "So in teaching as in the public sector as a whole, the numbers tell a clear story. So far, women have survived the job traumas of government cuts much better than men" (*Globe and Mail*, 2 December 1996).

Such facts are, of course, irrelevant to the practitioners of orthodoxy. A *Globe and Mail* article addressing women's issues in the 1997 election campaign quotes the views of U of T professor Sylvia Bashevkin: "You're talking about the *loss* of public-sector, often unionized jobs that women got in the welfare state after World War Two. Now they're talking about creating jobs through infrastructure, which overwhelmingly benefits men" (20 May 1997, emphasis added).

4 The rapidly changing demographic composition of Canada inevitably results in a lag in the representation of racial minorities, particularly in the context of downsizing. The Treasury Board policy makes no accommodation for this, offering instead the contradictory promise to "recruit, promote and retain qualified employees *on the basis of merit*" while proclaiming that in spite of the constraints posed by government cutbacks, "employment equity goals will remain a high priority, with *increased emphasis* on the development and retention of members of the designated groups" (Treasury Board 1994a: 2–7, emphasis added). The achievement of proportionate representation is transparently inconsistent with the merit principle, requiring disproportionate recruitment and promotion of targeted groups. This is achieved through the Special Measures Initiatives Program, which affords preferential recruitment, training, and promotion opportunities to specified designated groups. These programs provide explicit endorsement to the tendentious claim that under-representation is a function not of changing demographics but "systemic" or other barriers.

5 The case was brought by the tax-funded National Capital Alliance on Race Relations, whose president, Health Canada scientist Shiv Chopra, had had his own individual complaint dismissed by a separate tribunal.

6 The Annual Report for the Year Ending December 31, 1996 indicates overall expenditures of $683,803 for the chief and deputy commissioner (CHRC 1997: 101). Other staff are also enthusiasts for foreign travel. In September 1996, commission General Secretary John Hucker flew off to Tashkent, in Uzbekistan, to attend a seminar organized by the well known human rights activists at the Organization for Security and Cooperation in Europe (*Human Rights Forum* 6 no. 2, Fall/Winter 1996).

7 In 1996 as he prepared to leave the CHRC, Yalden was elected to the UN Human Rights Committee, where he will have an opportunity to

continue to give voice to what appears to be a less than consistent philosophy.

8 I wrote to Clancy querying the accuracy of her claims and asking her for statistical sources. Her office had advised me that they were compiled from a number of studies, including one on the Canadian trucking industry (sic). Clancy did not reply.

CHAPTER NINE

1 The enthusiasm with which such charges are levelled was evidenced in Alexa McDonough's response to the modest changes introduced by the Liberals: "Federal Liberal changes to the immigration law pander to xenophobia, racism and bigotry to pursue a narrow political and economic agenda ... a convenient politician [sic] cover for those advocating policies that are *fundamentally racist and sexist*, attacking the most vulnerable of immigrants – sponsored immigrant women and domestic workers, as well as those seeking refuge" (Alexa McDonough Home Page 1996, http://www.isisnet./com/alexa/fairness.html, emphasis added).

2 The charge of racist is frequently flung at Reform MPs in the House of Commons by their Liberal opponents, a charge no doubt the more offensive to those who are not racist. When Liberal MP John Cannis hurled it at Reform MP Darrell Stinson in a debate on prison reform, Stinson responded by rolling up his sleeves: "I hear the word racist from that side. Do you have the gonads to stand up here and say that to me, you son of a bitch?" Apparently explaining himself to the Speaker, Stinson added: "I will not have some asshole call me a racist" (*Globe and Mail*, 5 February 1997). Explaining his reaction to reporters, Stinson commented: "They can call me just about anything under the sun, but that is one thing I will not let anybody call me." Those European politicians who do indeed rest their appeal on racial prejudice display no similar sensitivity.

3 In addition, those under forty-four receive 10 points for age (with a reduction of 2 points a year, to a maximum of 10 for each additional year), 8 for work experience, 12 for language if a modest knowledge of French is added to English fluency (9 points are awarded for fluency in one of Canada's official languages, a further 6 for fluency in the other and 3 for more modest competence – there appears to be no mechanism for assuring any rigorous assessment of claimed proficiency). Eight points are awarded for so-called demographic factors and a suggested average of 6 for personal suitability (Canadian Immigration Self Assessment Guide). The rationale for many of the point determinations is not easily understood. A candidate gains 15 points for education to the BA

level but only one additional point for additional academic qualification whether at the Masters or PHD level.

4 When I reported in an article in the *Ottawa Citizen* that the "nearly
60 per cent" of claims are successful, Nurjehan Mawani, chair of the
Immigration and Refugee Board, responded with an article containing a
plethora of *ad hominems* about my "litany of allegations," and "misleading" "misinformation" and "groundless remarks" but notably failed
to address the substantive issues raised (Mawani 1997). She did explicitly refute my success figure: "Canada's acceptance rate stands at less
than 50 per cent." Canadians might be excused for assuming that this
stems from a calculation of the proportion of favourable decisions to
unfavourable decisions – those "whose claims are "accepted" by the
board and those whose claims are "rejected." Not so: to reach
Mawani's egregious figure you also have to include all those who have
withdrawn from the application process, including, no doubt, many
who simply used this as a stratagem to buy time in Canada. Since they
did not in fact ask the board to determine their case, it would have
been difficult for the board to "accept" them; but such logic is foreign
to those who prefer to massage numbers to buttress a weak case.
    Perhaps the most astonishing aspect of Mawani's reply was the claim
that "Canada has some of the toughest laws designed to deny criminals
access to permanent residence in this country."

5 In addition to local-authority social service departments, there are also
independent organizations like the National Society for the Prevention
of Cruelty to Children, which has an international reputation for its
work in dealing with abuse. The proposition that none of these would
pursue an allegation of child sexual abuse stretches credulity.

6 Citizenship and Immigration Backgrounder November 1995; News
Releases 20 March 1996; 7 January 1997; 9 January 1997; 28 February 1997; 14 March 1997; 26 March 1997.

7 A 1997 court case highlighted the way in which Canada's lax refugee
admission system could be easily abused by those whose intent was not
escape from persecution but crime. The principal defendant in a major
trial concerning the import and distribution of heroin had first entered
Canada in 1989 as a refugee claimant. Arrested in 1994, she had
(astonishingly) been freed on $75,000 bail – small change in drug-
trafficking circles. Not surprisingly, she failed to report to the court and
was believed to have returned to mainland China, leaving a seven-year-
old son in the care of a friend (*Globe and Mail*, 24 April 1997).

8 Immigrants who are convicted of crimes do not necessarily face any
efforts to deport them. A Jamaican immigrant, Evelyn Stewart, who
arrived in 1990, was charged with taking delivery of 1.5 kilograms of
marijuana, sent from Jamaica. While out on bail for that offence she

was charged, convicted, and jailed for trafficking cocaine. She received eighteen months on the trafficking charge, and a consecutive two-year penitentiary charge on the smuggling charge. Her defence counsel reported that no steps had been taken to send her back to Jamaica (*Toronto Star*, 2 August 1995).

9 Chief Inspector Stephen Carruthers, Hong Kong police, "Rough Cuts," CBC *Newsworld*, 9 December 1996.

10 Reed's sympathy for foreign-born criminals is not matched by any similar concern for the rights of those who have lived here for over three thousand years. In 1990 Justice Reed denied an injunction brought by the Labrador Innu to prevent continued military over-flying of an area subject to their land claim. The Innu had been engaged in a long peaceful struggle to assert their rights, which had led to numerous arrests and imprisonments. The Canadian government were hoping to transform the Goose Bay facility into a massive NATO air training centre which would have seen much of Labrador given over to low level flying, bombing ranges, and other military training exercises. Canada has signed no treaty with either the Innu or Inuit but has simply proceeded, in the manner of a colonial power, to ignore aboriginal interests. The NATO plan, which was ultimately rendered obsolescent by the end of the cold war, would have damaged traditional aboriginal harvesting and further harmed communities already experiencing massive social problems.

The injunction sought to prevent further over-flying, pending the completion of an environmental review. Reed questioned whether the Innu, who have been harvesting in the area for three millenia, made much use of the land, preferring to concern herself with damage that would result to the military and Canadians who had settled in Goose Bay, the base town (Wadden 1991: 191–3).

11 The reaction generated by this and similar cases resulted in the introduction of an expedited process. This permits those convicted of offences carrying a penalty of five years or more to be deported on a minister's opinion certificate, where the individual is a threat to public safety. The expedited process, which substantially reduced the possibility of lawyers engaging in lengthy legal-aid funded interventions on behalf of clients already convicted of a serious offence, resulted in strong protests from the immigration law section of the Canadian Bar Association (*Globe and Mail*, 28 August 1996). It is too soon to judge whether the new process will be effective, but the history of the Immigration Department in securing the removal of those ordered deported does not encourage optimism.

12 Richard Allen, chief economist at the Credit Union Central of British Columbia, has called the province's economic growth "an illusion." Allen notes: "The real growth rate for the '90s – if you include the estimated

zero growth in 1996 – was about 2 per cent. But the population growth rate was 2.5 per cent. So on a personal basis, our economy was actually shrinking" (Cernetig 1997: 52). B.C.'s spiralling deficits and growing provincial debt, in turn, are significantly impacted by population growth and the growing pressure on social services, reflected in a sharp increase in government spending per capita (ibid.: 53).

13 The *Globe and Mail* (27 February 1997) reported on the presidential ambitions of Serbian billionaire Bogoljub Karic, a former influential backer and intimate of Serbia's unsavoury President Slobodan Milosevic, who may face war crimes charges at The Hague (Borger 1997). The report suggested that with Milosevic facing increasing local opposition, Karic was now anxious "to distance himself." Curiously, Serbia's would-be president was reported, together with his four siblings, to be a Canadian landed immigrant. This status apparently involved neither actual or intended residence in Canada. Karic's Belgrade spokeswoman, Anna Bovan, said that while the family has businesses in Canada, Karic has no intention of living there: "He has some employees in Canada but to move there was never an option" (*Globe and Mail*, 27 February 1997).

14 There are no figures on the numbers of foreign nationals who have decided to acquire Canadian passports of convenience, but Raymond Chan, secretary of state for Asia-Pacific affairs, reported that Canada had a "normal" contingency plan in place to remove an estimated 100,000 "Canadians" in the event of unrest after the takeover by China (*Globe and Mail*, 5 March 1997). In fact, following the smooth transition to Chinese rule the number of those returning to Hong Kong increased, apparently encouraged by a desire to avoid the requirement to declare foreign holdings to the Canadian taxman. The *Globe and Mail* noted: "Since the July 1 takeover of Hong Kong by China, something most Vancouverites saw as improbable is occurring: Some of the West Coast's richest Chinese immigrants are heading back across the Pacific – and taking much of their money with them" (8 August 1997). Amidst reports of economic disruption and sharp falls in property values, the question of why Canada had afforded such generous treatment to those with the most opportunist attitude to their new country remained unanswered.

CHAPTER TEN

1 Typical of the NDP's preoccupation with symbolic politics was the release at the height of the recession of a booklet by the Ontario Women's Directorate, *Words that Count Women In*. As the government that had committed itself to abolish food banks watched the number of users soar, the highly paid femocrats in the Women's Directorate suggested the

world would be immeasurably improved by such changes as calling "mother earth" "sustaining earth." That the government assumed its mandate extended to revising the English language was symptomatic of a wider authoritarian trend which led to growing intervention in educational and cultural areas.

2 Lind notes the support of Ford Foundation head McGeorge Bundy for racial preferences in American college admissions: Bundy's argument in favour of such preferences did not extend to any attack on "legacy preferences, the largest affirmative action program in the United States, which chiefly benefited and continues to benefit whites of his class ... legacies are significantly less qualified than students admitted on the basis of merit" (Lind 1995: 164). In effect, Bundy, an elite member by birth, favoured enabling less qualified non-white students into select universities but without any implications for continuing privileged access to Ivy League schools for the children of the white elite. The enthusiasm of well-heeled progressives like Bob Rae and Stephen Lewis for a range of preferential policies equally entailed no personal costs; such costs would be borne by lower income white males.

3 Judy Wubnig observed on Lewis's apparent confusion about racism: "Is it judging the deeds of individuals according to their race, so that they are unequal under the law? No, not according to Lewis because he thinks it 'anti-racist' to treat individuals of different races *unequally* under the law, members of 'visible minorities' ... being treated preferentially ... Is it racism to judge ideas on the basis of the race of those who have them as did the National Socialists in Germany the ideas of 'Aryans' and 'non-Aryans' (Jews)? No, not according to Lewis, who thinks it "anti-racist" to have texts in the school curriculum chosen on the basis of the race of the authors" (SAFS *Newsletter*, November 1992, Society for Academic Freedom and Scholarship)

4 Among the recruits was Aderonke Akande, a twenty-one-year-old university drop-out, and daughter of then cabinet minister Zanana Akande (*Ottawa Citizen*, 7 December 1991).

5 Illustrative of the benefits of the shotgun marriage between Ontario's educrats and ethnocultural advocacy groups was the announcement that standardized testing, which would have done much to expose the failings of the public school system, was culturally racist (Emberley and Newell 1994: 33).

6 In their eagerness to appear at the forefront of progressive thinking, Education Minister Silipo and his successor, David Cooke, may not have known that the movement to reform the educational curriculum in the name of multiculturalism had not won universal support. Some had the temerity to suggest that perhaps some writers, musicians, and artists were more important than others and that schools had a legitimate

mandate to equip students with an understanding of the literary and historic traditions of the West (Schlesinger 1991, Bernstein 1994, Hoggart 1995). To the critics, the cultural relativism that underpinned the attack on the existing curriculum too readily resulted in schools that no longer had any coherent educational mission.

7 The 1991 Toronto Board of Education survey of the 74 per cent of students in the advanced level of high school students found 41 per cent of Chinese students to be "high" achievers in English and math, compared to 26 per cent of "English only" students (*Toronto Star*, 11 February 1995).

8 Writer Oakland Ross has recounted the detailed changes which a publisher demanded before one of his stories was deemed sufficiently sanitized to be included in a textbook that would pass muster for inclusion on Circular 14 (Ross 1995).

9 The clinic appeared at the inquest into the shooting death of Ian Clifford Coley, where its interrogation of a detective from the Metro police's black organized crime squad led to an "outburst" from the jury foreman who accused their lawyer of wasting the inquest's time (*Toronto Star*, 6 July 1995). The concerns of other members of the black community were evidenced by black detective David Mcleod, who was part of the squad involved in an anti-firearm operation outside a Scarborough club when Coley was shot. Mcleod told the inquest: "Gunmen … are only a very small percentage … Operations such as these have a great bearing on the safety of the black community." Citing concerns about dangers at nightclubs expressed to him by other blacks, Mcleod asked the inquest jury to recommend that the squad be expanded (*Toronto Star*, 9 July 1997).

10 There are undoubtedly a small number of virulent racists but black/ white race relations in Canada might be more fruitfully explored in the context of the views of both groups along with those of other Canadians of a variety of hues and ethnic backgrounds. There is ample evidence that some blacks, encouraged to view themselves as victims of the same kind of historic disadvantage that structured the American black experience, hold antagonistic and overtly racist attitudes towards whites. With the regular repetition of claims that all black failure must be laid at the door of white racism, any evidence that first-generation black immigrants and their descendants fail to attain immediate economic equality with longer-standing ethnic groups is seized as proof of bigotry. The negative attitudes and ethnic insularity that result from such a view merit concern.

Frances Henry's account, *The Caribbean Diaspora in Toronto*, contains a number of references to attitudes that are less than welcoming where white Canadians are concerned: the silence which descends on the black restaurant Raps as a group of whites take their food to a table, the woman who worries that in an interracial gathering she will "inadvertently make a derogatory comment about White people," or the fear of some Caribbean women that in a marriage or relationship with a white male they might "wind up with a blond child" (Henry 1994: 93–5, 177, and *passim*). Henry's account focuses exclusively on her belief that white racism is endemic and increasing; others might venture a more complex understanding of intergroup dynamics.

11 Doherty apparently believes that Lewis's opinions constitute some kind of factual evidence, citing with transparent approval Lewis's claims that the particular target of racism is black Canadians. Doherty quotes at length from Lewis's letter: "It is Blacks who are being shot, it is Black youth that is unemployed in excessive numbers, it is Black students who are disproportionately dropping out, it is housing communities with large concentrations of Black residents where the sense of vulnerability and disadvantage is most acute, it is Black employees, professional and non-professional, on whom the doors of equity slam shut" (R. v. Parks in 84 C.C.C. (3d): 369). Doherty notes, as though he had just finished surveying a scholarly summary of scientific research rather than the quickly drawn conclusions of a garrulous politician, "Mr. Lewis' report post-dates the trial in this case; however the conditions and attitudes he *describes* are obviously long standing" (emphasis added).

Lewis's polemic, not surprisingly, captures some of the problems that confront some members of the black community. The difficulty lies in the simplistic attribution of such problems to racism. Is it racism that causes a sense of vulnerability in certain areas or the disproportionate involvement of some local residents in drug dealing and other crime?

12 These questions posed no difficulty to Rae's Employment Equity Commissioner. Interviewed by a reporter for the *Hamilton Spectator*, Traoré was asked whether the son of an unemployed steelworker had greater employment opportunities than the daughter of an upper middle-class couple. The commissioner was in no doubt that the woman faced the greater employment barriers (Brown 1994: 8).

13 This was confirmed through a number of Freedom of Information requests to the Ministry of Citizenship probing the research that underpinned the assumptions that racial minorities experienced discrimination. These included:

• Is the Office of the Commissioner aware that some ethnic groups who are not racial minorities exhibit greater indications of disadvantage than some of those ethnic groups who are visible minorities? I request a copy of all material relating to the consideration of this question.

• Did the Office of the Commissioner undertake any review of the 1992 Economic Council of Canada study, *Earnings of Immigrants*? If such

a review has been undertaken I request a copy of all material relating
to it.

The Economic Council study found the evidence "goes against" the
view that immigrants face systemic discrimination based on colour
(deSilva 1992: 34). I was advised that there were no records: "the
Office of the Commissioner has not carried out this type of research";
"the Office of the Commissioner has not conducted any such research"
(Fleming, letter, 8 June 1993).

14 The Alliance for Employment Equity includes tax funded advocacy
organizations and companies that specialize in selling consultancy services, to assist businesses and public sector organizations in conforming
to the regulatory requirements of equity legislation. In 1991–92 the
group received $45,000 in direct funding from Citizenship, in 1993–94
$70,000. In the same year the Urban Alliance on Race Relations
received $25,000 for employment equity programming and a further
$25,000 for "networking" and information sharing in anti-racism work.
The United Food and Commercial Workers Union received $20,000 "to
promote and educate about the employment equity legislation of the
province."

Citizenship provided extensive funding to a wide range of ethnic organizations as well as traditional NDP clients – much of which might seem
little different than old-fashioned pork barrel politics. The anti-racism
program, premised on the belief that racism was a pervasive force in the
province, awarded ninety-six grants in 1993–94. The following are illustrative:
• Can-Sikh Cultural Centre: $8,000 – "To conduct seminars and work-
  shops for South Asian students designed to develop skills in identifying and dealing with systemic racism."
• Canadian Council of South Asian Christians: $10,000 – "Racism-
  proofing young adults and teaching them how to deal with racism."
• Gay Asians Toronto: $15,000 – "To produce a book on Gay Asians'
  experience on [sic] racism."
• United Steelworkers of America: $20,000 – "To hire an A/R coordina-
  tor to organize delivery of A/R sessions to steelworkers and union
  schools."
(Responses to FOI requests, Ministry of Citizenship, 14 December 1994;
13 January 1995).

15 In fact, as the highly sympathetic review goes on to report, the concept
of merit is under continuous assault from preferential hiring advocates.
Margaret Young, the Library of Parliament researcher who compiled the
review, notes in the following paragraphs the attempts of preferential
hiring advocates to redefine merit and qualification in ways that permit
more flexibility in appointing those with desirable group characteristics:

"Proponents of affirmative action offer a more complex assessment of the concept of merit than its detractors. Merit is not an objective test and is seldom defined ... Actual job performance is very difficult to predict accurately ... The idea that other factors in addition to merit can be relevant to employment decisions has been accepted in other areas, for example for veterans following both world wars.

"The notion of qualifications is sometimes elusive as well. In many cases it will be difficult to determine who is the best qualified for a job. Qualifications may be set without a serious assessment of how they relate to or predict job success."

Young captures the thrust of the frontal assault that preferential hiring advocates mount on notions of merit and qualification but fails to understand that this negates her assurance that hiring the unqualified would be "counterproductive." The Ontario Human Rights Commission, for example, has had no hesitation in hiring the unqualified, even as the agency becomes ever more fractious and less able to fulfil its statutory obligations.

16 Pressure to meet equity targets has led to a variety of institutional responses. The Kitchener Fire Department responded to demands for greater representation for designated group members by setting differential qualification thresholds: seventy for group members, eighty-five for able-bodied white males.

17 The information regarding this case was obtained under Freedom of Information (Management Board, 23 January 1995). In addition to measuring the coverage, civil servants were also directed to compile an exhaustive list of the news stories.

18 I first expressed concern to the Ontario Human Rights Commission in March 1991, querying the legality of such blatantly discriminatory recruitment practices and expressing concerns that my own candidacy would not be fairly considered. I hold a PHD in Social Administration from the London School of Economics and held a senior university position in the U.K. before returning to Canada. In addition to a fairly substantial publication record I also had direct expertise in the area of race relations and social work in a multicultural society (Loney 1975, Cheetham et al. 1981).

The investigating officer, according to the commission's procedures, should have sought to effect an "Early Settlement Initiative." This "provides a chance to solve matters without a lot of formal or complicated steps" (Ontario Human Rights Commission 1990). Instead the officer advised me that after investigation she had determined that Carleton did not intend to discriminate against white male candidates. It subsequently became clear that Carleton had proceeded exactly according to their advertised intention – in total, three of the four full-time positions, including the instructor position, were given to racial minority candidates who lacked PHDs.

In November I wrote to Esther Delph, the officer who had handled my initial query, to request a formal investigation. It seemed a relatively straightforward matter: if any employer had rejected qualified racial minority candidates and appointed unqualified white candidates, the matter would have been quickly addressed. In this case the commission's response was different; Delph simply ignored the letter.

In January I again wrote to Delph seeking an acknowledgment of my complaint. Delph, who had obviously been practising, ignored this letter as well.

In February I sent a recorded delivery letter to Leslie Lewis, executive director of the Ontario Human Rights Commission, advising her of my difficulties in securing any response from the Ottawa office. Lewis, perhaps intending to lead by example, did not reply. Unable to obtain any response from the Human Rights Commission, which has a statutory obligation to investigate such complaints, I sought the intervention of my MPP, Norman Sterling. On 5 May 1992, Sterling wrote to Lewis. Within a week Lewis wrote to acknowledge the complaint I had formally registered some six months previously. Perhaps conscious that my experience with Delph might have led me to doubt her enthusiasm for pursuing the matter, my complaint was assigned to another investigating officer, Lisa Taylor.

19 Carleton, inevitably, raised the argument that I had been denied appointment based on an earlier hiring process in the mid-1970s which had resulted in controversy. At that time I had been denied appointment to a permanent position from the temporary position I then held, following a dispute over the issue of whether faculty enthusiasm for pursuing lucrative private-contract research had a negative impact on teaching. But Carleton's argument failed to answer the question of why all the other *qualified* able-bodied white male candidates for full-time positions had failed to secure an interview, a question scrupulously avoided in the OHRC "investigation."

20 The school, with a faculty of less than twenty, already included two aboriginal Canadians.

21 Comments about organizational culture, for example, included:
• They always make statements about my handwriting in meetings. These are putdowns.
• In our office, they celebrated birthdays and missed mine twice. When confronted, they offered the poorest of excuses.
• One [white] employee has said that the problem with the Commission is lack of objectivity; community activists should not be employees.

• Some racial minorities do not support the methodology of the Anti-Racism Committee's preliminary report. Some [white] employees are using that as an argument that there is no racism at the Committee (Minors 1992: 14–17).

22 When Nathan Greenfield questioned Bob Rae on the issue in the course of reviewing his autobiography, Rae insisted that his government was not involved (personal communication).

23 On 11 May 1993 the Ontario Anti-Racism Secretariat reported on their activities concerning Show Boat to the "Stephen Lewis Report Coordinating Staff Committee." The Lewis report was regularly referenced in discussions about Show Boat and was used in defence of the provision of extensive financial support to many of the organizations involved in the coalition, though OARS denied that the financial support was provided to assist the coalition (Letter from A.D.M. Stewart to *Toronto Star*, original dated 27 September 1993).

24 Novelist Cecil Foster attempts, without obvious success, to account for the difference in response: "The show went ahead and opened to stellar reviews, even in the African-American press, 'how could this be?' ... Canadian Blacks are not African Americans" (Foster 1996: 13). Apparently, if the Barbadian-born Foster is to be believed, Caribbean blacks have a right to greater sensitivity to the material of Show Boat than those whose history actually forms its subject matter. Curiously, no such sensitivity surfaced among Caribbean-born Americans.

25 The records were initially requested on 27 October 1994. The ministry offered an extremely limited release at a cost of $80. On 16 August 1995 the Information and Privacy Commissioner ordered the release of a significant number of further documents (Order P-978).

26 This indication of minimal public concern had little impact on those who claim to know the views of the "black community." Three years later Judy Rebick was in no doubt: "The Black community in Toronto opposed the production of Showboat because they considered the play to be racist" (Rebick and Roach 1996: 75).

27 I specifically raised the question with Julie White, Trillium's executive director, of how a grant to an advocacy group such as the Urban Alliance fell within Trillium guidelines (3 March 1997). Trillium defended the grant on the grounds that the training would increase opportunities for "disadvantaged" groups.

The potential for harm in the explosion of diversity training and similar raced-based training of the kind apparently envisaged by the Alliance lies not simply in the frequent repetition of dubious statistics that purport to evidence gross discrimination, the stock in trade of the industry, or in the encouragement given to a festering culture of grievance.

Some "trainers" have been quick to label those who fail to exhibit the desired characteristics. At the University of Cincinnati a woman faculty member was told to stand up, and was identified as one of the privileged white elite: blonde, blue-eyed and well-educated. The trainer suggested that her three degrees were a result less of merit than genetic entitlement. Told to stand again, presumably for further denunciation, the woman sat and sobbed, while not one of her hundred or so colleagues intervened (Bork 1996: 246).

28 On 6 February 1997, I wrote to Trillium's executive director, Julie White, querying a particular gender-based grant and asked, "What research has Trillium funded which is explicitly or exclusively concerned with the real or putative disadvantages experienced by Canadian males?" My letter was immediately faxed to the organization that had successfully obtained the grant to which my query related, but in her subsequent reply White did not offer any answer to my question.

CHAPTER ELEVEN

1 Sandra Martin, in a critical chronicling of the UBC debacle, commented: "Giving a feminist labour lawyer carte blanche to find racism and sexism is like asking someone from the Flat Earth Society if it's possible to fall over the edge of the world" (Martin 1996).

2 The mandate of the U of T committee was indicative of the pressures for "sanitizing" the curriculum that ultimately resulted in the Rae government's 1993 zero tolerance policy. This called on universities and colleges to protect students from harassment and discrimination, concepts that stretched to include "negative environments." CAUT president Alan Andrews offered support to the Ontario initiative in the face of international criticism ("Letters," *Guardian Weekly*, 27 February 1994).

3 The officers constitute an activist core with a particular commitment to pushing the politics of identity. When Erindale College, for example, established a women's caucus, one of its founders was Rona Abramovitch, U of T women's officer (*Varsity*, University of Toronto, 24 January 1995).

4 In the U.K., internationally renowned philosophy professor John Cottingham was cleared by the courts of sexually assaulting two students at Reading University. Cottingham claimed the students had attempted to "humiliate, seduce or entice" him, and when they failed, sought to discredit him with the charges. One of the complainants had made a similar charge against a man in the United States, but the charge had been dropped when she refused to take a lie-detector test (*Guardian Weekly* 3 August 1997).

5 In Vancouver, for example, there are three daily newspapers, two television stations, and three radio stations targeting the Chinese language market.

6 The *Bulletin*'s less than inclusive editorial stance has even attracted attention from the *Toronto Sun*, which featured an article by editorial board member Lorrie Goldstein (27 April 1992). This was prompted by the *Bulletin*'s refusal to print a letter from U of T psychology professor John Furedy, who had criticized an earlier article in the *Bulletin* by official languages commissioner Victor Goldbloom for failing to confront Quebec's illiberal language laws. Furedy saw the refusal as a classic example of PC politics. The *Bulletin* took refuge in the spurious claim that Furedy's letter was libellous, a view not shared by the *Sun*'s legal counsel.

7 It is usually difficult to secure direct, attributable evidence of the operation of discriminatory hiring. The author's personal experiences include being phoned by a graduate student, who had known me many years earlier, after he heard I had applied for a position in his department. With an amicable gale of laughter at my naiveté, he assured me the position was reserved for a woman. This proved correct: the position was offered to a woman, and, since women candidates are often wooed by more than one department, a second woman was identified as the fall-back candidate. Seven books that I had written or edited were in the university's library; the successful candidate had none.

In another social science appointment at a prominent Ontario university, a highly qualified male candidate with numerous publications was rejected in favour of a visible minority woman who had had to switch universities in order to find a department prepared to grant her a PHD.

Professor Heinz Klatt, unusually, has provided documentary evidence of the preferential hiring practices in the Department of Psychology at the University of Western Ontario's King's College. The department agreed in 1995 to make an appointment on merit, taking into account research and teaching experience. A ranking system established a clear winner with thirteen publications and considerable teaching experience. The first woman was ranked number four, with one publication and no teaching experience. The department proceeded to vote to hire her. Only when Klatt promised to publicize the discriminatory hiring process and advise the highest ranked candidate what had happened did the department reverse its position and vote to hire him (personal communication, 25 November 1996).

8 The complaint was brought by the author, and, at the time of writing, remains unresolved. UBC's lawyers on the matter are Alexander Holburn

Beadin and Lang. The extract is from their letter of 2 May 1997, to the
B.C. Human Rights Council.

9 Paula Caplan makes a similar and equally unevidenced claim in her
polemic *Lifting a Ton of Feathers* (1993: 176). The claim that visible
minorities experience pervasive discrimination in academic hiring is fundamental to orthodoxy. Since Canada is a profoundly sexist and racist
society, what Caplan calls "non-dominant groups" (a categorization
explicitly designed to emphasize the "dominance" of another group)
must be continually marginalized. In contrast to this myopic ideological
vision, the evidence, as we will see, provides no support to claims that
visible minorities are under-represented in academic employment.

10 One of the male appointments was shared with the Faculty of Law;
thus four out of 5.5 appointments went to women (Sumner 1996: 385).

11 Sumner is not alone in turning to anecdote. A report on the debate at
the University of Toronto on employment equity, sponsored by the Society for Academic Freedom and Democracy, notes: "The only side using
systematic evidence, however was the anti-equity side ... The pro-equity
side supported their argument with anecdotal evidence" (*The Newspaper*, University of Toronto, 8 February 1995). The "pro-equity" side was
headed by James Brown of the university's Department of Philosophy.

12 The response to an article in the *Globe and Mail* by Donna Laframboise, an outspoken critic of feminist excesses (Laframboise 1996), illustrates the institutional power of feminist orthodoxy. Laframboise had
highlighted the anti-male bias in child custody disputes (Laframboise
1997a). Writing from their tenured positions at the University of British
Columbia, Susan Boyd (chairwoman, Feminist Legal Studies, Faculty of
Law), and Veronica Strong-Boag (director, Centre for Research in
Women's Studies and Gender Relations), wrote to assure any readers
who might have been led astray by Laframboise that the real problem
was "systemic anti-women bias" ("Letters," 26 April 1997). As for the
problems raised by Laframboise of denial of divorced fathers' access to
their children, "it is mainly when a man has gone seriously awry in his
dealings with the mother and children that problems arise." There are,
of course, no ideologues who might enter the debate as "chairman of
Masculinist Legal Studies" or "director, Centre for Research in Men's
Studies."

13 I have no direct experience of the University of Victoria, but in contrast to the colourful picture of sixteen-hour days, a visitor of my
acquaintance from a British university expressed some astonishment at
the faculty's minimal teaching obligations and his difficulty in locating
many of them at their place of work. A recent report on the crisis in
Canada's universities highlights not the pressures faced by academics but

the large number who have effectively retired in post (Bercuson *et al.* 1997: 125–52).

14 Accurate figures were supplied by Kenneth Heyworth of University of Toronto's statistical services (memo and attachments, 5 December 1996).

15 The figures were obviously too low for some. Wearing his heart on his sleeve, David Rayside, vice-principal of University College, told the university's alumnae that while he was a believer "in the shift to more assertive equity measures, including those now in force in Ontario," he regretted the failure "to pair [its] employment equity legislation with an educational equity program" (Rayside 1995). Rayside has been equally eager to advertise his "progressive" views in endorsing ill-considered demands for curriculum reform, arguing that too little attention is given to areas other than Europe and North America, "and in teaching about Canada and other countries, race and immigration are paid scant attention" ("Letters," *University of Toronto Bulletin*, 25 January 1995). It is possible that Rayside's colleagues in history and the social sciences manage to teach about Canada without addressing such issues, but it must make for a very odd curriculum. Where do U of T students think 97 per cent of the population come from? Do Rayside's colleagues really give "scant attention" to the issue of race in teaching about the United States?

16 Elsewhere, in a genuflection to fashionable wisdom on such matters, Emberley observes, in a discussion of the protection of incompetent academics through tenure, "there is a vast army of nonemployed, scholars, *usually young women*, with significant publications and an enviable record of teaching" (Emberley 1996: 65, emphasis added). The fact that men significantly outnumber women in the qualified pool and that qualified women are more likely to be hired than qualified men suggests that the "army" is overwhelmingly male.

17 In practice, as we have seen, Dalhousie has established a series of racially exclusive academic positions for which non-black candidates, however meritorious, will not be considered. The first successful applicant lacked a PHD, normally the prerequisite for a professorial appointment.

18 In addition to the suggestion of widespread institutionally induced schizophrenia, and the insistence (see below) on the equal claims of subjectivity, it is notable that the women and minorities whose learning and research is so profoundly vulnerable make up at least 70 per cent of the undergraduate population (visible minorities, aboriginals, the disabled, gay students, and [in some accounts] the poor, the unemployed, transvestites, bisexuals, Jews, etc.) The authors of this insight hold academic positions at the universities of Windsor, Dalhousie, and Concordia.

19 Carty obtained a PHD in sociology at the Ontario Institute for Studies in Education, an institute which has done much to lead the embrace of grievance politics. Feminism, she notes, is "the primary political discourse among faculty and students" at OISE, but she reports that racism is rampant: "terms like 'primitive' were thrown around loosely, always in reference to Blacks and/or pre-capitalist societies" (Carty 1991: 39). There is a considerable difference between these two usages. It seems unlikely that Carty's OISE professors described blacks as "primitive." The use of the term to describe particular social formations contains no pejorative connotations regarding ethnic or racial groups, applying to all societies at some historical juncture. It is surprising that a successful OISE doctoral student could be unaware of this distinction.

20 There are numerous examples that illustrate the difference in treatment, some of which were discussed earlier. A large number of contemporary sponsored immigrants have claimed social assistance, though the terms of sponsorship are supposed to preclude such claims. Contrast this with the policies of the Department of Immigration towards unemployed immigrants in the Depression: "From the summer of 1930 to the fall of 1935, the official policy was one of automatic deportation of the unemployed, while claiming that they were unemployable and undesirable" (Roberts 1988: 160). The one group that secured some amelioration was the British, since deportation angered London.

21 It is not clear what research methodology informs the work of Henry and her colleagues. One of her co-authors, fellow anthropology professor Carol Tator, was quoted in an *Ottawa Citizen* article that described studies (discussed elsewhere) purporting to show earnings penalties of 19.9 per cent for South Asians and 15.7 per cent for blacks, as against 5.6 per cent for Chinese and a mere 2.3 per cent for Southeast Asians. Tator found the Benjamin-Baker (1997) study mirrored the order of the "hit parade in terms of racist attitudes" (*Ottawa Citizen*, 19 January 1997).

It is unclear by what mechanisms Canadians have created a pyramid of prejudice that distinguishes between South Asians (highly unfavourable) and Southeast Asians (hardly unfavourable at all). I tried to explore with Professor Tator (described by the *Ottawa Citizen* as "a specialist in anti-racism studies") the labour market mechanisms that might create such gross disparities (personal communication, 13 February 1997). In many areas of the economy, wages are closely regulated and strongly driven by seniority. There may be scope for discrimination in promotion or recruitment, though there is little evidence for this in detailed industry data. Tator said she was unfamiliar with the research on earnings and had no answer to a question as to why, if such profound discrimination exists, visible minorities are so successful in accessing post-secondary education, particularly at the graduate level. Tator did refer me to a study undertaken by the highly partisan Urban Alliance on Race Relations, dating back to 1984, which used actors to measure discrimination against applicants for employment, and a subsequent telephone survey that measured discrimination against those who spoke with foreign accents (Caribbean, South Asian and Southern European), *No Discrimination Here: Who Gets the Work*. Tator also claimed support for her views based on her many years of "experience" working with racial minority "communities."

22 The commission was established, as its name suggests, to demonstrate that the problem the province faced was not that of the disproportionate involvement of some blacks in crime but the differential treatment of blacks in the criminal justice system. In consequence there was no attempt to separate the experience of different black ethnic groups. Had the commission done so, it might well have found that the groups had very different levels of involvement in the criminal justice system, and that the experience of those of Ghanaian origin and Jamaican origin was highly divergent. This would have proved inconvenient to the commission and its political sponsors, since it would have challenged the claim the problem was "systemic racism" rather than crime.

The obvious conclusion to be drawn from the remand data escaped commission co-chair Judge David Cole, who suggested that the figures simply reflected policing activity: had similar levels of policing occurred in Rosedale as in areas with large black populations, similar remand figures would have resulted. Those who have lacked Judge Cole's opportunity to study the problem at such extensive public expense might be puzzled by the absence of demands for more vigorous policing in Rosedale, in comparison to the continual pressure the Toronto police force face to take more effective action against the drug dealing, prostitution, and other street crime prevalent in some less salubrious areas of the city.

CHAPTER TWELVE

1 Such taxation proposals generally pursue the fiction that there are two sets of taxpayers: corporations and people. In the real world, corporate profit is distributed to executives and shareholders and is more effectively captured by taxes on those groups. Corporations have far more ability than individuals to shift earnings to jurisdictions with lower tax regimes.

Bibliography

Abella, I. 1996a. "Jewish Refugees Need Not Apply." *Globe and Mail*, 14 March.
– 1996b. "A Few Last Reflections on the Roux Affair." *Globe and Mail*, 21 November.
Abella, I., and H. Troper. 1982. *None Is Too Many: Canada and the Jews of Europe, 1933–48*. Toronto.
Abella, R. 1984. *Report of the Commission on Equality in Employment*. Ottawa: Supply and Services.
– 1985. *Research Studies of the Commission on Equality in Employment*. Ottawa: Supply and Services.
– 1991. "The New 'isms.'" In Granatstein and McNaught, eds., *"English Canada" Speaks Out*.
Abt Associates. 1988. "Employment Equity Status Report on Visible Minorities." Draft report for Ontario Ministry of Citizenship. Toronto. Mimeo.
– 1992. *Report on Focus Groups with Members of Designated Groups*. Technical Report no. 3. Employment and Immigration Canada.
Adachi, K. 1976. *The Enemy That Never Was*. Toronto: McClelland & Stewart.
Adelman H., A. Borowski, M. Burstein, and L. Foster., eds. 1994. *Immigration and Refugee Policy: Australia and Canada Compared*. 2 vols. Toronto: University of Toronto Press.
Adsett, M., and J. Kralt. 1997. "Discrimination or Inadequate Measurement? A Critical Review of Studies on Earnings Inequality among Immigrant and Canadian Born Ethnic Groups in Canada." Canadian Heritage. Mimeo.
Aiken, S. 1996. "No Visa, No Boarding Pass, No Refuge." *Globe and Mail*, 16 October.
Alexander, K., and A. Glaze. 1996. *Towards Freedom: The African-Canadian Experience*. Toronto: Umbrella Press.
Alexander, M. 1985. "Unjustified Quotas." *Policy Options* 6, no. 6.
Alibhai-Brown, Y. 1994. "The Age of the Baby Mother." *Guardian Weekly*, July 10.

Andrew, C. 1996. "A Small Wedding." *Globe and Mail*, 1 June.

Appiah, K.A. 1994. "Identity, Authenticity, Survival: Multicultural Societies and Social Reproduction." In Guttman, ed., *Multiculturalism: Examining the Politics of Recognition*.

Auditor General of Canada. 1997. "Citizenship and Immigration Canada and Immigration and Refugee Board: The Processing of Refugee Claims." Chapter 25 in *Report of the Auditor General of Canada to the House of Commons*. Ottawa: Minister of Public Works and Government Services.

Avery, D.H. 1995. *Reluctant Host: Canada's Response to Immigrant Workers 1986–1994*. Toronto: McClelland & Stewart.

Bannerji, H., ed. 1993a. *Returning the Gaze: Essays on Racism, Feminism and Politics*. Toronto: Sister Vision.

Bannerji, H. 1993b. *The Writing on the Wall: Essays on Culture and Politics*. Toronto: Tsar.

– 1995. "Re: Turning the Gaze." In Richer and Weir, eds., *Beyond Political Correctness*.

Bannerji, H., L. Carty, K. Dehli, S. Heald, and K. McKenna. 1991. *Unsettling Relations: The University as a Site of Feminist Struggles*. Toronto: Women's Press.

Barrett, S.R. 1991. "White Supremacists and Neo-Fascists: Laboratories for the Analysis of Racism in Wider Society." In McKague, ed., *Racism in Canada*.

Beck, R. 1996. *The Case against Immigration: The Moral, Economic, Social, and Environmental Reasons for Reducing U.S. Immigration back to Traditional Levels*. New York: Norton.

Bercuson, D., R. Bothwell, and J. Granatstein. 1997. *Petrified Campus: The Crisis in Canadian Universities*. Toronto: Random House.

Berger, T.R. 1977. *Northern Frontier Northern Homeland: The Report of the Mackenzie Valley Pipeline Inquiry*. 2 vols. Ottawa: Supply and Services.

Berkowitz, P. 1996. "More Alike Than Different." *University Affairs*, January.

Bernstein, R. 1994. *Dictatorship of Virtue: Multiculturalism and the Battle for America's Future*. New York: Knopf.

Bissoondath, N. 1994. *Selling Illusions: The Cult of Multiculturalism in Canada*. Toronto: Penguin.

Bloom, H. 1994 *The Western Cannon*. New York: Harcourt Brace.

Boothby, D. 1992. *Job Changes, Wage Changes and Employment Equity Groups*. Study prepared for the Interdepartmental Working Group on Employment Equity Data. Statistics Canada.

Borger, J. 1997. "The President's Secret Henchmen." *Guardian Weekly*, 16 February.

Bork, R.H. 1996. *Slouching toward Gomorrah: Modern Liberalism and American Decline*. New York: HarperCollins.

Borowski A., and D. Thomas. 1994. "Immigration and Crime." In Adelman et al., eds., *Immigration and Refugee Policy*.

Boxhill, W. Undated. *Approaches to the Collection of Data on Visible Minorities in Canada: A Review and Commentary*. Statistics Canada.

Boyd, M. 1991. "Gender, Visible Minority and Immigrant Earnings Inequality: Reassessing an Employment Equity Premise." In Satzewich, ed., *Immigration and Refugee Policy: Australia and Canada Compared*.

Brand, D. 1994. *Bread out of Stone*. Toronto: Coach House.

– 1996. *In Another Place, Not Here*. Toronto: Knopf.

Breedon Research. 1988. *Report on Focus Groups to Study Reactions to Ethnicity/Race Questions for the 1991 Census*. Report for Housing Family and Social Statistics Division, Statistics Canada.

Bricker, D. 1985. "What's Wrong with Affirmation." *Policy Options* 6, no. 7.

Brighton Research. 1996. *Strategic Evaluation of Multicultural Programs*. Final Report. Canadian Heritage.

Brodie, J., ed. 1996. *Women and Canadian Public Policy*. Toronto: Harcourt Brace.

Brown, G. 1992. *The Employment Equity Empress Has No Clothes: An Inquiry into Preferential Hiring in Canadian Universities*. Edmonton: Gender Issues Education Foundation.

– 1994a. "Brief to the House of Commons Standing Committee on Human Rights and the Status of the Disabled." November 29.

– 1994b. "Discrimination in University Hiring: Against Women or Men." *Inroads* no. 3, Summer.

Brown, R. 1991. "Overcoming Racism and Sexism – How?" In McKague, ed., *Racism in Canada*.

Bryden, J. 1994. "Special Interest Group Funding." MP's Report. Ottawa: House of Commons. Mimeo.

– 1996. "Canada's Charities: A Need for Reform." MP's Report. Ottawa: House of Commons. Mimeo.

Buckley, S. 1996. "African Women Fight Abuse." *Guardian Weekly*, 12 May.

Burgess, J.H. 1997. "Low Marks in Canadian History." *Globe and Mail*, 4 January.

Calliste, A. 1989. "Canada's Immigration Policy and Domestics from the Caribbean: The Second Domestic Scheme." In Vorst et al., eds., *Race, Class, Gender: Bonds and Barriers*.

Callwood, J. 1995. *Trial without End: A Shocking Story of Women and AIDS*. Toronto: Knopf.

Cameron, D.M. 1996. "Academic Freedom and the Canadian University." Research File 1, no. 3, March. Association of Universities and Colleges of Canada.

Canada. 1982. *The Charter of Rights and Freedoms: A Guide for Canadians*. Ottawa: Supply and Services.

– 1996. *Estimates 1996–97*, part 2, *The Main Estimates*. Ottawa: Supply and Services.

Canadian Broadcasting Corporation. 1993. *Journalistic Standards and Practices*. Canadian Broadcasting Corporation.

Canadian Civil Liberties Association. 1995. "The Role of Education in Combatting Racism." Submission to John Snobelen, Minister of Education and Training for Ontario. Toronto. Mimeo.

Canadian Heritage 1994a. "Opinion Poll Bullets." Michelle Rae Fraser. Mimeo.

– 1994b. "Selected Statistics on Ethnic Origins and Economic Activity Data." Policy Coordination and Strategic Planning Citizenship and Canadian Identity. Mimeo.

– 1996. *Annual Report on the Operation of the Canadian Multiculturalism Act*. Ottawa: Supply and Services.

– 1997. *Annual Report on the Operation of the Canadian Multiculturalism Act*. Ottawa: Public Works and Government Services.

Canadian Human Rights Commission. 1995. *Annual Report 1994*. Ottawa: Ministry of Supply and Services.

– 1997a. *Visible Minorities and the Public Service of Canada*. Report by John Samuel and Associates Inc. Ottawa: Canadian Human Rights Commission.

– 1997b. "Tribunal Decision." National Capital Alliance on Race Relations and Health and Welfare Canada. Decision date 19 March.

– 1997c. *Annual Report 1996*. Ottawa: Government Works and Public Services Canada.

Canadian Labour Congress. 1997. *Women's Work: A Report*. Ottawa: CLC.

Cannon, M. 1995. *The Invisible Empire: Racism in Canada*. Toronto: Random House.

Caplan, P. 1993. *Lifting a Ton of Feathers: A Woman's Guide to Surviving in the Academic World*. Toronto: University of Toronto Press.

Cardozo, A. 1993. "Levelling the Playing Field." *Policy Options*, March.

Cardozo, A., and L. Musto, eds. 1997. *The Battle over Multiculturalism: Does It Help or Hinder Canadian Unity?* Ottawa: Pearson Shoyama Institute.

Carleton University. 1993. *This is Carleton University School of Social Work*. Office of Admissions and Academic Records.

Carty, L. 1991. "Black Women in Academia: A Statement from the Periphery." In Bannerji *et al.*, *Unsettling Relations*.

Carty, L. ed. 1993. *And Still We Rise: Feminist Political Mobilizing in Contemporary Canada*. Toronto: Women's Press.

Cernetig, M. 1997. "Under Siege." *Globe and Mail's Report on Business*, May.

Champion, C. 1996. "Fast-Track to Discrimination." *Alberta Report*, 30 September.

Chavez, L., and R. Lerner. 1997. "Blacks May Get Easier Justice," *Globe and Mail*, 1 March.

Cheetham J., W. James, B. Mayor, M. Loney, and B. Prescott. 1981. *Social and Community Work in a Multi-Racial Society*. London: Harper and Row.

Child Poverty Action Group, Family Service Association of Metropolitan Toronto, Social Planning Council of Metropolitan Toronto. 1994. *The Outsiders*. A Report on the Prospects for Young Families in Metropolitan Toronto.

Citizenship and Immigration. 1994. "The Relative Performance of Selected Independents and Family Class Immigrants in the Labour Market." Economic and Demographic Research and Analysis Division, Strategic Research and Analysis Branch, Policy Sector. November. Mimeo.

– 1996. *Staying the Course: 1997 Annual Immigration Plan*. Ottawa: Supply and Services.

City of Ottawa. 1994. "Special Program Proposal for Hiring Qualified Aboriginal People, Racial Minorities and Women in the Ottawa Fire Department." Report to City Council meeting, February 16. Mimeo.

– 1996. "Executive Summary." Multicultural Centre. Mimeo.

City of Toronto. 1995. "Submission to the General Government Committee Regarding Employment Equity." Speaker's notes for Councillor Kyle Rae and Background Reports on City of Toronto Equal Opportunity Policies 1993–1995. Toronto. Mimeo.

Clark, C. 1997. *Public Sector Downsizing: The Impact on Job Quality in Canada*. Ottawa: Canadian Council on Social Development.

Cohen, M.G. 1993. "Social Policy and Social Services." In Pierson *et al.* eds., *Strong Voices*.

Collins, J., and F. Henry. 1994. "Racism, Ethnicity and Immigration." In Adelman *et al.*, eds., *Immigration and Refugee Policy*.

Commission on Systemic Racism. 1995. *Report of the Commission on Systemic Racism in the Ontario Criminal Justice System*. Toronto.

Consultation Group. 1992. *Gender Balance: More than Numbers*. Report of the Consultation Group on Employment Equity for Women. Ottawa: Government of Canada.

– 1993. *More than Numbers: Case Studies on Best Practices in the Employment of Women*. A Report by the Consultation Group on Employment Equity for Women. Ottawa: Government of Canada.

Conway, J. 1990. *The Canadian Family in Crisis*. Toronto: Lorimer.

Cook, D. 1996. "Unmasking the Dreaded 'L' Word: The Political Context of the Equity Debate." *Newsletter*, Society for Academic Freedom and Scholarship, no. 15, December.

Corcoran, T. 1996. "Ottawa's Tobacco Pork Barrel." *Globe and Mail*, 28 September.

– 1997. "The Case for Total Pension Reform." *Globe and Mail*, 14 November.

Coren, M.N. 1995. *Lewis Carroll: A Biography*. New York: Knopf.

Cox, D., and P. Glenn. 1994. "Illegal Immigration and Refugee Claims." In Adelman *et al.*, *Immigration and Refugee Policy*.

Coyne, A. 1996. "Privatize or Perish: The Case for Blowing Up Our Ivory Towers." *Globe and Mail*, 4 May.

Criminal Intelligence Service Canada. 1996. *Annual Report on Organized Crime in Canada*. Ottawa: CISC.

Crowley, B.L. 1994. *The Road to Equity: Gender, Ethnicity, and Language*. Toronto: Stoddart.

Cutt, J., and C. Hodgkinson. 1992. "Equity and Excellence in the University." *Policy Options*. September.

Dagg, A.I. 1993. "Toward a Feminist Academy." *Policy Options*, March.

Dahlin, K. 1996. "Politically Speaking." *University of Toronto Magazine*, Autumn.

Davies, N. 1997. "How the Yardies Duped the Yard." *Guardian Weekly*, 9 March.

Davis, B. 1995. *Whatever Happened to High School History?* Toronto: Lorimer.

Dawson, A. 1996. "So Near, and Yet So Far to Go." *Ottawa Sun*, 27 October.

Dean, M. 1995. "Shock Troops on Campus." *Canadian Forum*, July/August.

Dehli, K. 1991. "Leaving the Comfort of Home: Working through Feminisms." In Bannerji *et al.*, *Unsettling Relations:*

de Silva, A. 1992. *Earnings of Immigrants: A Comparative Analysis*. Ottawa: Economic Council of Canada.

– 1996. *Discrimination against Visible Minority Men*. Working Paper W-96-6E. Applied Research Branch Strategic Policy, Human Resources Development Canada. Hull.

DeVoretz, D.J., ed. 1995. *Diminishing Returns: The Economics of Canada's Immigration Policy*. Toronto: C.D. Howe Institute, Laurier Institution.

DeVoretz, D.J. 1996. "How Central Canadian Labour Difficulties Drive the Immigration Debate." *Vancouver Sun*, 21 May.

Dewar, E. 1995. *Cloak of Green*. Toronto: Lorimer.

Donald, L. 1997. *Aboriginal Slavery on the Northwest Coast of North America*. Los Angeles: University of California Press.

Drakich J., M. Taylor, and J. Bankier. 1996. "Academic Freedom Is the Inclusive University." In Riches and Weir, eds., *Beyond Political Correctness*.

D'Souza, D. 1992. *Illiberal Education: The Politics of Race and Sex on Campus*. New York: Vintage.

– 1995. *The End of Racism*. New York: Free Press.

Dwyer, V. 1997. "Who Should Pay for ESL? The Backlash against Teaching Immigrants English." *Maclean's*, 14 April.

Eccles, W.J. 1969. *The Canadian Frontier 1534–1760*. New York: Holt, Rinehart and Winston.

Economic Council of Canada. 1990. *Good Jobs, Bad Jobs: Employment in the Service Economy*. Ottawa: Supply and Services.

Edmonds, J., J. Côté-O'Hara, E. MacKenzie. 1990a. *Beneath the Veneer: The Report of the Task Force on Barriers to Women in the Public Service*. Vol. 1. Ottawa: Supply and Services.

– 1990b. *Beneath the Veneer*. Report of the Task Force on Barriers to Women in the Public Service. Vol. 2. Ottawa: Supply and Services.

Ehring, G., and W. Roberts. 1993. *Giving away a Miracle: Lost Dreams Broken Promises and the Ontario NDP*. Oakville: Mosaic Press.

Emberley, P.C. 1996. *Zero Tolerance: Hot Button Politics in Canadian Universities*. Toronto: Penguin.

Emberley, P.C., and W.R. Newell. 1994. *Bankrupt Education: The Decline of Liberal Education in Canada*. Toronto: University of Toronto Press.

Employment and Immigration Canada. 1991. *Employment Equity: A Guide for Employers*. Ottawa.

External Affairs. 1997. "Minister Axworthy Announces New Guidelines for the Promotion of Canadian Culture Abroad." News Release.

Fekete, J. 1994. *Moral Panic: Biopolitics Rising*. Montreal: Robert Davies.

Ferguson, E. 1997. "Drowned in a Sea of Apathy." *Guardian Weekly*, 26 January.

Ferro, M. 1997. *Colonization: A Global History*. London: Routledge.

Findlay, B. 1992. "Racism: Learning to Change." In Pierson *et al.*, *Strong Voices*.

Findlay, S. 1987. "Facing the State: The Politics of the Women's Movement Reconsidered." In Maroney and Luxton, eds., *Feminism and Political Economy*.

– 1991. "Making Sense of Pay Equity: Issues for a Feminist Political Practice." In Fudge and McDermott, eds., *Just Wages*.

– 1993a. "Problematizing Privilege." In Carty, ed., *And Still We Rise*.

– 1993b. "Reinventing the 'Community': A First Step in the Process of Democratization." *Studies in Political Economy* 42, Autumn.

– 1995. "Democracy and the Politics of Representation Feminist Struggles with the Canadian State." PHD thesis, Political Science, University of Toronto.

Finlayson, J. 1995. *Against the Current: Canadian Women Talk about 50 Years of Life on the Job*. Toronto: Doubleday.

Flanagan, T. 1995. "Political Correctness, Ontario Style." *Globe and Mail*, 6 January.

Foot, D., and D. Stoffman. 1996. *Boom, Bust and Echo: How to Profit from the Coming Demographic Shift*. Toronto: Macfarlane, Walter and Ross.

Fortin, P. 1996. "Raise the Inflation Target and Let Canada Recover." *Globe and Mail*, 26 September.

Foster, C. 1991. *Distorted Mirror: Canada's Racist Face*. Toronto: HarperCollins.

– 1996. *A Place Called Heaven: The Meaning of Being Black in Canada*. Toronto: HarperCollins.

Fox-Genovese, E. 1996. *Feminism is Not the Story of My Life*. New York: Doubleday.

Frank, T. 1996. "Employers of Women." *University Affairs*, January.

Freedland, J. 1996. "Seeking Rights for Ugly Americans." *Globe and Mail*, 27 July.

Fried, M. 1996. "Pulling the Plug." *New Internationalist* 285, November.

Friedman, M. 1962. *Capitalism and Freedom*. Chicago: University of Chicago Press.

Fry, H. 1996. Speaking Notes. Juliette Cuenco Seminar, Pearson Shoyama Institute. Ottawa. Mimeo.

Fudge, J. 1996. "Fragmentation and Feminization: The Challenge of Equity for Labour-Relations Policy." In Brodie, ed., *Women and Canadian Public Policy*.

Fudge, J., and P. McDermott, eds. 1991. *Just Wages: A Feminist Assessment of Pay Equity*. Toronto: University of Toronto Press.

Furedy, J.J. 1994. "Ice Station Academe." *Gravitas* 1, no. 3, Autumn.

– 1995. "CAUT's Defence of Academic Freedom under Attack." CAUT *Bulletin* 42, no. 4, February.

– 1996. "Academic Freedom and the UBC Administrators: Errors of Judgment vs. Professional Misconduct." SAFS *Newsletter*, December 1996.

Gabriel, C. 1996. "One or the Other? 'Race,' Gender and the Limits of Official Multiculturalism." In Brodie, ed., *Women and Canadian Public Policy*.

Gabriel, C., and K. Scott. 1993. "Women's Press at Twenty: The Politics of Feminist Publishing." In Carty, ed., *And Still We Rise*.

Gagnon, L. 1996. "How Laws Make Marriage a Less Appealing Option." *Globe and Mail*. 27 April.

Gavigan, S. 1996. "Familial Ideology and the Limits of Difference." In Brodie, ed., *Women and Canadian Public Policy*.

Gentium Consulting. 1994. "Working towards Addressing Conflict." Report prepared for Interval House staff and board collective. Ottawa. Mimeo.

Gilbert, S., and A. Pomfret. 1995. "Gender Tracking in University Programs." Occasional Paper no. 4. Industry Canada.

Gillmoor, D. 1995. "Promised Land." *Canadian Geographic*, July/August 1995.

Glazer, N. 1987. *Affirmative Discrimination, Ethnic Inequality and Public Policy*. 2nd ed. Cambridge: Harvard University Press.

Gotlieb, A. 1993. "What About Us? Organizing Inclusively in the National Action Committee on the Status of Women." In Carty, ed., *And Still We Rise*.

Government of Ontario. 1992. *Opening Doors: A Report on the Employment Equity Consultations*. Toronto: Office of the Employment Equity Commissioner.

Granatstein, J.L., and K. McNaught, eds. 1991. *"English Canada" Speaks Out*. Toronto: Doubleday.

Greenfield, N. 1994. "Interest Groups Doth Protest Too Much about Shakespeare." *Ottawa Citizen*, 25 May.

– 1995. "The Irony of Nationalism in Canada and Abroad." *Ottawa X Press*, 13 December.

Groarke, L. 1996a. "What's in a Number? Consequentialism and Employment Equity in Hall, Hurka, Sumner and Baker *et al.*" *Dialogue* 35.

– 1996b. "A Reply to Professor Sumner." *Dialogue* 35.

Guttman, A., ed. 1994. *Multiculturalism: Examining the Politics of Recognition.* Princeton University Press.

Gwyn, R. 1995. *Nationalism without Walls: The Unbearable Lightness of Being Canadian.* Toronto: McClelland & Stewart.

Hacker, A. 1992. *Two Nations: Black and White, Separate, Hostile, Unequal.* New York: Ballantine.

Harney, R., and H. Troper. 1975. *Immigrants: A Portrait of the Urban Experience, 1890–1930.* Toronto: Van Nostrand Reinhold.

Harrison, K. 1996. "Open Season on White Males? Hardly." *Globe and Mail,* 20 September.

Harvey, E.B., and N.S. Wortley. 1993. *Patterns of Socioeconomic Disadvantage for Selected Ethnocultural Groups, Canada, 1986.* Report prepared for the Interdepartmental Working Group on Employment Equity Data. Working Paper 4.15. Statistics Canada.

Henighan, T. 1996. *The Presumption of Culture.* Vancouver: Raincoast.

Henry, F. 1994. *The Caribbean Diaspora in Toronto: Learning to Live with Racism.* Toronto: University of Toronto Press.

Henry, F., C. Tator, W. Mattis, and T. Rees. 1995. *The Colour of Democracy.* Toronto: Harcourt Brace.

Hill, D.G. 1981. *The Freedom Seekers: Blacks in Early Canada.* Agincourt: Book Society of Canada.

Hobsbawm, E. 1994. *The Age of Extremes: A History of the World, 1914–1991.* New York: Pantheon.

Hoggart, R. 1995. *The Way We Live Now.* London: Cape.

House of Commons. 1995. *Employment Equity: A Commitment to Merit.* Report of the Standing Committee on Human Rights and the Status of Disabled Persons.

Hum, D., and W. Simpson. 1994. *Sources of Income of Persons with Disabilities in Canada.* Study prepared for Employment Equity Data Program, Housing, Family and Social Statistics Division. Working Paper 5.14. Statistics Canada.

Human Resources and Development Canada. 1993. *Annual Report Employment Equity Act 1993.* Ottawa: Supply and Services.

– 1994a. *Annual Report Employment Equity Act 1994.* Ottawa: Supply and Services.

– 1994b. *Profile of Post-secondary Education in Canada.* Ottawa: Supply and Services.

– 1995a. *Annual Report Employment Equity Act 1995.* Ottawa: Supply and Services.

– 1995b. *Federal and Provincial Support to Post-Secondary Education in Canada.* Tenth Annual Report. Ottawa: Supply and Services.

– 1997. *Applied Research Bulletin* 3, no. 1.

Interdepartmental Working Group on Employment Equity Data. 1993. *The Labour Market Activity of Groups Designated under the Employment Equity Act 1988–1989*. Part 1. Employment Equity Data Program, Report 1.15. Statistics Canada.

Ignatieff, M. 1996. "The Narcissism of Minor Difference." In Littleton, ed., *Clash of Identities*.

Immigration and Refugee Board. 1997. "Country of Persecution." Analysis Report, Current (1 October 1996 to 31 December 1996) and Year to Date (1 January 1996 to 31 December 1996). Ottawa. Mimeo.

Industry Canada. 1990. *Canada Scholarships Program 1989–90 Report Card*. Ottawa.

– 1991. *Canada Scholarships Program 1990–91 Report Card*. Ottawa.

Irvine, A.D. 1996. "Jack and Jill and Employment Equity." *Dialogue* 35.

Jamieson, R. 1997. Letter from the Ontario Ombudsman. File no. 109428.

Jerome-Forget, M. 1997. "Looking for the Answers to High Unemployment." *Financial Post*, 3 May.

Juriansz, R. 1993. "Under-Reporting in Employment Equity Surveys." *Managing Diversity* 2, no. 1.

Kallen, E. 1995. *Ethnicity and Human Rights*. Don Mills, ON: Oxford University Press.

Kaplan, W. ed. 1993. *Belonging: The Meaning and Future of Canadian Citizenship*. Montreal and Kingston: McGill-Queen's University Press.

Kashmeri, Z. 1996. "Hirings Spark New Furore over Firefighter Jobs." *Toronto Star*, 23 May.

Keene, J. 1992. *Human Rights in Ontario*. Toronto: Carswell.

Kelly, K. 1995. "Visible Minorities a Diverse Group." *Canadian Social Trends*, Summer.

Kierans, T.E. 1994. Foreword. In Crowley, *The Road to Equity*.

Kierans, T.E., and R. Kunin. 1995. Foreword. In DeVoretz, ed., *Diminishing Returns*.

Klein, N. 1994. "Why Universities Feel Harrassed by Zero Tolerance." *Globe and Mail*, 6 January.

Kline, M. 1989. "Women's Oppression and Racism: A Critique of the 'Feminist Standpoint.'" In Vorst *et al.* eds., *Race, Class, Gender*.

Kohli, R. 1993. "Power or Empowerment: Questions of Agency in the Shelter Movement." In Carty, ed., *And Still We Rise*.

Kralt, J. and A. Allen. 1992. "Overview of Black Canadians in Toronto CMA." Canadian Heritage. Mimeo.

Kreuger, L. 1996. "Teachers-to-be Get 2nd (or 16th) Chance at York." *Globe and Mail*, 12 January.

Laframboise, D. 1996. *The Princess at the Window: A New Gender Morality*. Toronto: Penguin.

– 1997a. "Oh Dad, Poor Dad." *Globe and Mail*, 2 April.

– 1997b. "The Case of the Brie and the Baguettes." *Ottawa Citizen*, 21 September.

Lalonde, M.E. 1993. *Profiling Designated Group Presence in Canada's Labour Market Based on 1988 National Graduate Survey Data*. Statistics Canada Employment Equity Data Program. Report 1.21.

Lampkin, L. 1985. "Visible Minorities in Canada." In Abella, ed., *Research Studies of the Commission on Equality in Employment*.

Langellier J.P. 1996. "Nepalese Girls Caught Up in Sexual Slavery." *Guardian Weekly*, 13 October.

Lasch, C. 1995. *The Revolt of the Elites and the Betrayal of Democracy*. New York: Norton.

Leah, R. 1989. "Linking the Struggles: Racism, Feminism and the Union Movement." In Vorst *et al.*, eds., *Race, Class, Gender*.

LeBor, A. 1996. "Xenophobes Give Hungary's Reputation a Black Eye." *Globe and Mail*, 14 October.

Levan, A. 1996. "Violence against Women." In Brodie, ed., *Women and Canadian Public Policy*

Levitt, C.H., and W. Shaffir. 1987. *The Riot at Christie Pits*. Toronto: Lester and Orpen Dennys.

Lewington, J. 1996. "Program Upgrades Foreign Teachers." *Globe and Mail*, 19 August.

Lewis, S. 1992. "Dear Bob." Letter to the Premier. 9 June. Toronto. Mimeo.

Library of Parliament. 1989. "Affirmative Action Employment Equity." *Current Issue Review* 84–31.

Lind, M. 1995. *The Next American Nation: The New Nationalism and the Fourth American Revolution*. New York: Free Press.

Little, B. 1996. "Why It Pays to Stay in School." *Globe and Mail*, 26 August.

Littleton, J., ed. 1996. *Clash of Identities: Media Manipulation and Politics of the Self*. New Jersey: Prentice Hall.

Loney, M. 1975. *Rhodesia: White Racism and Imperial Response*. Harmondsworth: Penguin.

– 1977. "A Political Economy of Citizen Participation." In Panitch, ed., *The Canadian State*.

– 1986. *The Politics of Greed: The New Right and the Welfare State*. London: Pluto Press.

– 1987. "The Grand Rapids Hydro Project and the Construction of Dependency." *Canadian Journal of Native Studies* 7 no. 1.

– 1995a. "Social Problems, Community Trauma and Hydro Project Impacts." *Canadian Journal of Native Studies* 15, no. 2.

– 1995b. "New Facts Devalue Defence of Generous Payments." *Ottawa Citizen*, 5 April.

– 1996. "Identity Politics As Management Fad." *Books in Canada*. May.

Maart, R. 1990. "Resistance from the Tongue." *Fuse* 13, Summer.

Mahler, S.J. 1995. *American Dreaming: Immigrant Life on the Margins.* Princeton University Press.

Malvern, P. 1985. *Persuaders: Influence Peddling, Lobbying and Political Corruption in Canada.* Toronto: Methuen.

Management Board Secretariat. 1993. *The Ontario Employment Equity Annual Report.* Government of Ontario.

Marchak, P. 1996. *Sexism and the University: The Political Science Affair at the University of British Columbia.* Montreal: McGill-Queen's University Press.

Maroney, H.J., and M. Luxton, eds. 1987. *Feminism and Political Economy.* Toronto: Methuen.

Marsden, L. 1980. "The Role of the National Action Committee in Facilitating Equal Pay Policy in Canada." In Raimer, ed., *Equal Employment Policy for Women.*

Martin, L. 1995. *Chrétien.* Vol. 1: *The Will to Win.* Toronto: Lester.

Martin, R. 1993. "Challenging Orthodoxy: A Critical Analysis of Racially-Based Job Quotas." *Canadian Labour Law Journal* 1.

– 1995. "Orthodoxy and Research." Mimeo.

– 1996. "An Agenda for a Revived Canadian Left." *Inroads* 5.

Martin, S. 1996. "Sex, Race and Recriminations at UBC." *Globe and Mail*, 28 September.

Mawani, N. 1997. "Refugee-Determination System Fair, Efficient." *Ottawa Citizen*, 2 January.

McFarlane, P. 1996. "Ovide's Last Stand." *Globe and Mail*, 23 November.

McKague, O. 1991. *Racism in Canada.* Saskatoon: Fifth House.

McKenzie, M. 1987. "You Mean I Still Ain't." Reprinted in Pierson *et al.*, 1993. *Strong Voices.*

Ministry of Citizenship. Undated. *Shared Accountability Framework.* Part 4: *Workforce: Employment Equity.* Toronto.

– 1994. *Getting Ready: Preparing for Ontario's Employment Equity Act.* Toronto.

Ministry of Education and Training. 1993. *Antiracism and Ethnocultural Equity in School Boards.* Guidelines for Policy Development and Implementation. Toronto: Queen's Printer for Ontario.

Minors, A. 1992. *Towards Eliminating Racism at the Ontario Human Rights Commission.* Report to the Anti-Racism Committee. Toronto: OHRC.

Mohan, M. 1992. *Employment Disadvantage Among Women Who Are Members of Visible Minority Groups.* Mana Research Ltd., Statistics Canada Employment Equity Data Program. Report 1.18.

Moriba-Meadows, G., and J. Dale Tiller. 1995. "Understanding and Solidarity." In Riches and Weir, eds., *Beyond Political Correctness.*

Nazareth, E. 1996. "Infamous Riot." *Ottawa Sun's TV Sun*, 11 August.

Ng, R. 1989. "Sexism, Racism, and Canadian Nationalism." In Vorst *et al.* ed., *Race, Class, Gender.*

Nikiforuk, A. 1994. *If Learning Is So Natural, Why Am I Going to School?* Toronto: Penguin.

North York Board of Education. 1995. "Analysis of Demographic and Socio-Economic Characteristics of Low Achieving Grade 8 Students on the Mathematics Benchmarks Test."

Nourbese Philip, M. 1990. "Publish and Be Damned." *Fuse* 13, no. 6.

– 1992. *Frontiers.* Mercury: Stratford.

Ontario Council of Agencies Serving Immigrants. 1996. Fact Sheet 2. Toronto: OCASI.

Ontario Human Rights Commission. 1993. "A Proposed Plan of Action for Anti-Racism and Organizational Change in the Ontario Human Rights Commission." Anti-Racism Project Team. Toronto. Mimeo.

– 1995. Martin Loney vs. Carleton University. File no. 40-858R/E354.

Office of the Employment Equity Commissioner. 1992a. *Opening Doors: A Report on the Employment Equity Consultations.* Toronto: Ministry of Citizenship.

– 1992b. *Employment Equity Fact Sheets.* Toronto: Ministry of Citizenship.

O'Neil, M. 1993. "Citizenship and Social Change: Canadian Women's Struggle for Equality." In Kaplan, ed., *Belonging: The Meaning and Future of Canadian Citizenship*

Ontario Women's Directorate. 1993. Women in the Labour Market: Focus on Racial Minority Women. Toronto.

Osberg, L. 1988. *The Future of Work in Canada: Trends, Issues and Forces for Change.* Ottawa: Canadian Council on Social Development.

Pal, L.A. 1993. *Interests of State: The Politics of Language, Multiculturalism and Feminism in Canada.* Montreal and Kingston: McGill-Queen's University Press.

Panitch, L., ed. 1977. *The Canadian State: Political Economy and Political Power.* Toronto: University of Toronto Press.

Pay Equity Coalition of Saskatchewan *et al.* 1996. "Towards Workplace Equity." National Conference on Pay and Employment Equity Registration Brochure.

Pendakur, R., and K. Pendakur. 1995. *Earnings Differentials among Ethnic Groups in Canada.* Strategic Research and Analysis, Corporate and Intergovernmental Affairs, Canadian Heritage.

– 1996. "The Colour of Money: Earnings Differentials among Ethnic Groups in Canada." Canadian Heritage. Mimeo.

Phillips, K. 1990. *Politics of Rich and Poor: Wealth and the American Electorate in the Reagan Aftermath.* New York: HarperCollins.

Pierson, R.R., and M.G. Cohen. 1995. *Canadian Women's Issues.* Vol. 2: *Bold Visions.* Toronto: Lorimer.

Pierson, R.R., M.G. Cohen, P. Bourne, and P. Masters, eds. 1993. *Canadian Women's Issues.* Vol. 1: *Strong Voices.* Toronto: Lorimer.

Pilger, J. 1994. "Deathly Silence of the Diplomats." *Guardian Weekly*, 30 October.

Policy Coordination and Strategic Planning Citizenship and Canadian Identity. 1994. *Selected Statistics on Ethnic Origins and Economic Activity Data 1991 Census*. Public Use Microfile. Ottawa: Canadian Heritage.

Pool, H. 1996. "World's Top 10 Billionaires." *Guardian Weekly*, 28 July.

Prince, M., ed. *How Ottawa Spends, 1986–87: Tracking the Tories*. Toronto: Methuen.

Public Service Commission. 1993. *Annual Report 1992*. Ottawa: Supply and Services.

– 1994. *Annual Report 1993*. Ottawa: Supply and Services.

Rae, B. 1996. *From Power to Protest: Personal Reflections on a Life in Politics*. Toronto: Viking.

Raimer, R., ed. 1980. *Equal Employment Policy for Women*. Philadelphia: Temple University Press.

Rauch, J. 1993. *Kindly Inquisitors: The New Attacks on Free Thought*. Chicago: University of Chicago Press.

Rayside, D. 1995. "Equality in Reality." *University of Toronto Magazine*. Summer.

Rebick, J. 1996. "Bridging Identity: A Creative Response to Identity Politics." In Littleton, ed., *Clash of Identities*.

Rebick, J., and K. Roach. 1996. *Politically Speaking*. Toronto: Douglas and McIntyre.

Redway, Alan. 1992. *A Matter of Fairness: Canadian Parliamentary Report of the Special Committee on the Review of the Employment Equity Act*. Ottawa: Queen's Printer.

Reitz, J.G. 1993. "Statistics on Racial Discrimination in Canada." *Policy Options*, March.

Reitz, J.G., and R. Breton. 1994. *The Illusion of Difference: Realities of Ethnicity in Canada and the United States*. Toronto: C.D. Howe Institute.

Renner, K. 1996a. "Has Affirmative Action Gone Too Far? Canadian Academic Women." Technical Report no. 9: The Higher Education Series. Ottawa: K.E. Renner and Associates. Mimeo.

– 1996b. "Universities and Colleges Are on the Threshold of Change." Technical Report no. 7: The Higher Education Series. Ottawa: K.E. Renner and Associates. Mimeo.

Resnick, P. 1996. "No Discrimination Means No Reverse Discrimination." *Globe and Mail*, 12 September.

Richer, S. 1995. "Reaching the Men: Inclusion and Exclusion in Feminist Teaching." In Richer and Weir, eds., *Beyond Political Correctness*.

Richer, S., and L. Weir, eds. 1995. *Beyond Political Correctness: Toward the Inclusive University*. Toronto: University of Toronto Press.

Roberts, B. 1988. *Whence They Came: Deportation from Canada 1900–1935*. Ottawa: University of Ottawa Press.

Ross, I. 1996. "Courts Left to Shape Same-Sex Policy." *Globe and Mail*, 12 October.

Ross, O. 1995. "Rape and Torture, Yes, Smoking and Drinking, No." *Globe and Mail*, 7 January.

Roy, P.E. 1989. *White Man's Province: British Columbia Politicians and Chinese and Japanese Immigrants, 1858–1914*. Vancouver: University of British Columbia Press.

Salutin, R. 1996. "Journalistic Bards in the Court of Business." *Globe and Mail*, 2 February.

Satzewich, V., ed. 1991. *Deconstructing a Nation: Immigration, Multiculturalism and Racism in '90s Canada*. Halifax: Fernwood Publishing.

Saveland, W. 1993. *Systemic Discrimination and Employment Equity Programs: An Account of Evolving Statistical Definitions in Employment Equity*. Interdepartmental Working Group on Employment Equity Data. Statistics Canada Working Paper (1.13).

Schlesinger, A. 1991. *The Disuniting of America*. New York: Norton.

Scott, P. 1993. "Maintaining Employment Equity in a Recession." *Managing Diversity* 2, no. 1, April/May.

Sher, N.M. 1997. "Is a Nazi Criminal in Our Midst?" *Globe and Mail*, 12 April.

Sheth, A., and A. Handa. 1993. "A Jewel in the Frown: Striking Accord between Indian Feminists." In Bannerji, ed., *Returning the Gaze*.

Simms, G. 1993. "Racism As a Barrier to Canadian Citizenship." In Kaplan, ed., *Belonging: The Meaning and Future of Canadian Citizenship*

Simpson, J. 1993. *Faultlines: Struggling for a Canadian Vision*. Toronto: HarperCollins.

Simon Fraser University. 1995. *Twentieth Anniversary, Women's Studies*. Simon Fraser University.

Sivanandan, A. 1985. "RAT and the Degradation of Black Struggle." *Race and Class* 36, no. 12.

– 1997. *When Memory Dies*. London: Arcadia.

Social Sciences and Humanities Research Council of Canada/Citizenship and Immigration. 1996. *Backgrounder*. SSHRC-CIC Centre of Excellence for Research on Immigration and Settlement.

Sommers, C.H. 1995. *Who Stole Feminism? How Women Have Betrayed Women*. New York: Touchstone.

Sowell, T. 1990. *Preferential Policies: An International Perspective*. New York: William Morrow.

Stackhouse, J. 1996a. "Destino." *Globe and Mail*, 3 February.

– 1996b. "Ghana's Big, Red Tomatoes Pure Gold to Poor Farmers." *Globe and Mail*, 29 January.

– 1997a. "Hindu Extremists Keep the Faith." *Globe and Mail*, 5 August.

– 1997b. "A Passage through India." *Globe and Mail*, 2 August.

Stalker, J. 1995. "The Chill Women Feel at Canada's Universities." *Globe and Mail*, 25 July.

Statistics Canada. 1989. *Employment Equity Definitions of Visible Minorities, Aboriginal Peoples and Persons with Disabilities*. Census Operations Divisions.

– 1990. *Making the Tough Choices in Using Census Data to Count Visible Minorities in Canada*. W. Boxhill. Employment Equity Data Program. Working paper 4.12.

– 1995. *Labour Force Annual Averages, 1994*.

– 1995a. *Women in Canada*.

– 1997. *Earnings of Men and Women in 1995*.

Steiner, G. 1996. *No Passion Spent*. London: Faber and Faber.

Stephney, B. 1996. "Welfare: Blow It Up. Get Rid of It. It's Destroying the Black Family." *Globe and Mail*, 7 September.

Stoffman, D. 1993. *Toward a More Realistic Immigration Policy for Canada*. Toronto: C.D. Howe Institute.

– 1997. "Promised Land? Or Just Promises?" *Globe and Mail*, 26 April.

Sumner, L.W. "Why the Numbers Count." *Dialogue* 35.

Swimmer, G., and D. Gollesch. 1986. "Affirmative Action for Women in the Federal Public Service." In Prince, ed., *How Ottawa Spends*.

Taylor, L. 1994. *Case Analysis*. Case no. 40–858R (E-354). Toronto: Ontario Human Rights Commission.

Thobani, S. 1993. "Making a Commitment to Inclusion." *Ottawa Citizen*, 3 June.

Thomas, D. 1996. *The Social Welfare Implications of Immigrant Family Sponsorship Default: An Analysis of Data from the Census Metropolitan Area of Toronto: Final Report*. Ottawa: Citizenship and Immigration Canada.

Thornhill, E. 1989. "Focus on Black Women!" In Vorst *et al.*, eds., *Race, Class, Gender*.

Torczyner, J.L. 1997. *Diversity, Mobility and Change: The Dynamics of Black Communities in Canada*. Montreal: McGill School of Social Work.

Townson, M. 1985. "The Socio-Economic Costs and Benefits of Affirmative Action." In Abella, *Research Studies*.

– 1995. *Women's Financial Futures: Mid-Life Prospects for a Secure Retirement*. Ottawa: Canadian Advisory Council on the Status of Women.

Treasury Board. 1994. *Employment Equity in the Public Service: Annual Report 1992–93*. Ottawa: Supply and Services.

– 1994a. *Employment Equity in the Public Service of Canada*. Client Services Division. Ottawa: Supply and Services.

– 1995. *Employment Equity in the Public Service: Annual Report 1993–94*. Ottawa: Supply and Services.

Trempe, R. 1997. *Not Just Numbers: A Canadian Framework for Future Immigration*. Immigration Legislative Review. Ottawa: Citizenship and Immigration Canada.

Trillium Foundation. 1997. *Grants 1994–95, 1995–96, April-June 1996; Grant Information*. Canadian Council on Social Development. Approval date: January 16.

Turner, T. 1995. *The Composition and Implications of Metropolitan Toronto's Ethnic, Racial and Linguistic Populations 1991*. Report to Access and Equity Centre, Municipality of Metropolitan Toronto.

University of British Columbia. 1997. *Equity Office Annual Report 1996*. Vancouver: UBC.

Valpy, M. 1993. "The Storm around Show Boat." *Globe and Mail*, 12 March.

– 1995. "To Deal with the 'Crisis' of Black Schooling." *Globe and Mail*, 21 March.

Verburg, P. 1996. "Deconstructing the Arts Faculty." *Alberta Report*, 30 September.

Veuglers, J.W.P., and T.R. Klassen. 1994. "Continuity and Change in Canada's Unemployment-Immigration Linkage." *Canadian Journal of Sociology* 19, no. 3.

Vickers, J., P. Rankin, and C. Apelle. 1993. *Politics As If Women Mattered: A Political Analysis of the National Action Committee on the Status of Women*. Toronto: University of Toronto Press.

Visible Minority Consultation Group. 1992. *Breaking Through the Visibility Ceiling*. Report to the Secretary of Treasury Board. Ottawa: VMCG.

– 1993. *Distortions in the Mirror*. Report to the Secretary of Treasury Board. Ottawa: VMCG.

Vorst, J., et al., eds. 1989. *Race, Class, Gender: Bonds and Barriers*. Toronto: Between the Lines.

Wadden, M. 1991. *Nitassinan: The Innu Struggle to Reclaim Their Homeland*. Vancouver: Douglas & McIntyre.

Waldron, D., and E.J. Chambers. 1995. *Labour Market Experience of Immigrants to Alberta: A Panel Approach*. Edmonton: Western Centre for Economic Research, University of Alberta.

Walkom, T. 1994. *Rae Days: The Rise and Follies of the NDP*. Toronto: Key Porter.

Wallace, J. 1996. "The Equity Debate at the University of Alberta." In Richer and Weir, eds., *Beyond Political Correctness*:

Wannell, T. undated. "Measuring Employment Equity Designated Group Status." Ottawa: Statistics Canada. Mimeo.

Wannell, T., and N. Caron. 1994a. *A Look at Employment Equity Groups among Recent Postsecondary Graduates: Visible Minorities, Aboriginal Peoples and the Activity Limited*. Ottawa: Statistics Canada.

– 1994b. *The Gender Earnings Gap among Recent Postsecondary Graduates, 1984–92*. Ottawa: Statistics Canada.

Warskett, R. 1991. "Political Power, Technical Disputes, and Unequal Pay: A Federal Case." In Fudge and McDermott, eds., *Just Wages*.

Wente, M. 1994. "Who's Minding the Shelter?" *Globe and Mail*, 30 July.

Whitaker, R. 1987. *Double Standard: The Secret History of Canadian Immigration*. Toronto: Lester and Orpen Dennys.

White, P. 1988. "Testing 1991 Census Ethnic Ancestry, Ethnic Identity and Race Questions: Results of Two Surveys." Paper presented to Canadian Population Society, Windsor, ON. Statistics Canada. Mimeo.

Wilson, T. 1996. *Diversity at Work: The Business Case for Equity*. Toronto: Wiley.

Wilson, W.J. 1987. *The Truly Disadvantaged: The Inner City, the Underclass, and Public Policy*. Chicago: University of Chicago Press.

Winks, R. 1971. *The Blacks in Canada: A History*. Montreal: McGill-Queen's University Press.

Winn, C. 1985. "Affirmative Action and Visible Minorities: Eight Premises in Quest of Evidence." *Canadian Public Policy* 11, no. 4.

Wong, J. 1996a. "The Olympians Were Welcomed Home, but Not Me." *Globe and Mail*, 10 August.

– 1996b. "An Outpouring of Support but Still Some Nagging Doubts." *Globe and Mail*, 19 October.

Wong, L.S., and N.S. Netting. 1991. "Business Immigration to Canada: Social Impact and Racism." In Satzewich, ed., *Deconstructing a Nation*

Wright, C. 1993. "It's Not Just about Burning Crosses." *The Womanist* 4, no. 1.

Yau, M., M. Chang, and S. Zeigler. 1993. *The 1991 Every Secondary Student Survey*. Part 3: *Program Level and Student Achievement*. Report no. 205. Research Service, Toronto Board of Education.

Young, D. 1992. *The Handling of Race Discrimination Complaints at the Ontario Human Rights Commission*. Toronto: OHRC.

Young, H. 1996. "Nobel Prize Shames an Indifferent World." *Guardian Weekly*, 20 October.

Zong, L. 1997. "New Racism, Cultural Diversity and the Search for National Identity." In Cardozo and Musto, eds., *The Battle over Multiculturalism*.

Index

Davis, Rob, 44
Dean, Misao, 300–1, 308
Delellis, Linda, 99
Dempsey, James, 180
designated groups, definition, 173–80
de Silva, Arnold, 116
DeVoretz, Don, 213, 242
Dewar, Elaine, 137
Din, Ravinda, 70
disabled, 6
diversity training, x, xi, 4, 54, 90
Dobbin, Murray, 87
Doherty, Justice, 25
domestic workers, 94, 216
Donnelly, Liam, 293
Donner, Arthur, 214
double disadvantage: and federal employment, 189, 199; and visible minority women, 120–6, 127, 142, 171, 246
Drabinsky, Garth, 134
Drainie, Bronwyn, 75, 340n5
Drakich, J., 313, 316
Dresden, ON, 97, 105
D'Souza, Dinesh, 94, 104, 315
Dukakis, Michael, 79
Dvorkin, Jeffrey, 337n6

Eberts, Mary, 160–1, 350n1
education, in Ontario, 251–6
Emberley, Peter, 252, 312
Employment Equity Act: 1986, 172, 173, 183, 202; 1996, 209–11
equality rights, 160–3, 206–7
eurocentric curriculum, x, 256, 288, 312, 315, 323

families, and income, 45
Farrakhan, Louis, 78, 95, 341n1

Federal Contractors Program, 172
Federation des Femmes du Québec, 155
Fekete, John, 10, 39
findlay, barbara, 61
Findlay, Susan, 55–6, 60, 74, 128, 134–5
Finestone, Sheila, 146
Finlayson, Judith, 23–4
firefighters, and recruitment, 31–4
Flanagan, Thomas, 153
Fortier, Suzanne, 324
Foster, Cecil, 12, 118, 131, 346n2, 363n24
France, Anatole, 164
Franklin, Melissa, 303
Fry, Hedy, 88, 118, 151
Fudge, Judy, 263
Fulford, Robert, 42, 152, 156
funding by government of race and gender based groups, 133–55, 180. See also Canada Council, Canadian Heritage, grievance politics, Ontario Arts Council, Show Boat, and Trillium Foundation
Furedy, John, 290, 292, 333n1, 365n6
Fuse, 65–6

Gabriel, Christina, 22, 141, 318
Gardner, Beverley, 284
Gavignan, Shelley, 318
Gayle, Clinton, 231
Ghiz, Joe, 45, 98
Glazer, Nathan, 167–8
Globe and Mail, x
Go, Avvy, 19, 37, 336n7
Gordon, Charles, 12, 334n4
Gottell, Lise, 296
Goulet, Monica, 145
graduate earnings, 187, 203
Graham, Bill, 309

Grant, Oneil Rohan, 231
Grant-Cummings, Joan, 136, 143
Grey, Deborah, 86
grievance politics, xiii, 26, 42, 54, 89, 93, 129, 325, 327; funding of, x, 130, 284–6; and Rae government, 245, 255, 281–3, 326; and universities, 288–325. See also biopolitics; politics of identity
Gwyn, Richard, 156
Gzowski, Peter, 131

Hackney Borough, London, 279
Hageman, Margaret, 32
Hall, David, 238
Harrison, Kathryn, 298–300
Hasselfield, Ginny, 54, 219
Health Canada, 154, 205
Helsinki Watch Group, 230
Henderson, Brian, 101
Henigan, Thomas, 148, 280
Henry, Frances, 52, 97, 172, 358n10; and racism in universities, 309–12, 316–19; and Show Boat, 281, 322–3
Henry, Jeff, 281, 339n1
Henson, James, 94
Hill, Daniel, 95
Hillary, Sir Edmund, 105
Hobsbawm, Eric, 157
Homolka, Karla, 142
hooks, bell, 60–1
Horton, Willie, 79
Hosek, Chaviva, 137, 347n6
House of Commons Human Rights Committee, 19, 37, 204
Hubbard, William, 97
Hum, Derek, 24